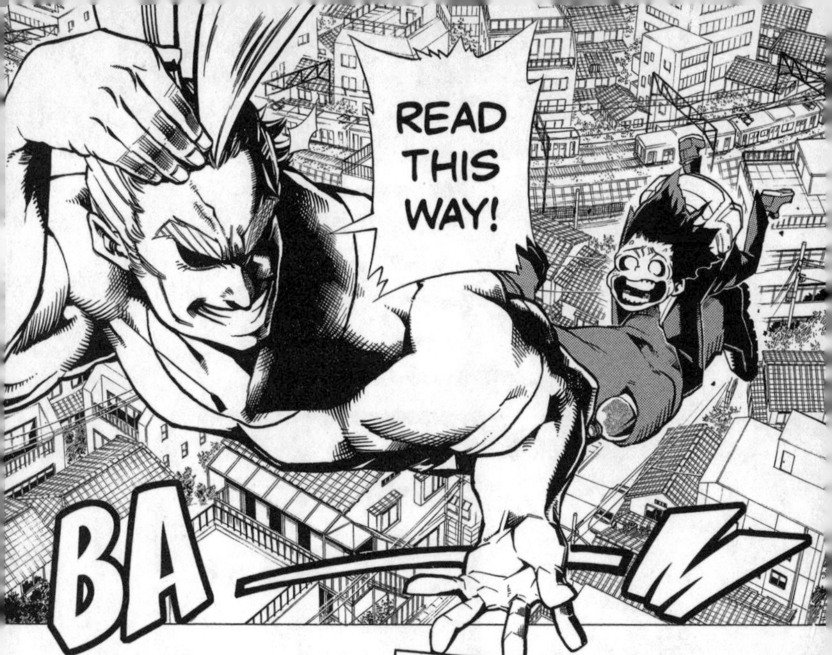
READ THIS WAY!
BA-M

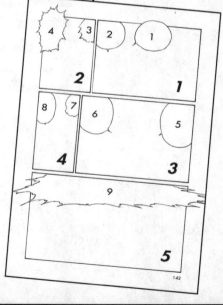

MY HERO ACADEMIA

reads from right to left, starting in the upper-right corner. Japanese is read from right to left, meaning that action, sound effects and word-balloon order are completely reversed from English order.

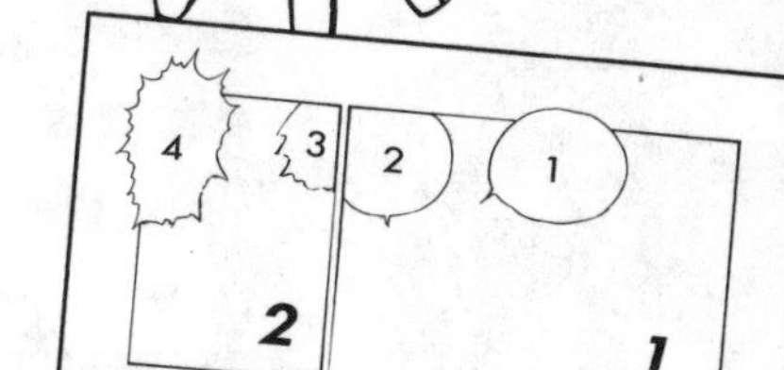
1
2
1
3
4
2
5
6
3
7
8
4
9
5
142

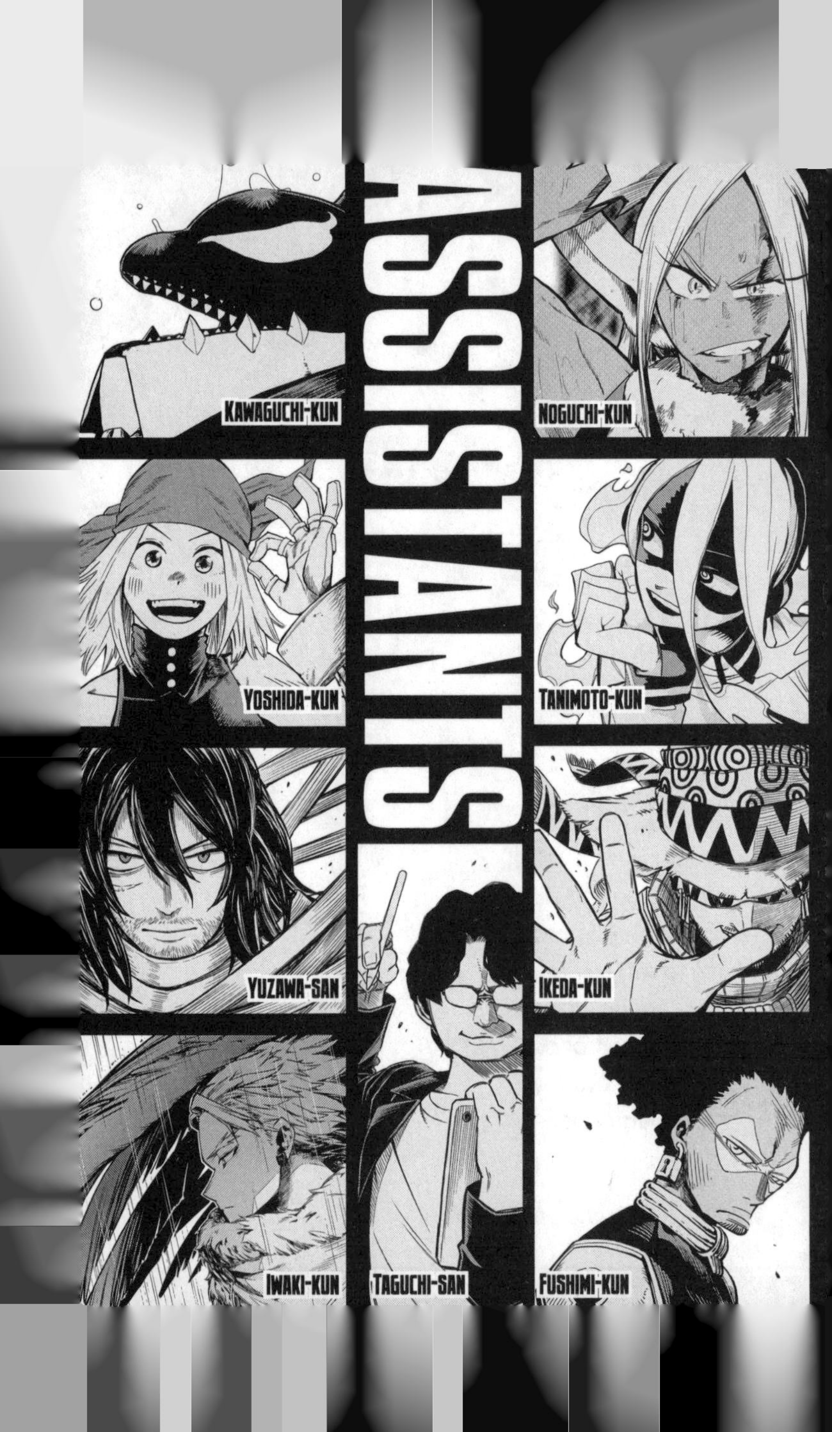
ASSISTANTS
NOGUCHI-KUN
KAWAGUCHI-KUN
TANIMOTO-KUN
YOSHIDA-KUN
IKEDA-KUN
YUZAWA-SAN
FUSHIMI-KUN
TAGUCHI-SAN
IWAKI-KUN

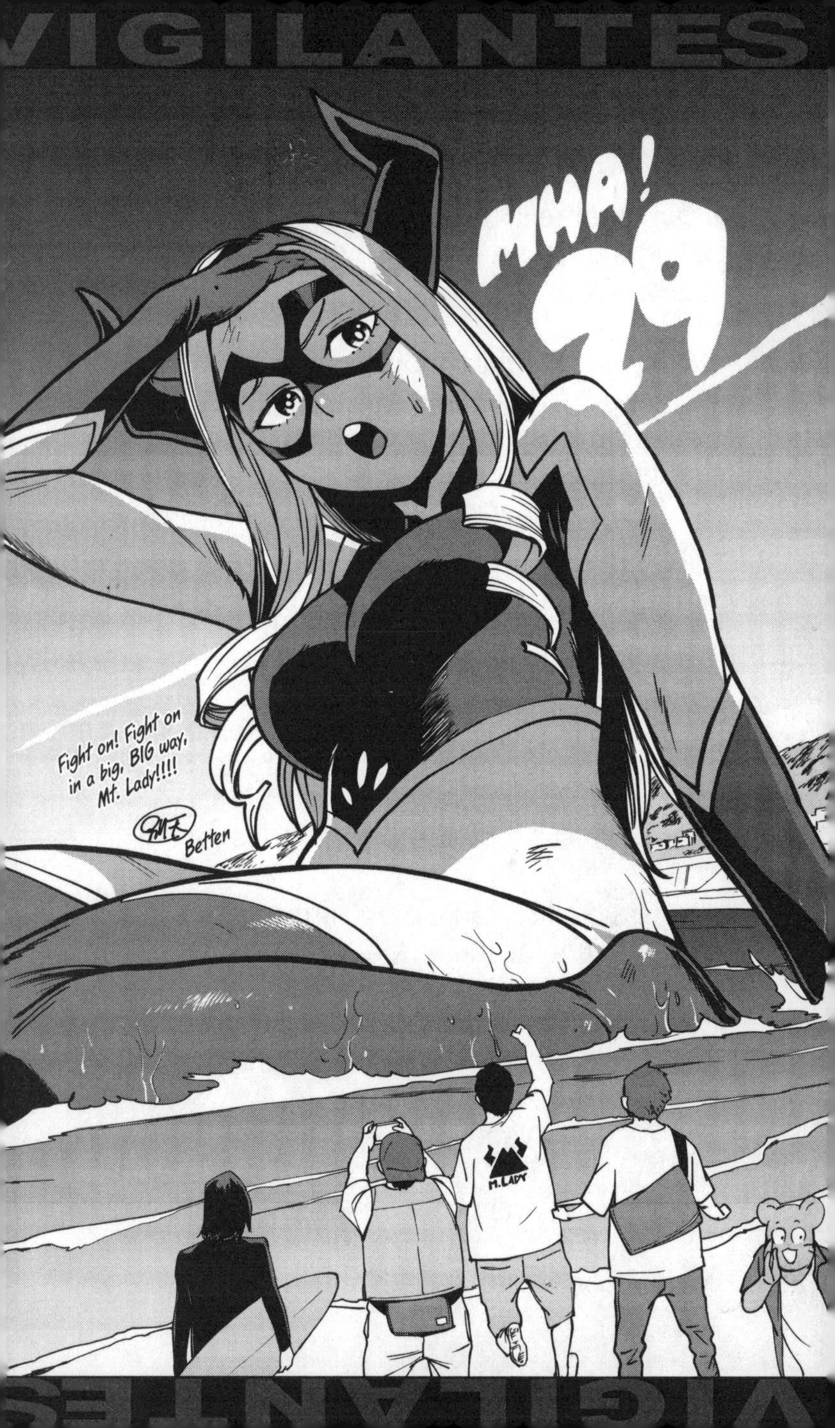
VIGILANTES
MHA! 29
Fight on! Fight on in a big, BIG way, Mt. Lady!!!!
Betten
M.LADY

THE AFTERWORD

I've got an art exhibition coming up! In preparation, I'm putting together a collection of original art, including stuff you literally can't see anywhere else.

And the third movie was announced!

What's a guy s'posed to do when the thing he could never imagine happening even once in his life ends up happening three whole times?

I'm spinning around and bowing my head and saying "Thank you!" in every compass direction, to everyone.

I'm at the point where just looking at some grass makes me start bawling.

Bizarre.

The next volume marks a big turning point in the story, so thank you to all the readers who've come this far. In the hopes that you'll keep enjoying the story to the very end, me and Deku and the whole gang won't be letting up on our PLUS ULTRA approach!

Also!! Mind your health!!

Don't forget to wash your hands and gargle regularly!!

Make sure you're warm and cozy while sleeping!!

See ya!!

MHA: Vigilantes volume 11 came out in Japan the same day as this book, and I've received another art contribution from the artist, Betten Sensei!!

Much appreciated, every time!!

It's coming up in two pages, so you've got plenty to look forward to when you turn the page!

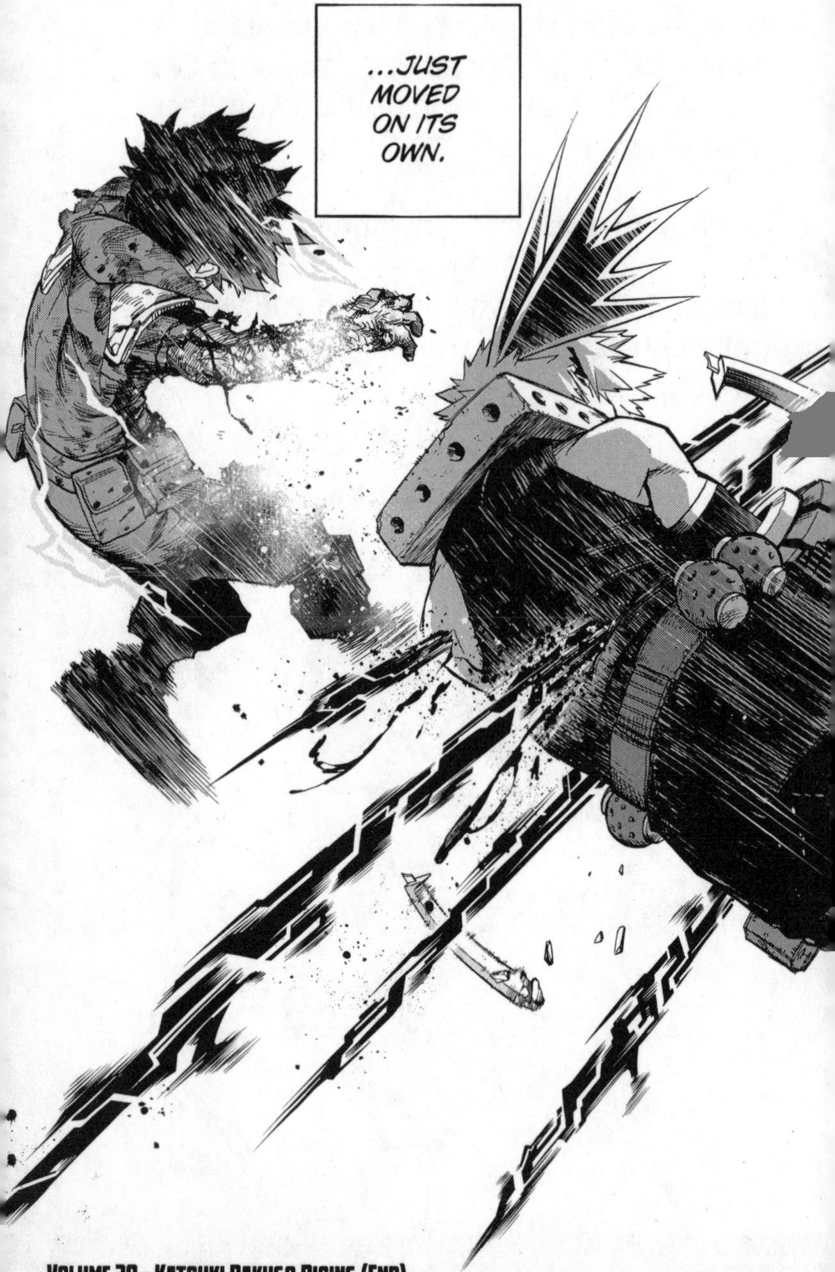
...JUST MOVED ON ITS OWN.

VOLUME 29 - KATSUKI BAKUGO RISING (END)

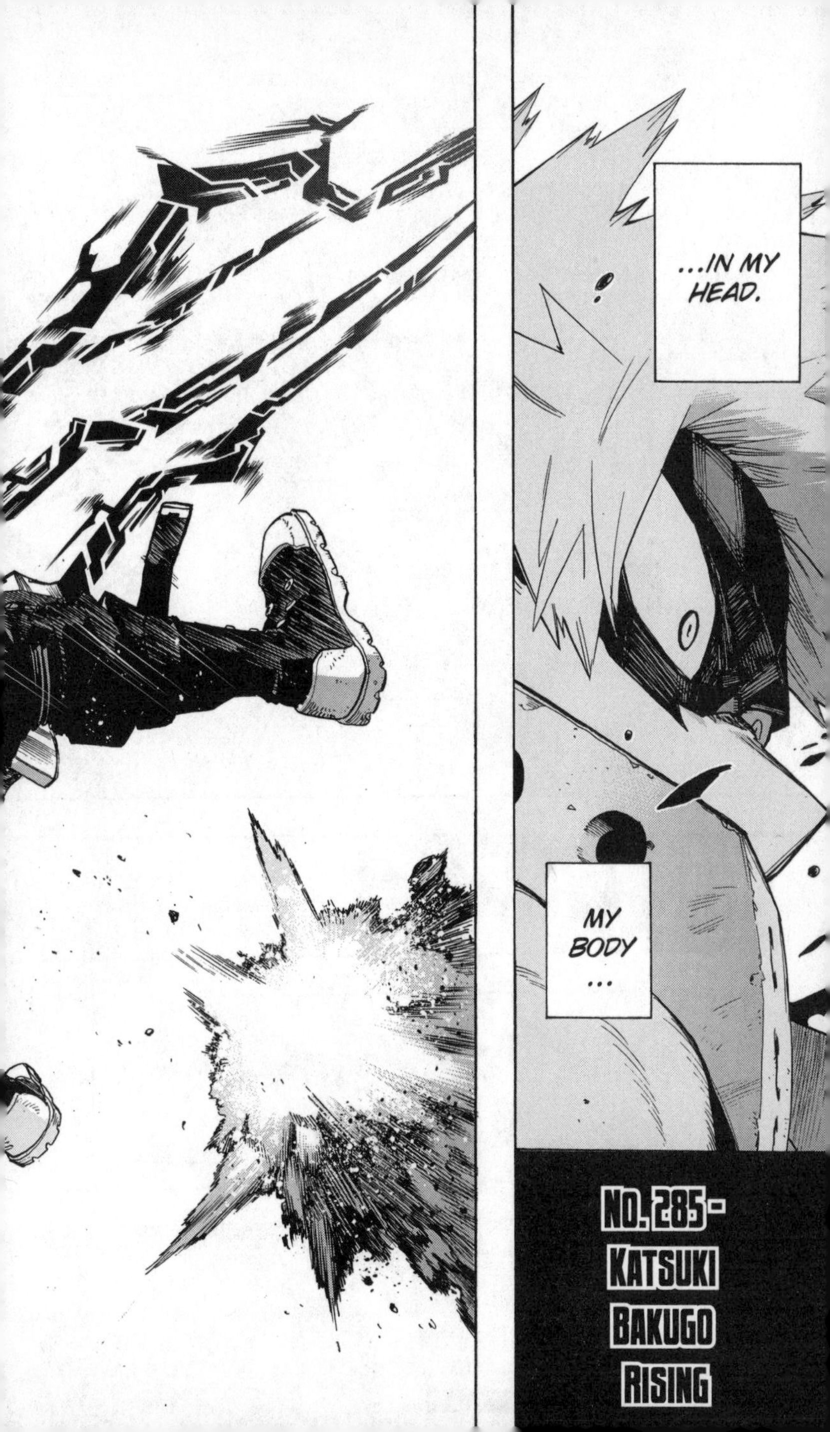
...IN MY HEAD.
MY BODY ...
NO. 285- KATSUKI BAKUGO RISING

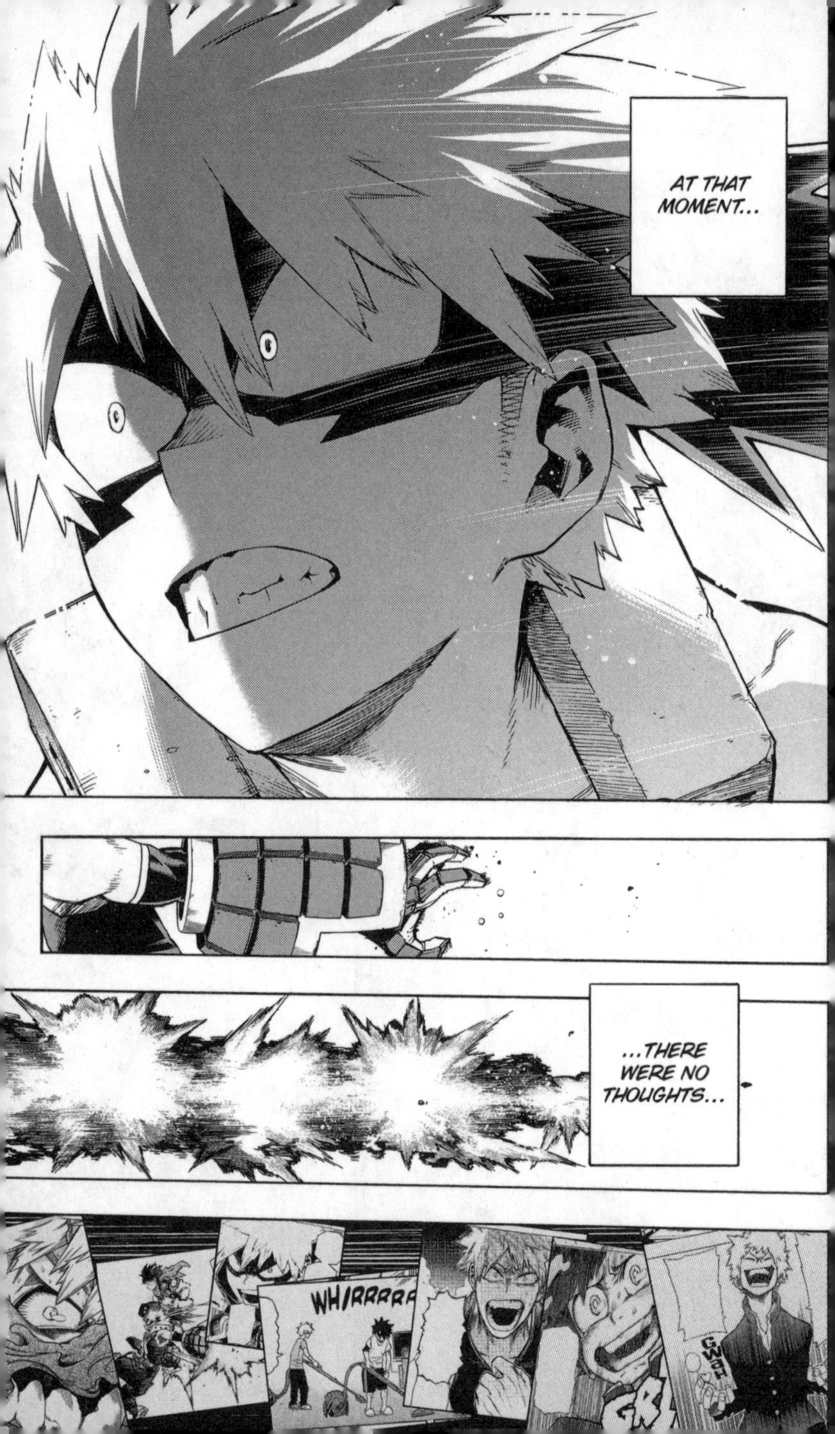
AT THAT MOMENT...
...THERE WERE NO THOUGHTS...
GWAH

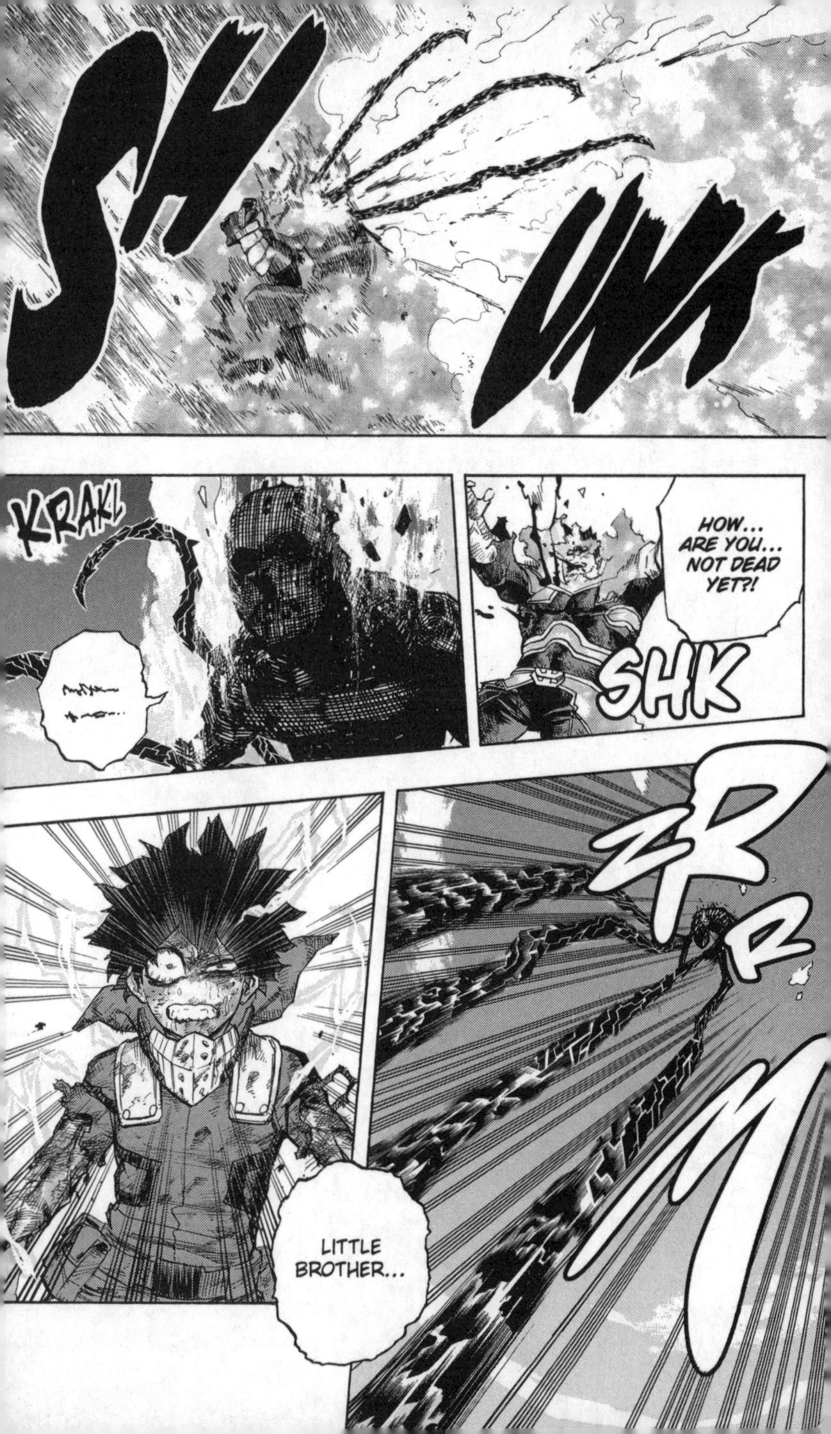
SHUNK
HOW... ARE YOU... NOT DEAD YET?!
SHK
KRAKL
ZRR
LITTLE BROTHER...

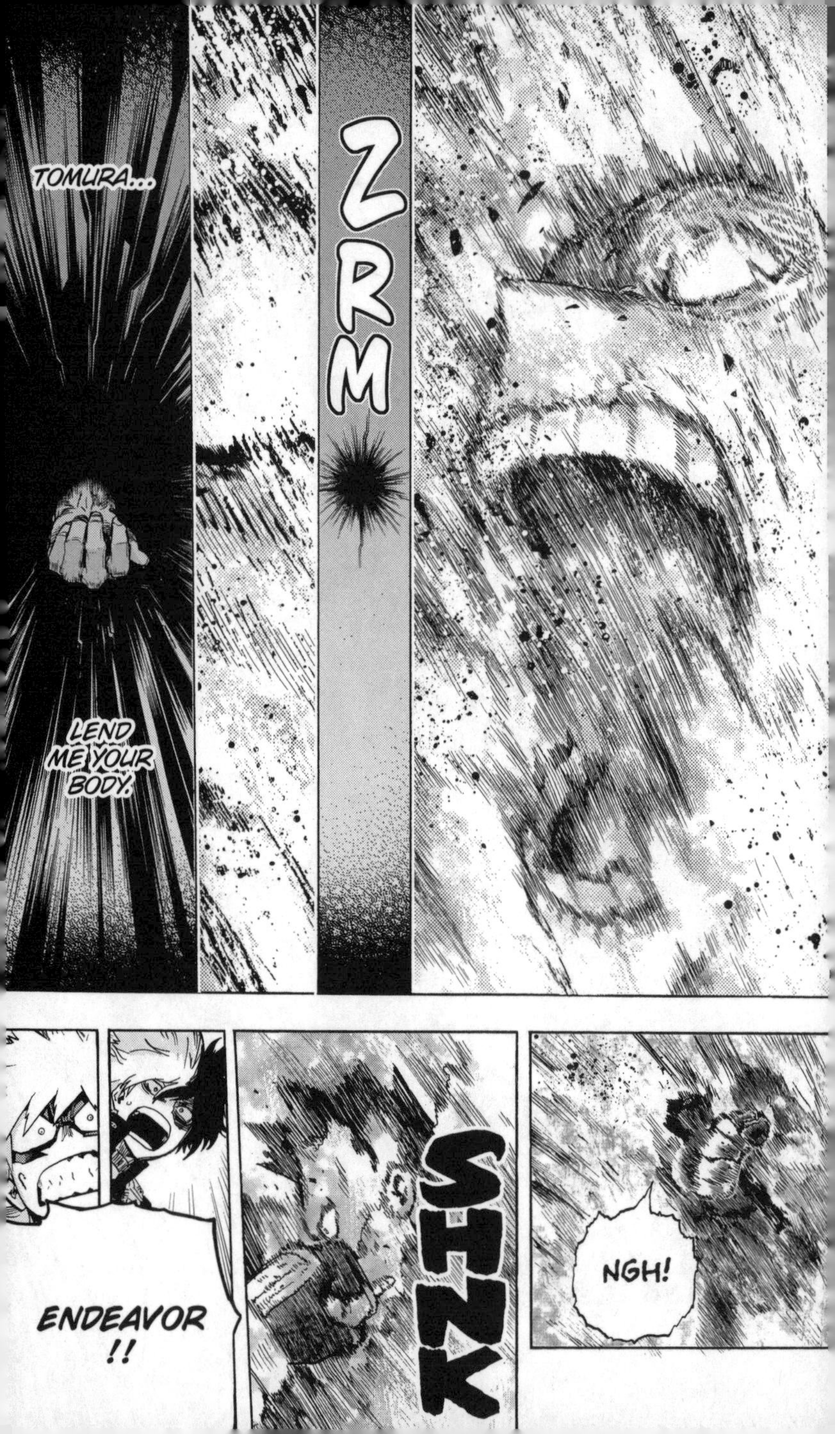
ZRM
TOMURA...
LEND ME YOUR BODY.
NGH!
SHNK
ENDEAVOR!!

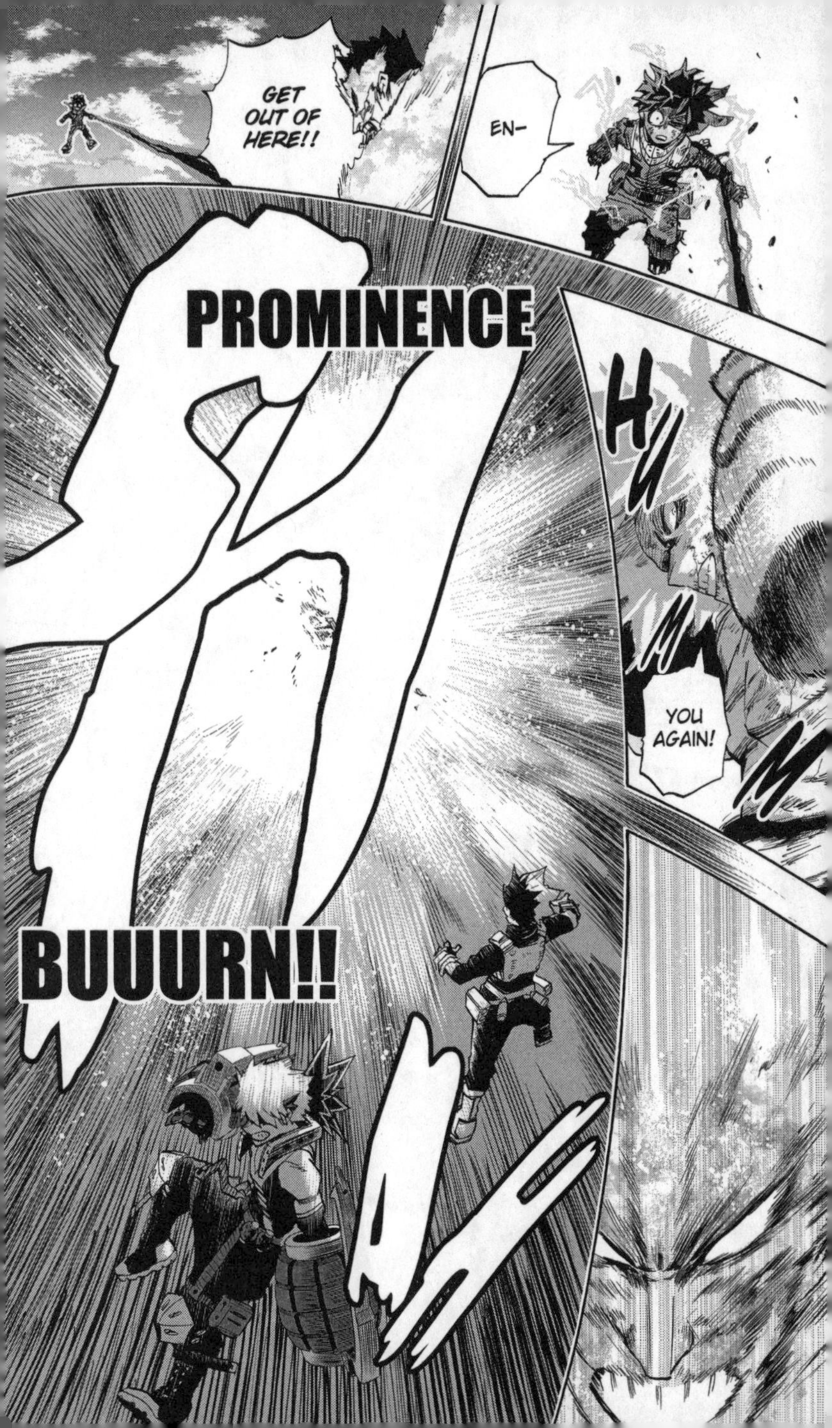

EN-
GET OUT OF HERE!!
HUMMM
YOU AGAIN!
PROMINENCE
BUUURN!!

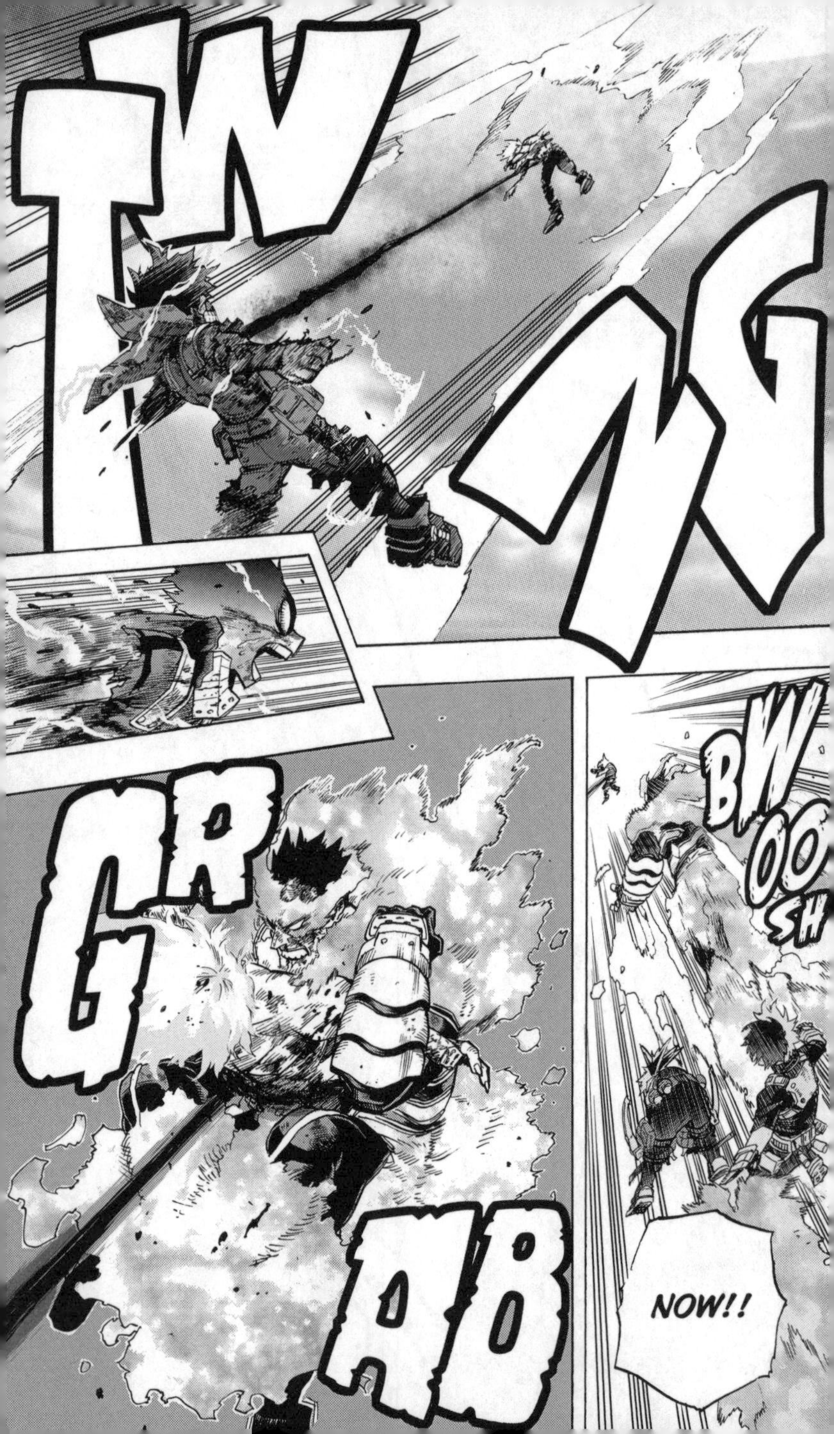

TWNG
BWOOSH
GRAB
NOW!!

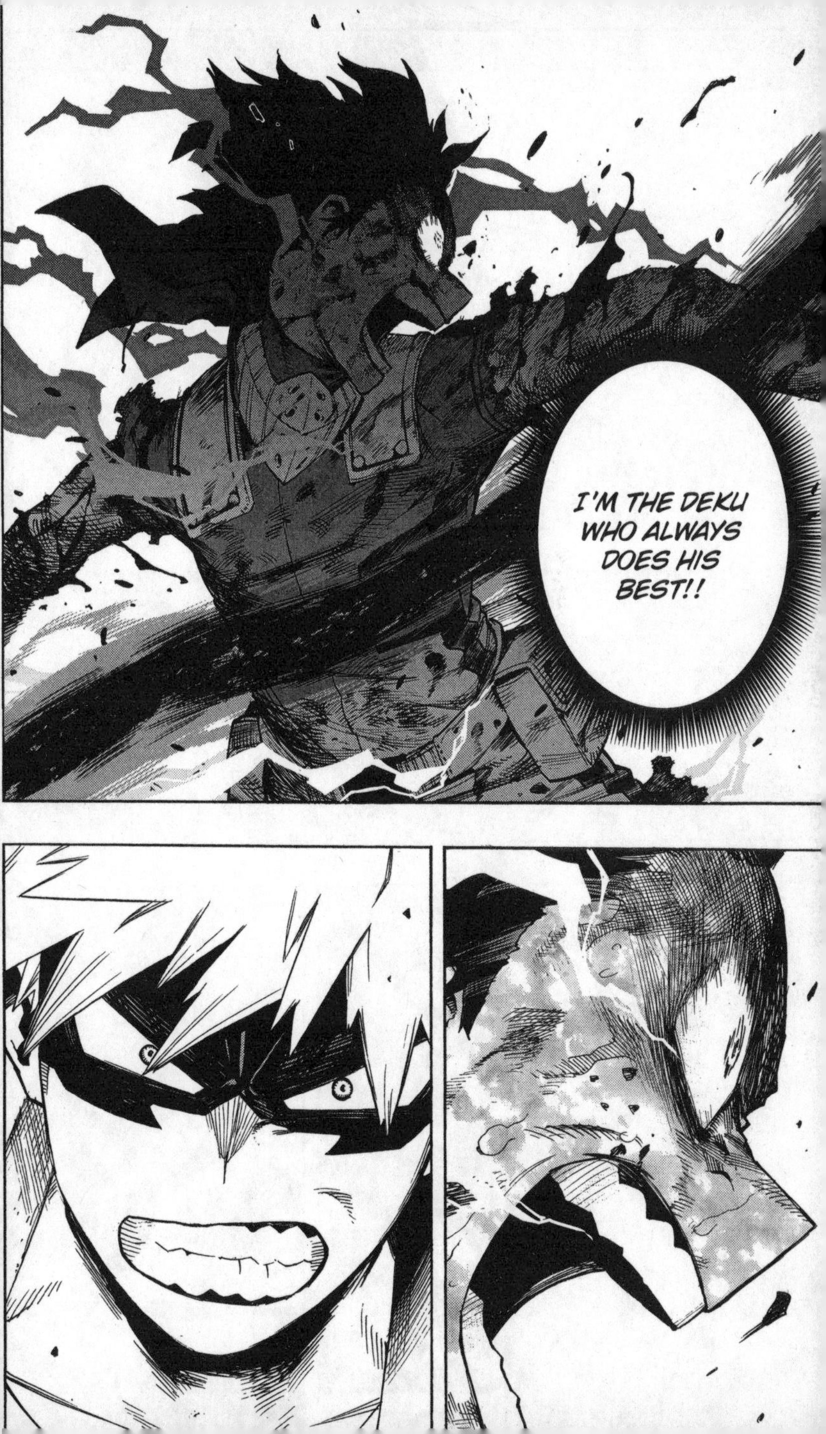
I'M THE DEKU WHO ALWAYS DOES HIS BEST!!

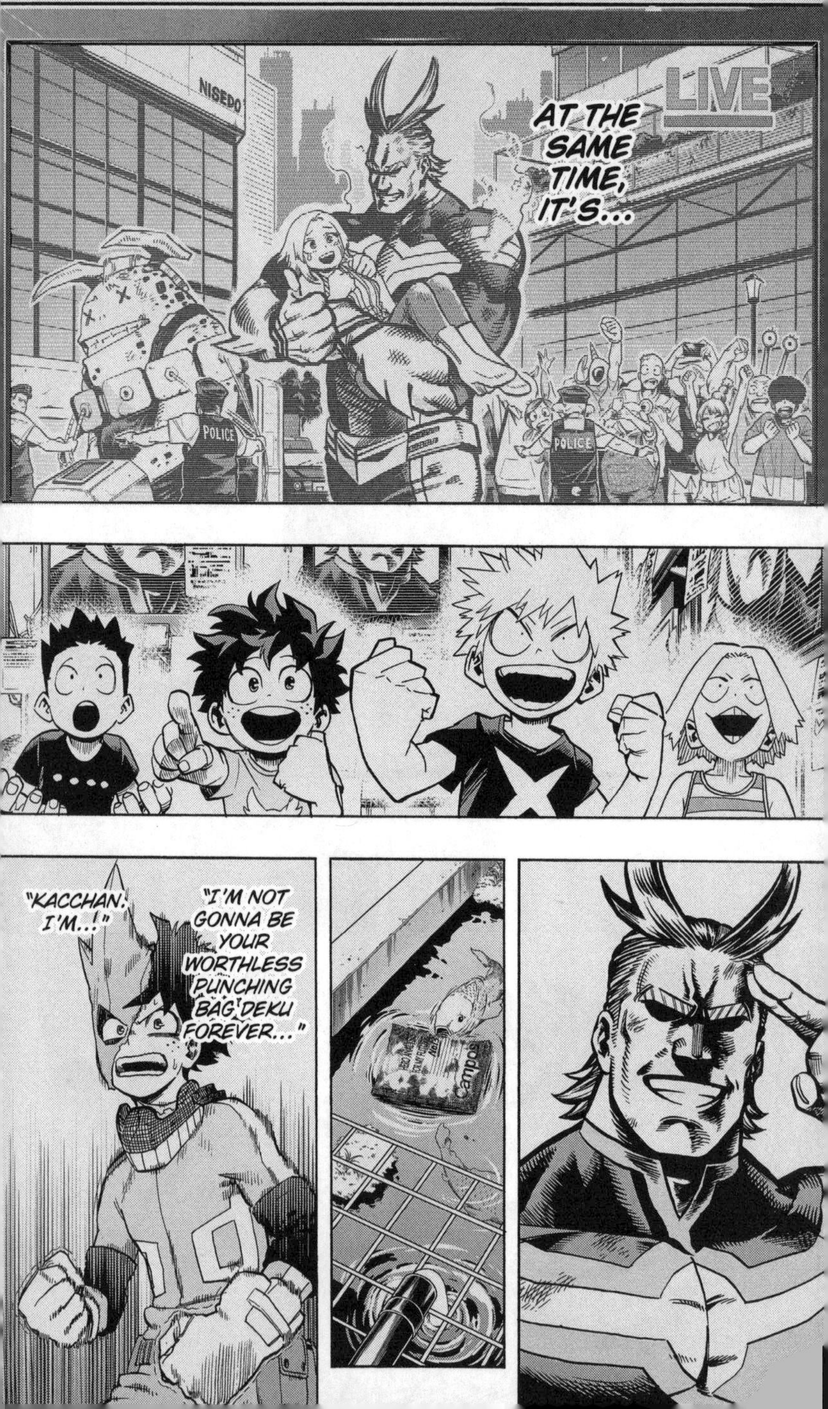
LIVE
NISEDO
AT THE SAME TIME, IT'S...
POLICE
POLICE
"I'M NOT GONNA BE YOUR WORTHLESS PUNCHING BAG DEKU FOREVER..."
"KACCHAN. I'M...!"

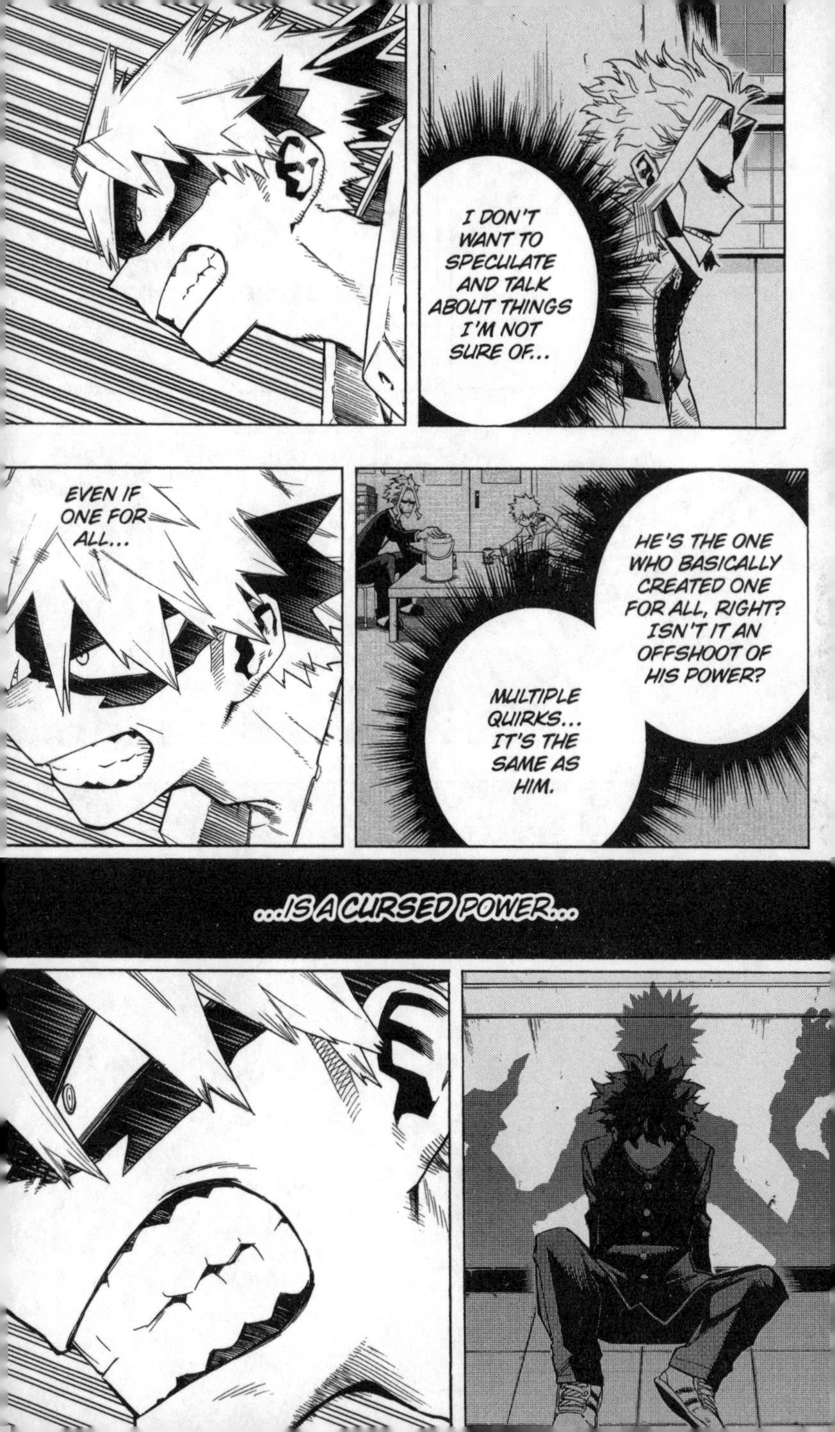
I DON'T WANT TO SPECULATE AND TALK ABOUT THINGS I'M NOT SURE OF...
HE'S THE ONE WHO BASICALLY CREATED ONE FOR ALL, RIGHT? ISN'T IT AN OFFSHOOT OF HIS POWER?
MULTIPLE QUIRKS... IT'S THE SAME AS HIM.
EVEN IF ONE FOR ALL...
...IS A CURSED POWER...

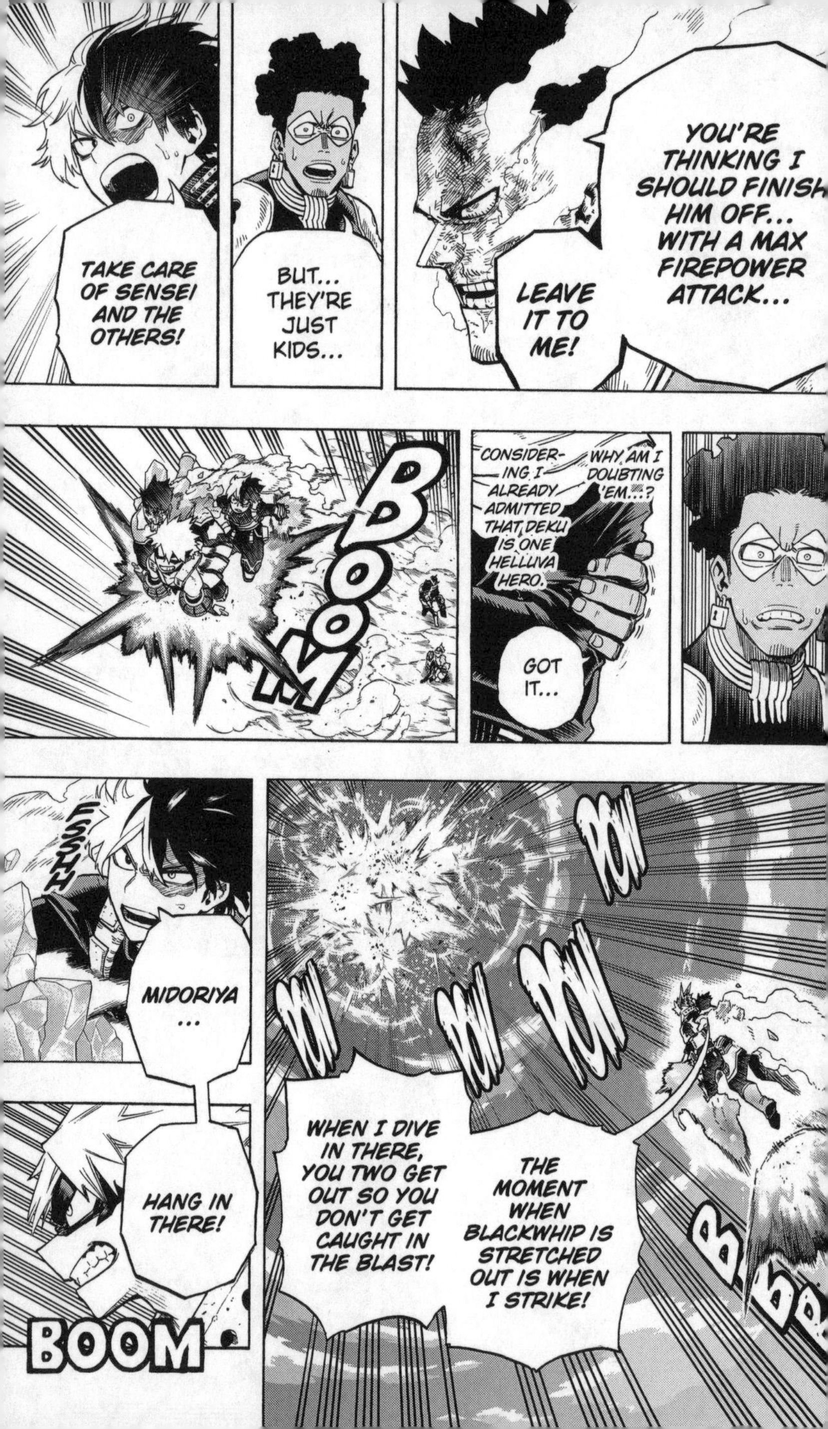

YOU'RE THINKING I SHOULD FINISH HIM OFF... WITH A MAX FIREPOWER ATTACK...
LEAVE IT TO ME!
BUT... THEY'RE JUST KIDS...
TAKE CARE OF SENSEI AND THE OTHERS!
WHY AM I DOUBTING 'EM...?
CONSIDERING I ALREADY ADMITTED THAT DEKU IS ONE HELLUVA HERO.
GOT IT...
BOOOOM
BOW
THE MOMENT WHEN BLACKWHIP IS STRETCHED OUT IS WHEN I STRIKE!
WHEN I DIVE IN THERE, YOU TWO GET OUT SO YOU DON'T GET CAUGHT IN THE BLAST!
BOW BOW BOW BOW
FSSHH
MIDORIYA...
HANG IN THERE!
BOOM

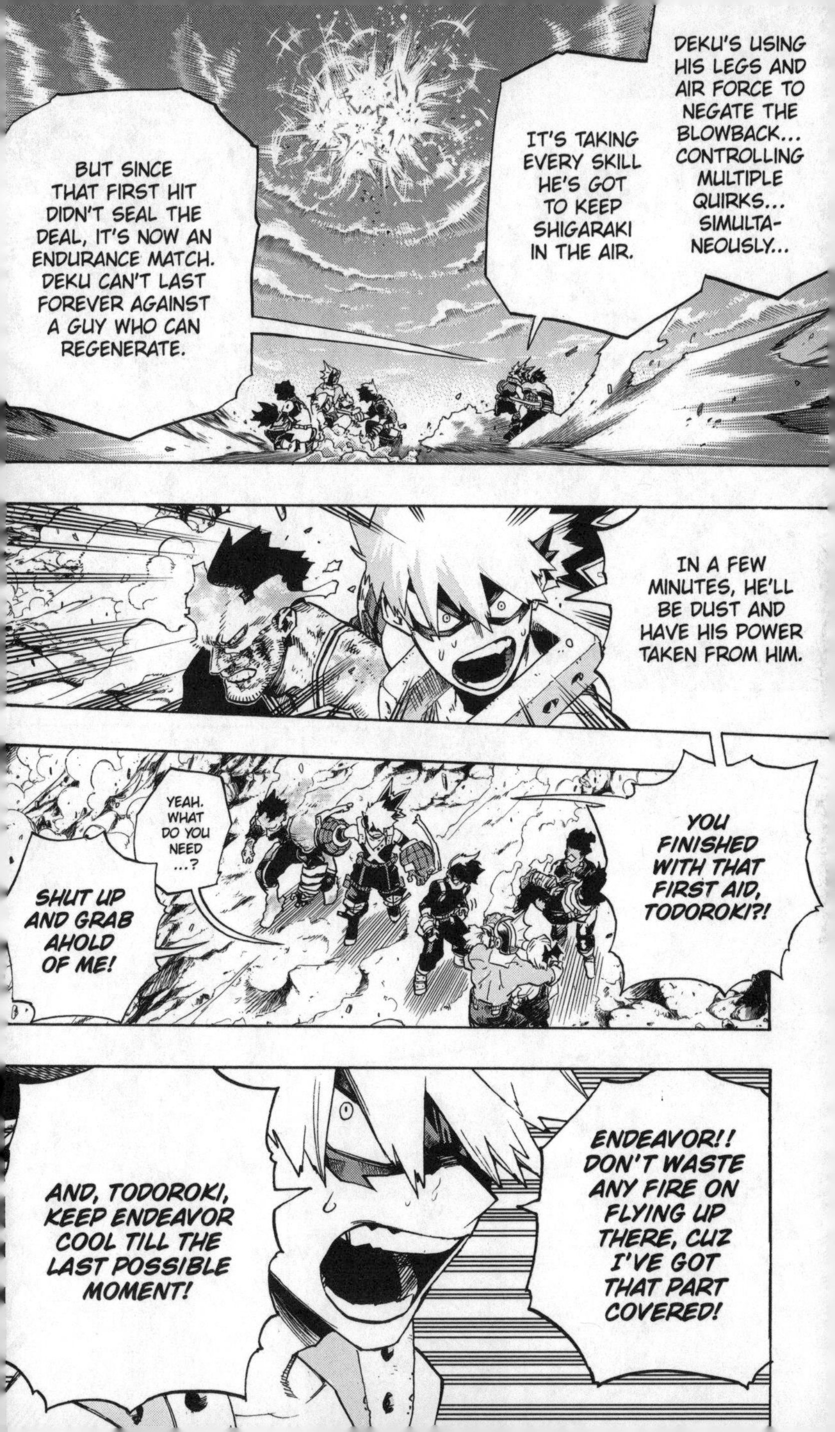
DEKU'S USING HIS LEGS AND AIR FORCE TO NEGATE THE BLOWBACK... CONTROLLING MULTIPLE QUIRKS... SIMULTA-NEOUSLY...
IT'S TAKING EVERY SKILL HE'S GOT TO KEEP SHIGARAKI IN THE AIR.
BUT SINCE THAT FIRST HIT DIDN'T SEAL THE DEAL, IT'S NOW AN ENDURANCE MATCH. DEKU CAN'T LAST FOREVER AGAINST A GUY WHO CAN REGENERATE.
IN A FEW MINUTES, HE'LL BE DUST AND HAVE HIS POWER TAKEN FROM HIM.
YOU FINISHED WITH THAT FIRST AID, TODOROKI?!
YEAH. WHAT DO YOU NEED ...?
SHUT UP AND GRAB AHOLD OF ME!
ENDEAVOR!! DON'T WASTE ANY FIRE ON FLYING UP THERE, CUZ I'VE GOT THAT PART COVERED!
AND, TODOROKI, KEEP ENDEAVOR COOL TILL THE LAST POSSIBLE MOMENT!

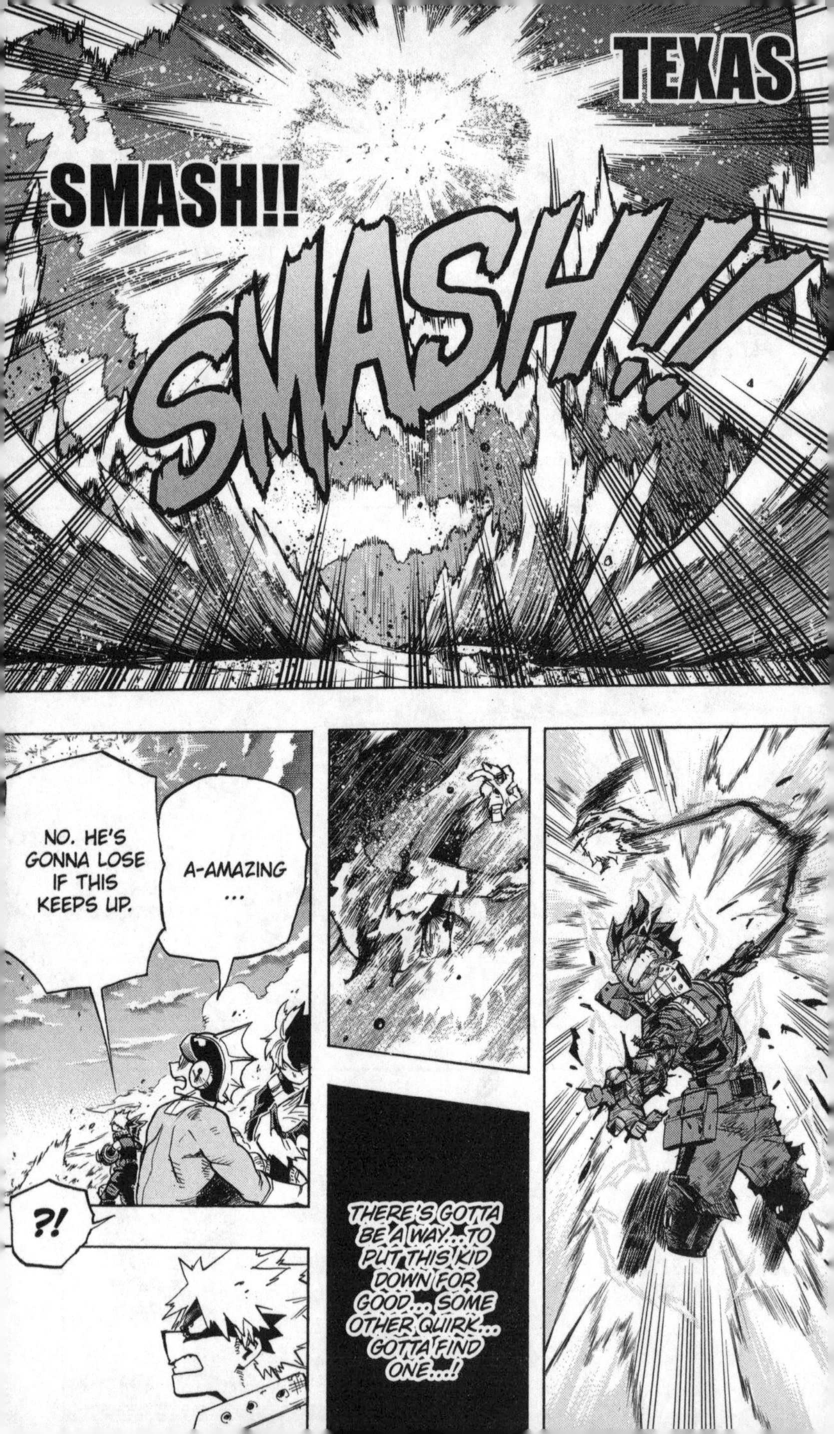
TEXAS
SMASH!!
SMASH!!
THERE'S GOTTA BE A WAY... TO PUT THIS KID DOWN FOR GOOD... SOME OTHER QUIRK... GOTTA FIND ONE...!
A-AMAZING...
NO. HE'S GONNA LOSE IF THIS KEEPS UP.
?!

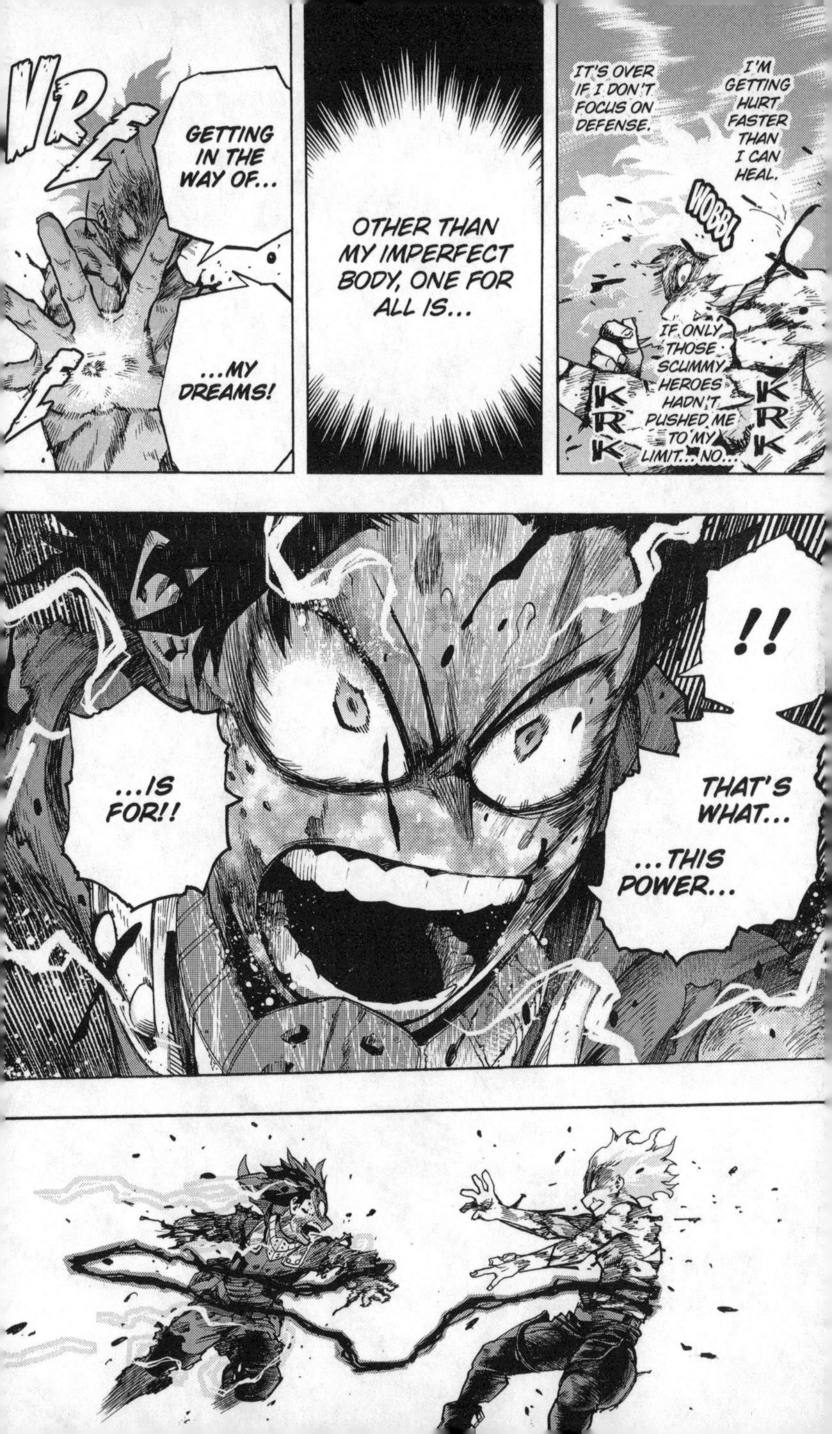

I'M GETTING HURT FASTER THAN I CAN HEAL.
IT'S OVER IF I DON'T FOCUS ON DEFENSE.
WOBBL
IF ONLY THOSE SCUMMY HEROES HADN'T PUSHED ME TO MY LIMIT... NO...
KRK
KRK
OTHER THAN MY IMPERFECT BODY, ONE FOR ALL IS...
VRF
GETTING IN THE WAY OF...
...MY DREAMS!
!!
THAT'S WHAT...
...THIS POWER...
...IS FOR!!

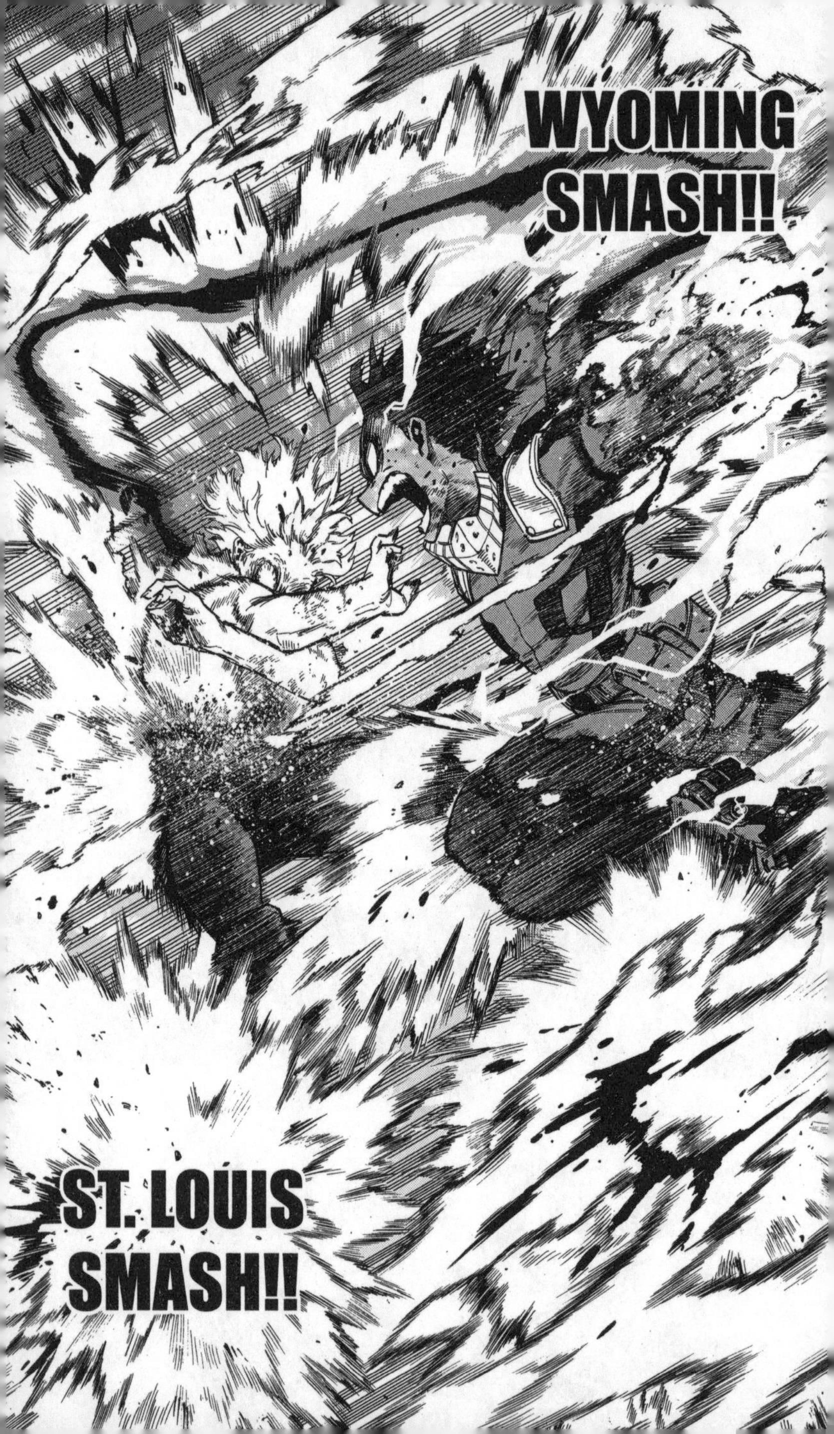
WYOMING SMASH!!
ST. LOUIS SMASH!!

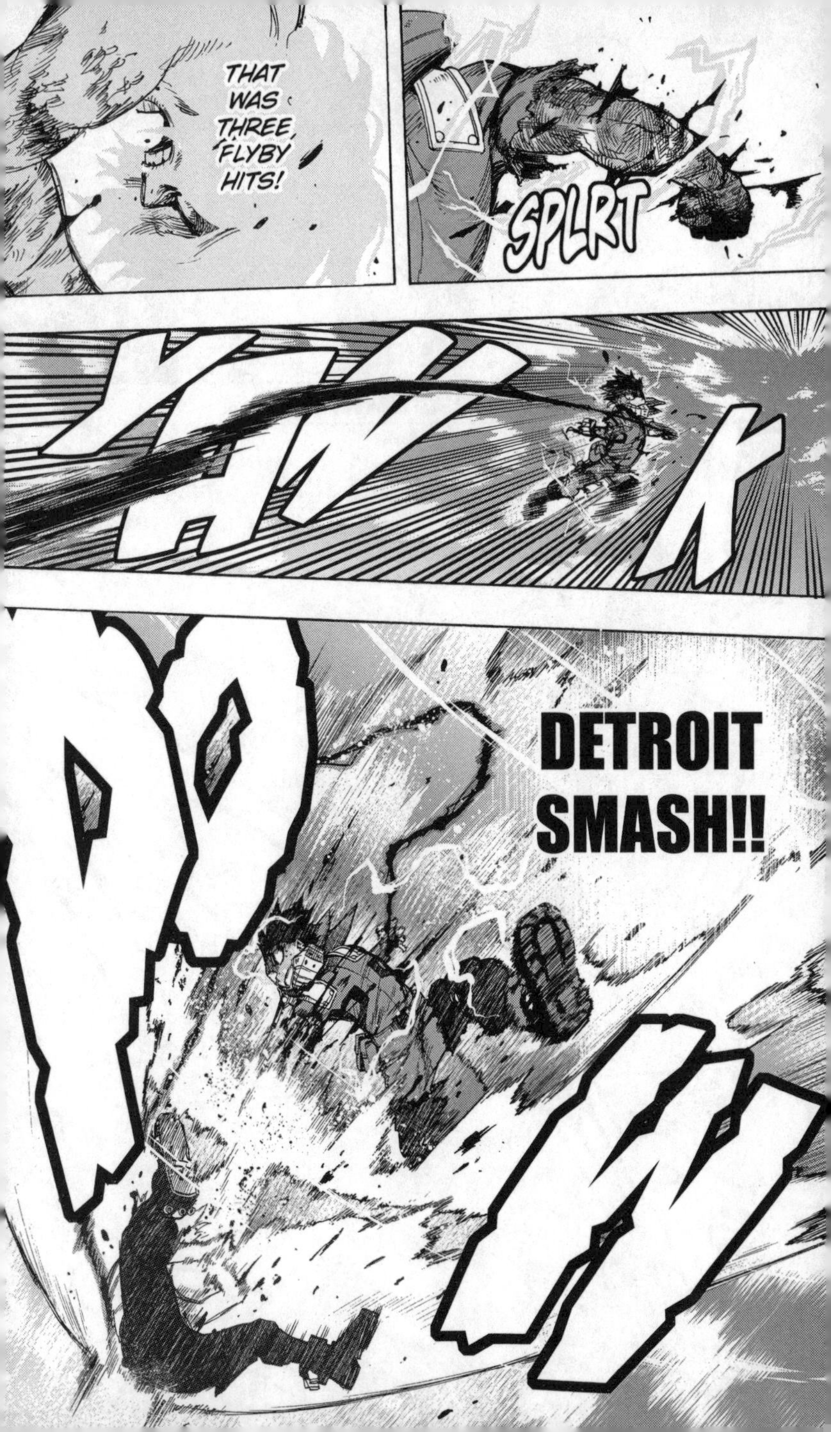
SPLRT
THAT WAS THREE, FLYBY HITS!
DETROIT SMASH!!

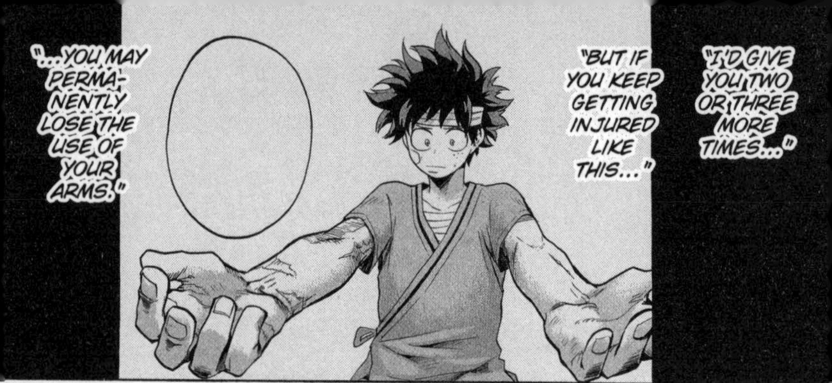
"I'D GIVE YOU TWO OR THREE MORE TIMES..."
"BUT IF YOU KEEP GETTING INJURED LIKE THIS..."
"...YOU MAY PERMANENTLY LOSE THE USE OF YOUR ARMS."

No. 285 - Katsuki Bakugo Rising

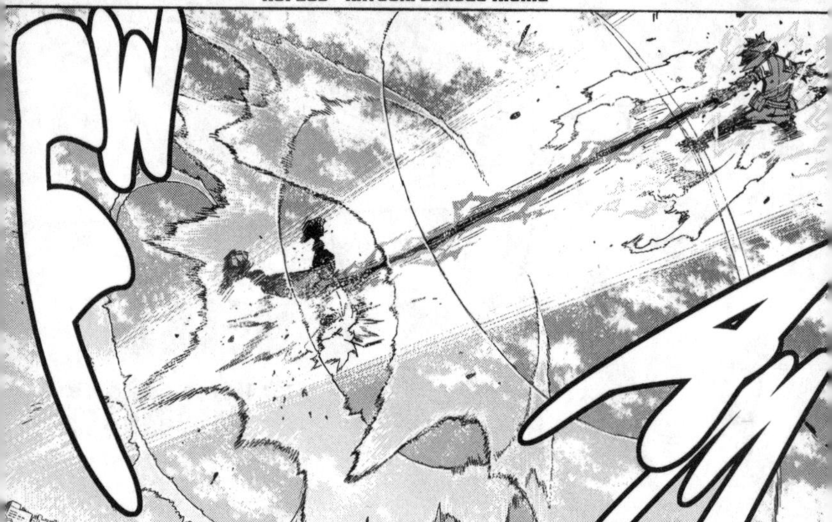
FW
AM

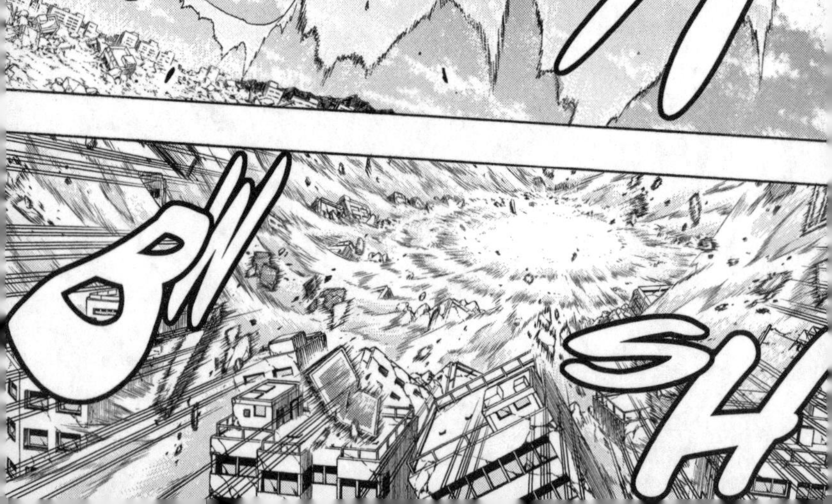
BW
SH

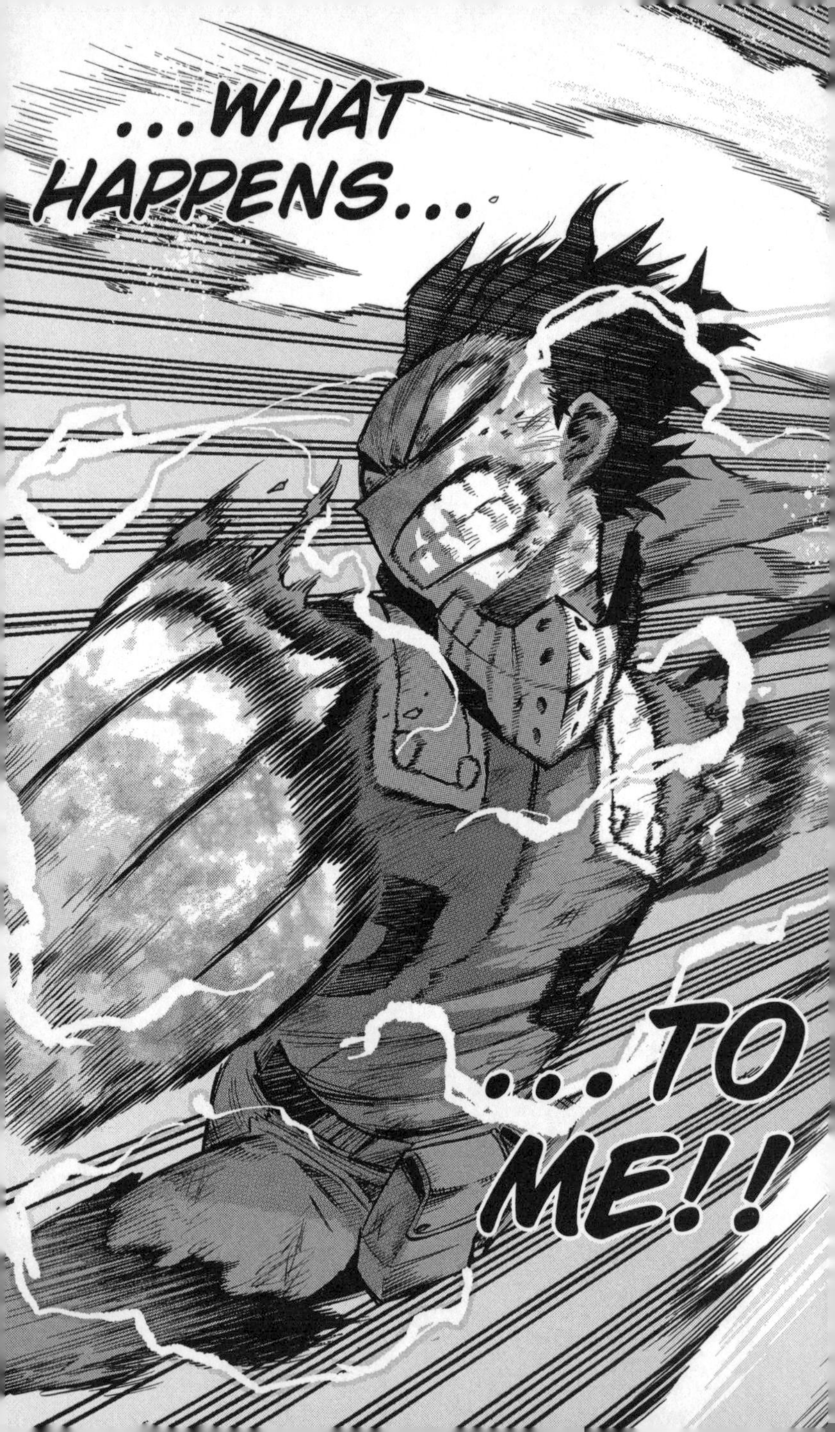
...WHAT HAPPENS...
...TO ME!!

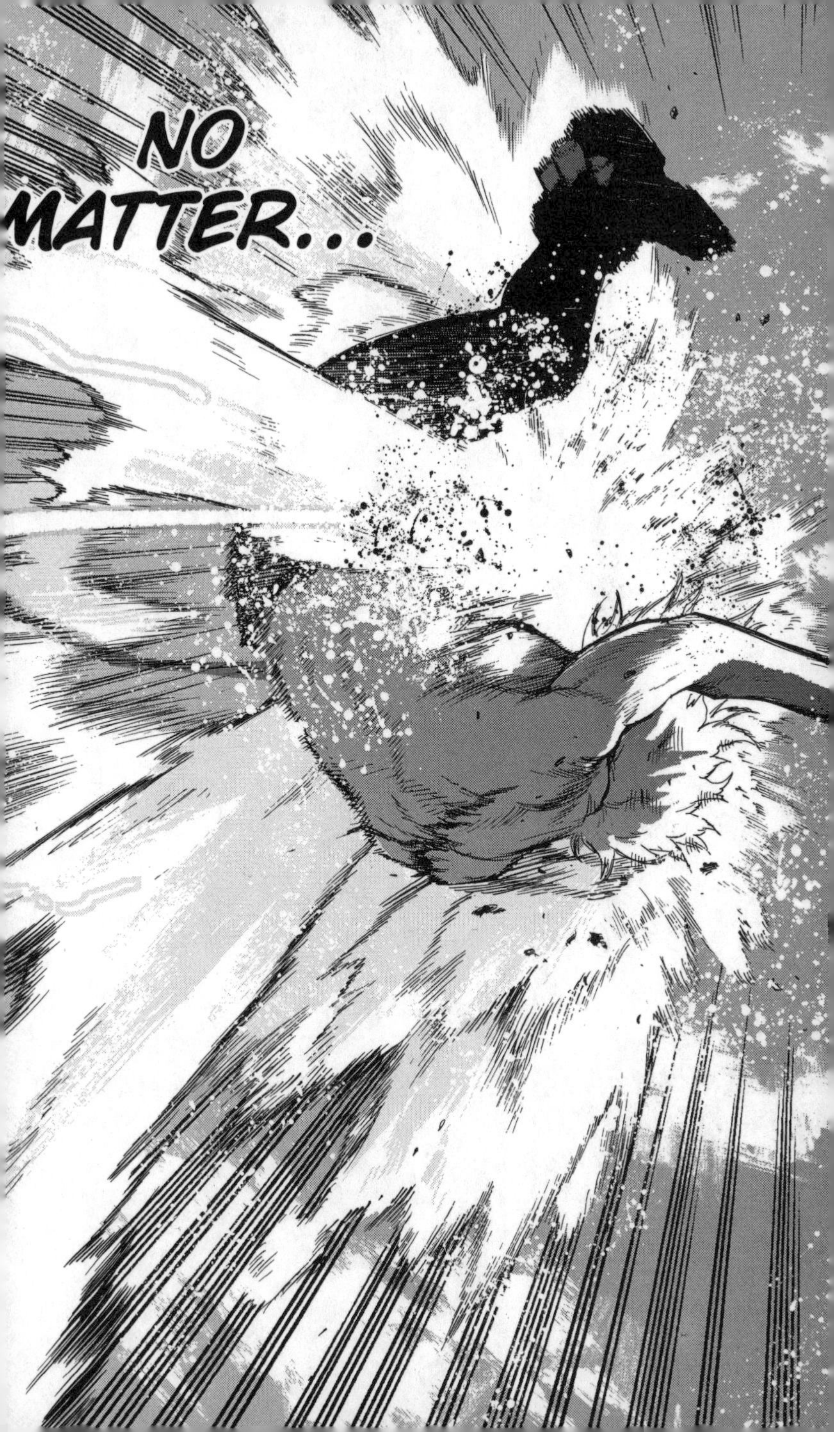
NO MATTER...

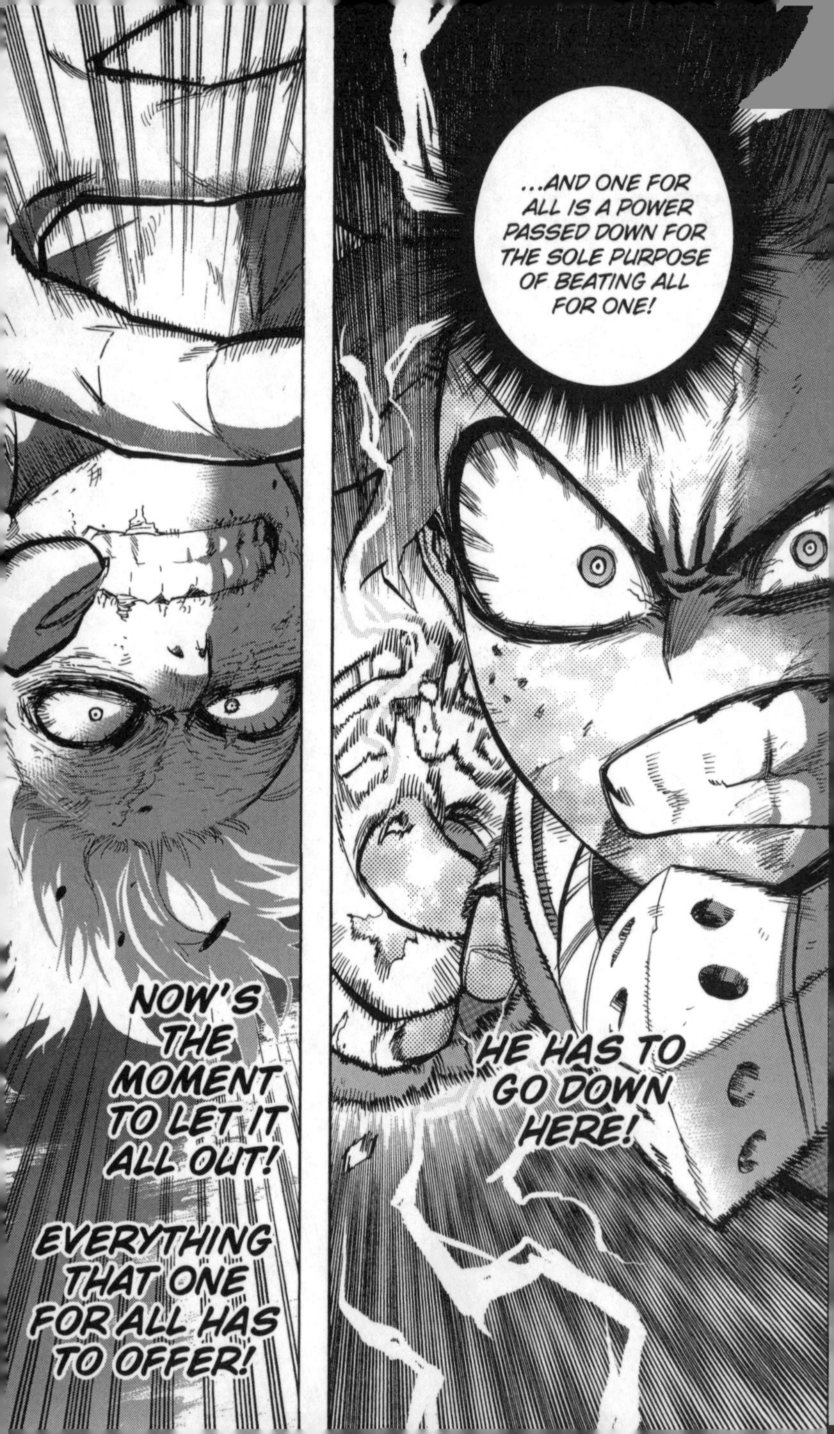
...AND ONE FOR ALL IS A POWER PASSED DOWN FOR THE SOLE PURPOSE OF BEATING ALL FOR ONE!
HE HAS TO GO DOWN HERE!
NOW'S THE MOMENT TO LET IT ALL OUT!
EVERYTHING THAT ONE FOR ALL HAS TO OFFER!

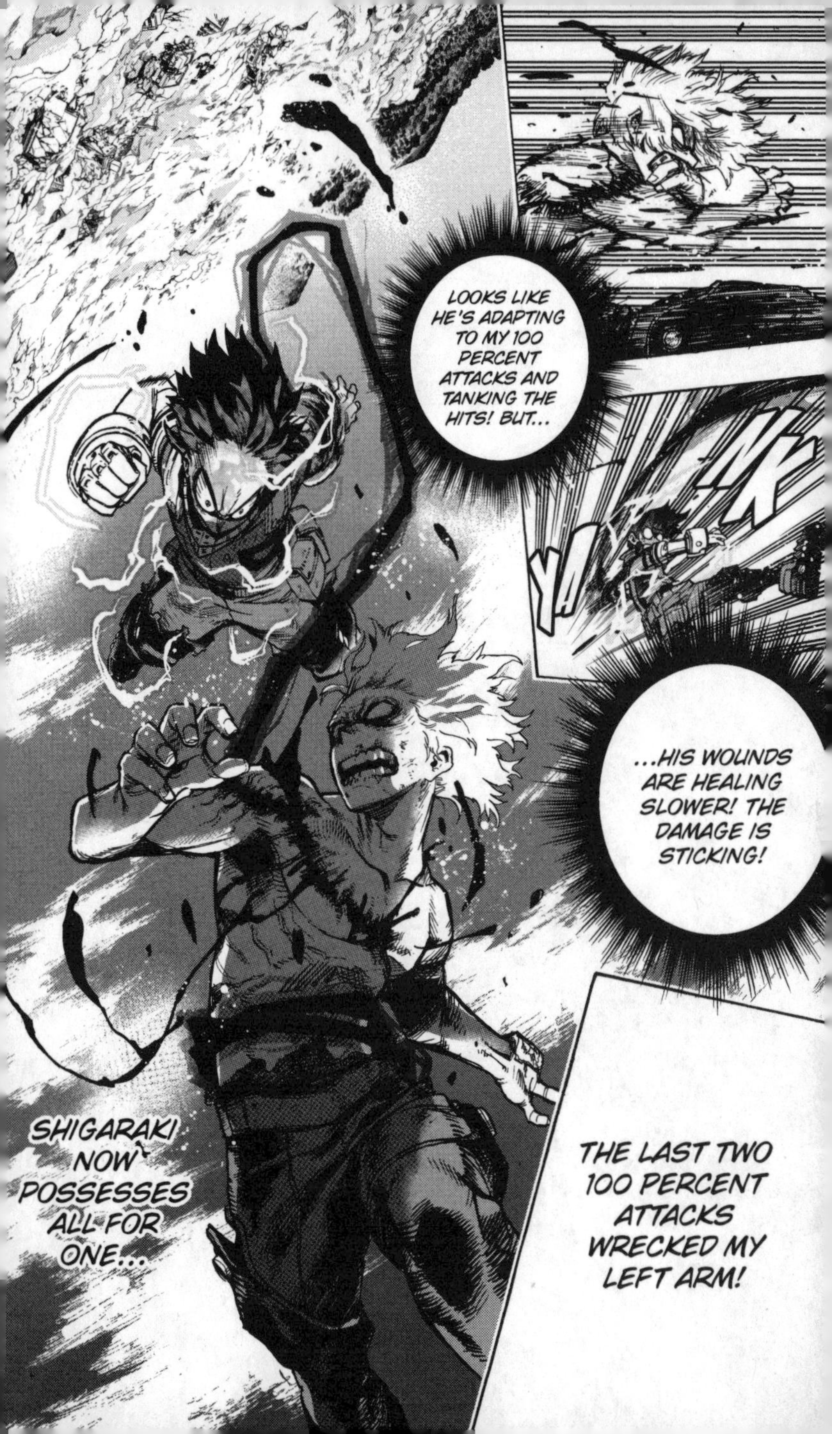
LOOKS LIKE HE'S ADAPTING TO MY 100 PERCENT ATTACKS AND TANKING THE HITS! BUT...
YANK
...HIS WOUNDS ARE HEALING SLOWER! THE DAMAGE IS STICKING!
SHIGARAKI NOW POSSESSES ALL FOR ONE...
THE LAST TWO 100 PERCENT ATTACKS WRECKED MY LEFT ARM!

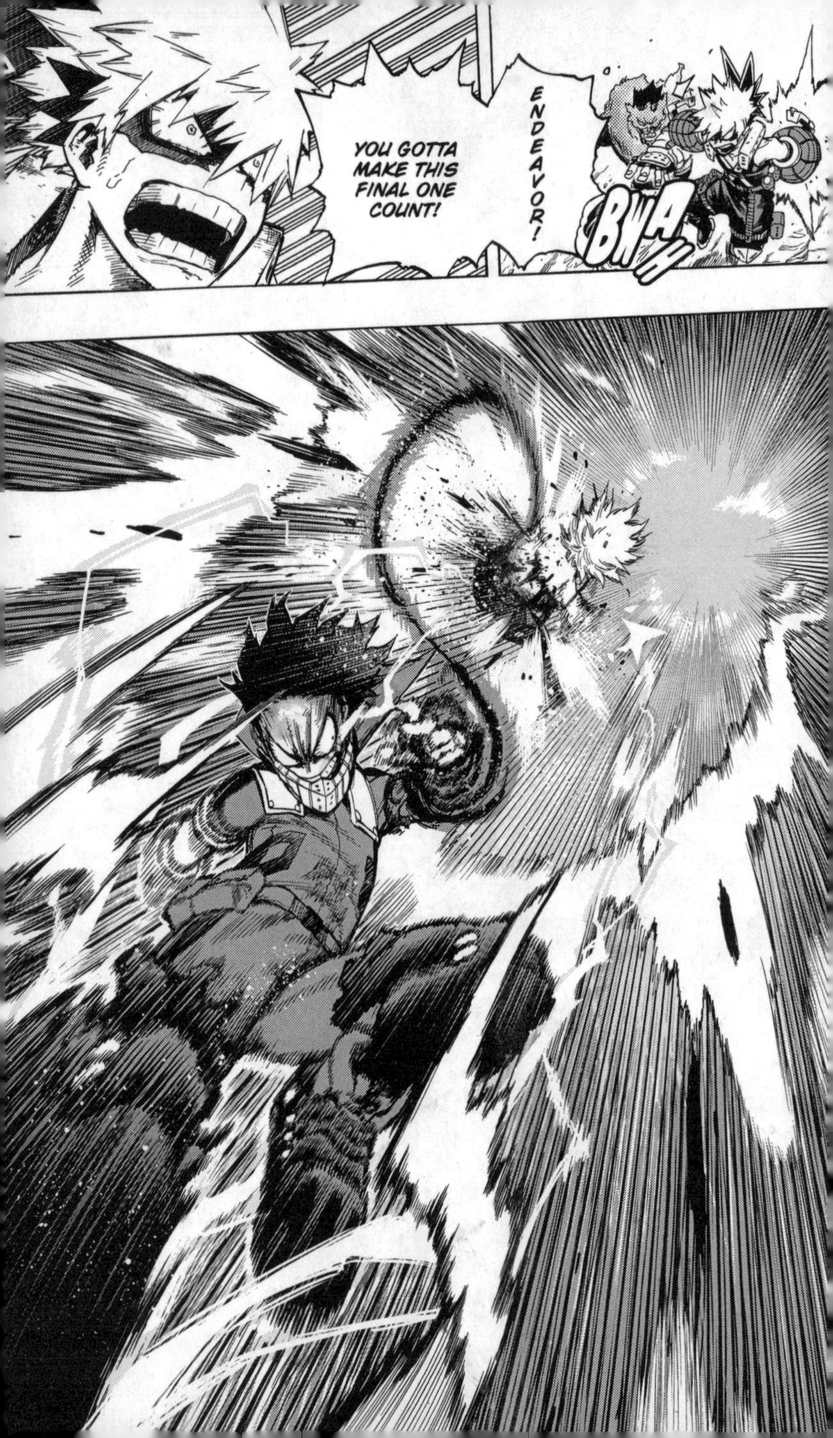
ENDEAVOR!
BWAH
YOU GOTTA MAKE THIS FINAL ONE COUNT!

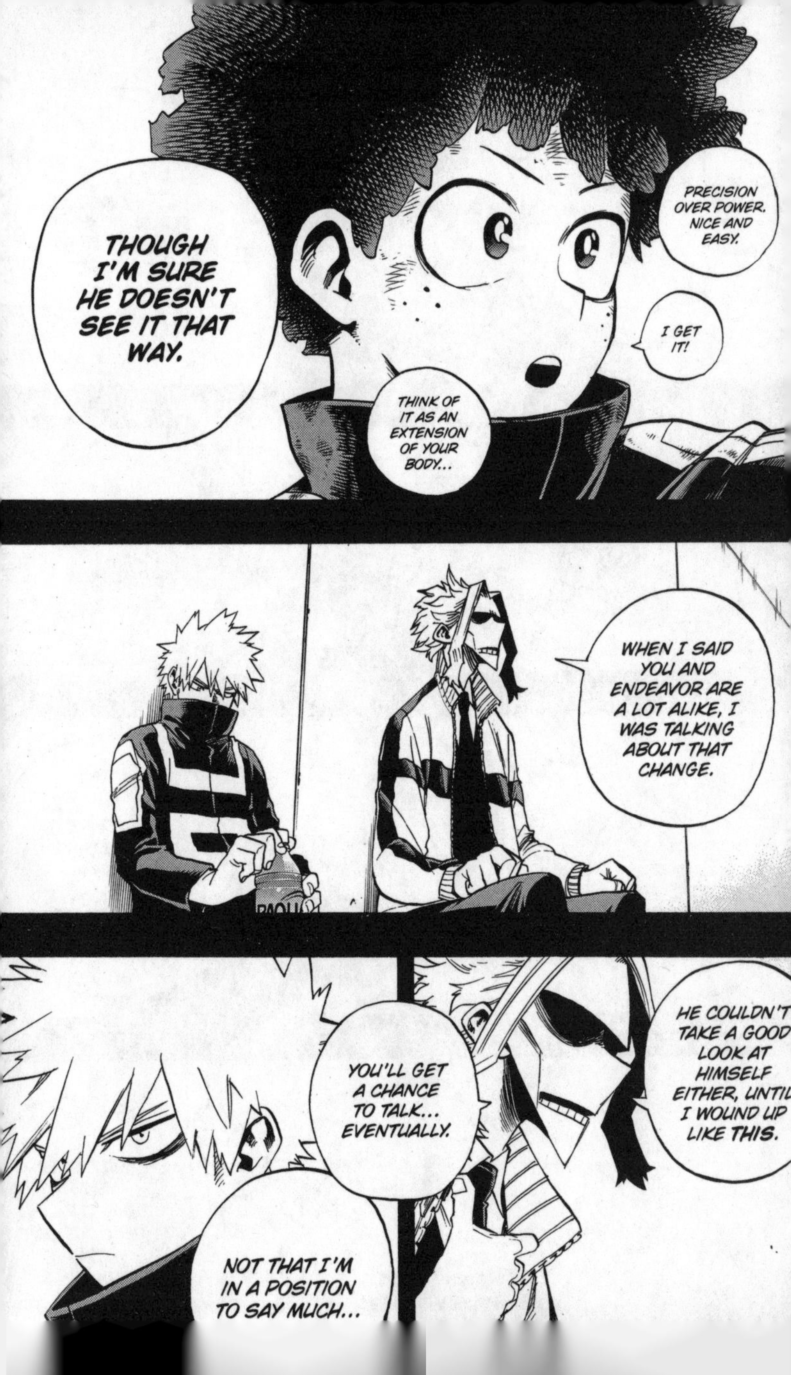
PRECISION OVER POWER. NICE AND EASY.
I GET IT!
THINK OF IT AS AN EXTENSION OF YOUR BODY...
THOUGH I'M SURE HE DOESN'T SEE IT THAT WAY.
WHEN I SAID YOU AND ENDEAVOR ARE A LOT ALIKE, I WAS TALKING ABOUT THAT CHANGE.
HE COULDN'T TAKE A GOOD LOOK AT HIMSELF EITHER, UNTIL I WOUND UP LIKE THIS.
YOU'LL GET A CHANCE TO TALK... EVENTUALLY.
NOT THAT I'M IN A POSITION TO SAY MUCH...

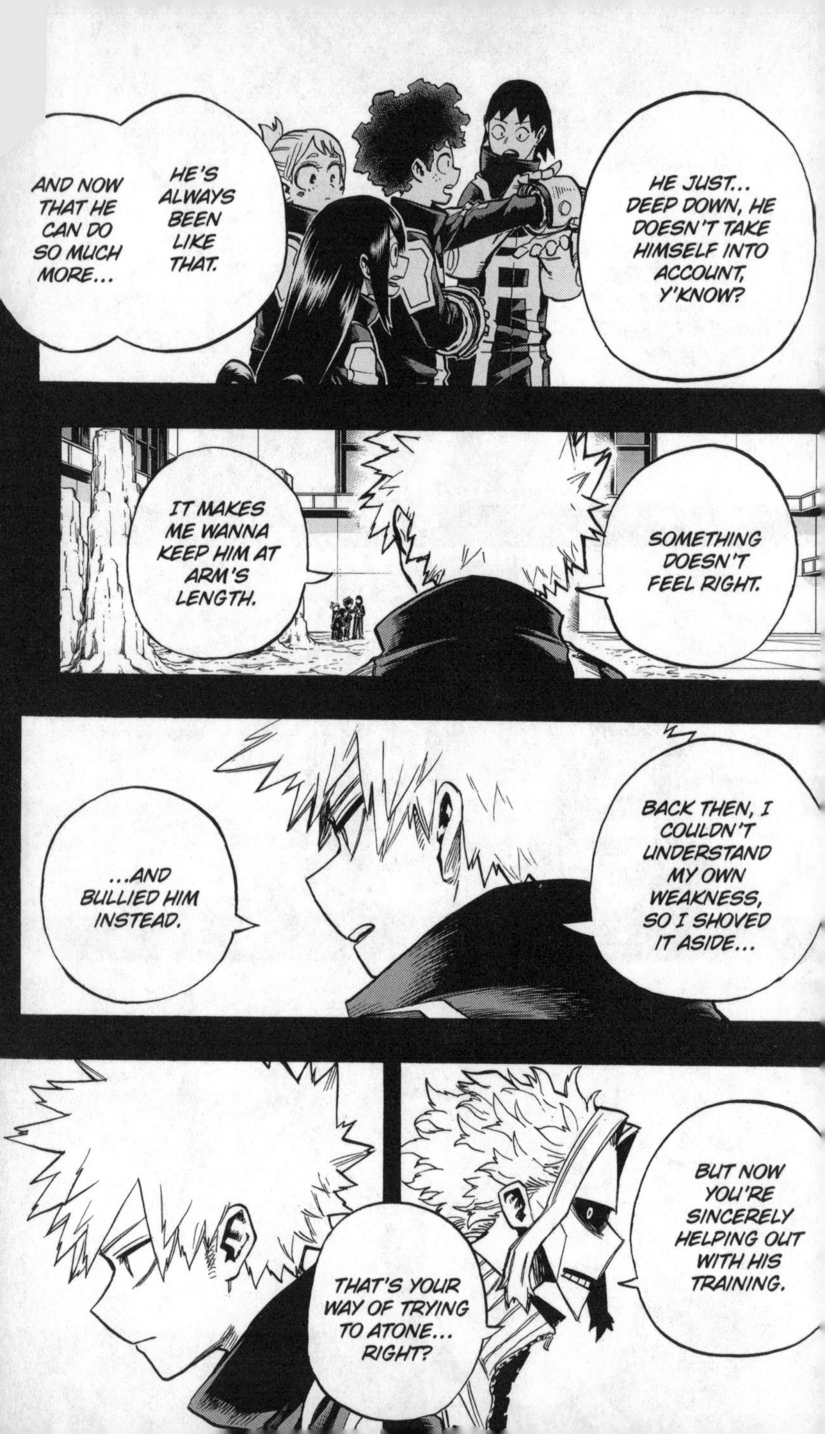
HE JUST... DEEP DOWN, HE DOESN'T TAKE HIMSELF INTO ACCOUNT, Y'KNOW?
HE'S ALWAYS BEEN LIKE THAT.
AND NOW THAT HE CAN DO SO MUCH MORE...
SOMETHING DOESN'T FEEL RIGHT.
IT MAKES ME WANNA KEEP HIM AT ARM'S LENGTH.
BACK THEN, I COULDN'T UNDERSTAND MY OWN WEAKNESS, SO I SHOVED IT ASIDE...
...AND BULLIED HIM INSTEAD.
BUT NOW YOU'RE SINCERELY HELPING OUT WITH HIS TRAINING.
THAT'S YOUR WAY OF TRYING TO ATONE... RIGHT?

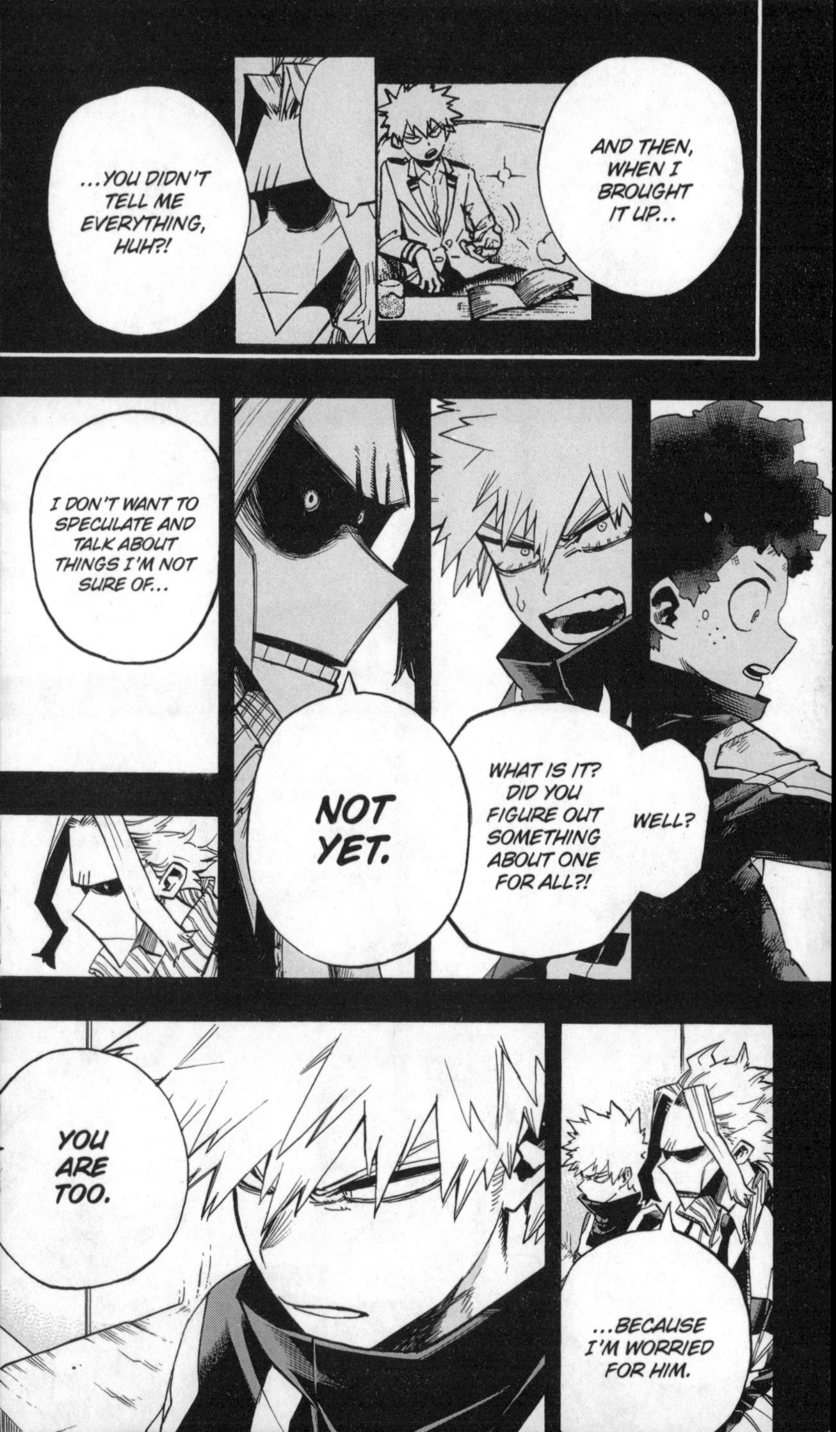
AND THEN, WHEN I BROUGHT IT UP...
...YOU DIDN'T TELL ME EVERYTHING, HUH?!
WELL?
WHAT IS IT? DID YOU FIGURE OUT SOMETHING ABOUT ONE FOR ALL?!
NOT YET.
I DON'T WANT TO SPECULATE AND TALK ABOUT THINGS I'M NOT SURE OF...
...BECAUSE I'M WORRIED FOR HIM.
YOU ARE TOO.

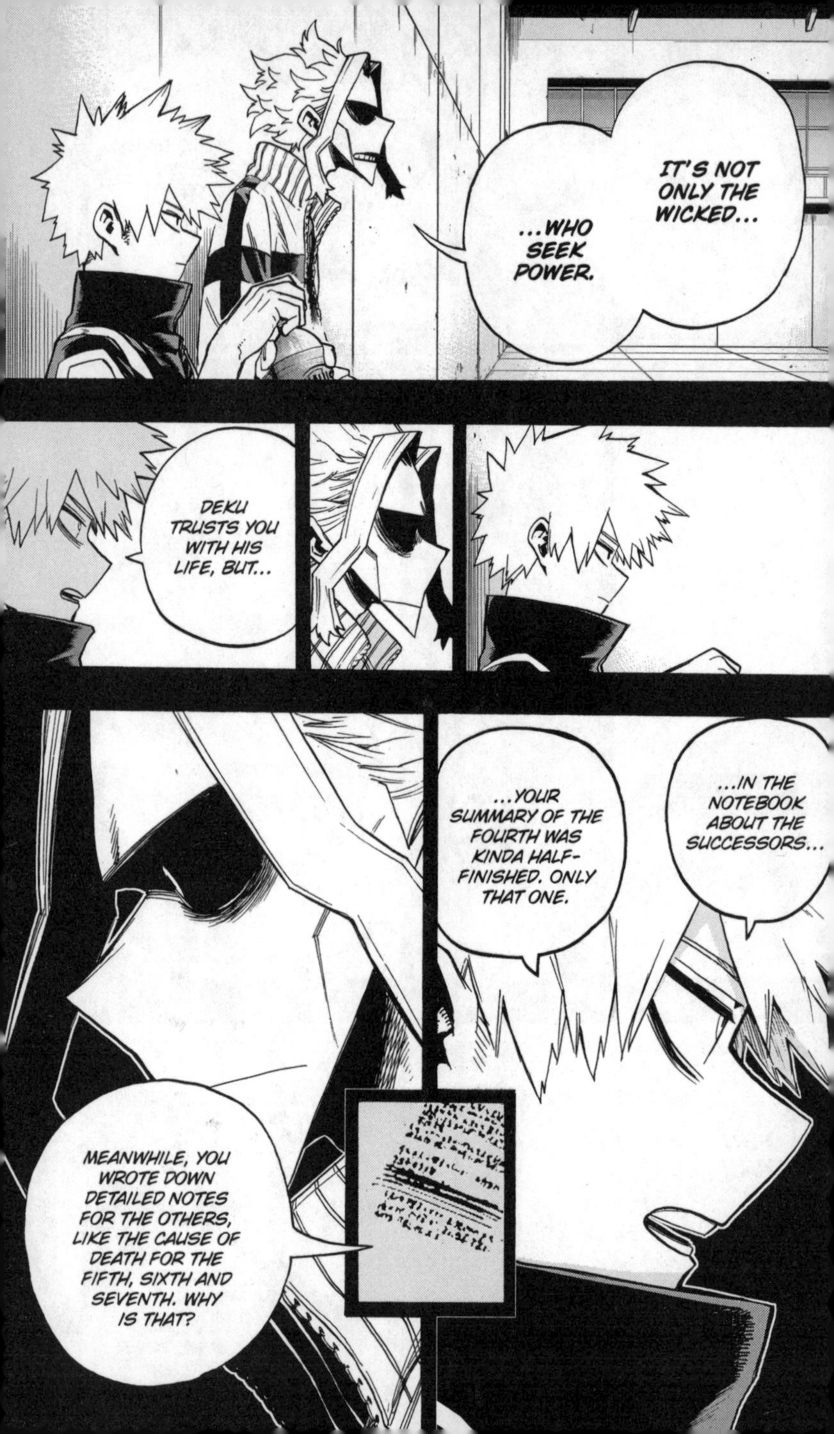
IT'S NOT ONLY THE WICKED...
...WHO SEEK POWER.
DEKU TRUSTS YOU WITH HIS LIFE, BUT...
...IN THE NOTEBOOK ABOUT THE SUCCESSORS...
...YOUR SUMMARY OF THE FOURTH WAS KINDA HALF-FINISHED. ONLY THAT ONE.
MEANWHILE, YOU WROTE DOWN DETAILED NOTES FOR THE OTHERS, LIKE THE CAUSE OF DEATH FOR THE FIFTH, SIXTH AND SEVENTH. WHY IS THAT?

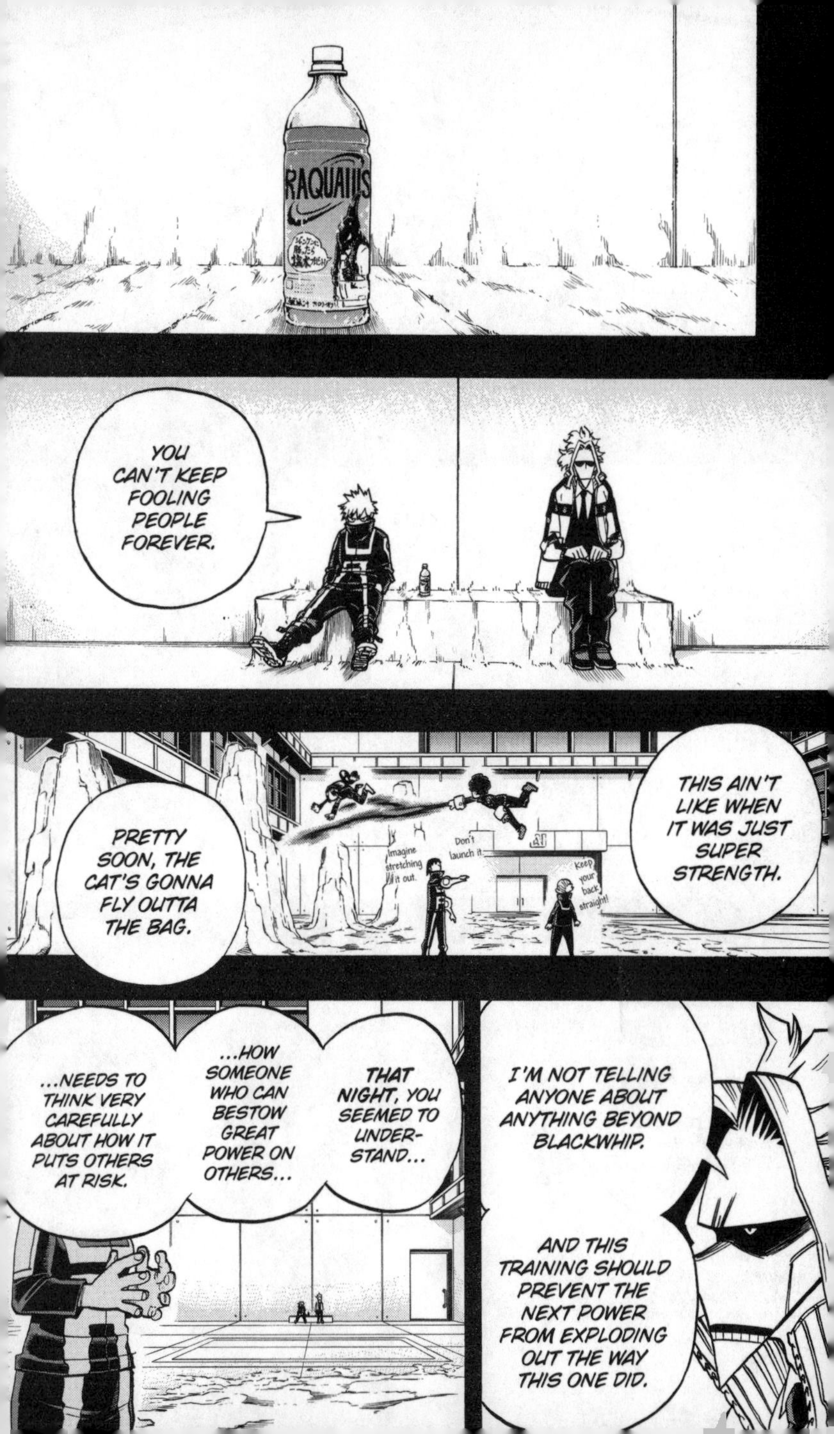
RAQUAIUS
YOU CAN'T KEEP FOOLING PEOPLE FOREVER.
THIS AIN'T LIKE WHEN IT WAS JUST SUPER STRENGTH.
Keep your back straight!
Don't launch it.
Imagine stretching it out.
PRETTY SOON, THE CAT'S GONNA FLY OUTTA THE BAG.
I'M NOT TELLING ANYONE ABOUT ANYTHING BEYOND BLACKWHIP.
AND THIS TRAINING SHOULD PREVENT THE NEXT POWER FROM EXPLODING OUT THE WAY THIS ONE DID.
THAT NIGHT, YOU SEEMED TO UNDERSTAND...
...HOW SOMEONE WHO CAN BESTOW GREAT POWER ON OTHERS...
...NEEDS TO THINK VERY CAREFULLY ABOUT HOW IT PUTS OTHERS AT RISK.

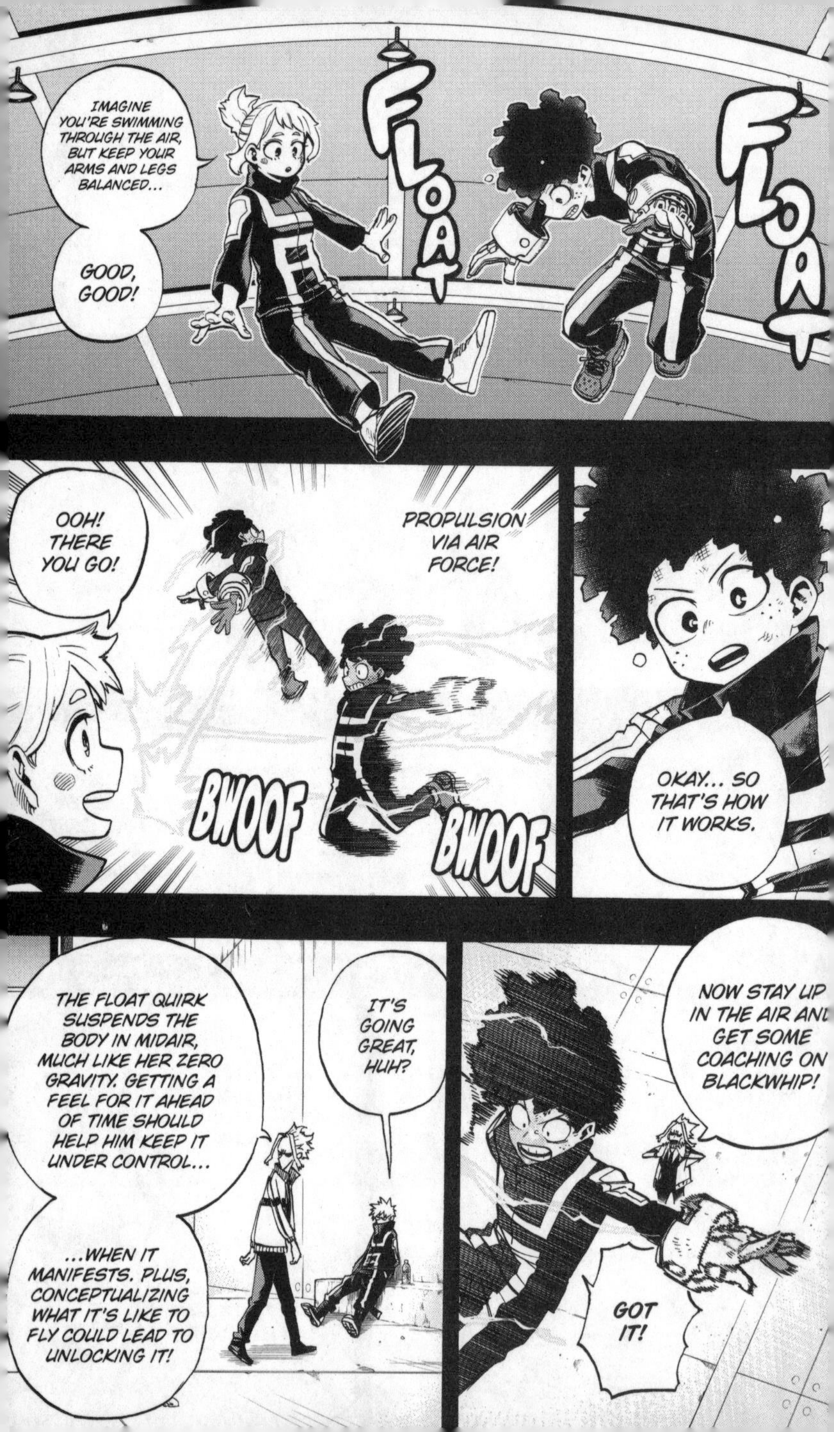
FLOAT
FLOAT
IMAGINE YOU'RE SWIMMING THROUGH THE AIR, BUT KEEP YOUR ARMS AND LEGS BALANCED...
GOOD, GOOD!
OKAY... SO THAT'S HOW IT WORKS.
PROPULSION VIA AIR FORCE!
OOH! THERE YOU GO!
BWOOF
BWOOF
NOW STAY UP IN THE AIR AND GET SOME COACHING ON BLACKWHIP!
GOT IT!
IT'S GOING GREAT, HUH?
THE FLOAT QUIRK SUSPENDS THE BODY IN MIDAIR, MUCH LIKE HER ZERO GRAVITY. GETTING A FEEL FOR IT AHEAD OF TIME SHOULD HELP HIM KEEP IT UNDER CONTROL...
...WHEN IT MANIFESTS. PLUS, CONCEPTUALIZING WHAT IT'S LIKE TO FLY COULD LEAD TO UNLOCKING IT!

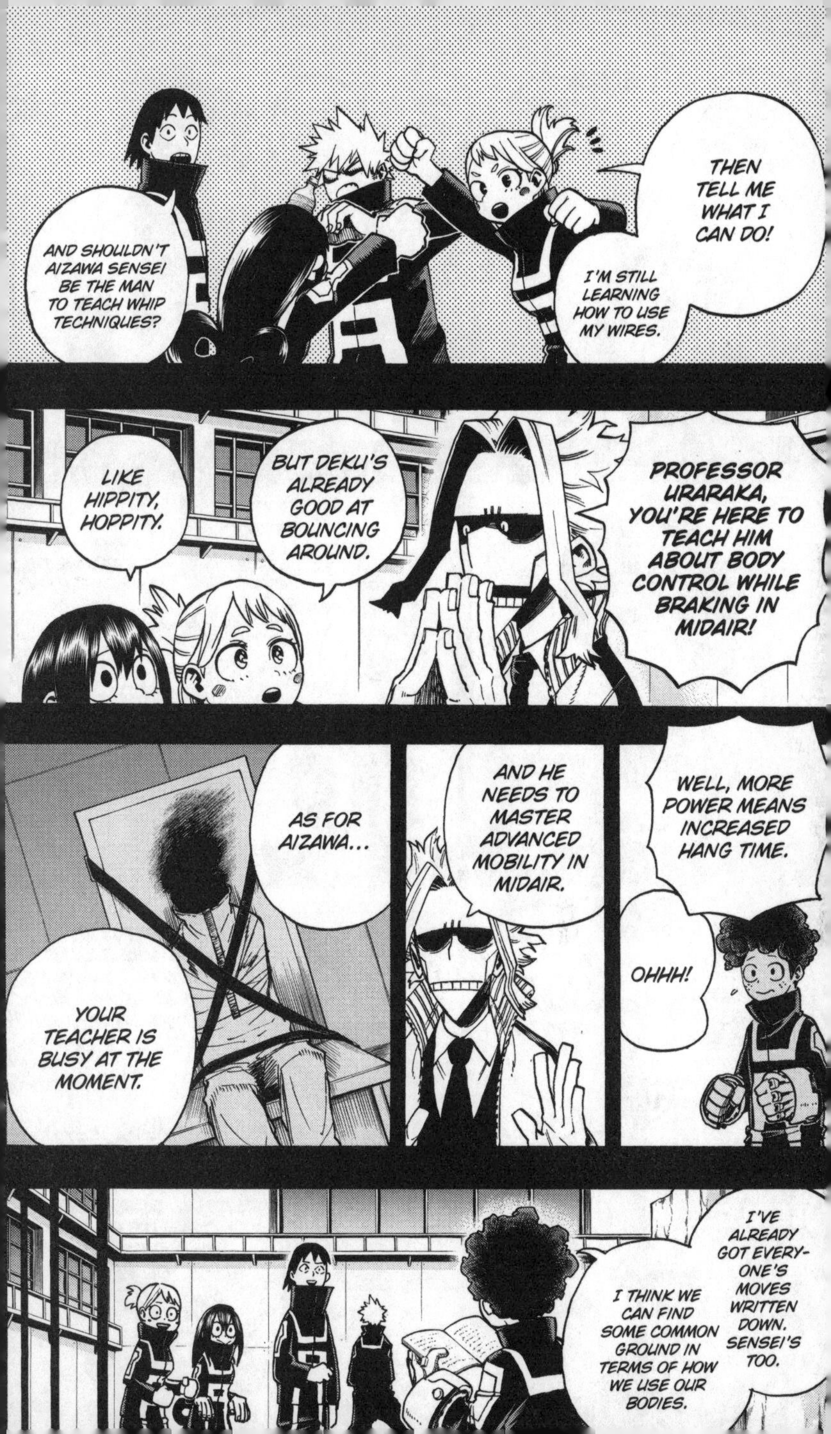
THEN TELL ME WHAT I CAN DO!
I'M STILL LEARNING HOW TO USE MY WIRES.
AND SHOULDN'T AIZAWA SENSEI BE THE MAN TO TEACH WHIP TECHNIQUES?
PROFESSOR URARAKA, YOU'RE HERE TO TEACH HIM ABOUT BODY CONTROL WHILE BRAKING IN MIDAIR!
BUT DEKU'S ALREADY GOOD AT BOUNCING AROUND.
LIKE HIPPITY, HOPPITY.
WELL, MORE POWER MEANS INCREASED HANG TIME.
OHHH!
AND HE NEEDS TO MASTER ADVANCED MOBILITY IN MIDAIR.
AS FOR AIZAWA...
YOUR TEACHER IS BUSY AT THE MOMENT.
I'VE ALREADY GOT EVERY-ONE'S MOVES WRITTEN DOWN. SENSEI'S TOO.
I THINK WE CAN FIND SOME COMMON GROUND IN TERMS OF HOW WE USE OUR BODIES.

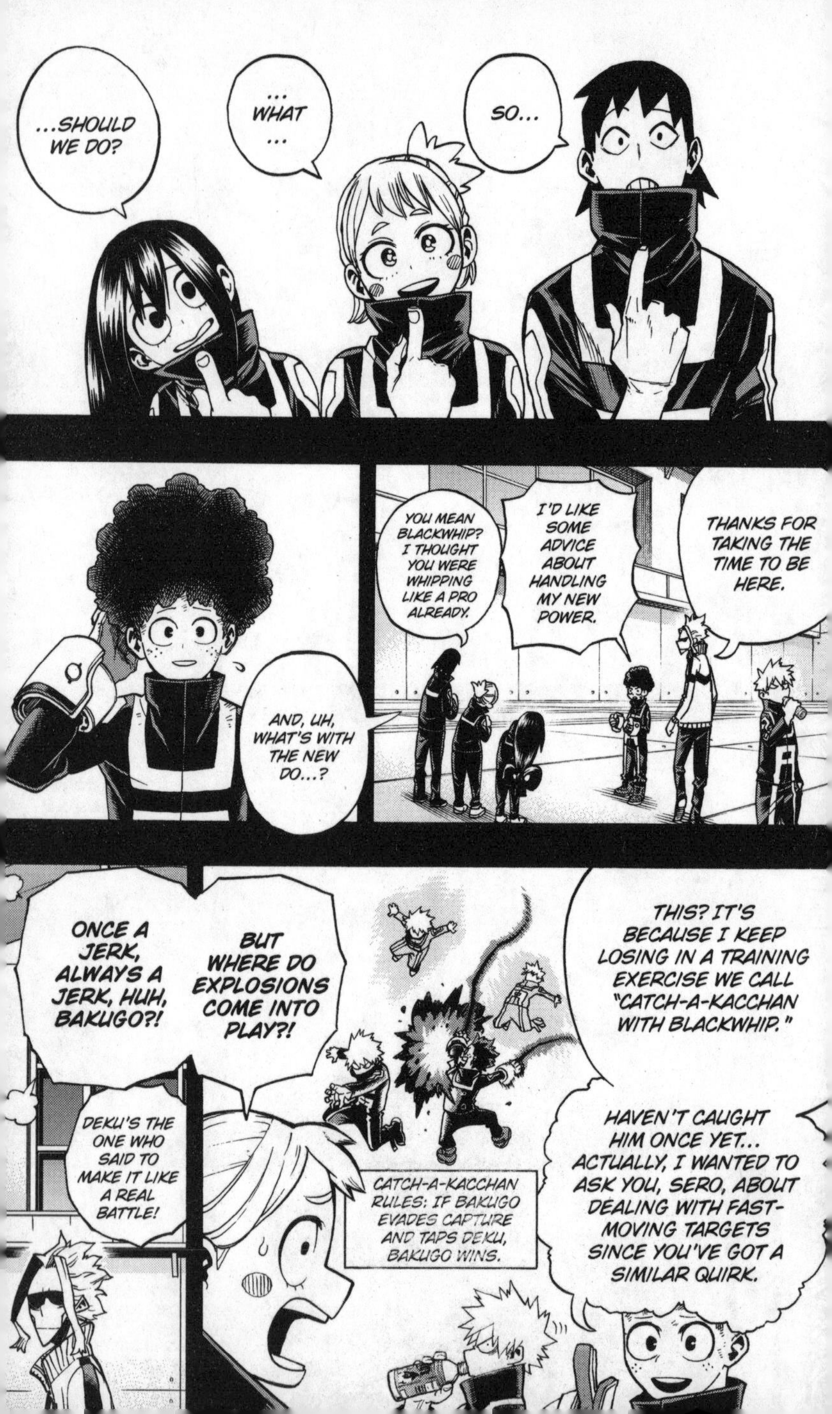
SO...
... WHAT ...
...SHOULD WE DO?
THANKS FOR TAKING THE TIME TO BE HERE.
I'D LIKE SOME ADVICE ABOUT HANDLING MY NEW POWER.
YOU MEAN BLACKWHIP? I THOUGHT YOU WERE WHIPPING LIKE A PRO ALREADY.
AND, UH, WHAT'S WITH THE NEW DO...?
THIS? IT'S BECAUSE I KEEP LOSING IN A TRAINING EXERCISE WE CALL "CATCH-A-KACCHAN WITH BLACKWHIP."
CATCH-A-KACCHAN RULES: IF BAKUGO EVADES CAPTURE AND TAPS DEKU, BAKUGO WINS.
HAVEN'T CAUGHT HIM ONCE YET... ACTUALLY, I WANTED TO ASK YOU, SERO, ABOUT DEALING WITH FAST-MOVING TARGETS SINCE YOU'VE GOT A SIMILAR QUIRK.
BUT WHERE DO EXPLOSIONS COME INTO PLAY?!
ONCE A JERK, ALWAYS A JERK, HUH, BAKUGO?!
DEKU'S THE ONE WHO SAID TO MAKE IT LIKE A REAL BATTLE!

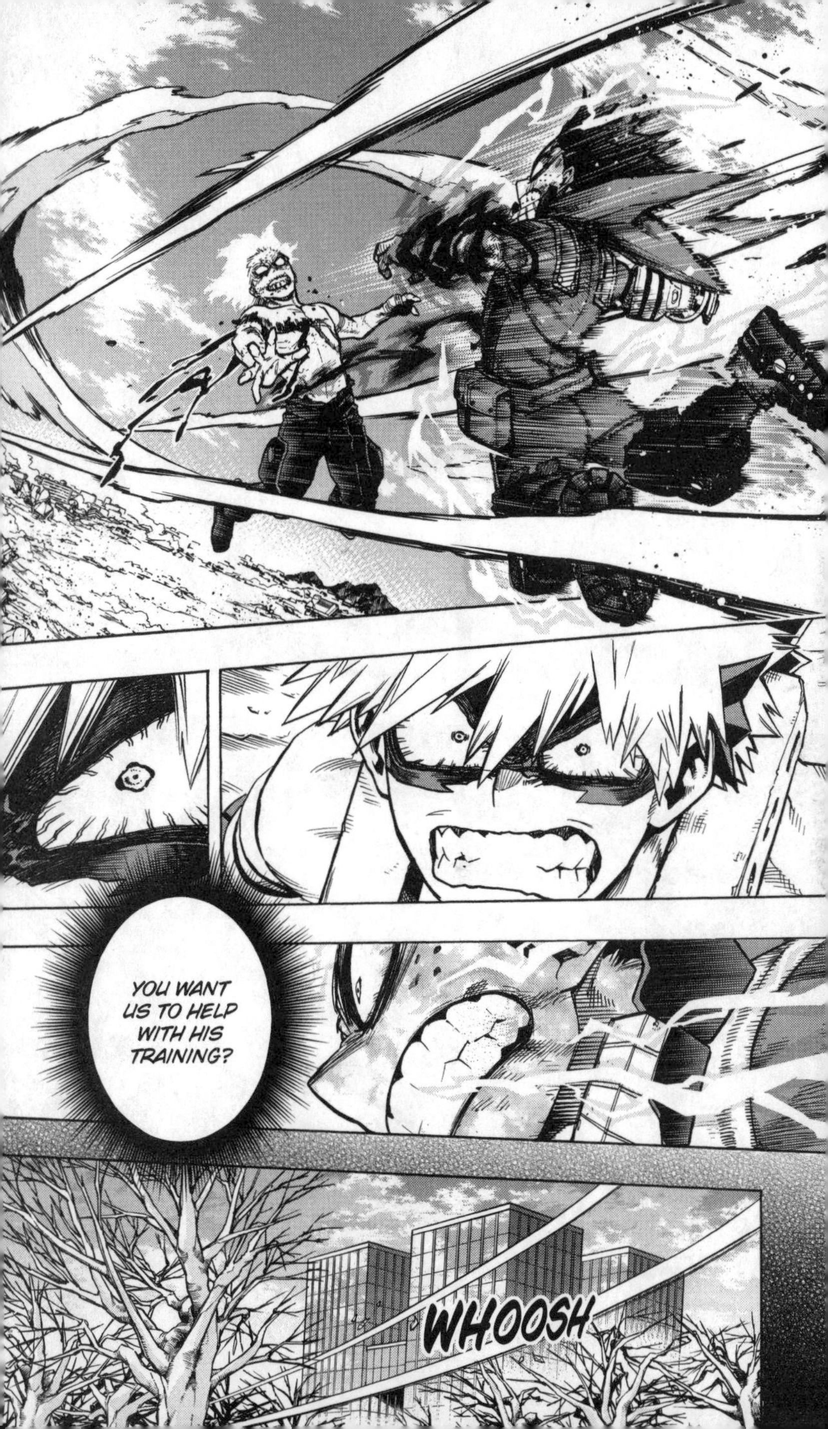
YOU WANT US TO HELP WITH HIS TRAINING?
WHOOSH

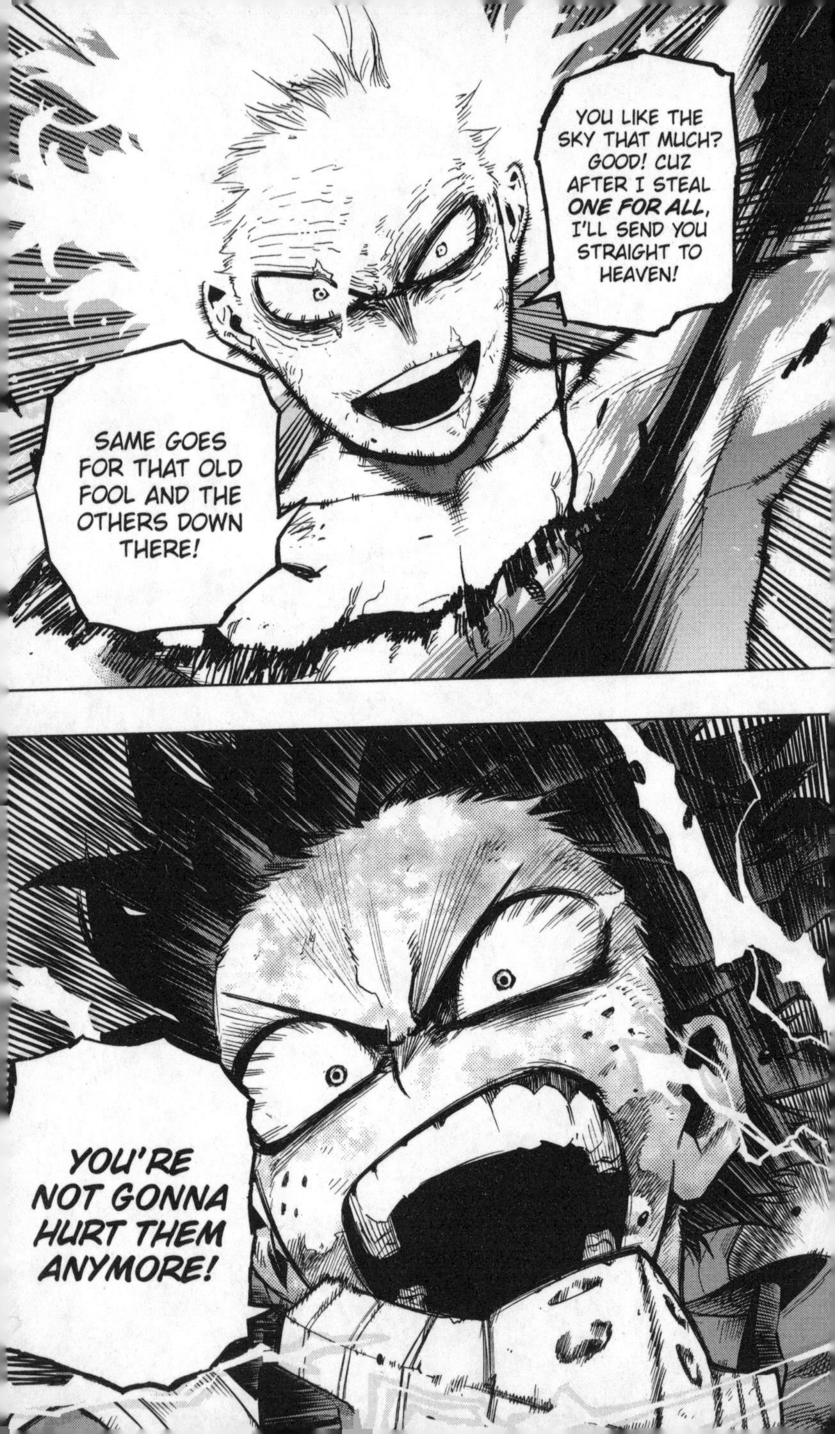
YOU LIKE THE SKY THAT MUCH? GOOD! CUZ AFTER I STEAL ONE FOR ALL, I'LL SEND YOU STRAIGHT TO HEAVEN!
SAME GOES FOR THAT OLD FOOL AND THE OTHERS DOWN THERE!
YOU'RE NOT GONNA HURT THEM ANYMORE!

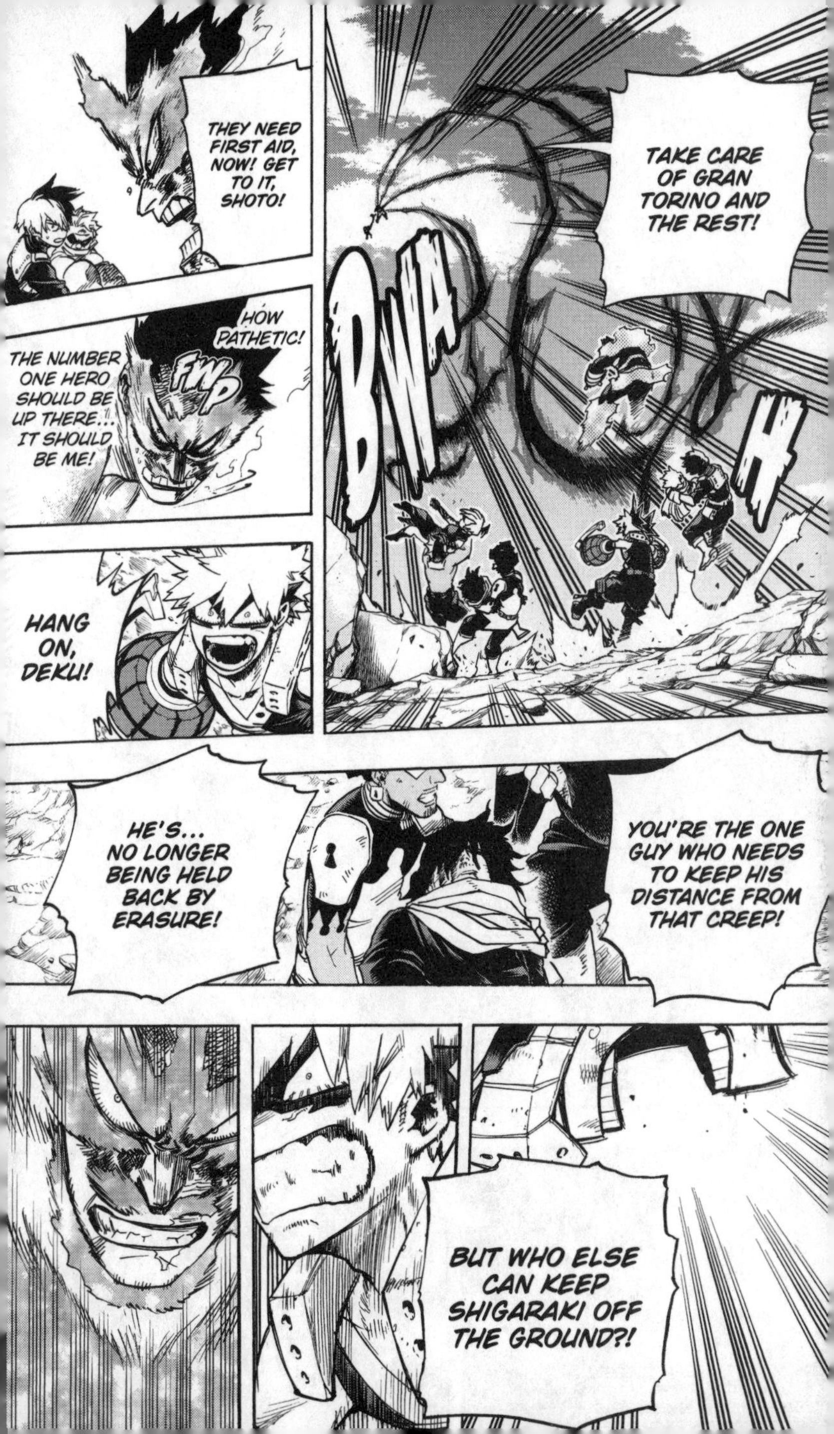
TAKE CARE OF GRAN TORINO AND THE REST!
BWAH
THEY NEED FIRST AID, NOW! GET TO IT, SHOTO!
HOW PATHETIC!
FWP
THE NUMBER ONE HERO SHOULD BE UP THERE... IT SHOULD BE ME!
HANG ON, DEKU!
YOU'RE THE ONE GUY WHO NEEDS TO KEEP HIS DISTANCE FROM THAT CREEP!
HE'S... NO LONGER BEING HELD BACK BY ERASURE!
BUT WHO ELSE CAN KEEP SHIGARAKI OFF THE GROUND?!

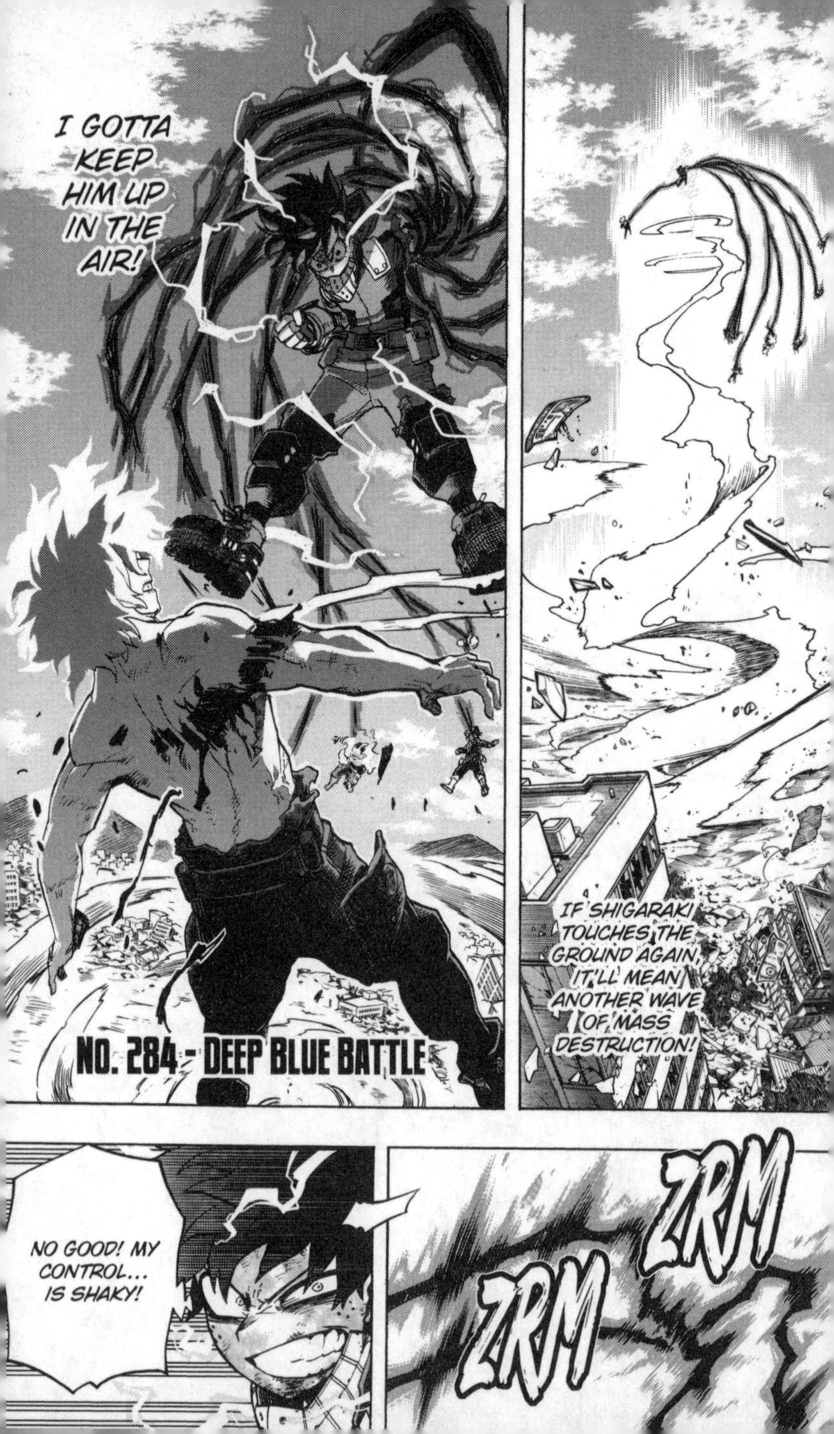
IF SHIGARAKI TOUCHES THE GROUND AGAIN, IT'LL MEAN ANOTHER WAVE OF MASS DESTRUCTION!
I GOTTA KEEP HIM UP IN THE AIR!
NO. 284 - DEEP BLUE BATTLE
ZRM
ZRM
NO GOOD! MY CONTROL... IS SHAKY!

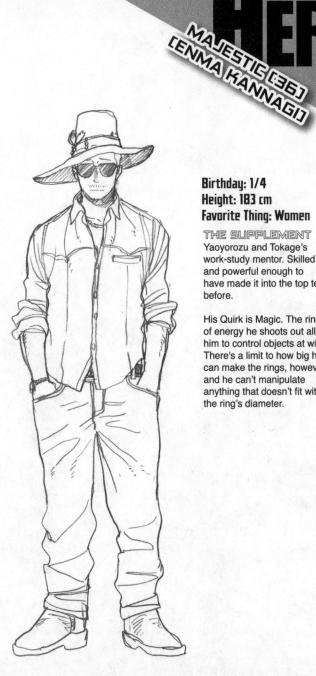

HERO

MAJESTIC [36]
[ENMA KANNAGI]

Birthday: 1/4
Height: 183 cm
Favorite Thing: Women

THE SUPPLEMENT

Yaoyorozu and Tokage's work-study mentor. Skilled and powerful enough to have made it into the top ten before.

His Quirk is Magic. The rings of energy he shoots out allow him to control objects at will. There's a limit to how big he can make the rings, however, and he can't manipulate anything that doesn't fit within the ring's diameter.

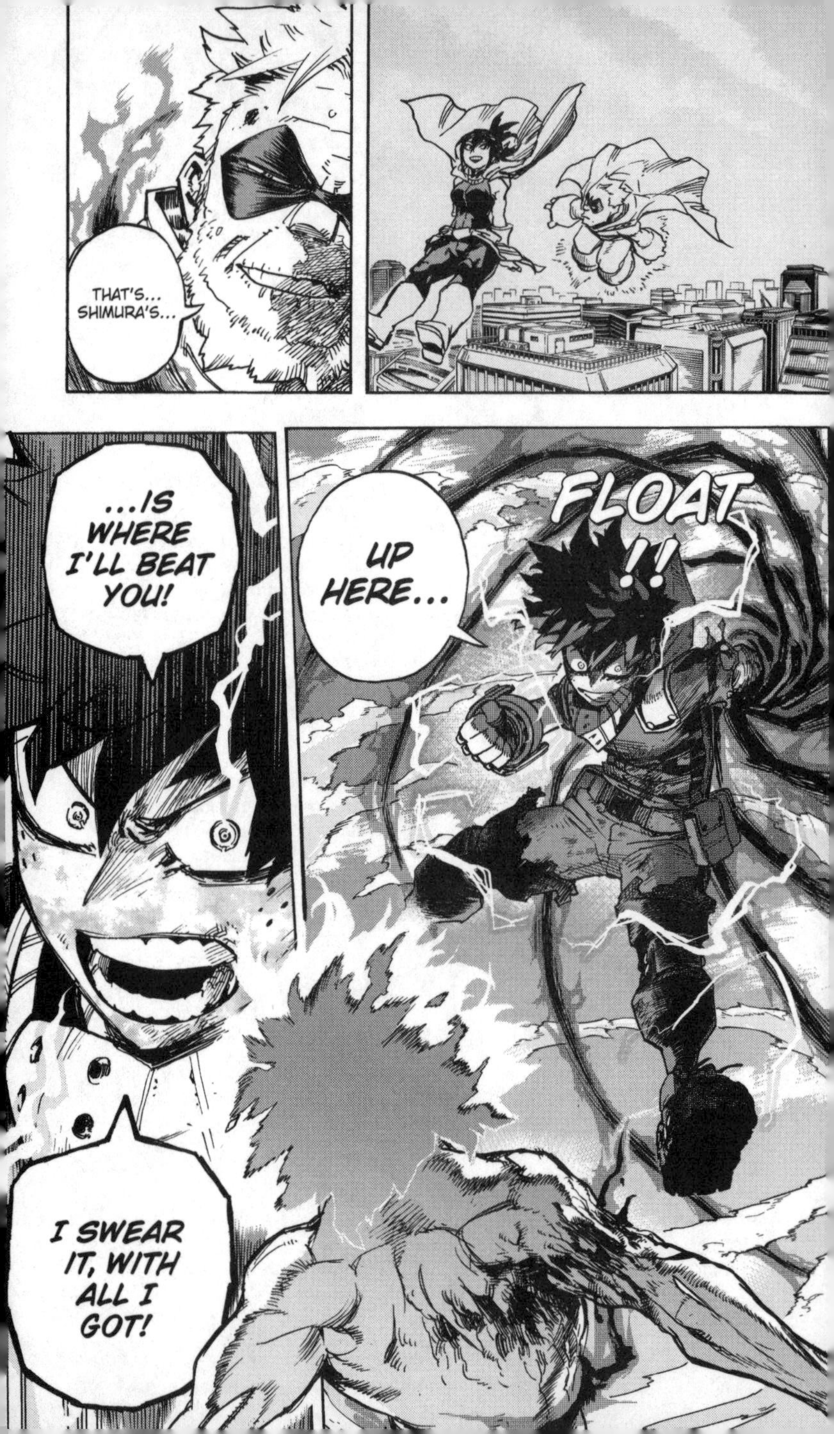
THAT'S... SHIMURA'S...
FLOAT !!
UP HERE...
...IS WHERE I'LL BEAT YOU!
I SWEAR IT, WITH ALL I GOT!

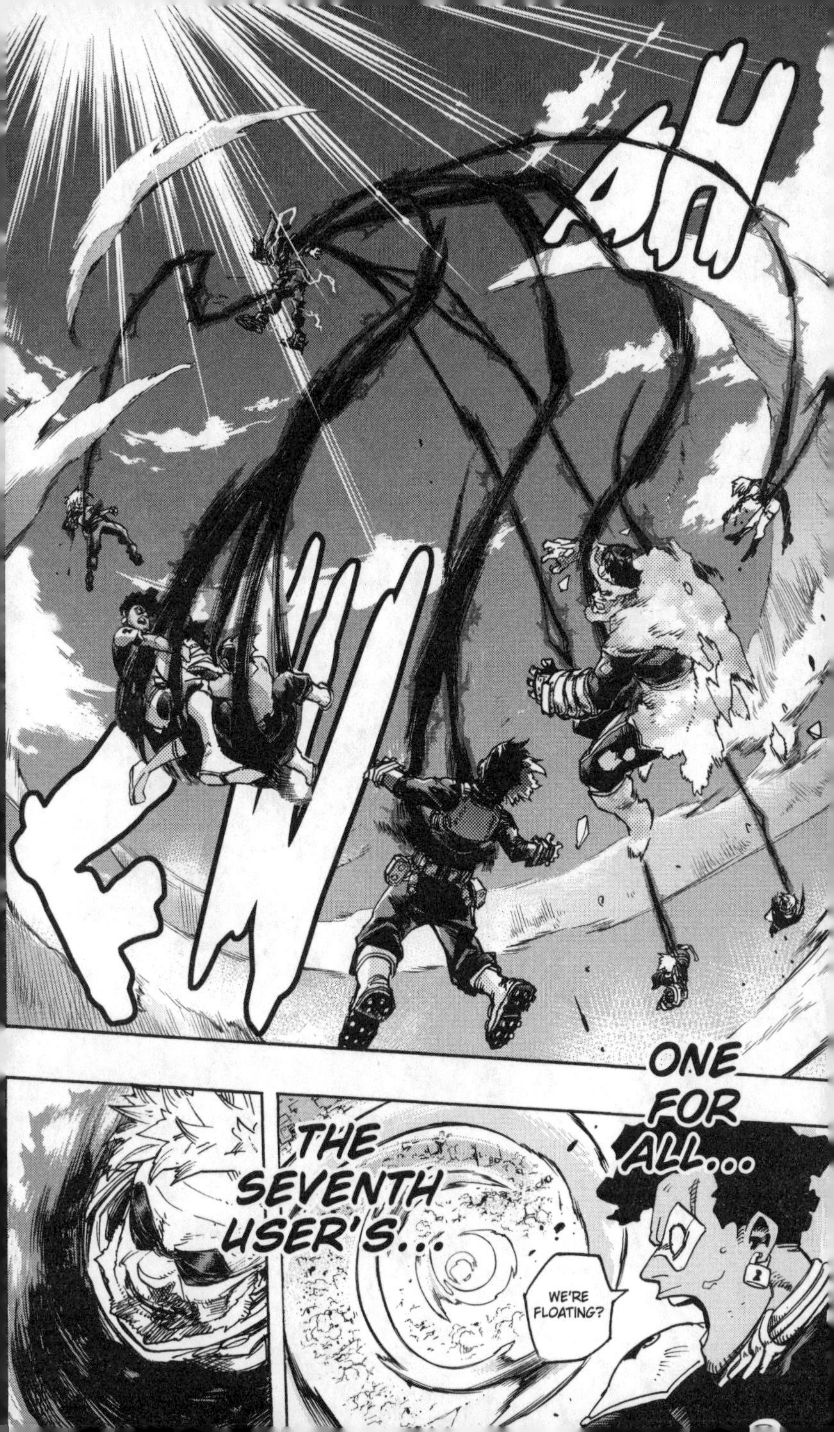
WE'RE FLOATING?
THE SEVENTH USER'S...
ONE FOR ALL...

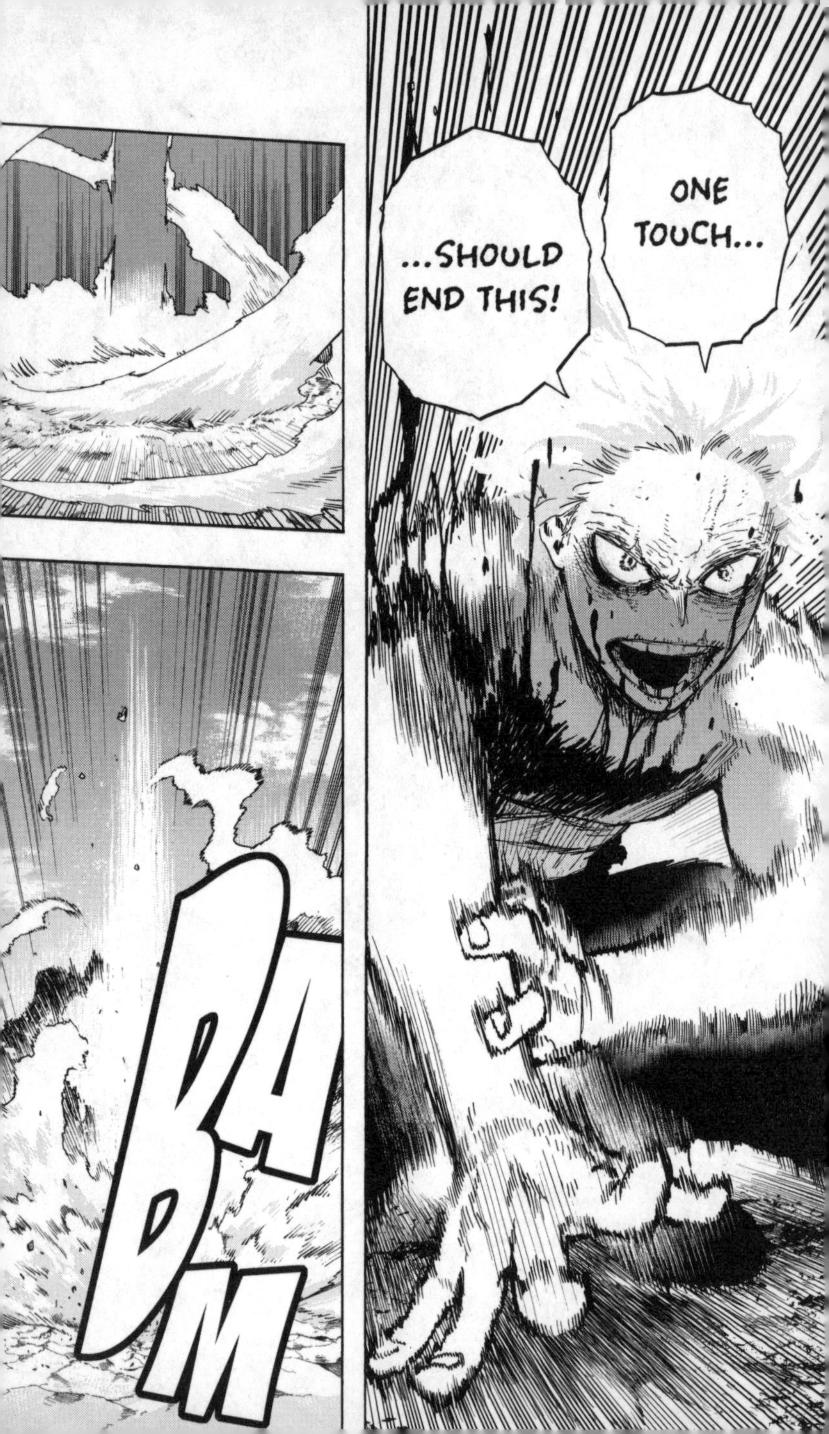
ONE TOUCH...
...SHOULD END THIS!
BADM

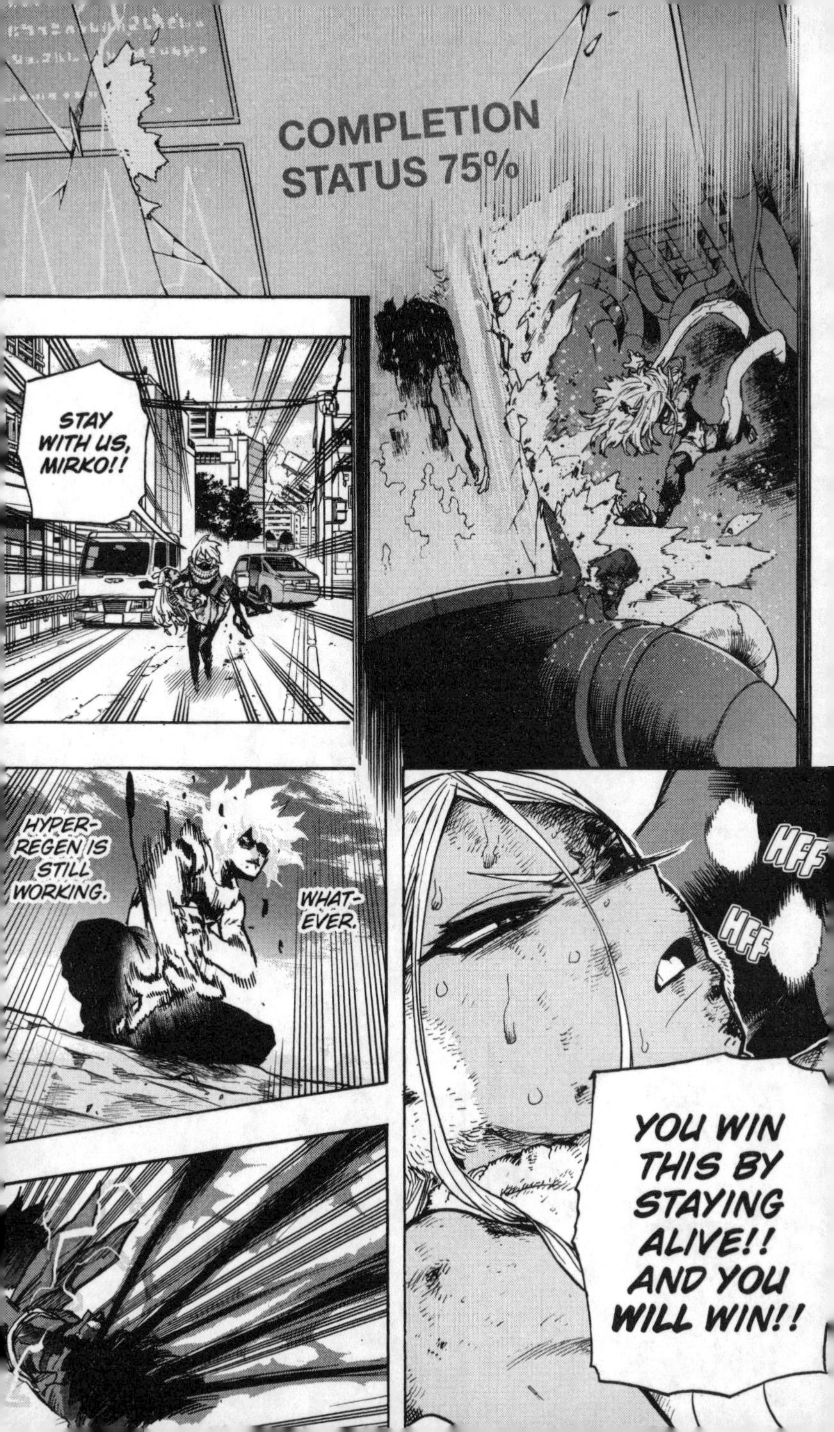
COMPLETION STATUS 75%
STAY WITH US, MIRKO!!
HFF
HFF
YOU WIN THIS BY STAYING ALIVE!! AND YOU WILL WIN!!
HYPER-REGEN IS STILL WORKING.
WHAT-EVER.

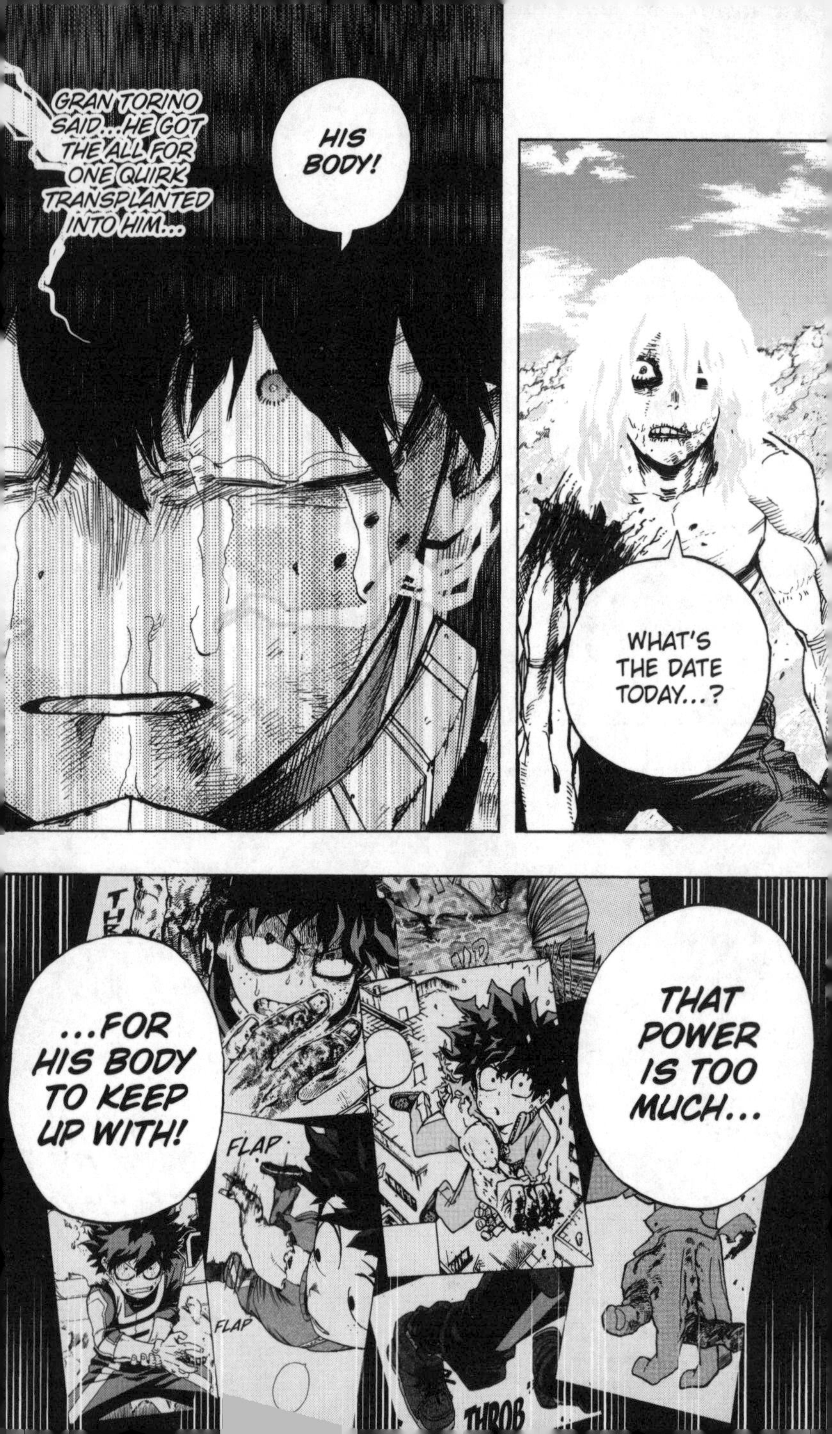
WHAT'S THE DATE TODAY...?
GRAN TORINO SAID...HE GOT THE ALL FOR ONE QUIRK TRANSPLANTED INTO HIM...
HIS BODY!
THAT POWER IS TOO MUCH...
...FOR HIS BODY TO KEEP UP WITH!
FLAP
FLAP
THROB

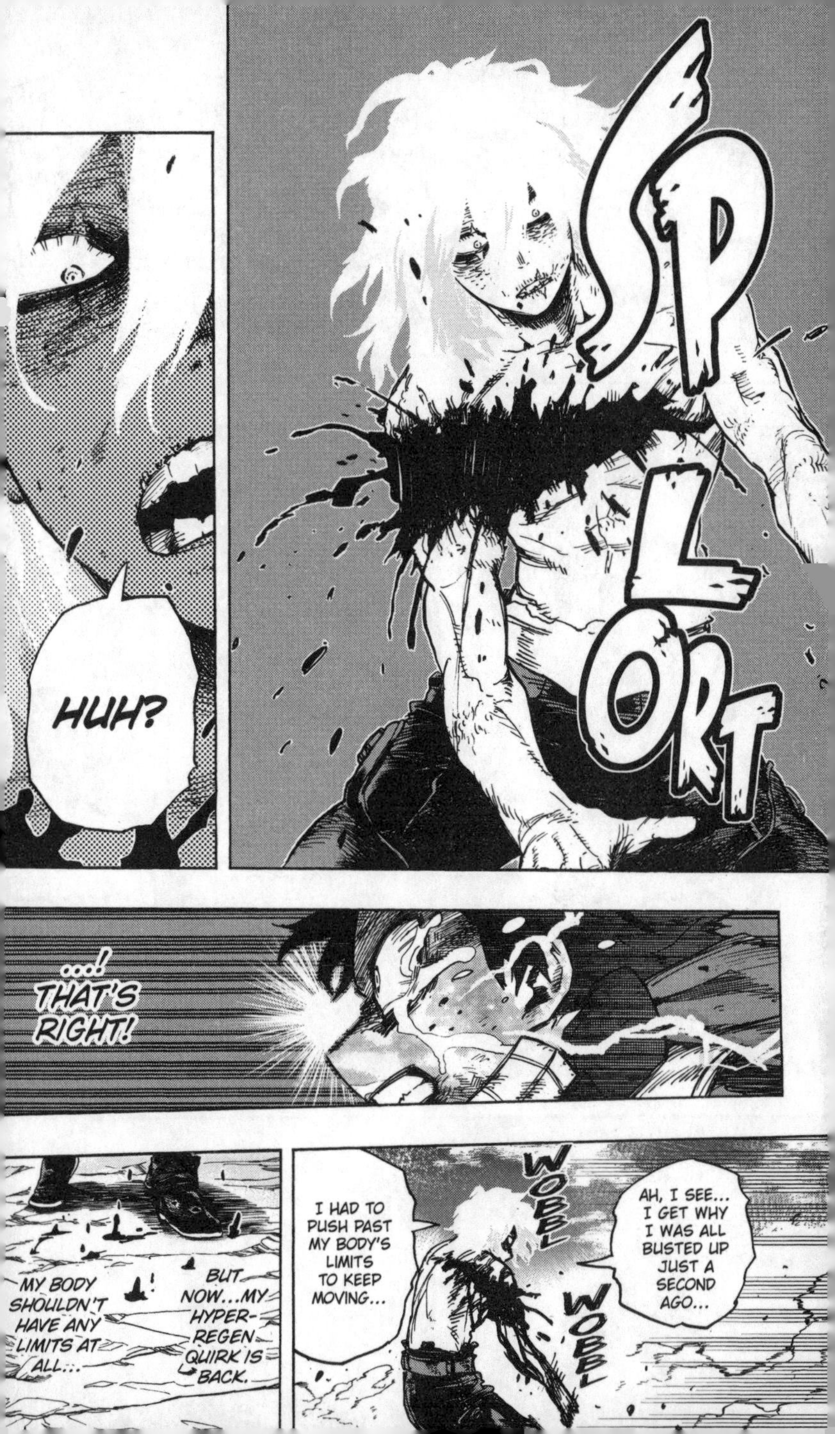
SPLORT
HUH?
...! THAT'S RIGHT!
AH, I SEE... I GET WHY I WAS ALL BUSTED UP JUST A SECOND AGO...
WOBBL
WOBBL
I HAD TO PUSH PAST MY BODY'S LIMITS TO KEEP MOVING...
BUT NOW... MY HYPER-REGEN QUIRK IS BACK.
MY BODY SHOULDN'T HAVE ANY LIMITS AT ALL...

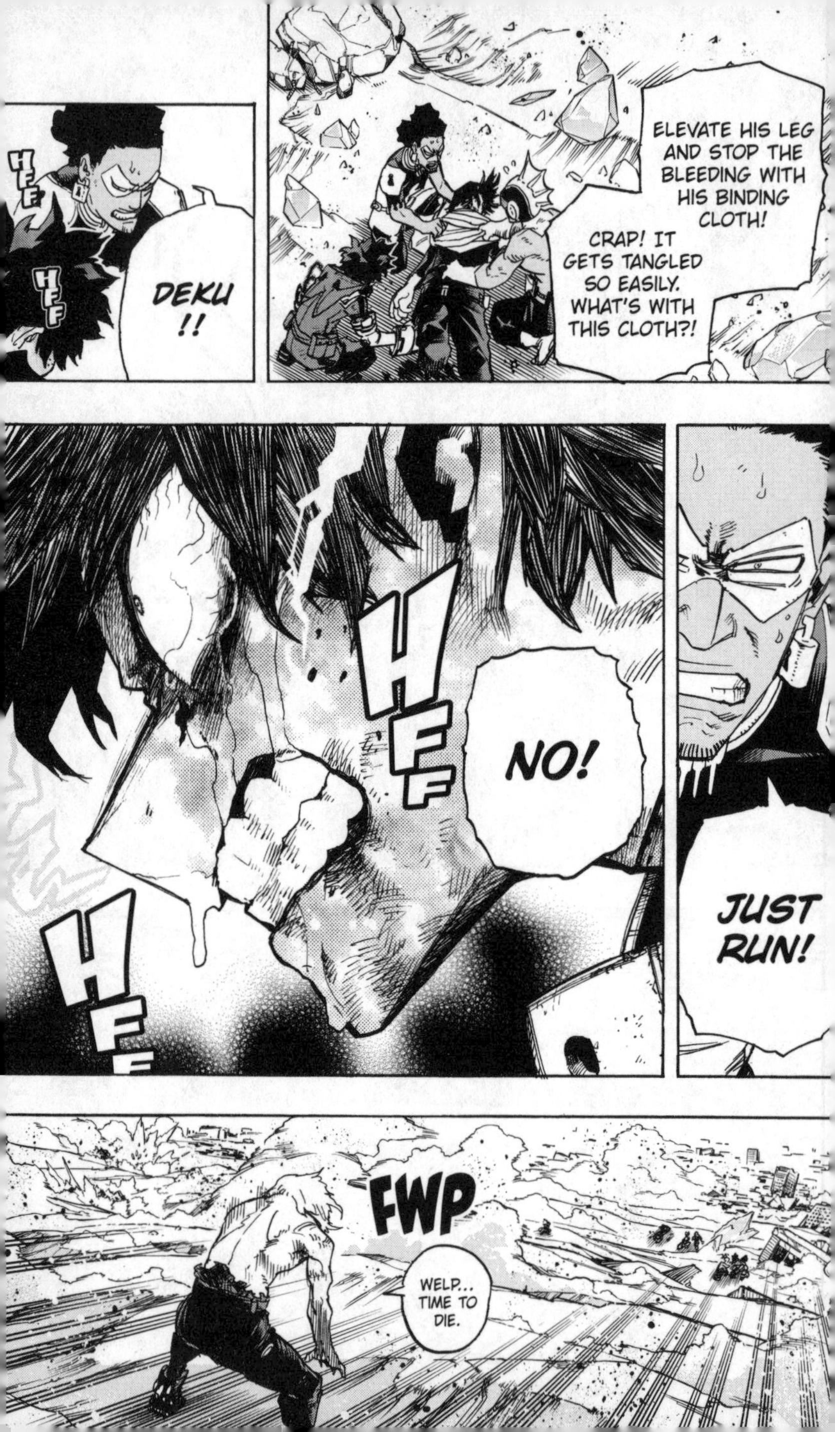
ELEVATE HIS LEG AND STOP THE BLEEDING WITH HIS BINDING CLOTH!
CRAP! IT GETS TANGLED SO EASILY. WHAT'S WITH THIS CLOTH?!
HFF
HFF
DEKU !!
JUST RUN!
HFF
NO!
HFF
FWP
WELP... TIME TO DIE.

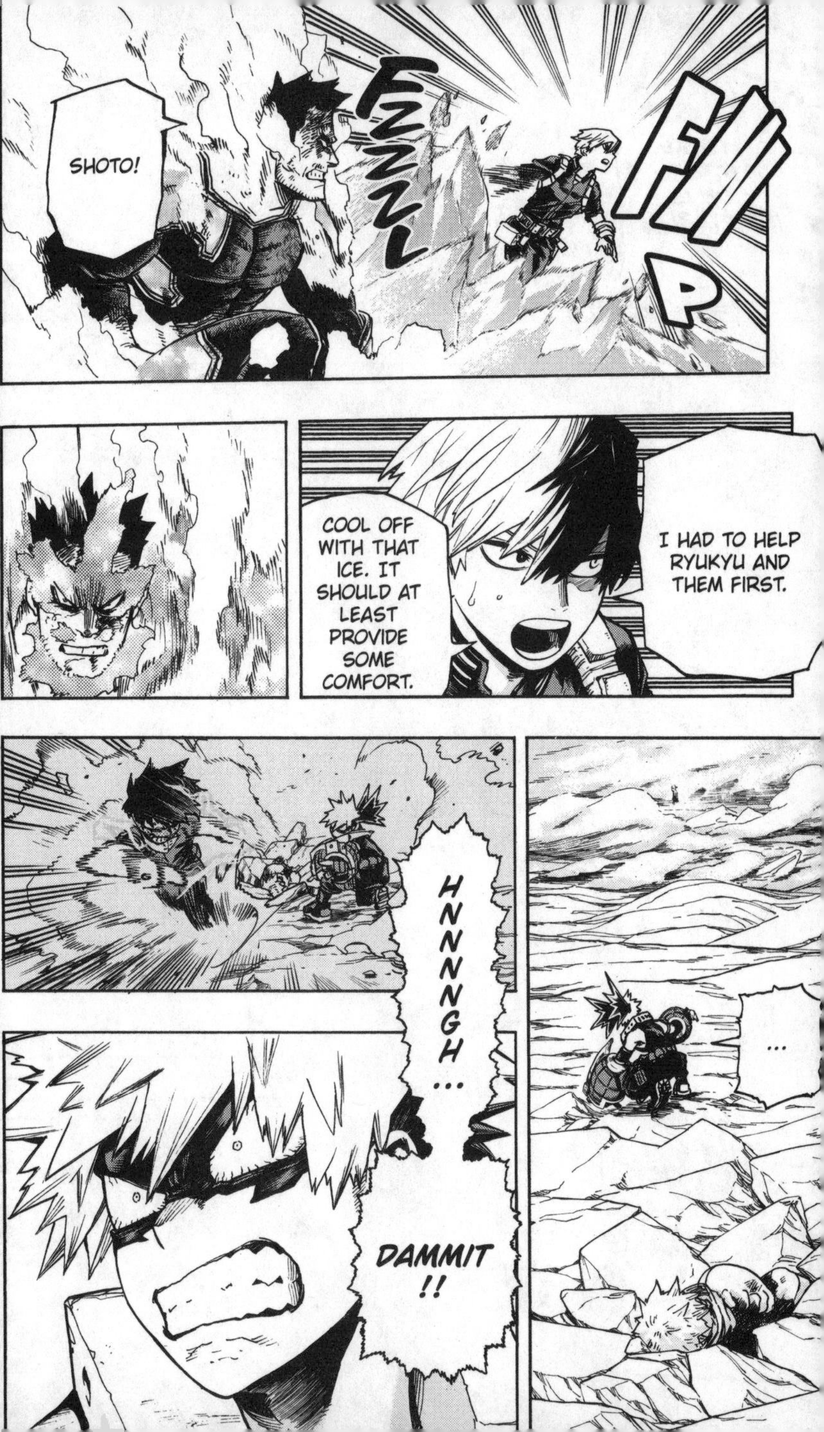
FWIP
FZZZL
SHOTO!
I HAD TO HELP RYUKYU AND THEM FIRST.
COOL OFF WITH THAT ICE. IT SHOULD AT LEAST PROVIDE SOME COMFORT.
...
HNNNNGH...
DAMMIT!!

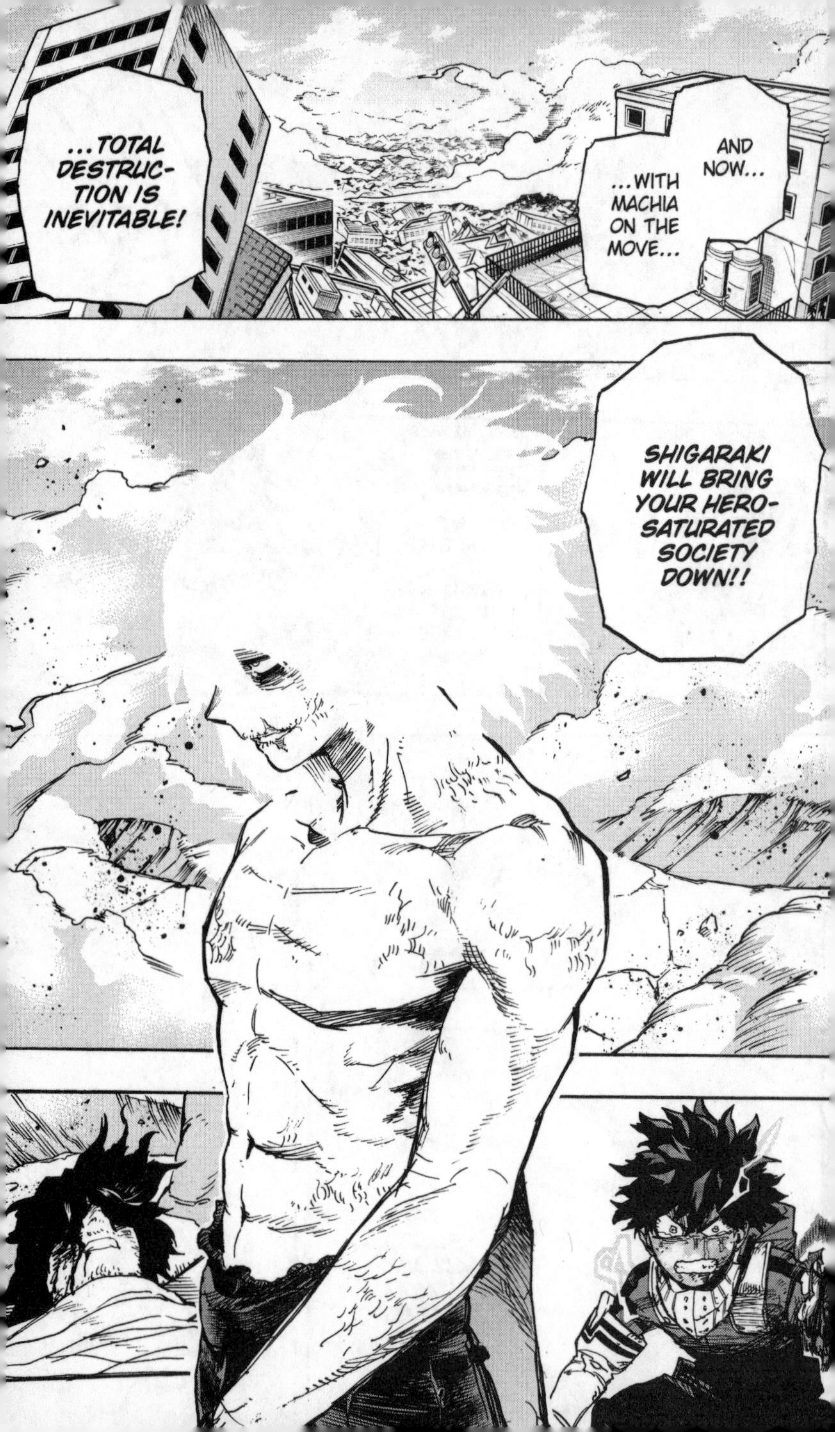
AND NOW...
...WITH MACHIA ON THE MOVE...
...TOTAL DESTRUCTION IS INEVITABLE!
SHIGARAKI WILL BRING YOUR HERO-SATURATED SOCIETY DOWN!!

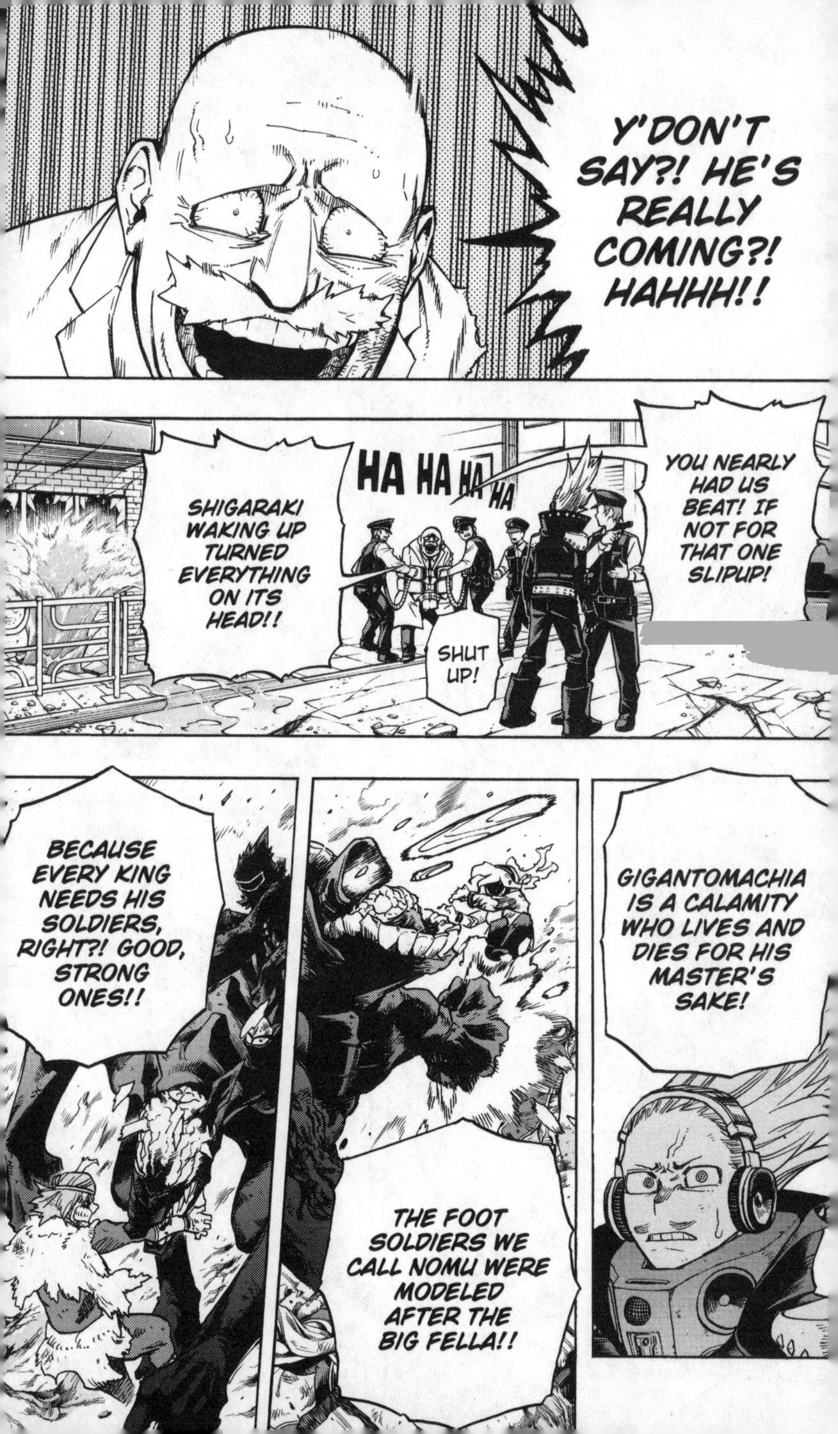
Y'DON'T SAY?! HE'S REALLY COMING?! HAHHH!!
YOU NEARLY HAD US BEAT! IF NOT FOR THAT ONE SLIPUP!
HA HA HA HA
SHUT UP!
SHIGARAKI WAKING UP TURNED EVERYTHING ON ITS HEAD!!
GIGANTOMACHIA IS A CALAMITY WHO LIVES AND DIES FOR HIS MASTER'S SAKE!
THE FOOT SOLDIERS WE CALL NOMU WERE MODELED AFTER THE BIG FELLA!!
BECAUSE EVERY KING NEEDS HIS SOLDIERS, RIGHT?! GOOD, STRONG ONES!!

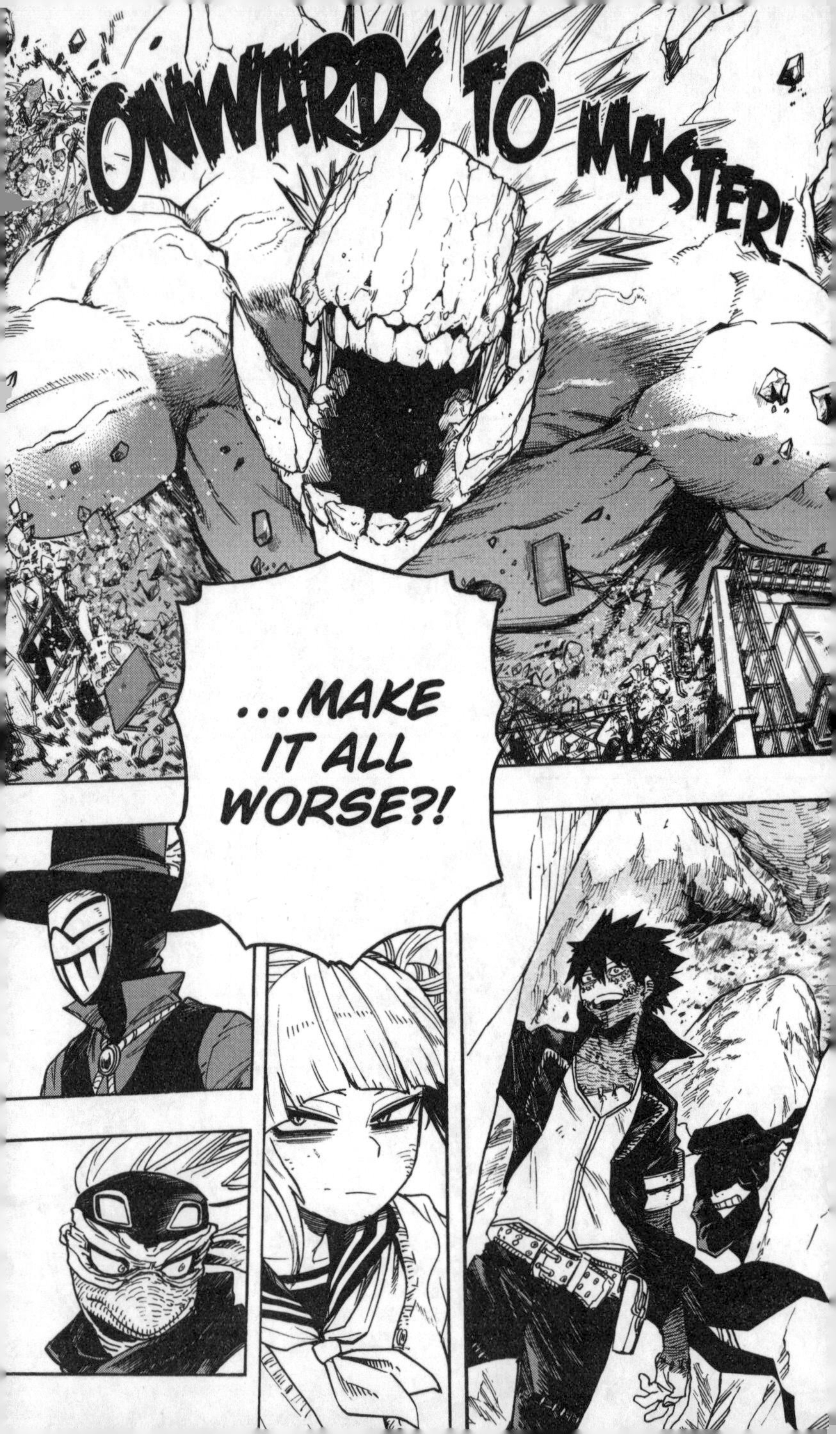
ONWARDS TO MASTER!
...MAKE IT ALL WORSE?!

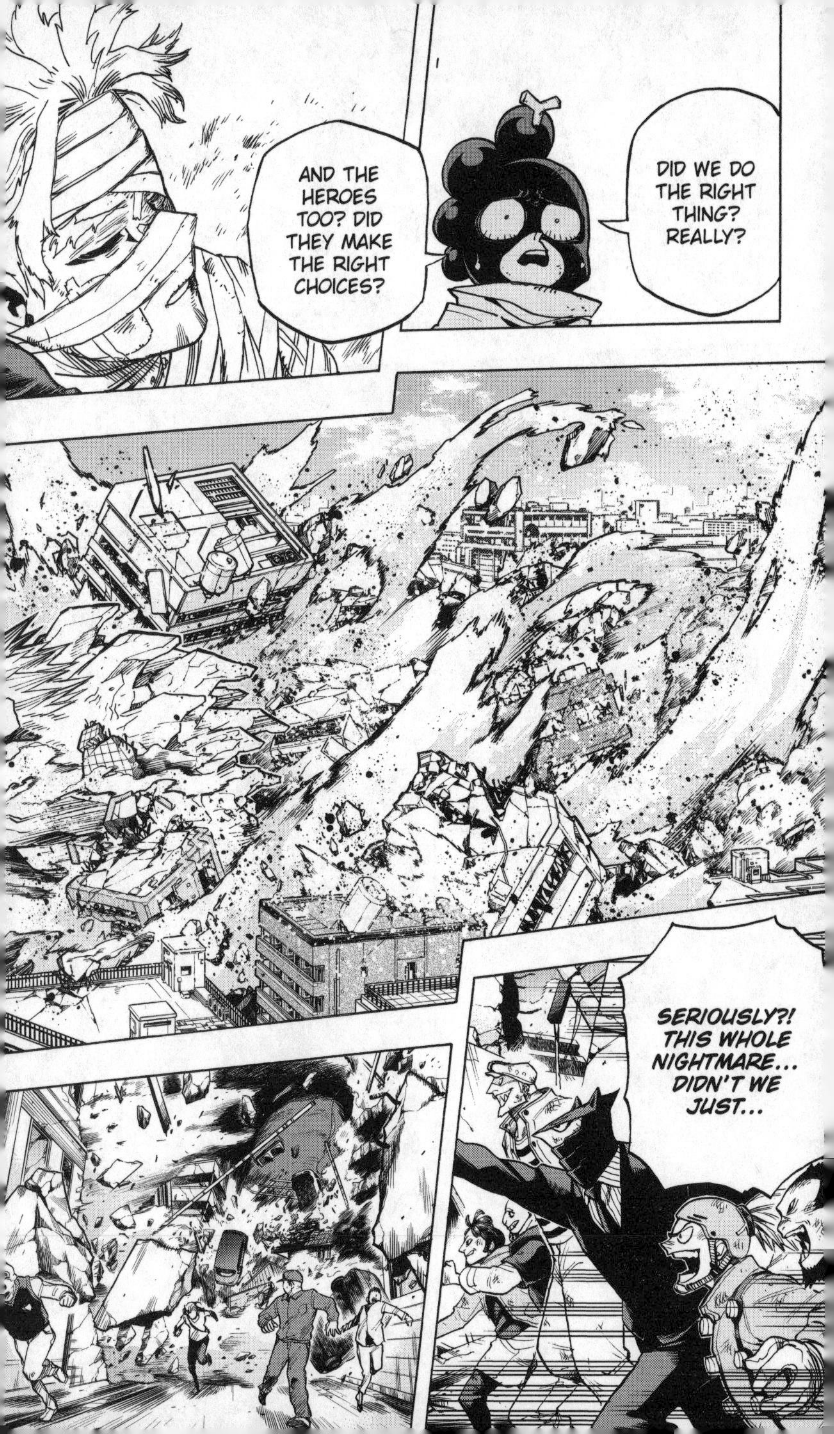
DID WE DO THE RIGHT THING? REALLY?
AND THE HEROES TOO? DID THEY MAKE THE RIGHT CHOICES?
SERIOUSLY?! THIS WHOLE NIGHTMARE... DIDN'T WE JUST...

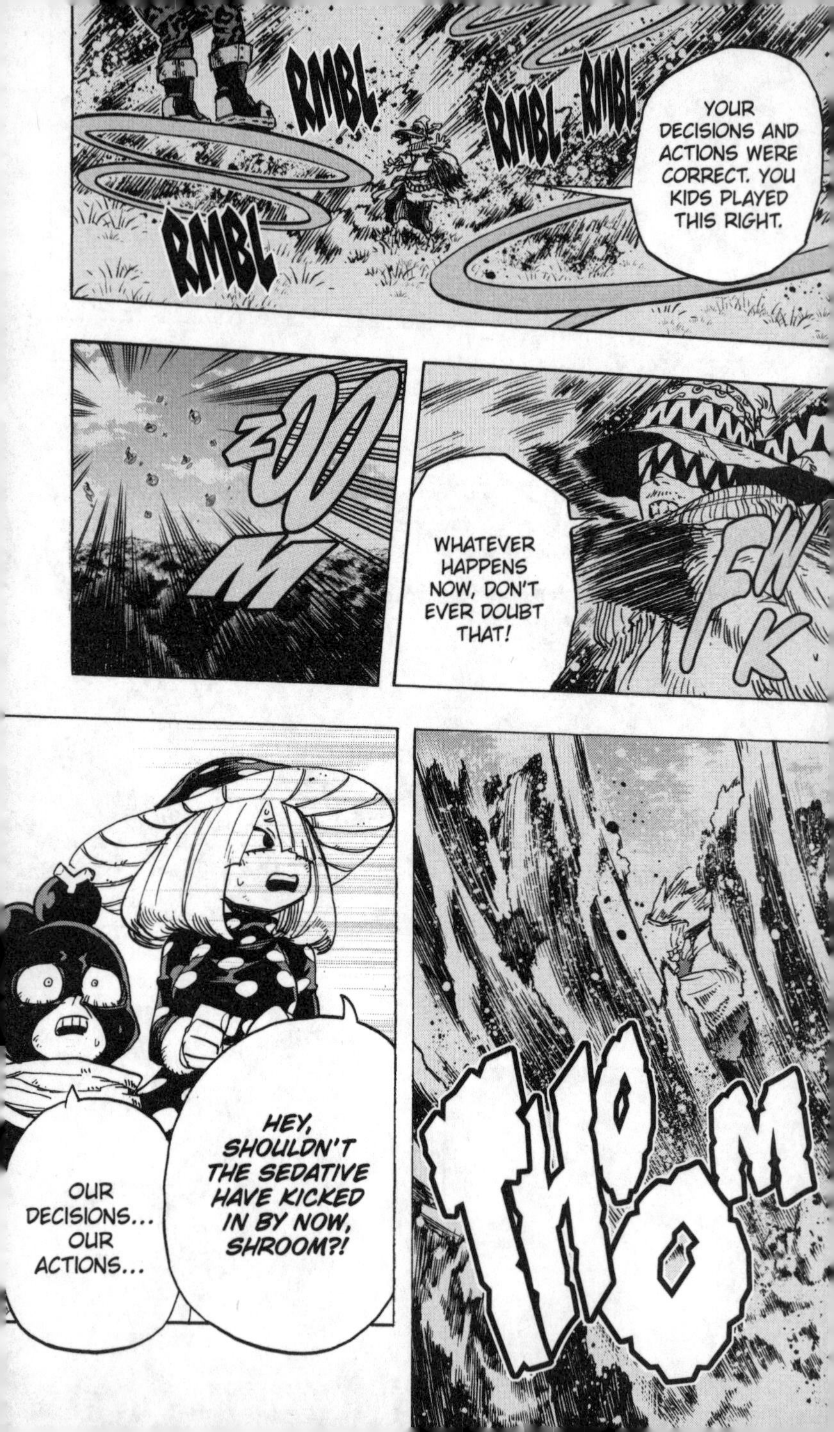
RMBL
RMBL RMBL
RMBL
YOUR DECISIONS AND ACTIONS WERE CORRECT. YOU KIDS PLAYED THIS RIGHT.
WHATEVER HAPPENS NOW, DON'T EVER DOUBT THAT!
FWK
ZOOOM
THOOM
HEY, SHOULDN'T THE SEDATIVE HAVE KICKED IN BY NOW, SHROOM?!
OUR DECISIONS... OUR ACTIONS...

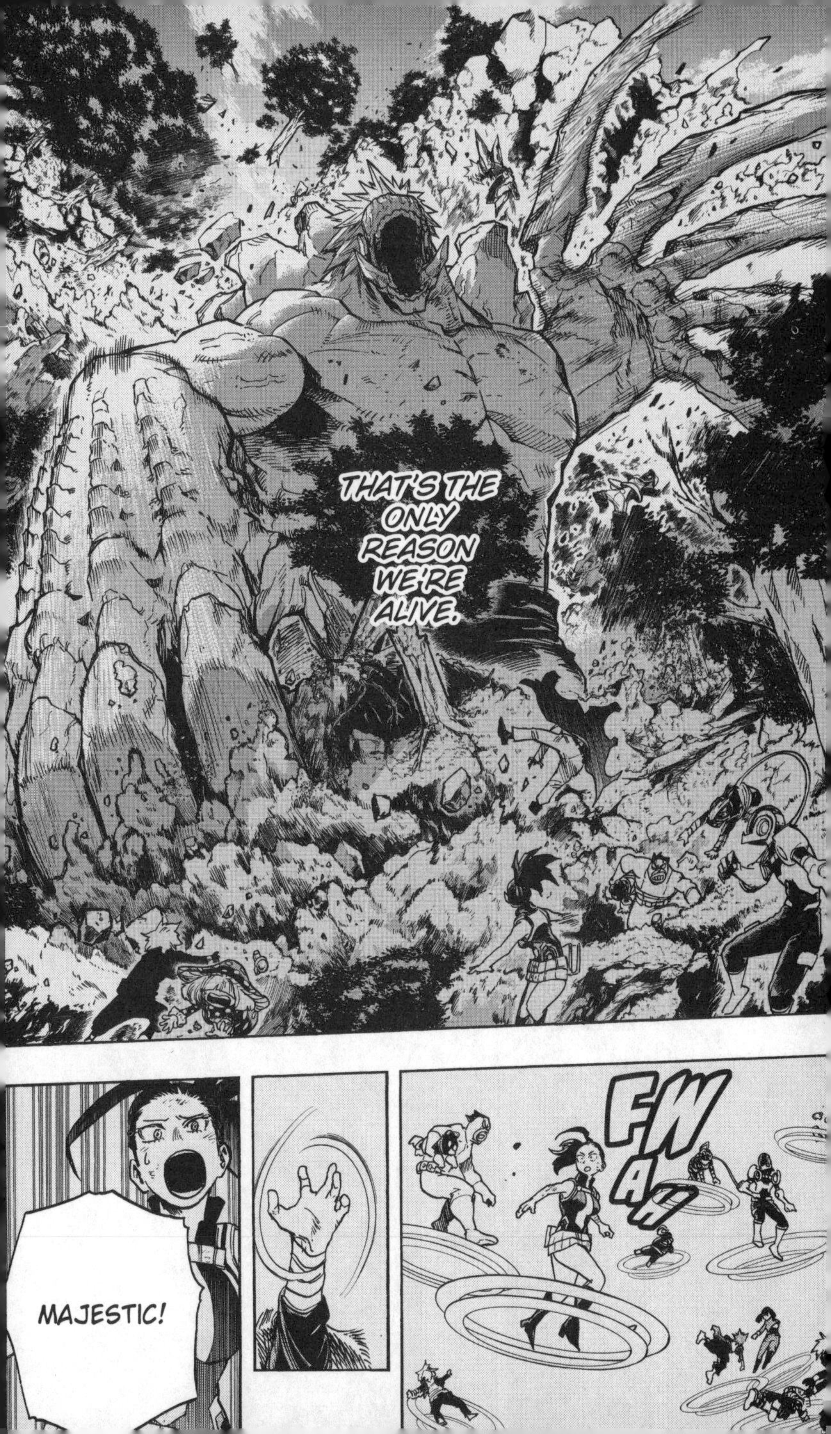
THAT'S THE ONLY REASON WE'RE ALIVE.
FWAH!
MAJESTIC!

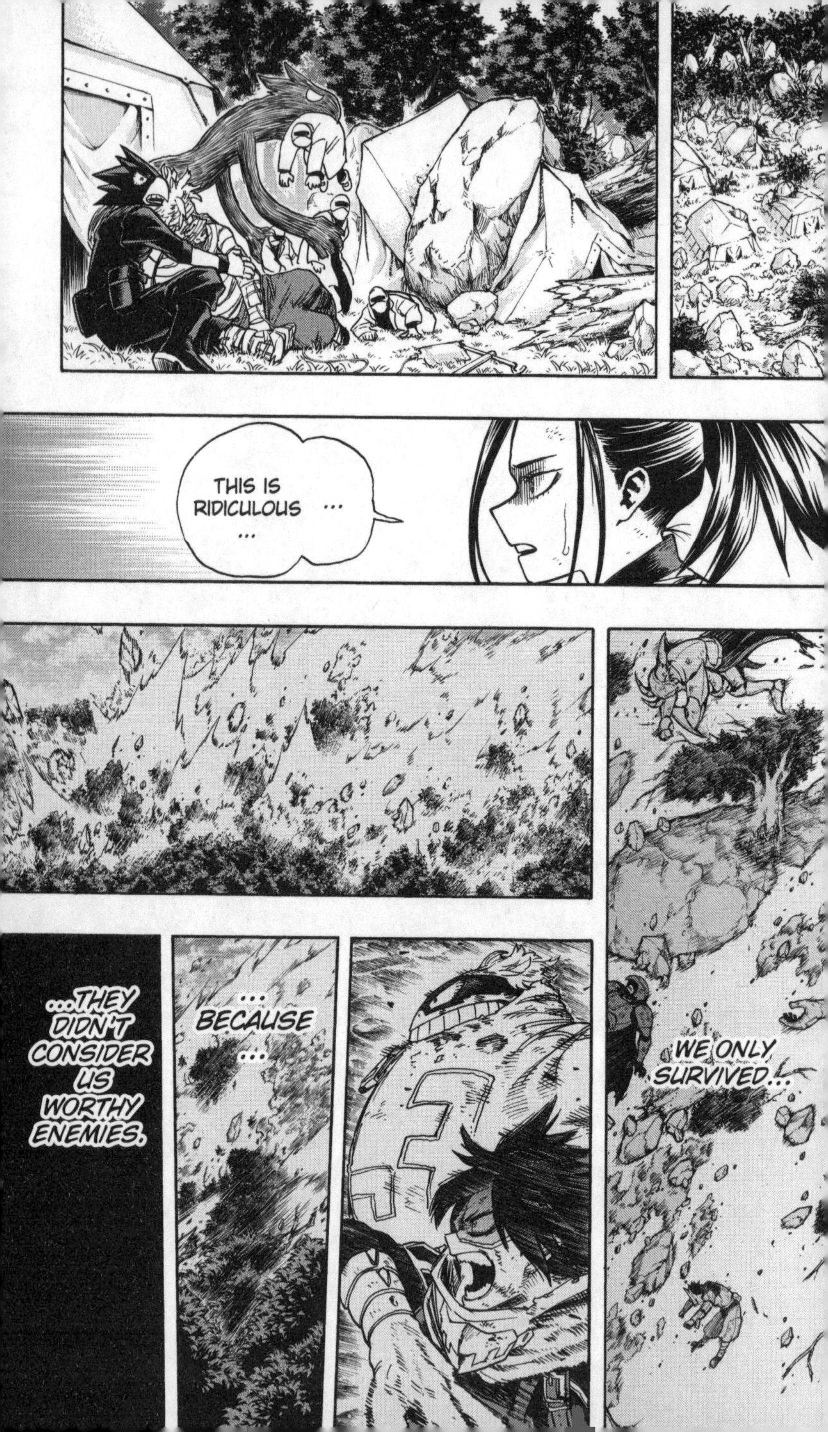
THIS IS RIDICULOUS ... ...
WE ONLY SURVIVED...
... BECAUSE ...
...THEY DIDN'T CONSIDER US WORTHY ENEMIES.

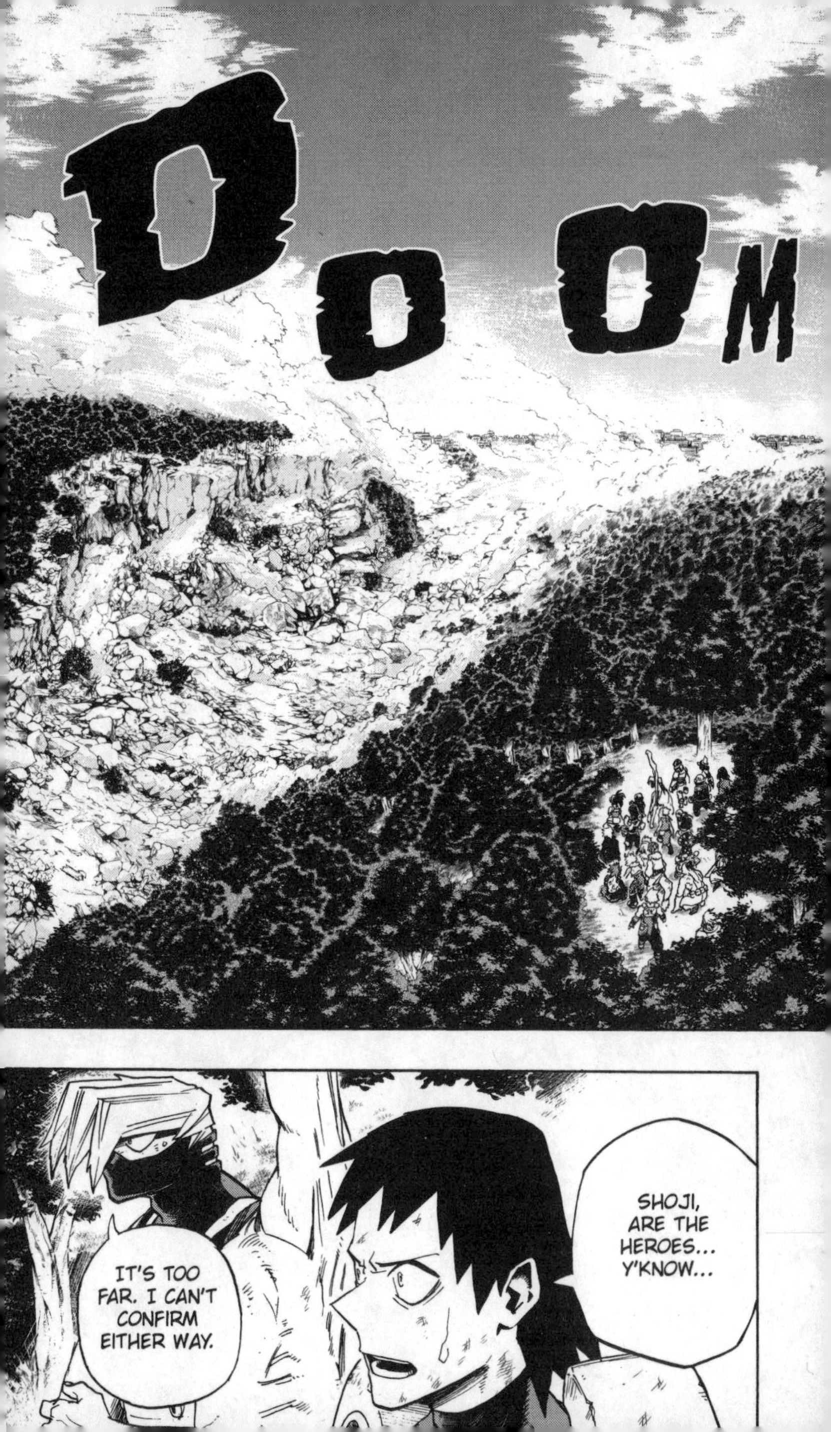
DOOM
SHOJI, ARE THE HEROES... Y'KNOW...
IT'S TOO FAR. I CAN'T CONFIRM EITHER WAY.

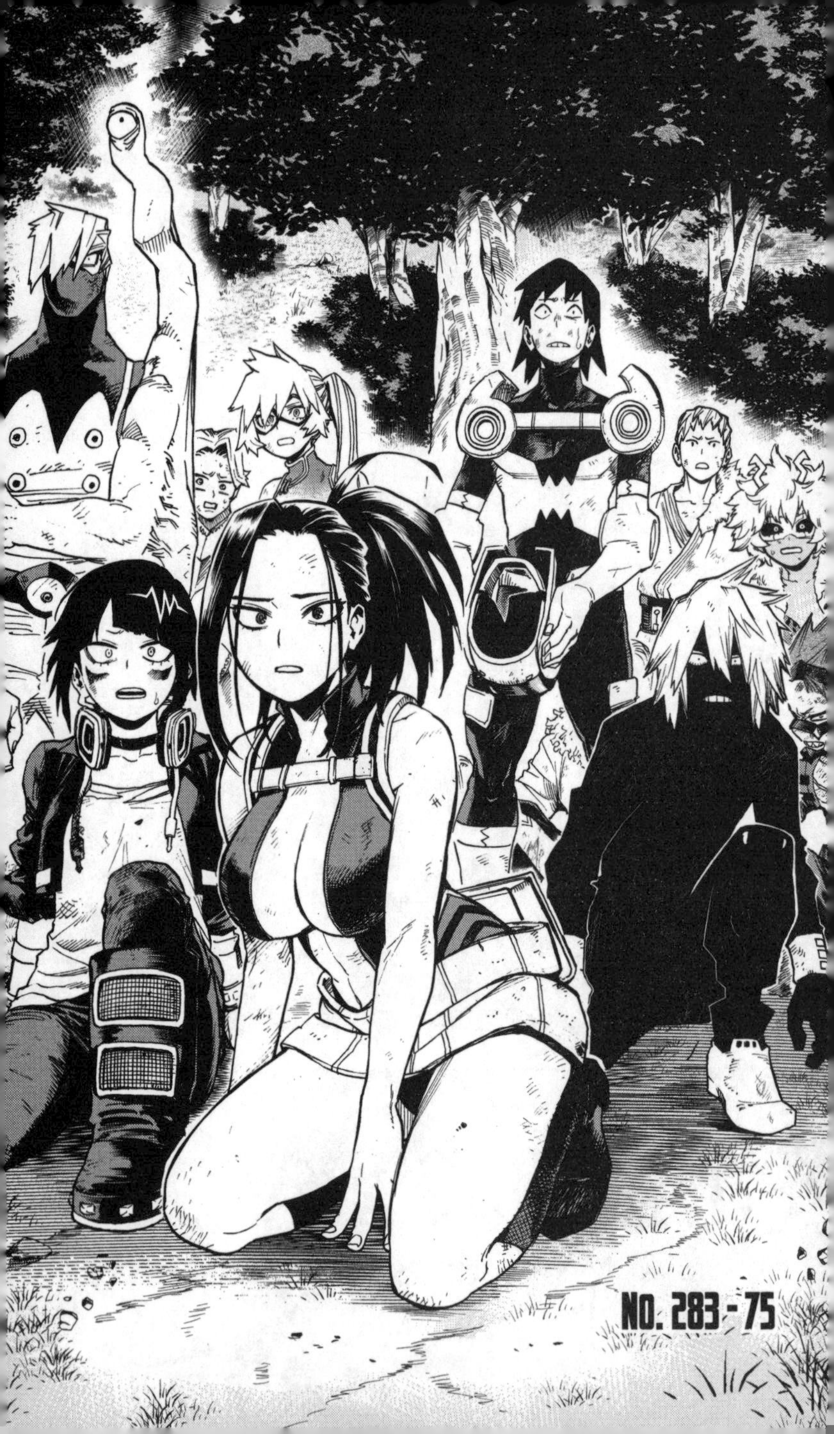
NO. 283 - 75

All of my assistants are incredible.
I'm so grateful for them.

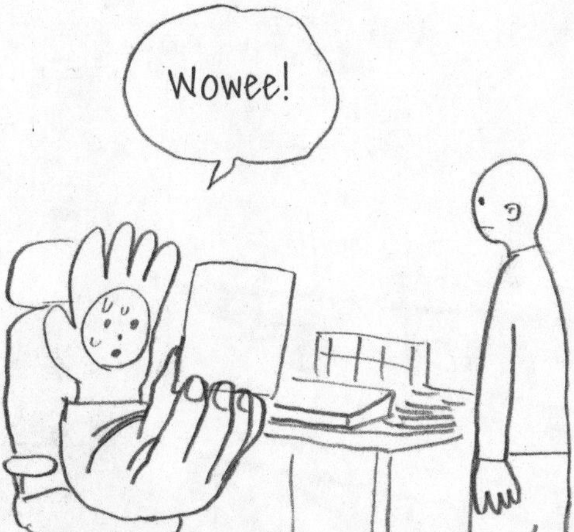
Wowee!

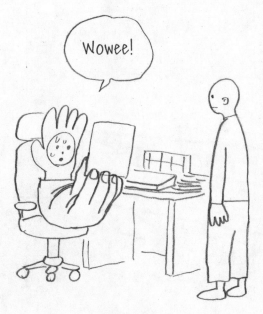

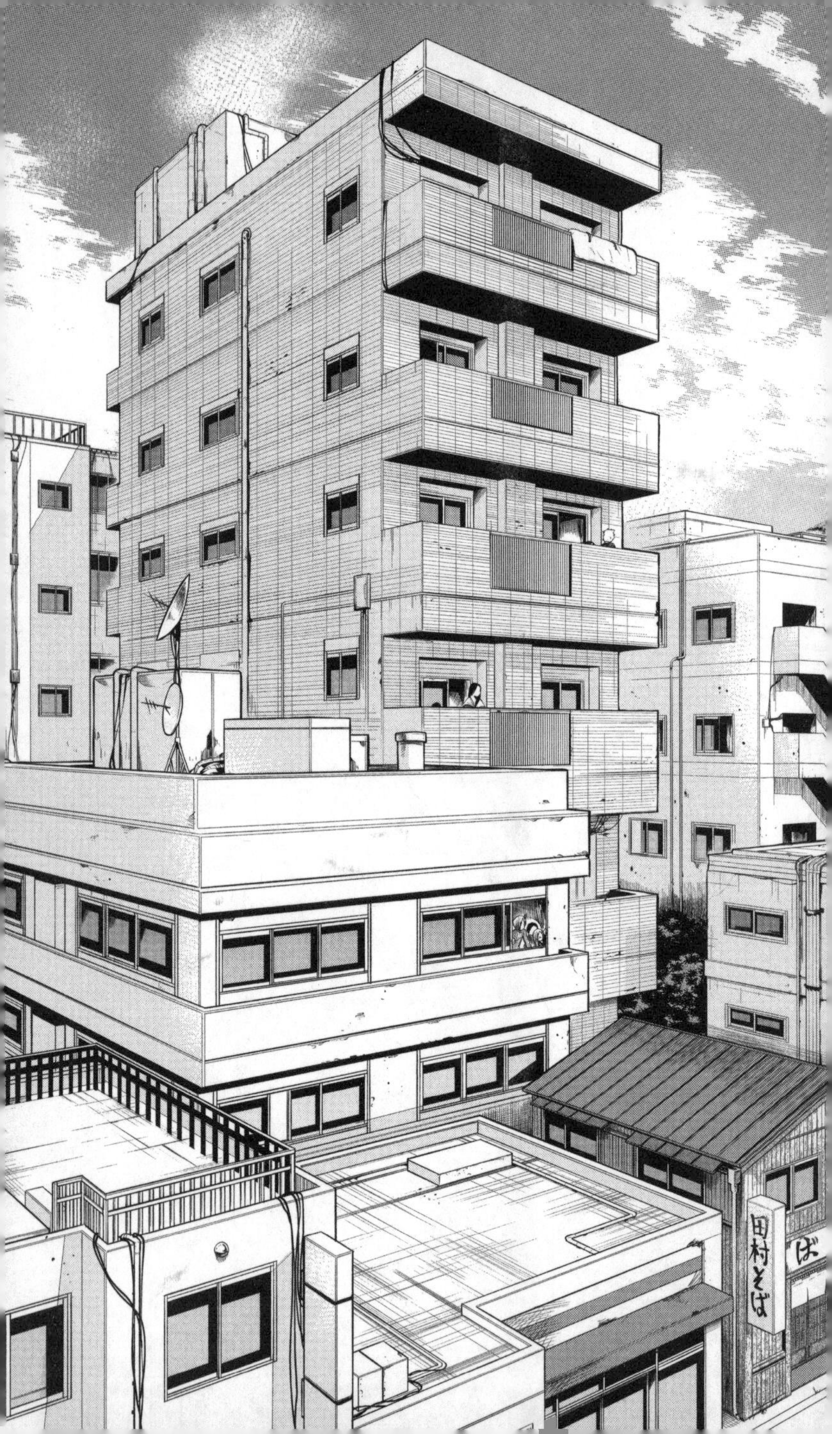
田村そば
ば

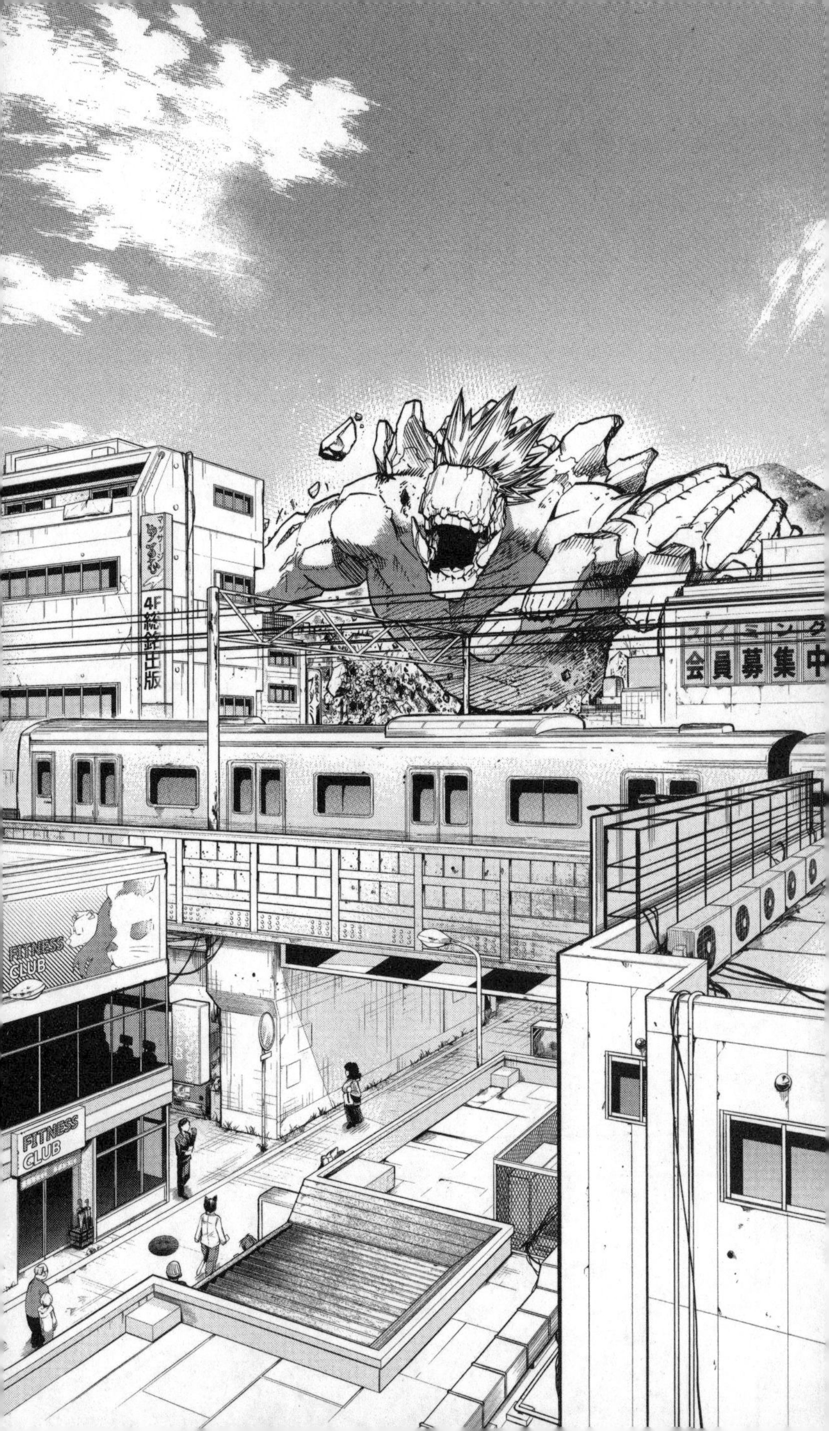

マッサージ
4F 総鉄出版
会員募集中
FITNESS CLUB
FITNESS CLUB

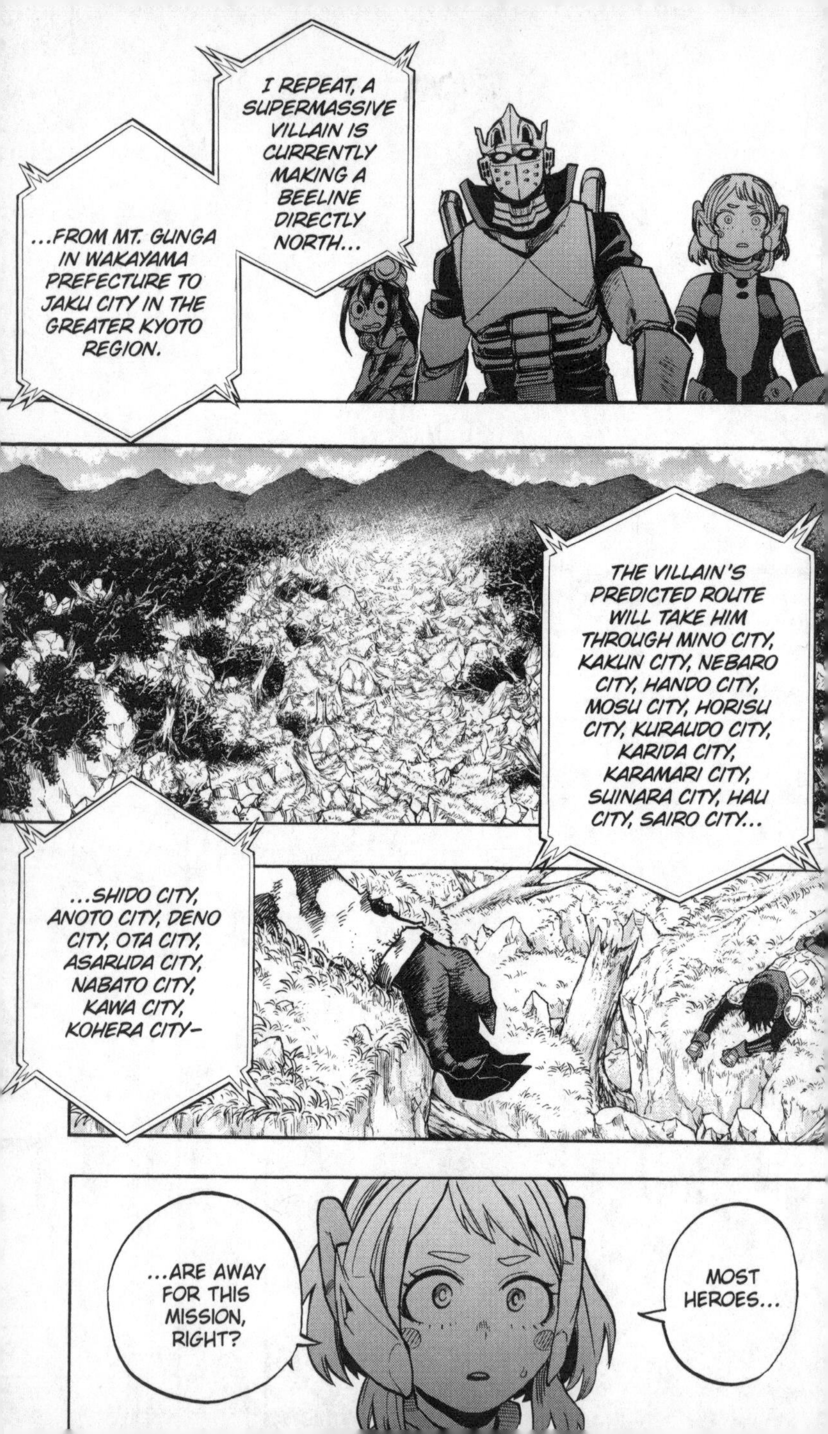
I REPEAT, A SUPERMASSIVE VILLAIN IS CURRENTLY MAKING A BEELINE DIRECTLY NORTH...
...FROM MT. GUNGA IN WAKAYAMA PREFECTURE TO JAKU CITY IN THE GREATER KYOTO REGION.
THE VILLAIN'S PREDICTED ROUTE WILL TAKE HIM THROUGH MINO CITY, KAKUN CITY, NEBARO CITY, HANDO CITY, MOSU CITY, HORISU CITY, KURAUDO CITY, KARIDA CITY, KARAMARI CITY, SUINARA CITY, HAU CITY, SAIRO CITY...
...SHIDO CITY, ANOTO CITY, DENO CITY, OTA CITY, ASARUDA CITY, NABATO CITY, KAWA CITY, KOHERA CITY-
MOST HEROES...
...ARE AWAY FOR THIS MISSION, RIGHT?

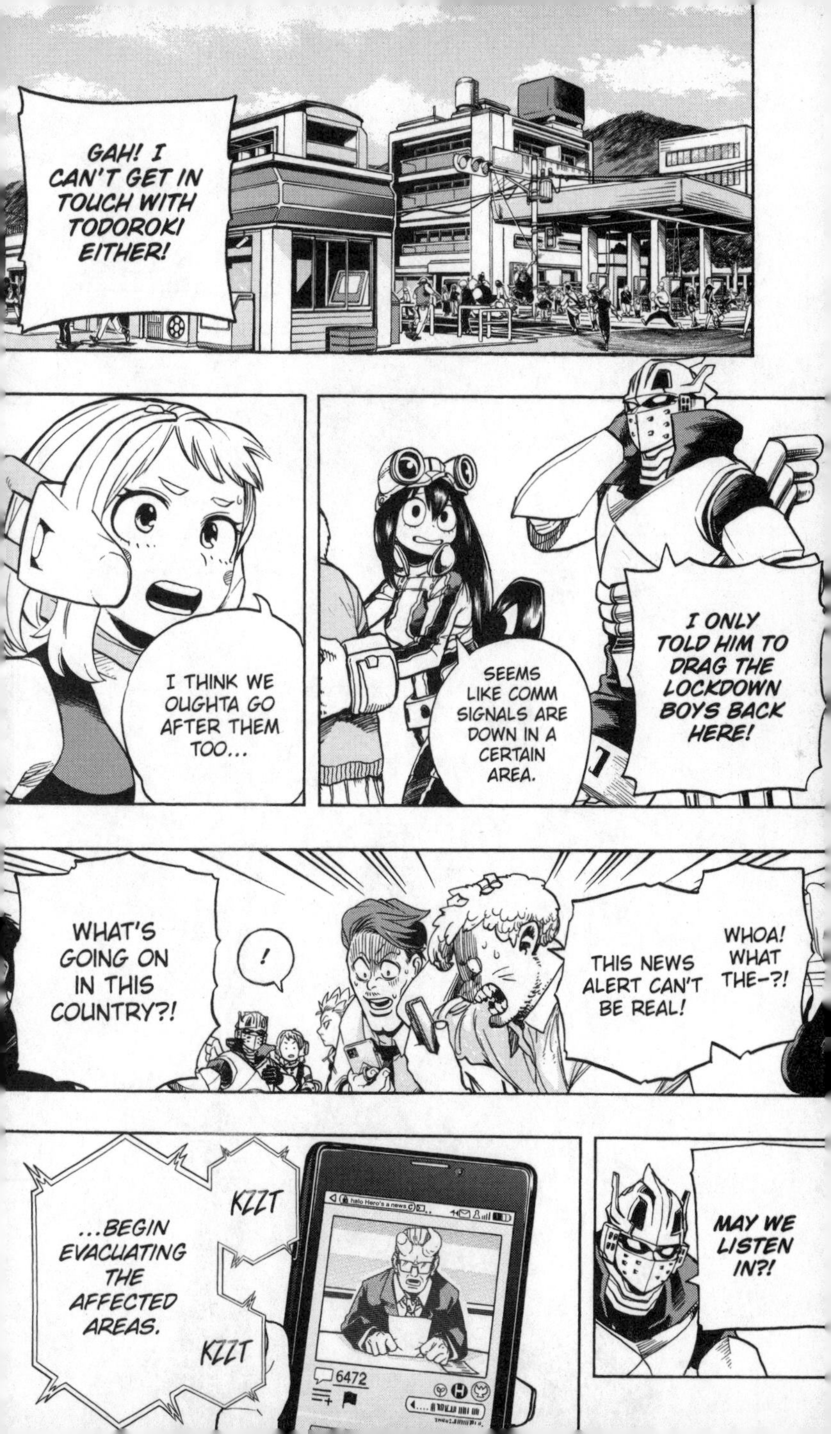
GAH! I CAN'T GET IN TOUCH WITH TODOROKI EITHER!
I ONLY TOLD HIM TO DRAG THE LOCKDOWN BOYS BACK HERE!
SEEMS LIKE COMM SIGNALS ARE DOWN IN A CERTAIN AREA.
I THINK WE OUGHTA GO AFTER THEM TOO...
WHOA! WHAT THE-?!
THIS NEWS ALERT CAN'T BE REAL!
!
WHAT'S GOING ON IN THIS COUNTRY?!
MAY WE LISTEN IN?!
KZZT
...BEGIN EVACUATING THE AFFECTED AREAS.
KZZT
6472

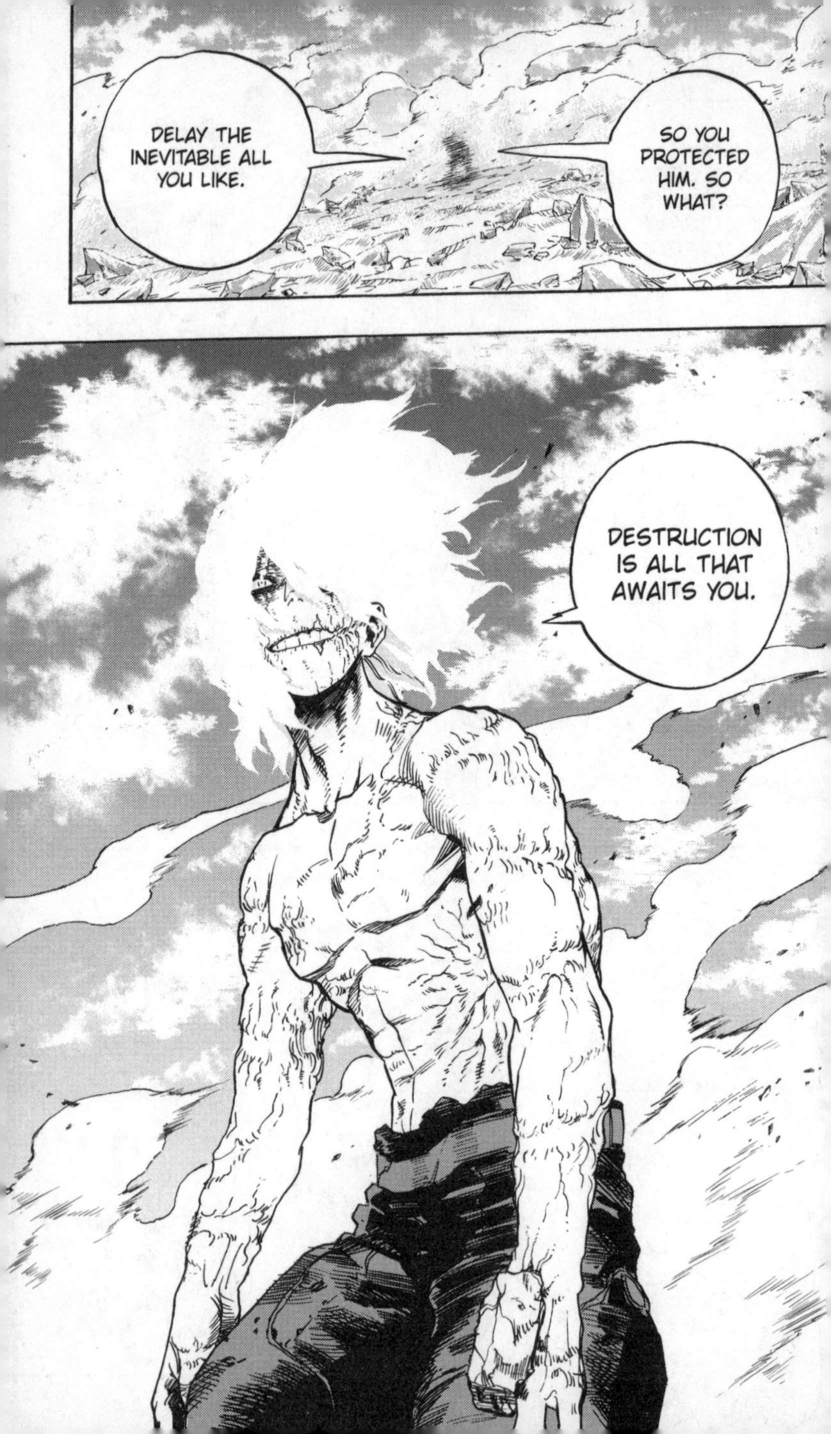
SO YOU PROTECTED HIM. SO WHAT?
DELAY THE INEVITABLE ALL YOU LIKE.
DESTRUCTION IS ALL THAT AWAITS YOU.

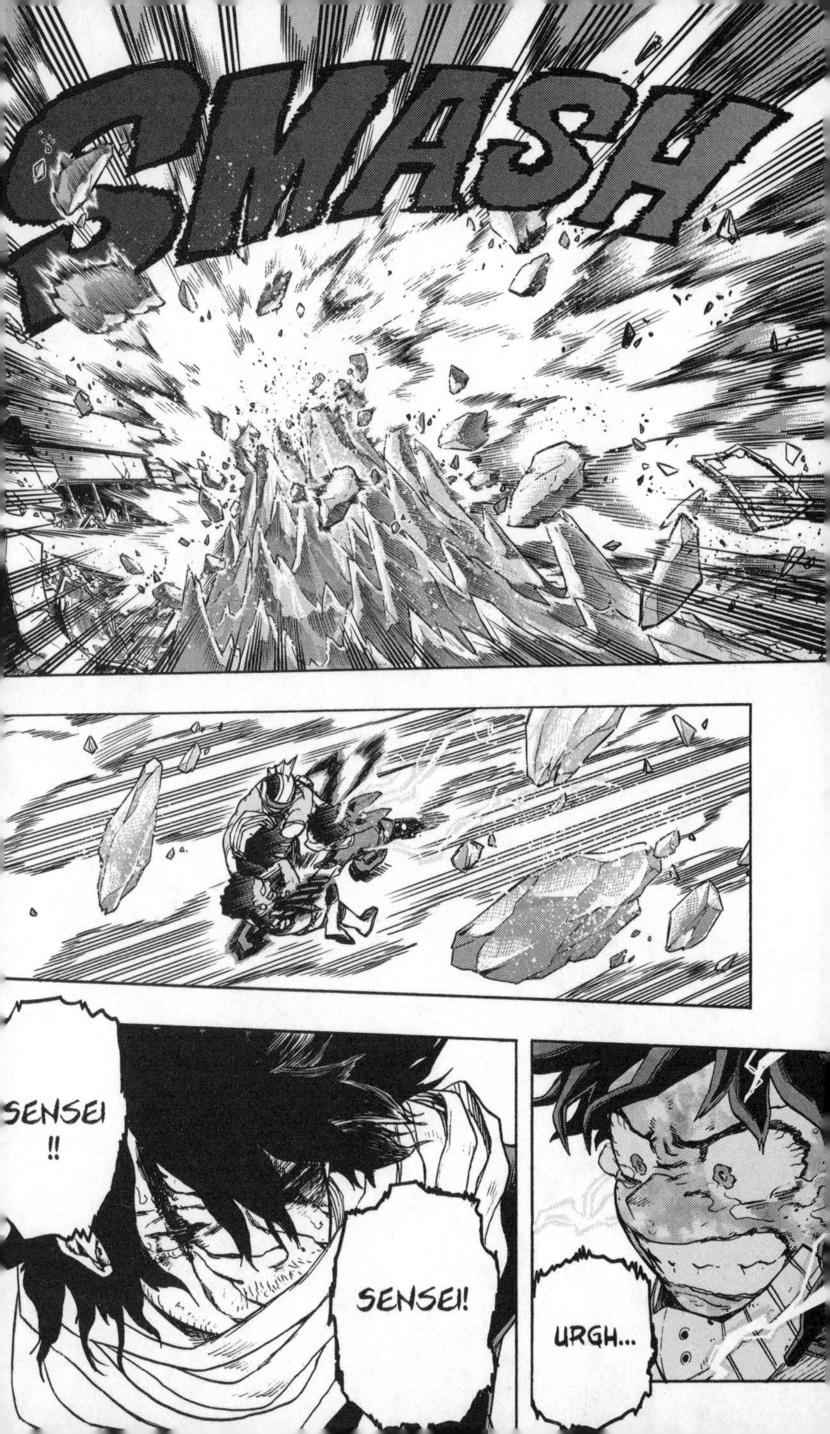
SMASH
URGH...
SENSEI !!
SENSEI!

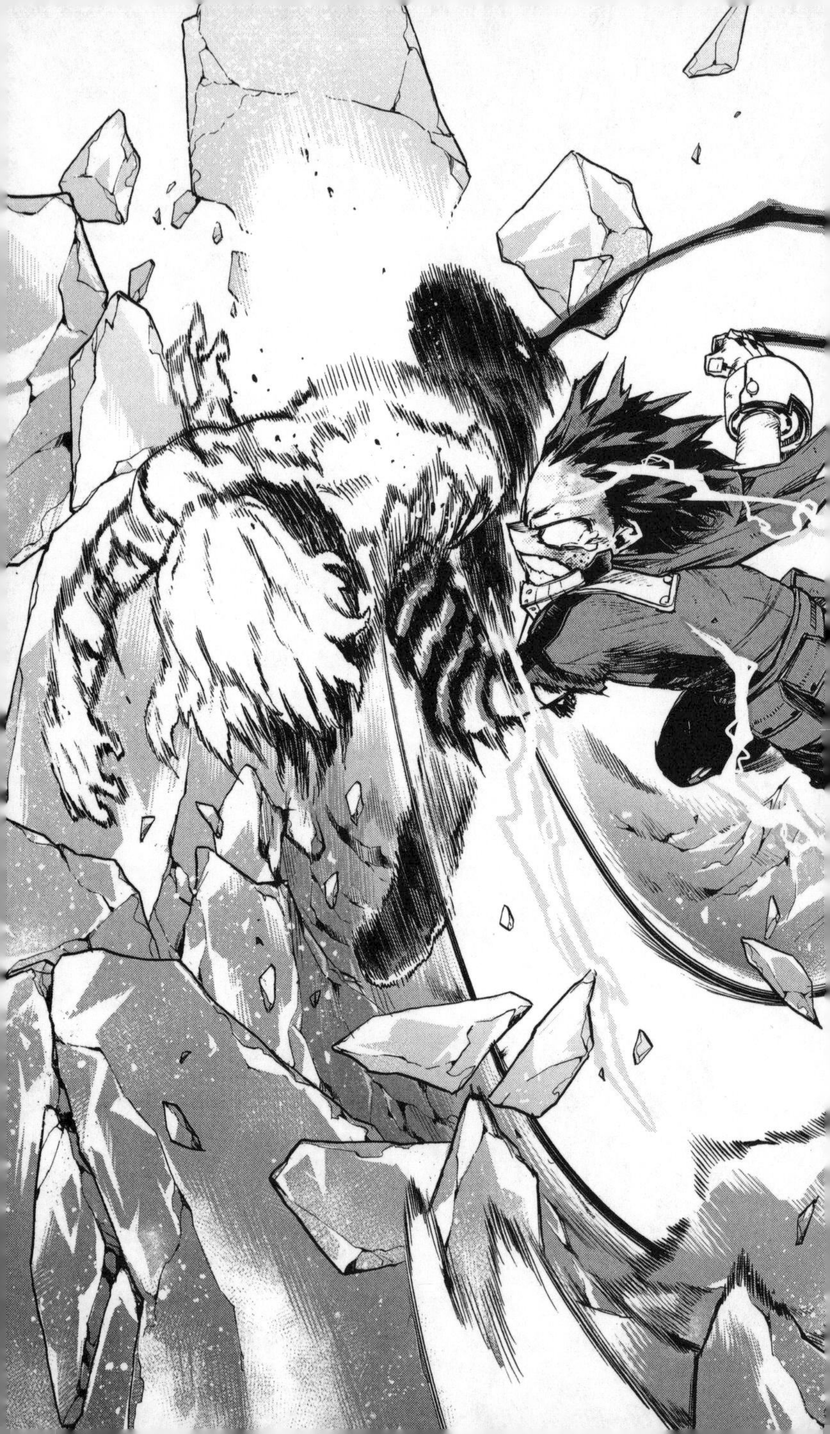

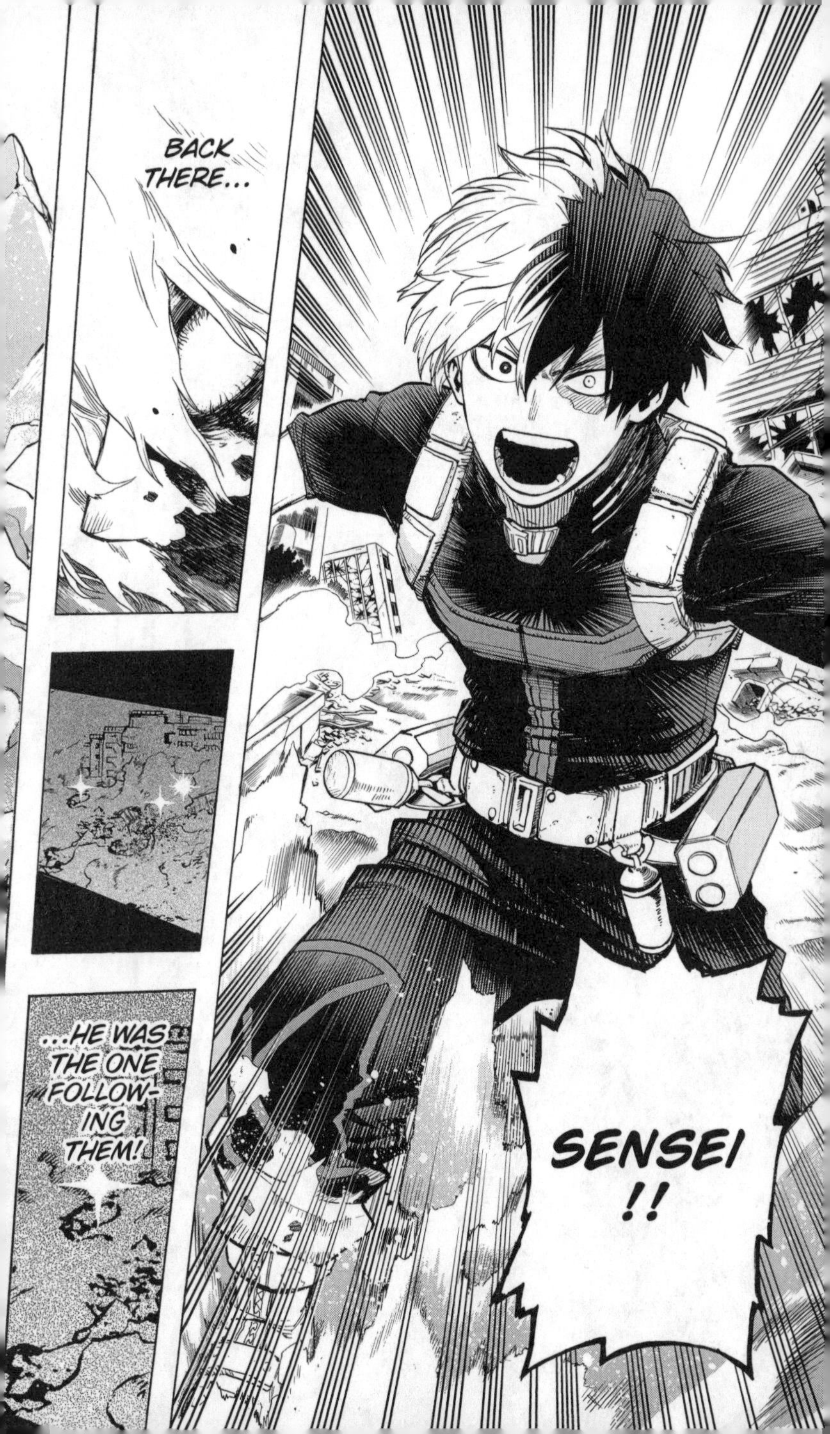
SENSEI !!
BACK THERE...
...HE WAS THE ONE FOLLOWING THEM!

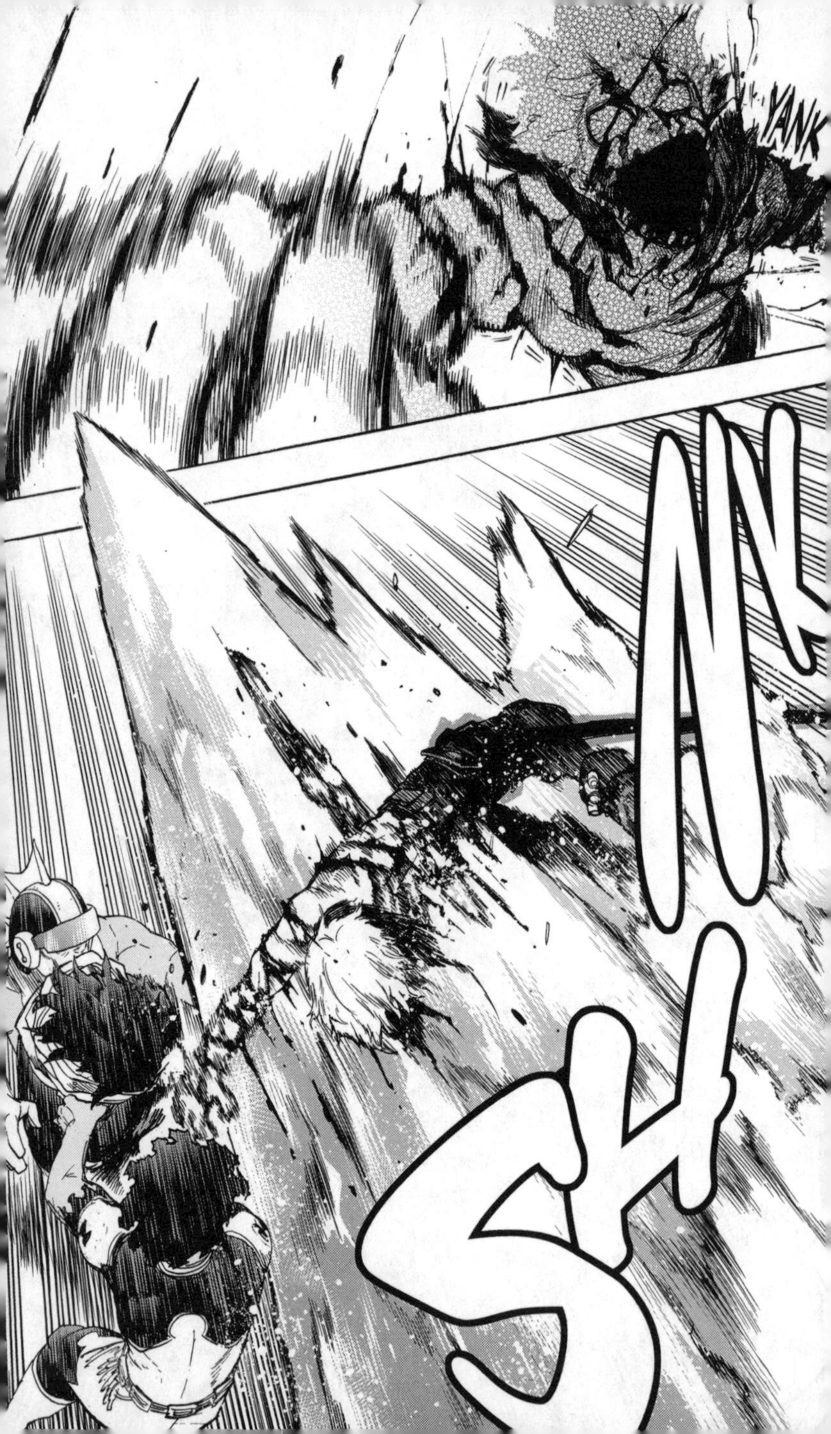
YANK
SHANK

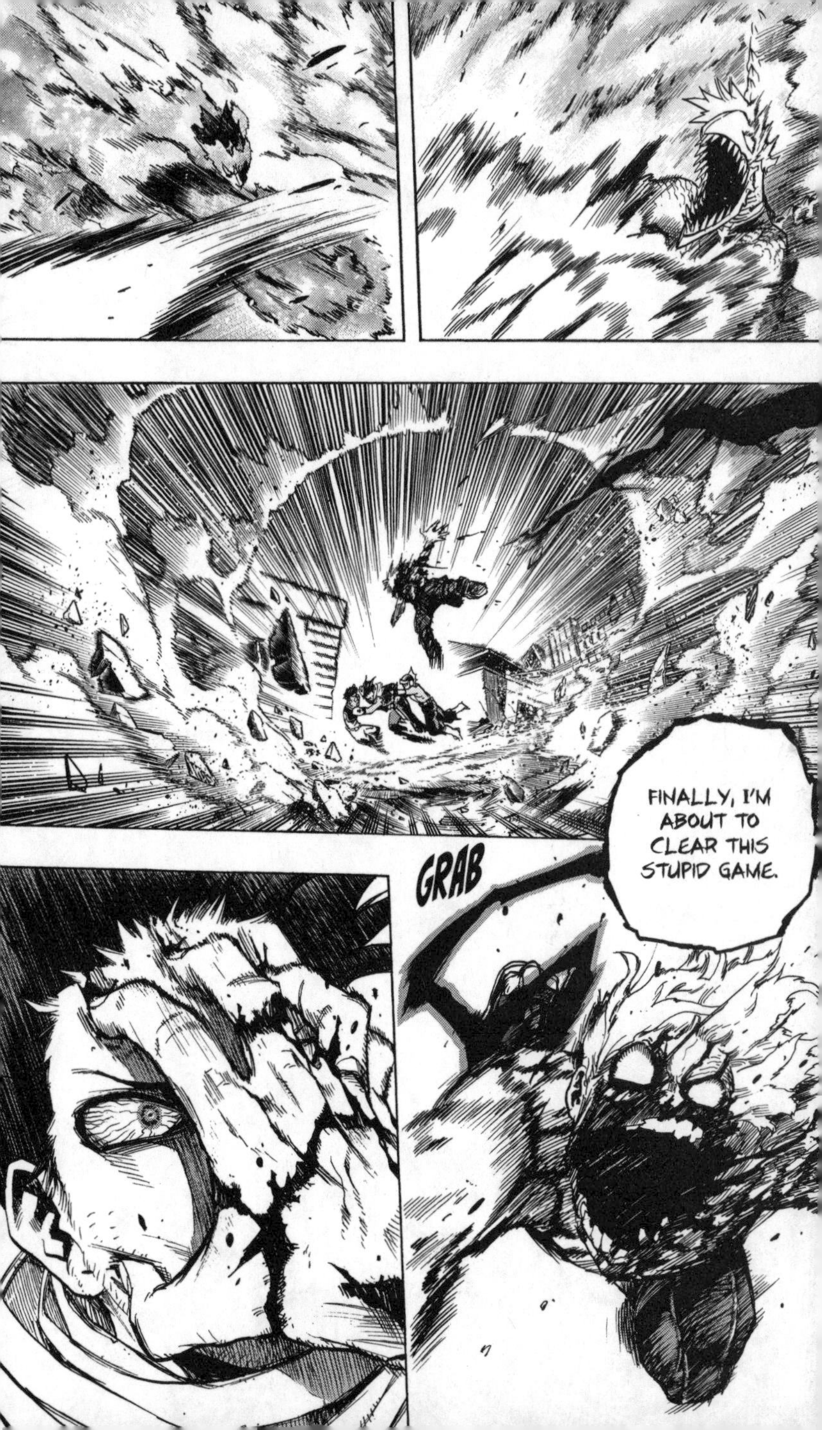
FINALLY, I'M ABOUT TO CLEAR THIS STUPID GAME.
GRAB

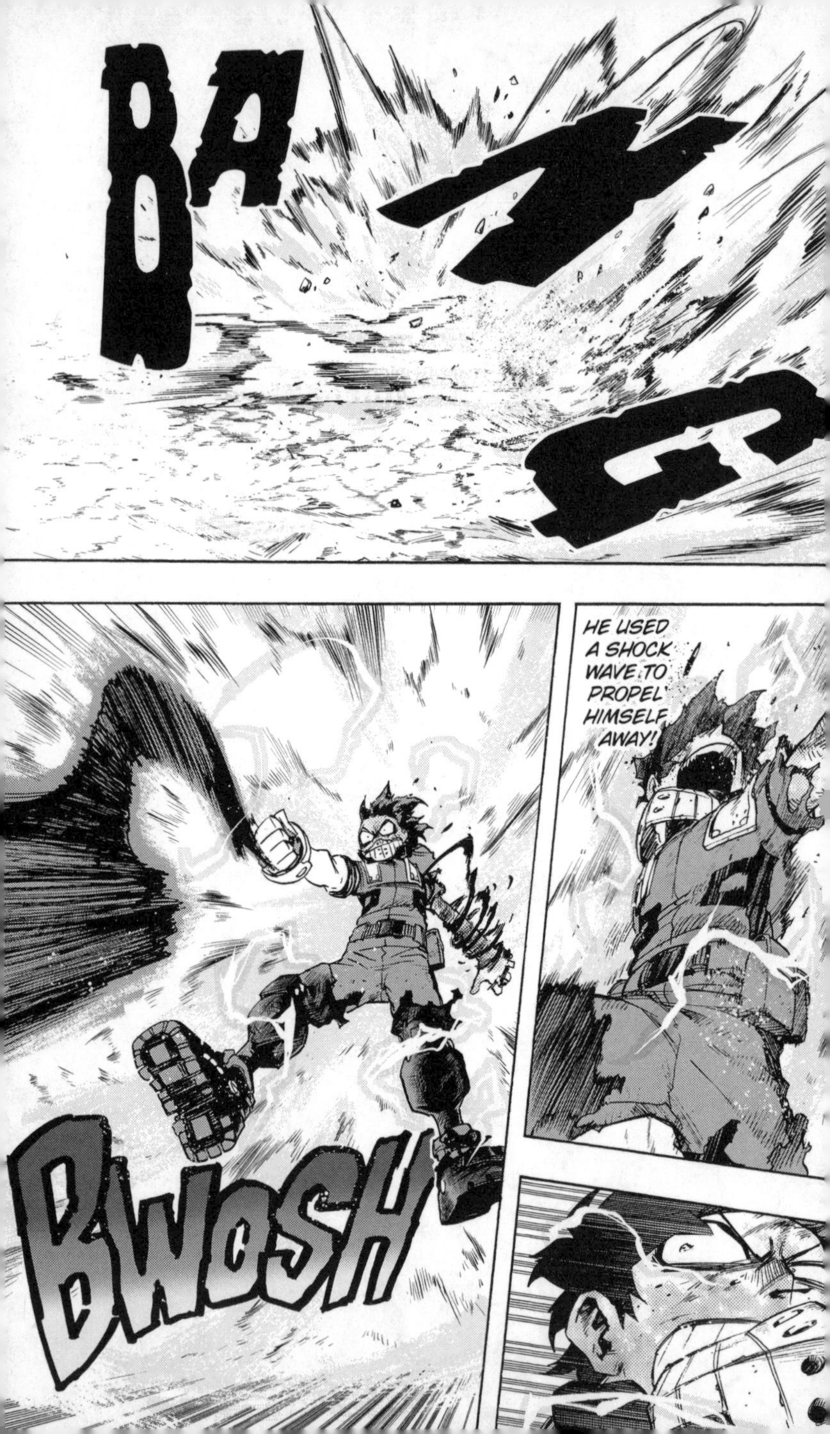
BANG
HE USED A SHOCK WAVE TO PROPEL HIMSELF AWAY!
BWOSH

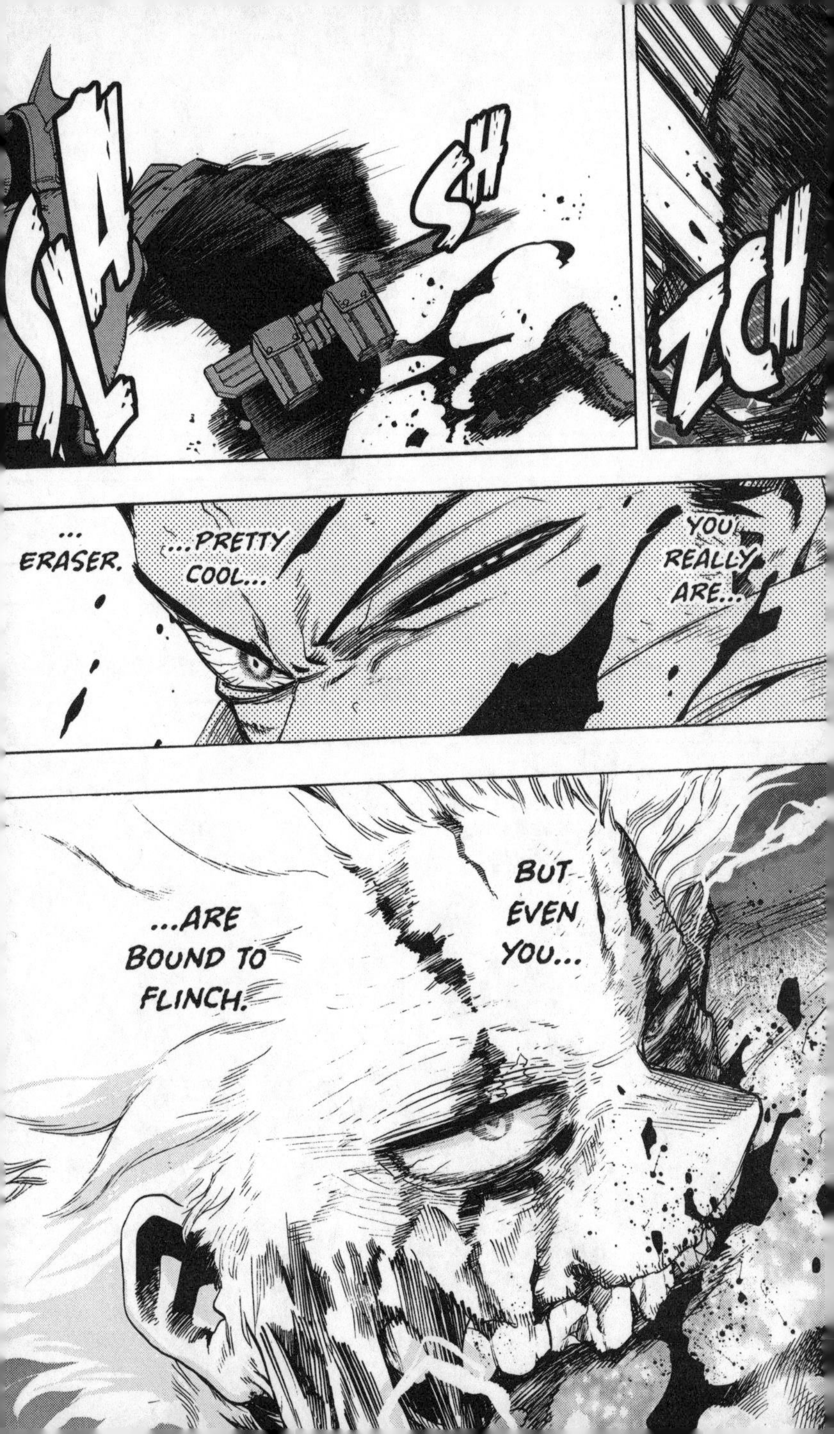
ZCH
SH
YOU REALLY ARE...
...PRETTY COOL...
... ERASER.
BUT EVEN YOU...
...ARE BOUND TO FLINCH.

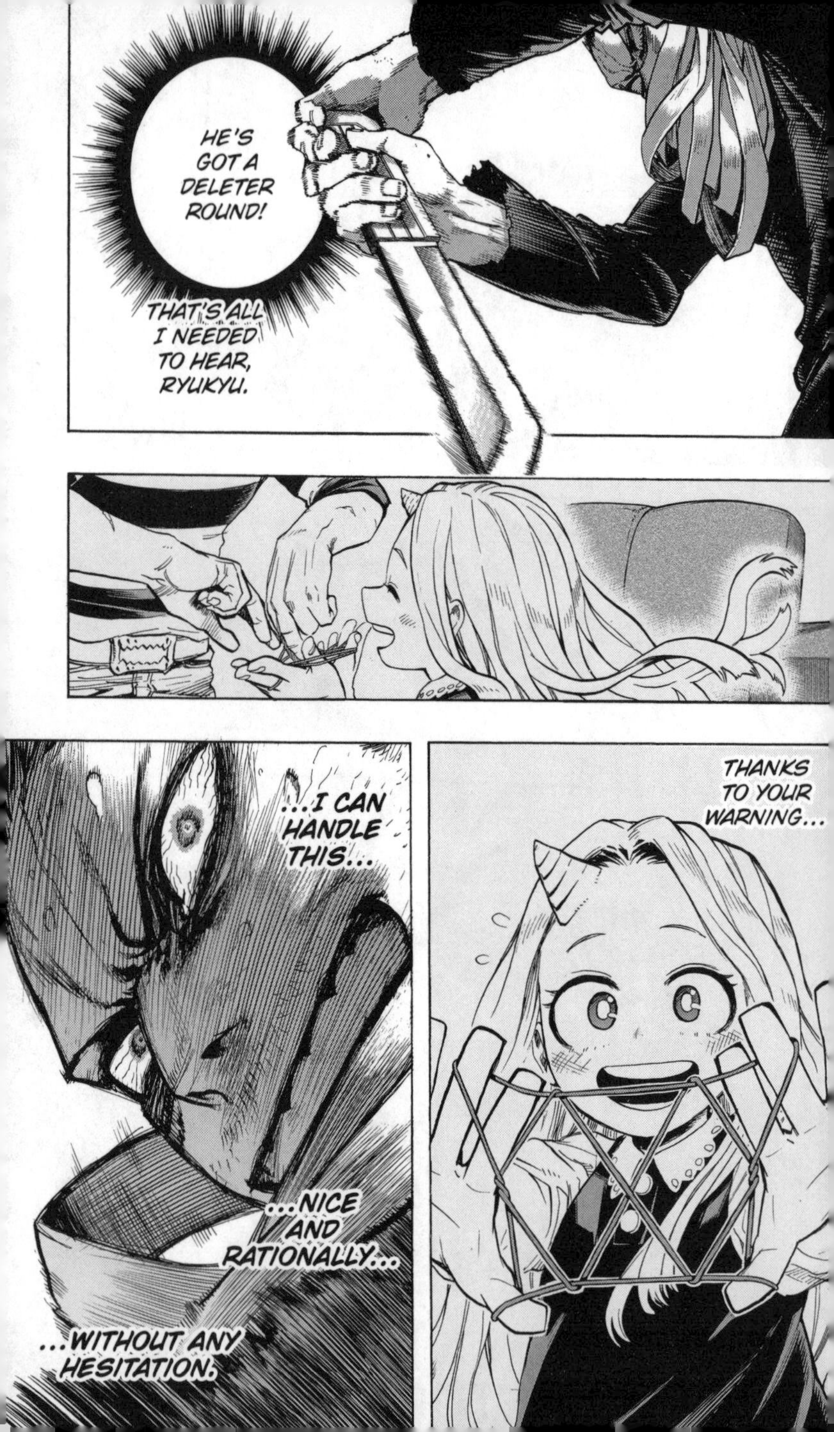
HE'S GOT A DELETER ROUND!
THAT'S ALL I NEEDED TO HEAR, RYUKYU.
THANKS TO YOUR WARNING...
...I CAN HANDLE THIS...
...NICE AND RATIONALLY...
...WITHOUT ANY HESITATION.

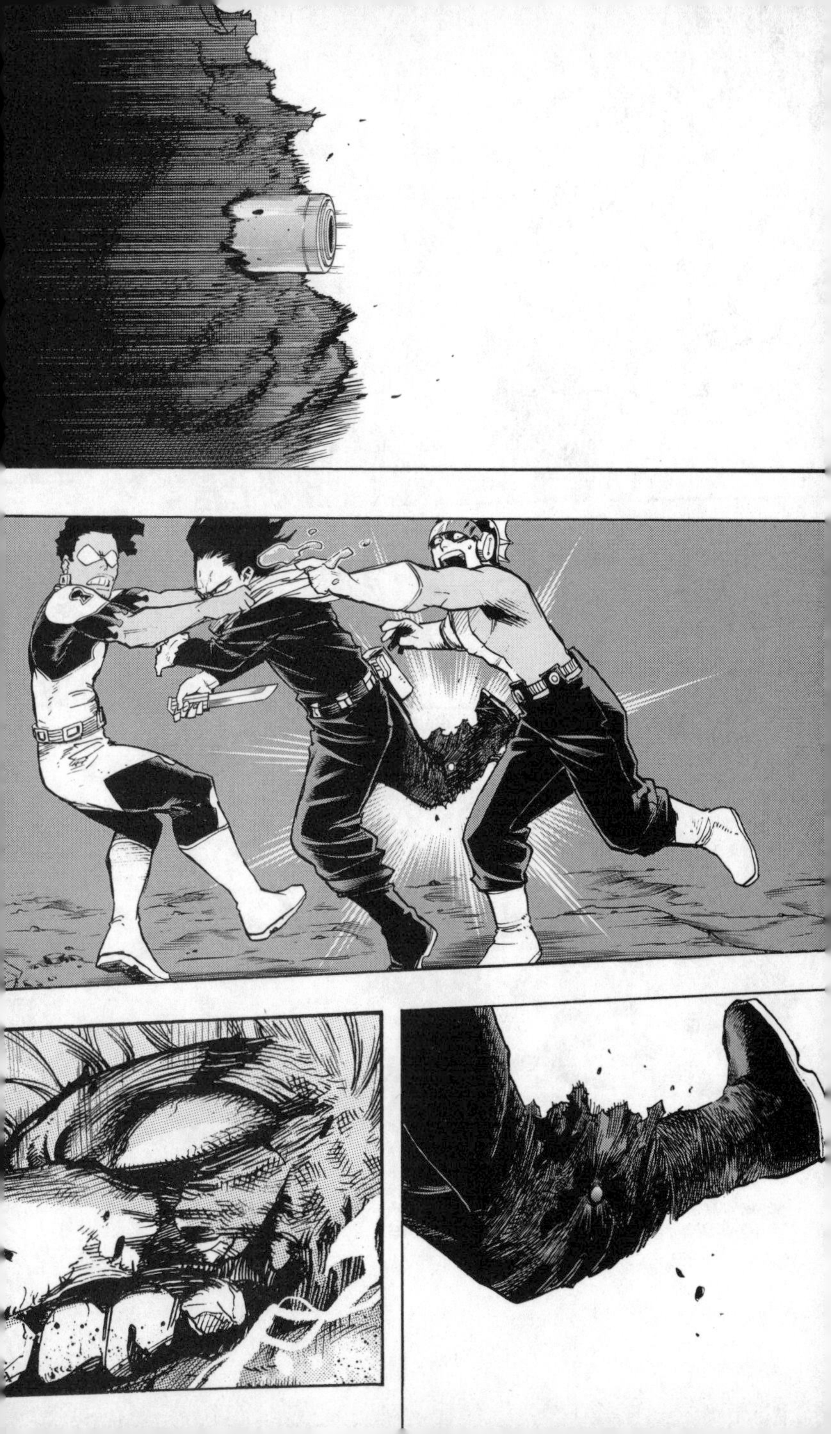

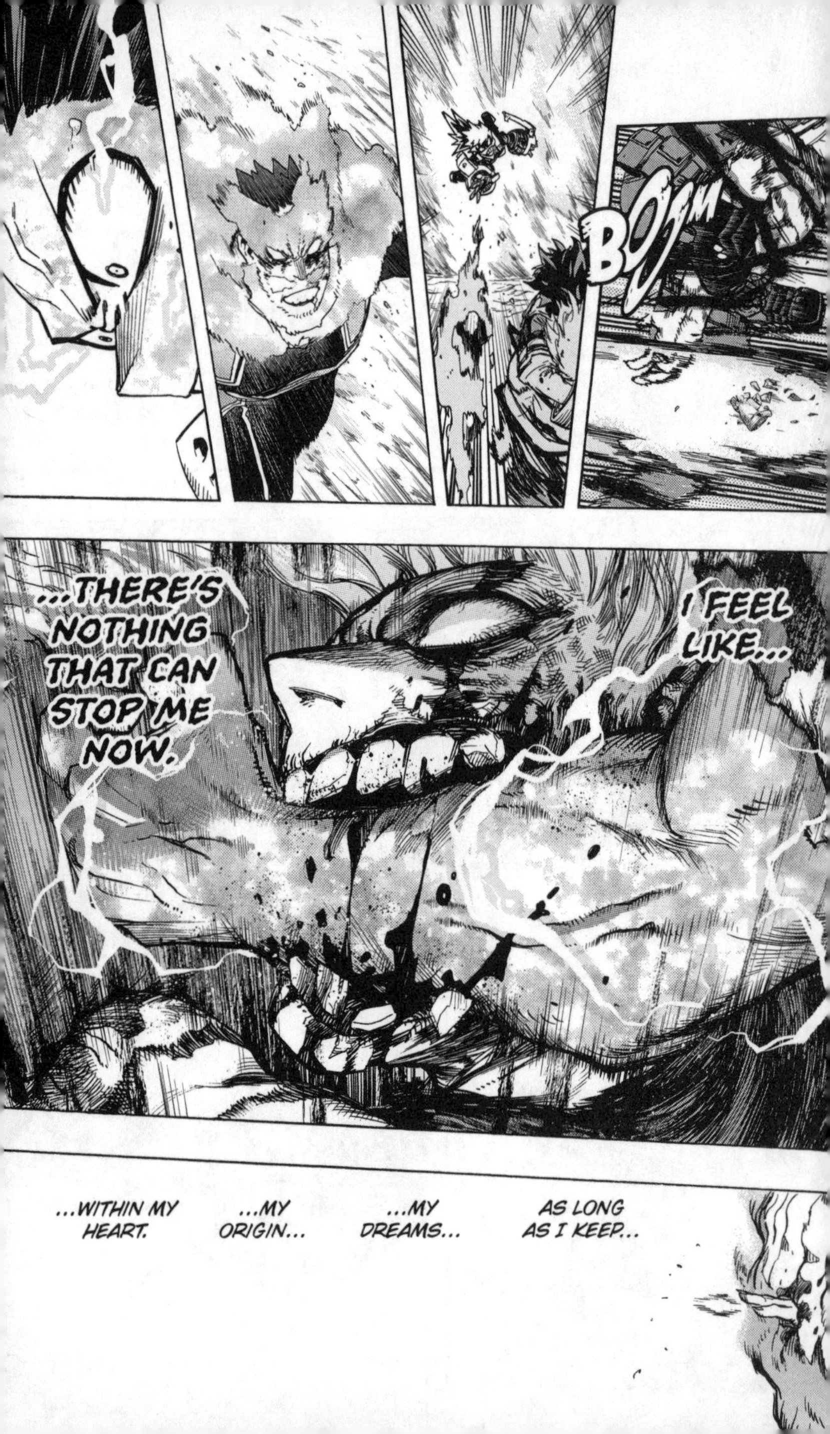
BOOM
I FEEL LIKE...
...THERE'S NOTHING THAT CAN STOP ME NOW.
AS LONG AS I KEEP...
...MY DREAMS...
...MY ORIGIN...
...WITHIN MY HEART.

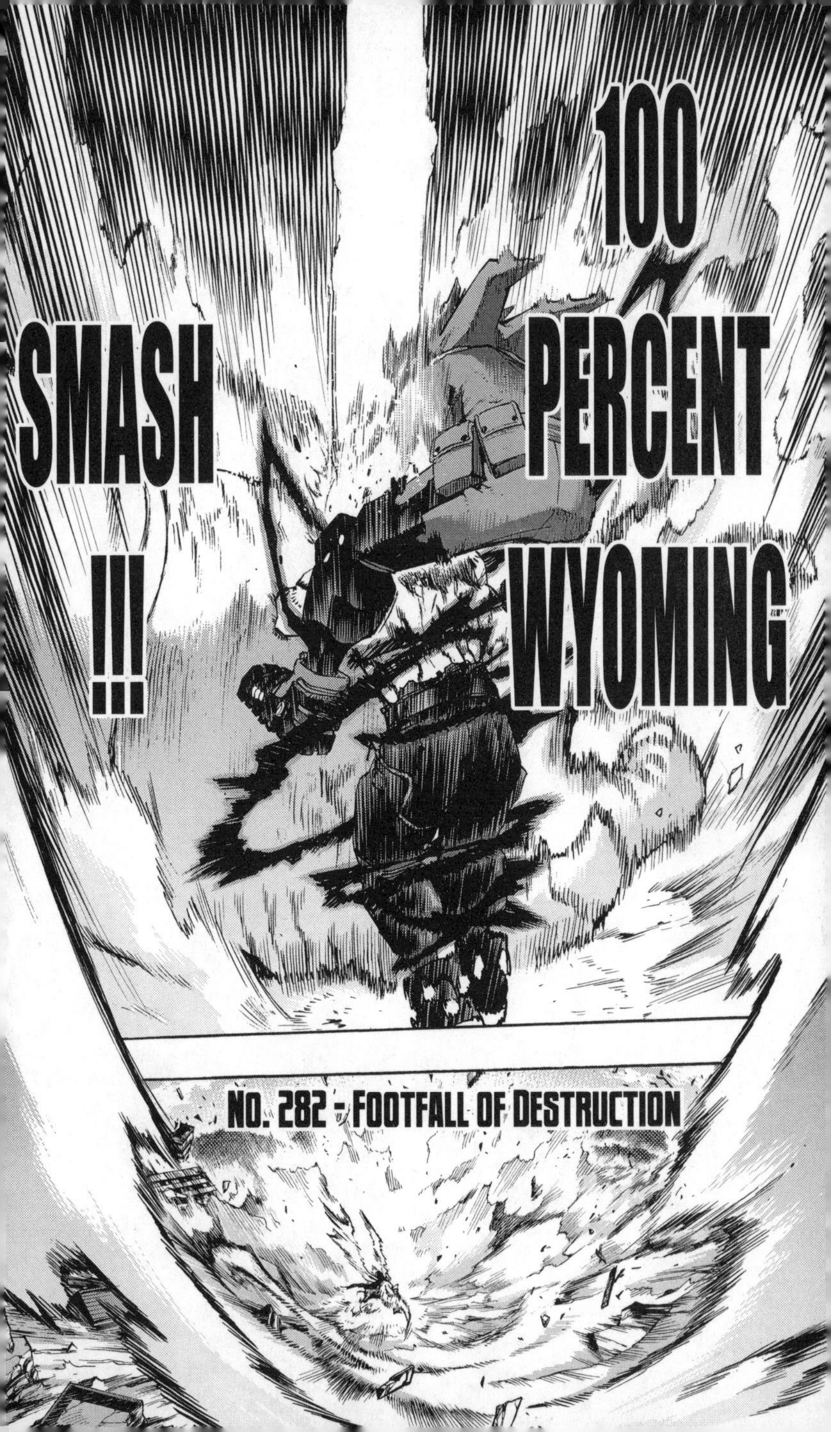

100 PERCENT WYOMING
SMASH !!!
No. 282 - Footfall of Destruction

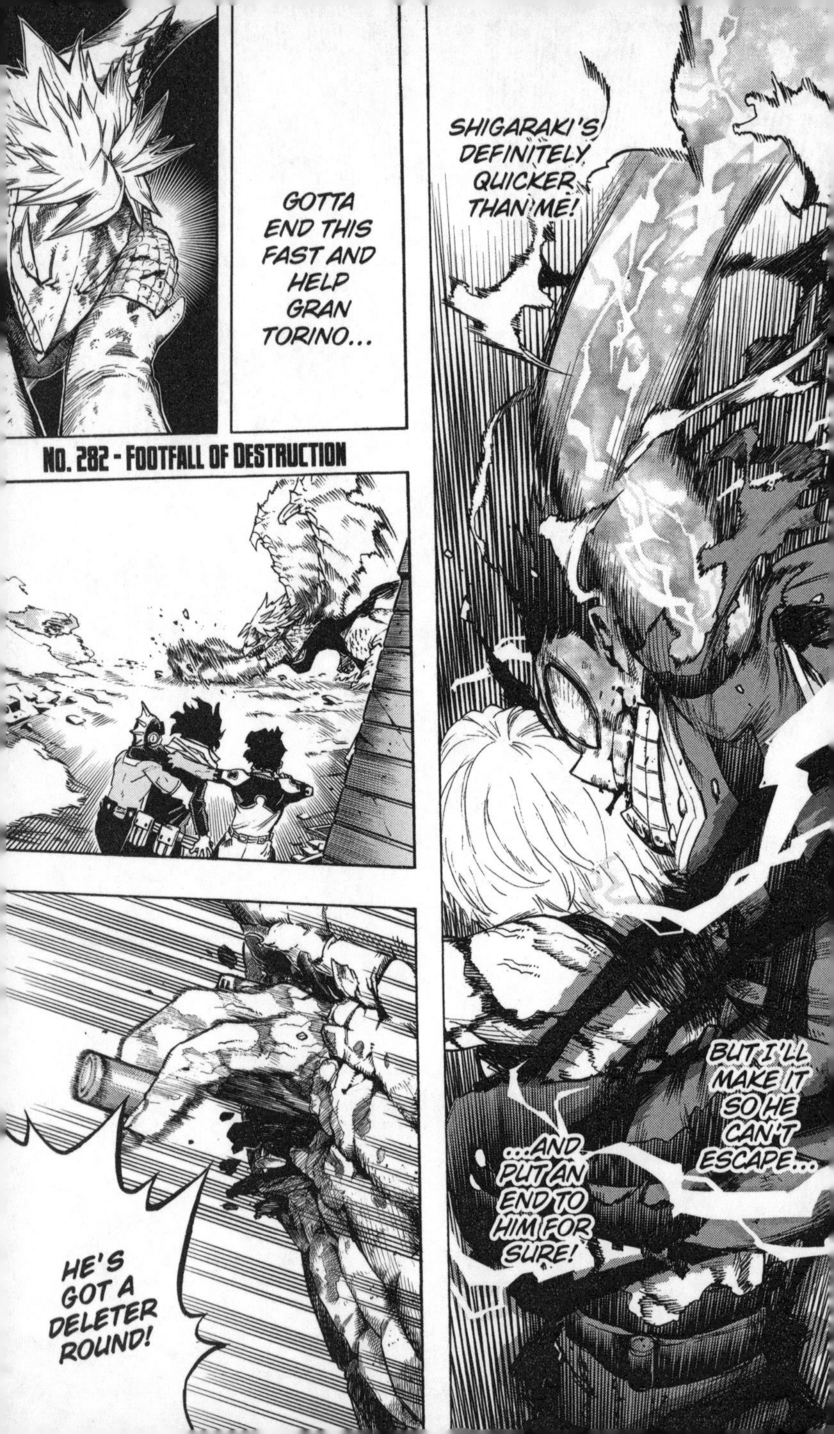
SHIGARAKI'S DEFINITELY QUICKER THAN ME!
BUT I'LL MAKE IT SO HE CAN'T ESCAPE...
...AND PUT AN END TO HIM FOR SURE!
GOTTA END THIS FAST AND HELP GRAN TORINO...
No. 282 - Footfall of Destruction
HE'S GOT A DELETER ROUND!

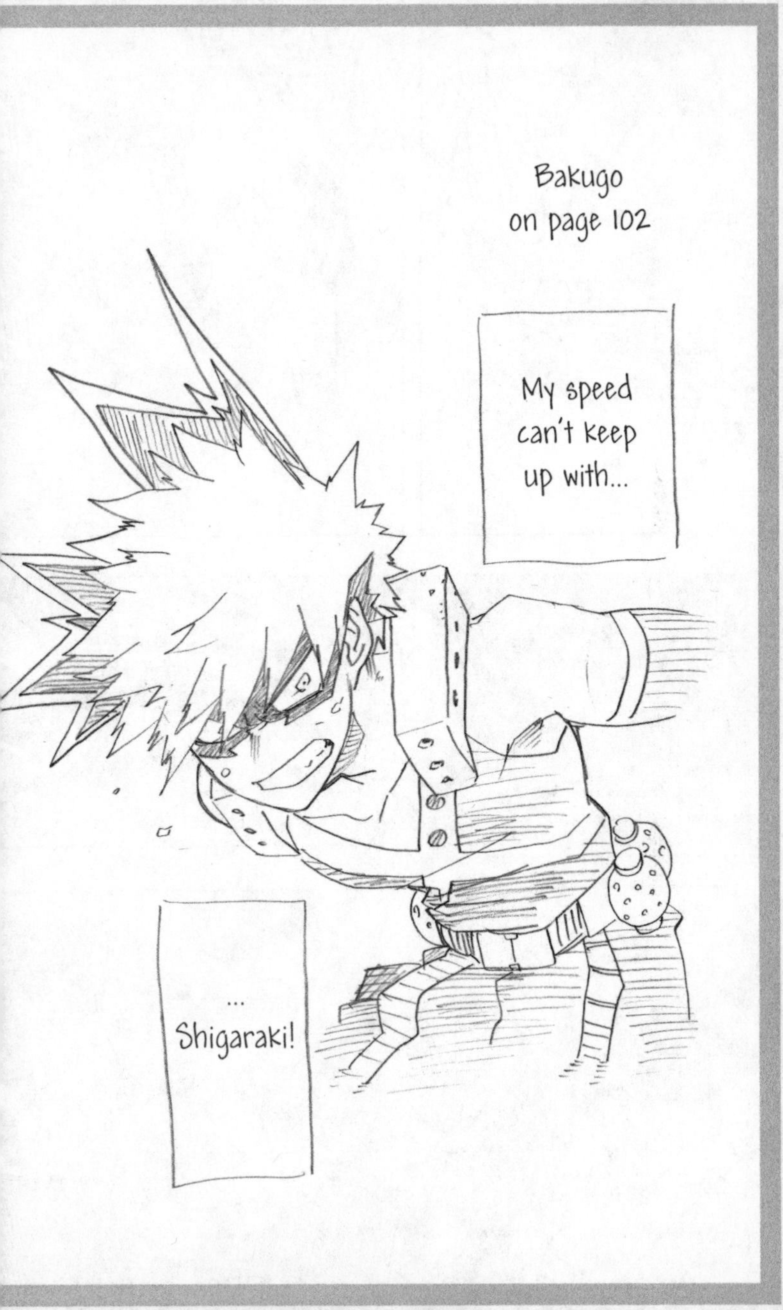
Bakugo on page 102
My speed can't keep up with...
...Shigaraki!

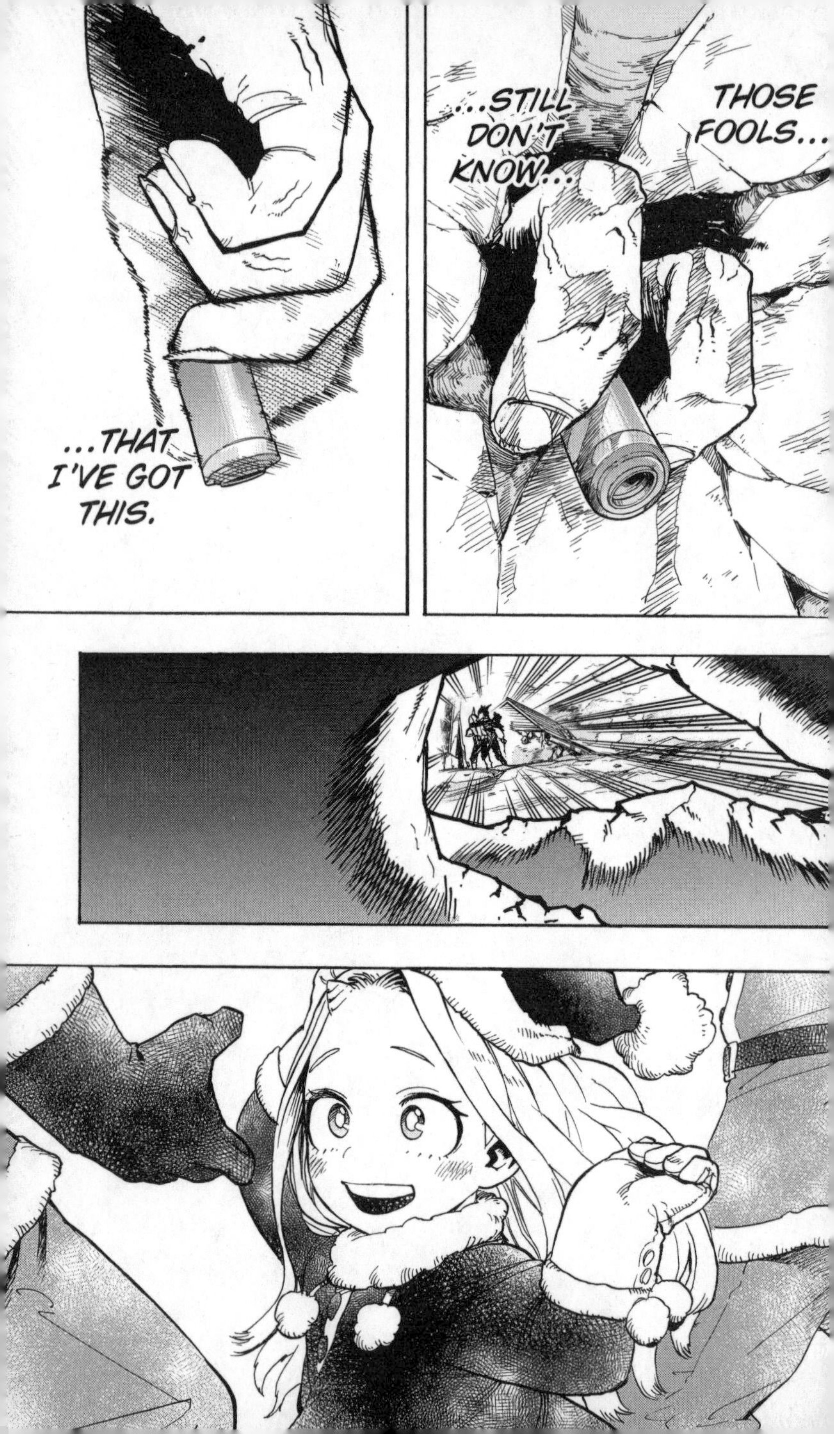
THOSE FOOLS...
...STILL DON'T KNOW...
...THAT I'VE GOT THIS.

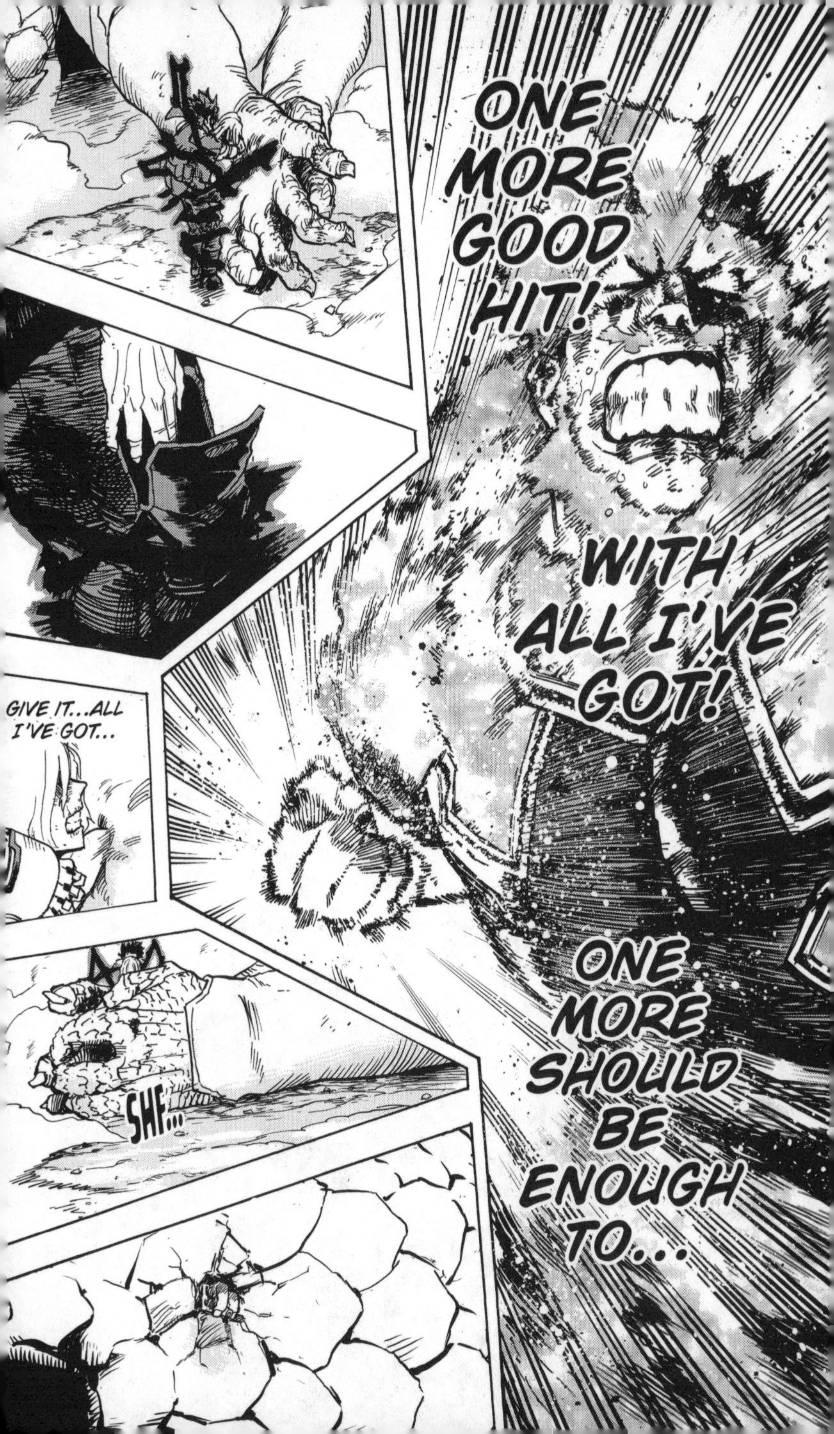
ONE MORE GOOD HIT!
WITH ALL I'VE GOT!
ONE MORE SHOULD BE ENOUGH TO...
GIVE IT...ALL I'VE GOT...
SHF...

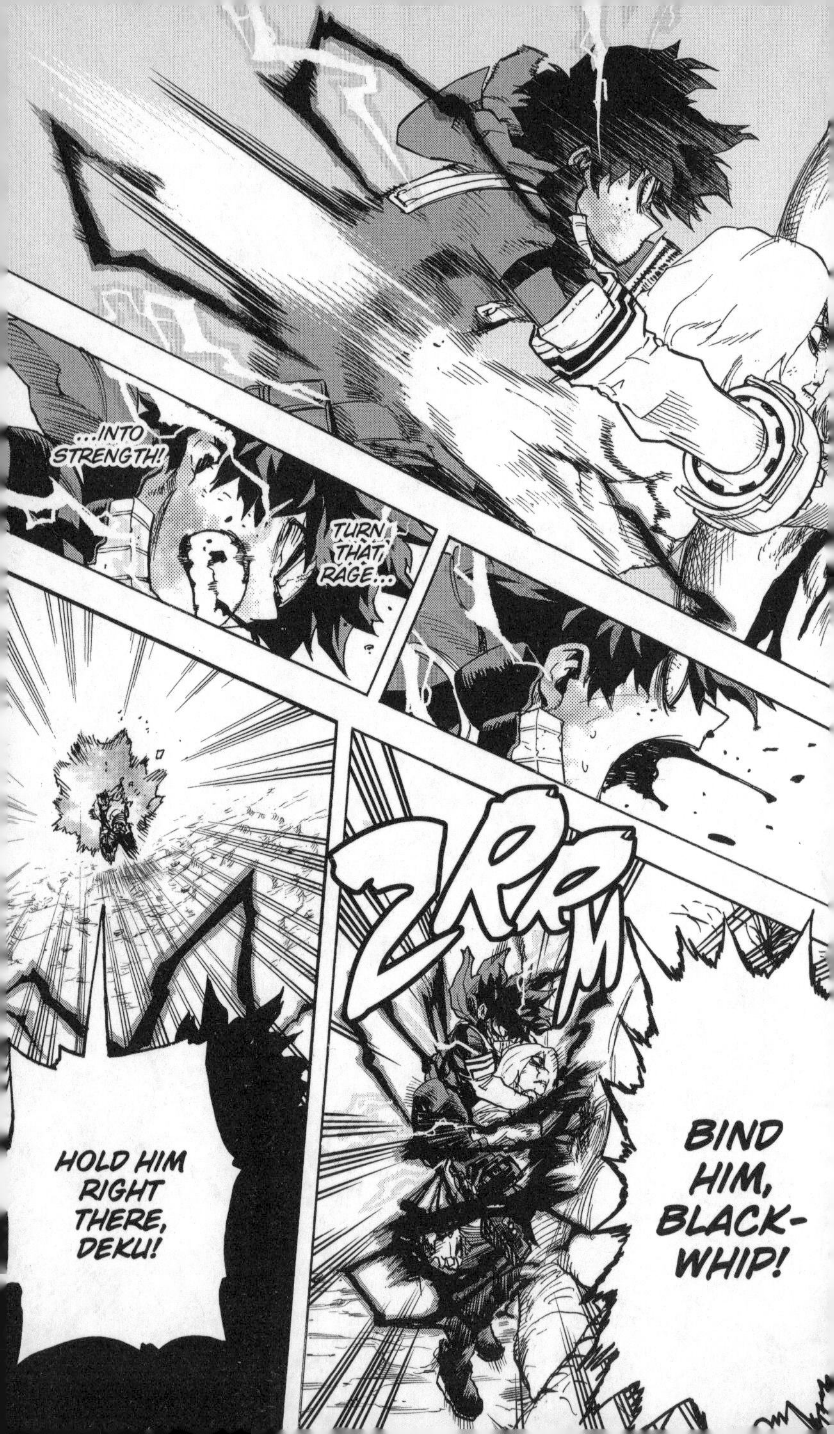
TURN THAT RAGE...
...INTO STRENGTH!
ZRRM
BIND HIM, BLACK-WHIP!
HOLD HIM RIGHT THERE, DEKU!

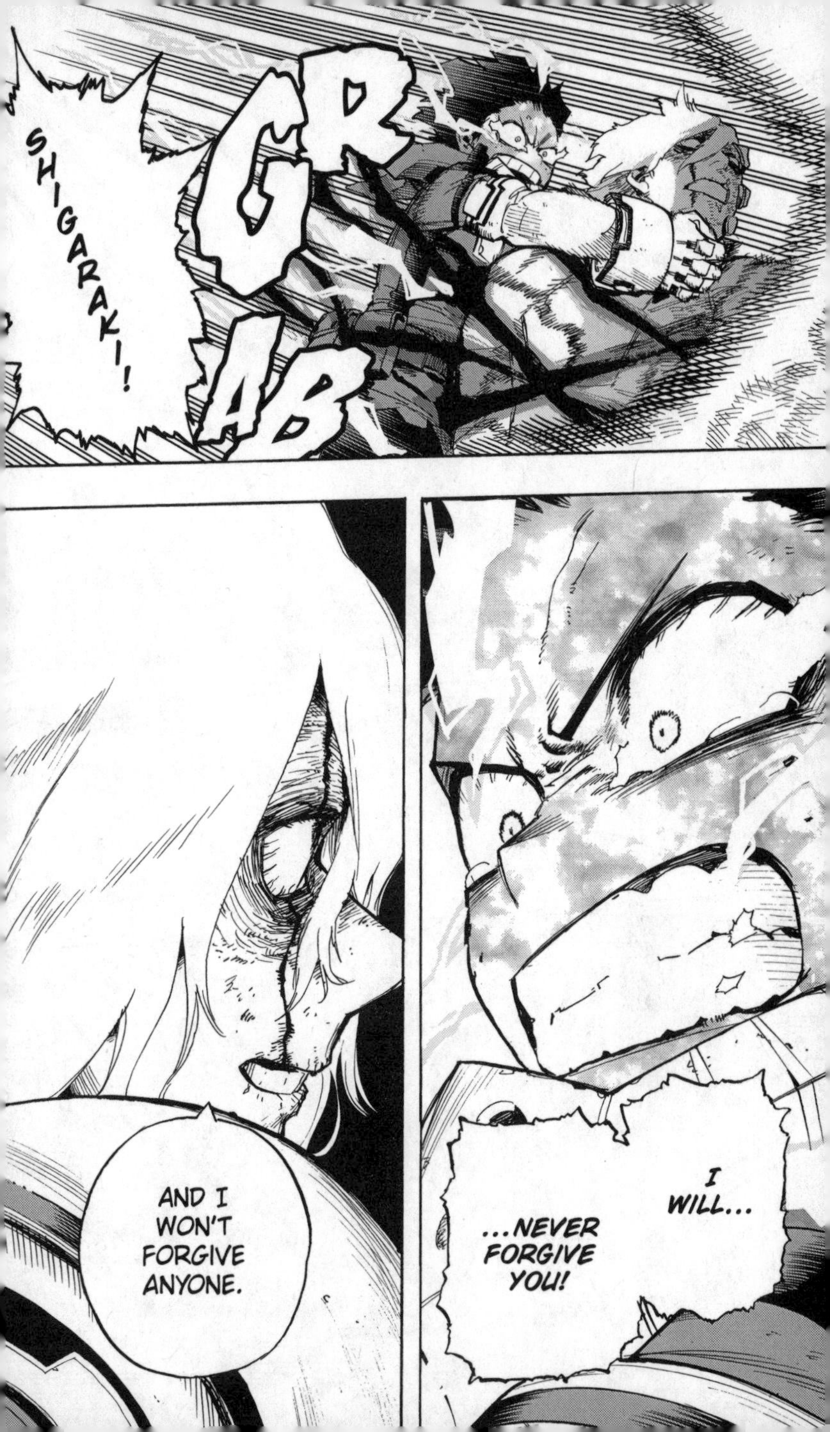
SHIGARAKI!
GRAB
I WILL...
...NEVER FORGIVE YOU!
AND I WON'T FORGIVE ANYONE.

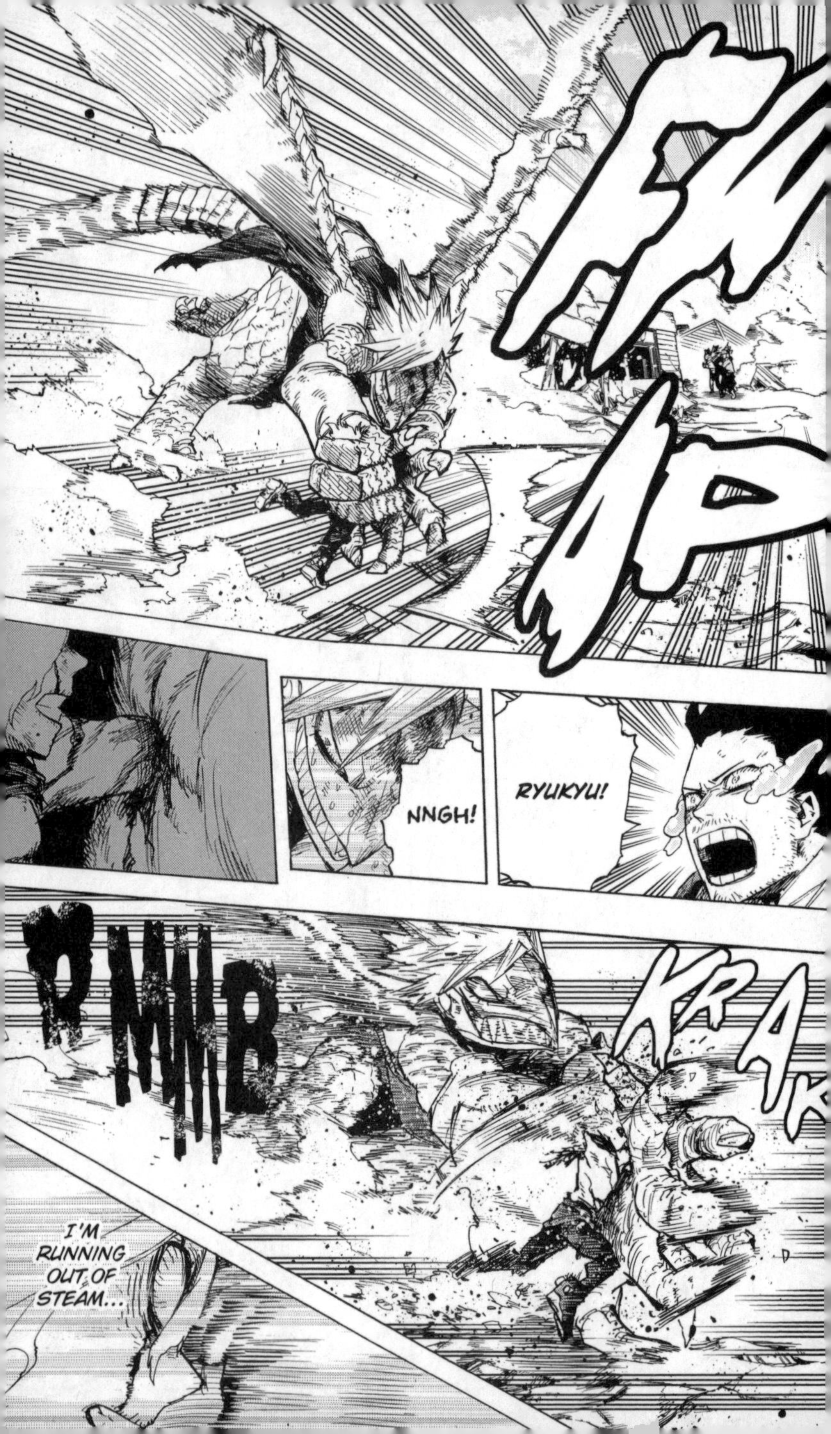
RYUKYU!
NNGH!
I'M RUNNING OUT OF STEAM...

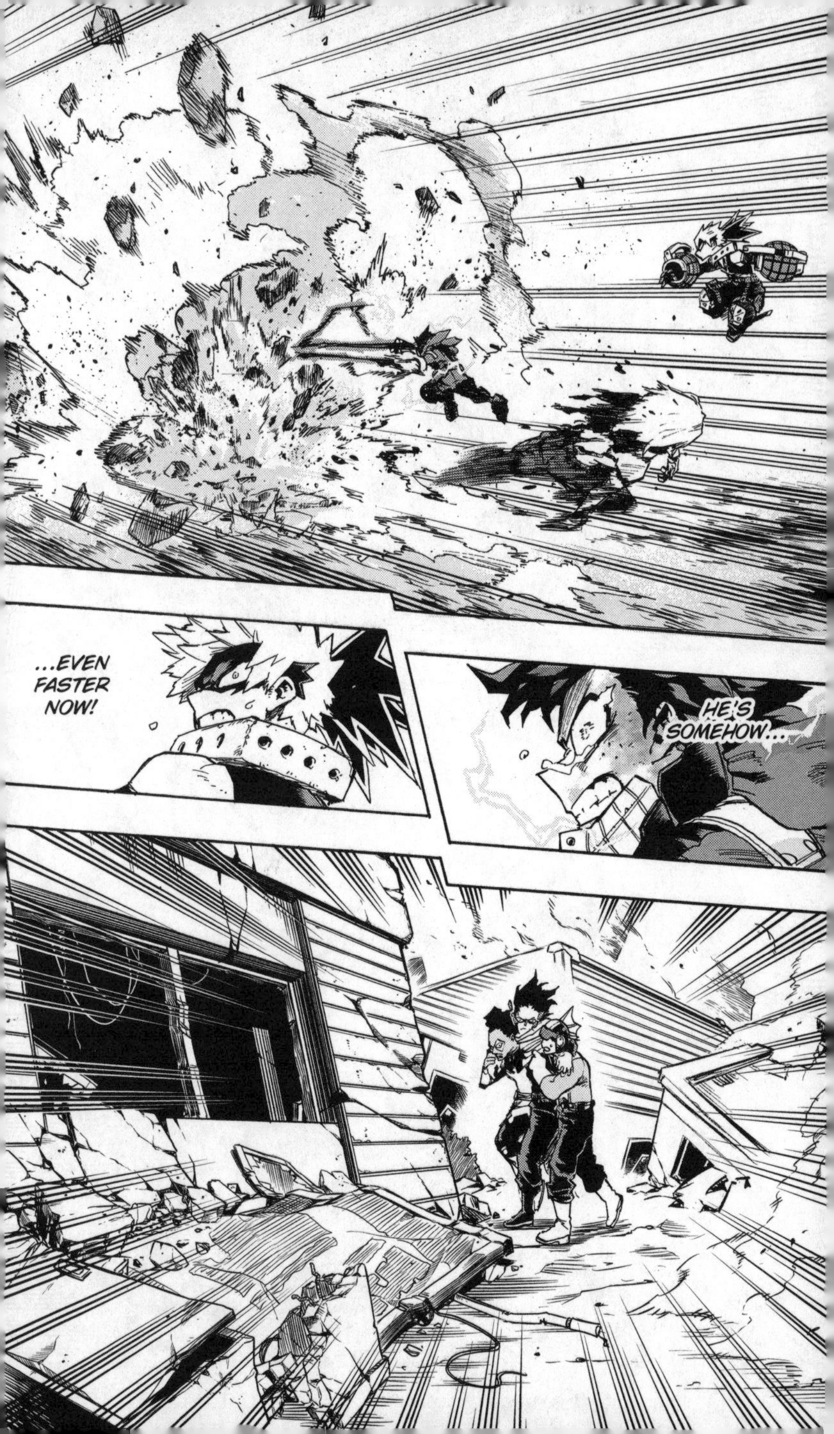
HE'S SOMEHOW...
...EVEN FASTER NOW!

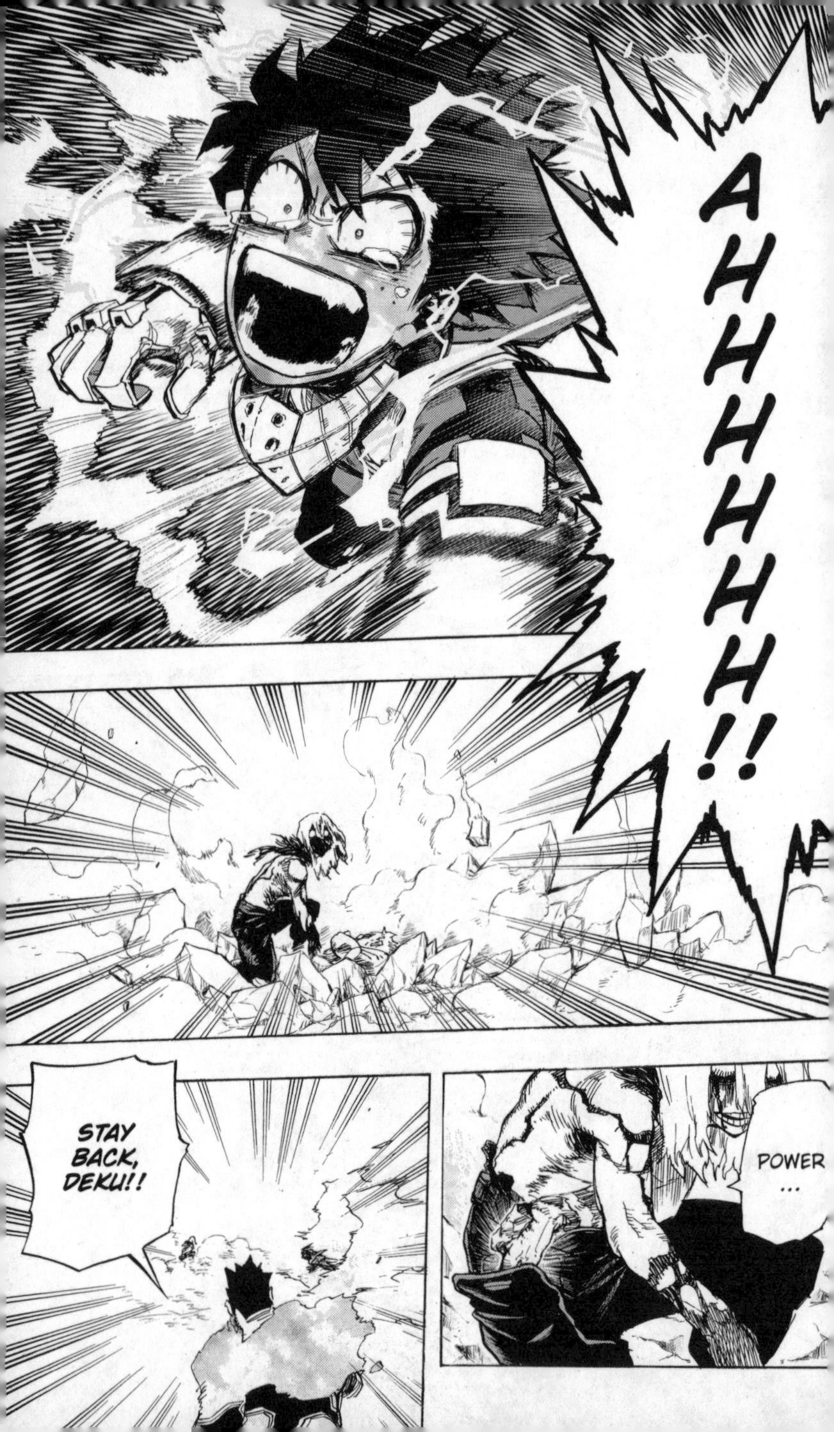
AHHHHHH!!
POWER ...
STAY BACK, DEKU!!

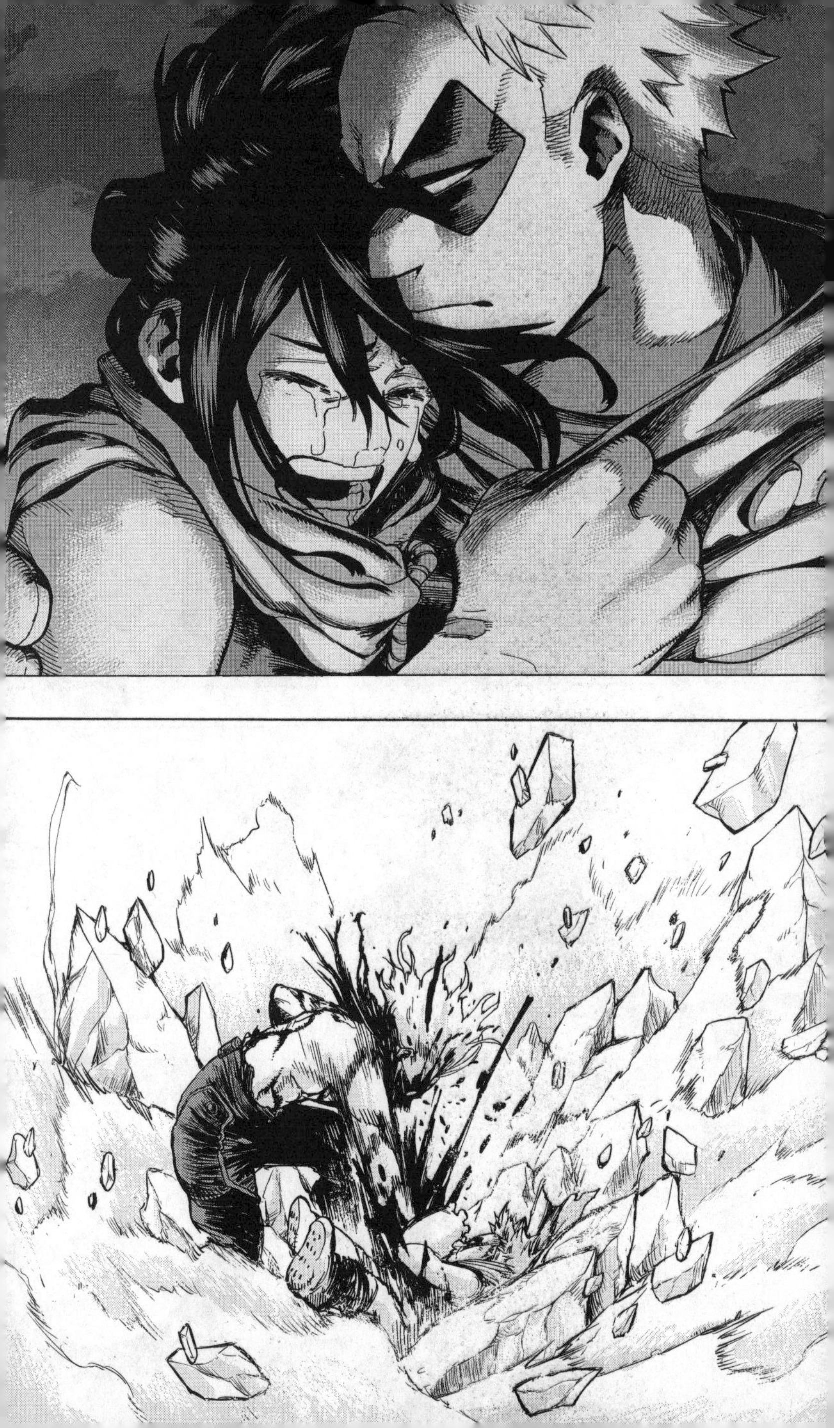

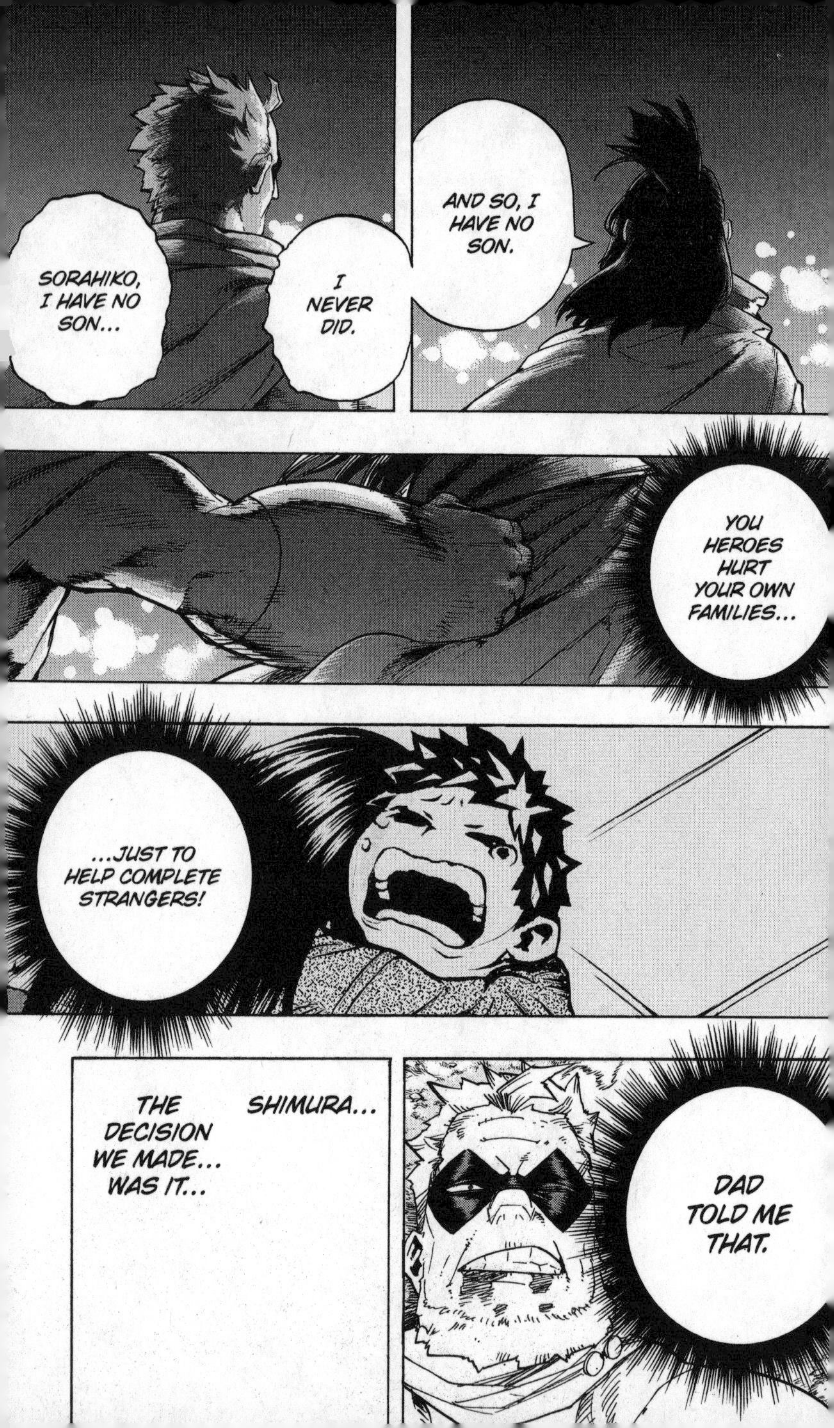
AND SO, I HAVE NO SON.
I NEVER DID.
SORAHIKO, I HAVE NO SON...
YOU HEROES HURT YOUR OWN FAMILIES...
...JUST TO HELP COMPLETE STRANGERS!
DAD TOLD ME THAT.
SHIMURA...
THE DECISION WE MADE... WAS IT...

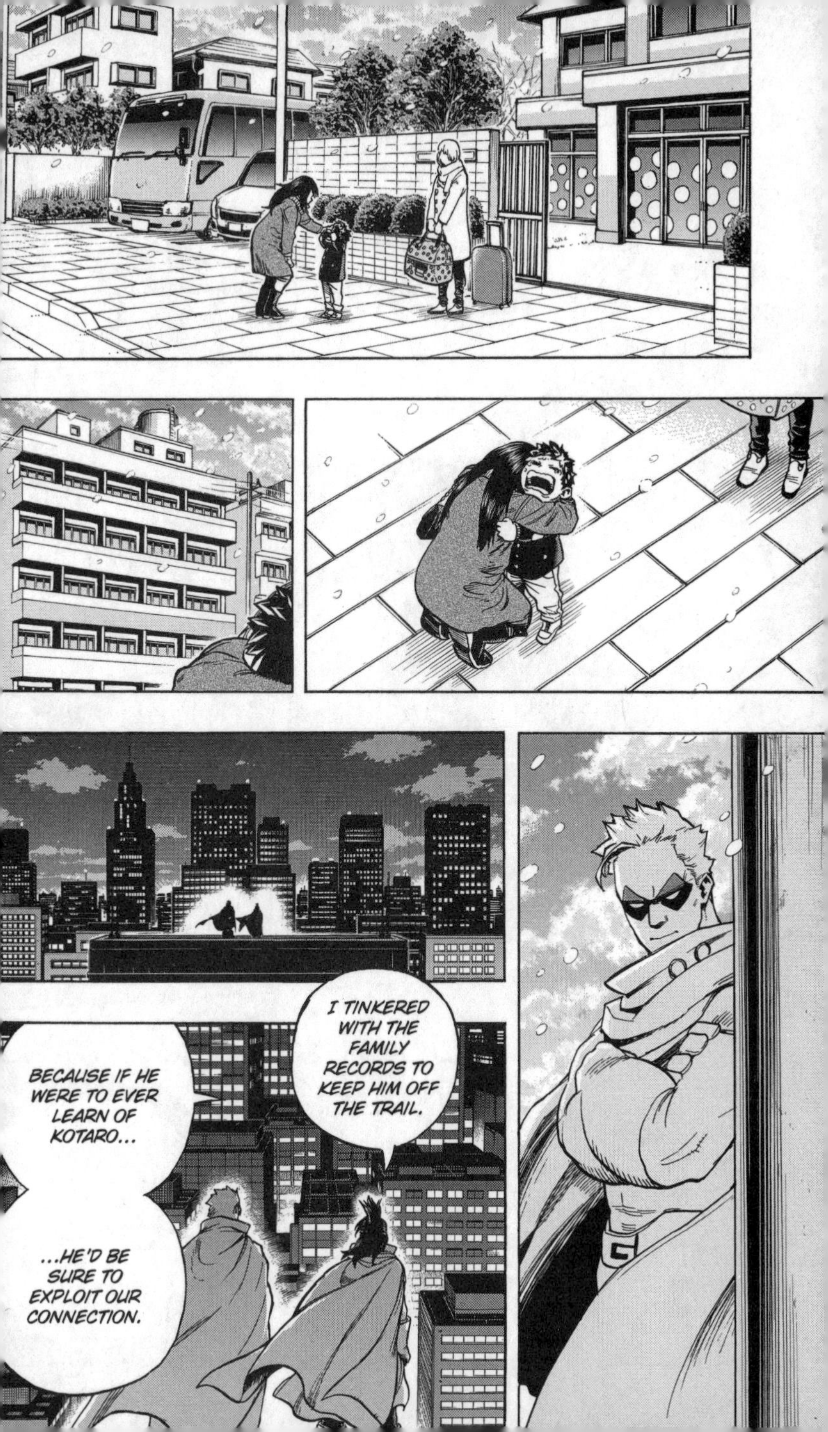
I TINKERED WITH THE FAMILY RECORDS TO KEEP HIM OFF THE TRAIL.
BECAUSE IF HE WERE TO EVER LEARN OF KOTARO...
...HE'D BE SURE TO EXPLOIT OUR CONNECTION.

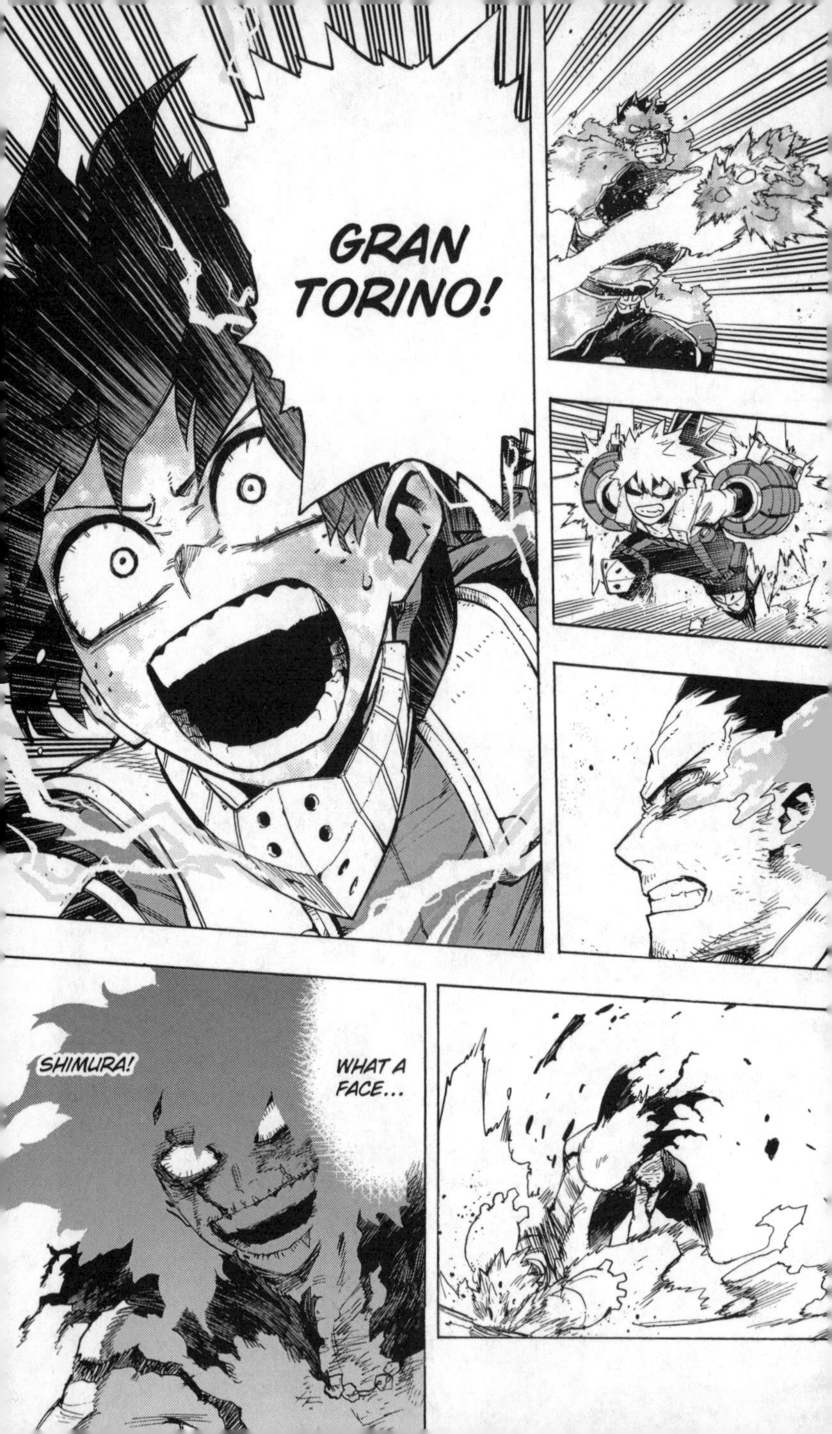
GRAN TORINO!
WHAT A FACE...
SHIMURA!

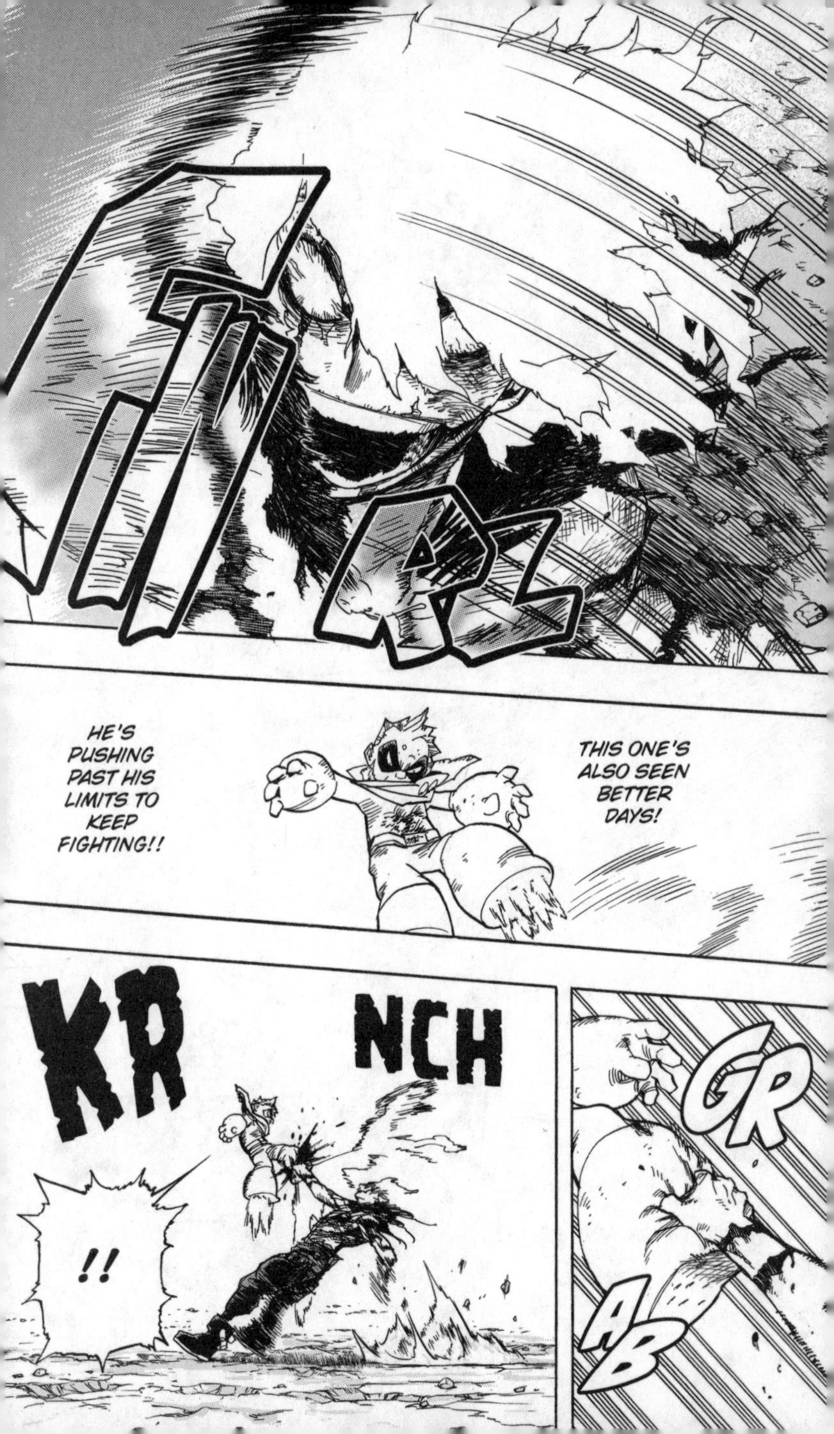

THIS ONE'S ALSO SEEN BETTER DAYS!
HE'S PUSHING PAST HIS LIMITS TO KEEP FIGHTING!!
GR AB
KR NCH
!!

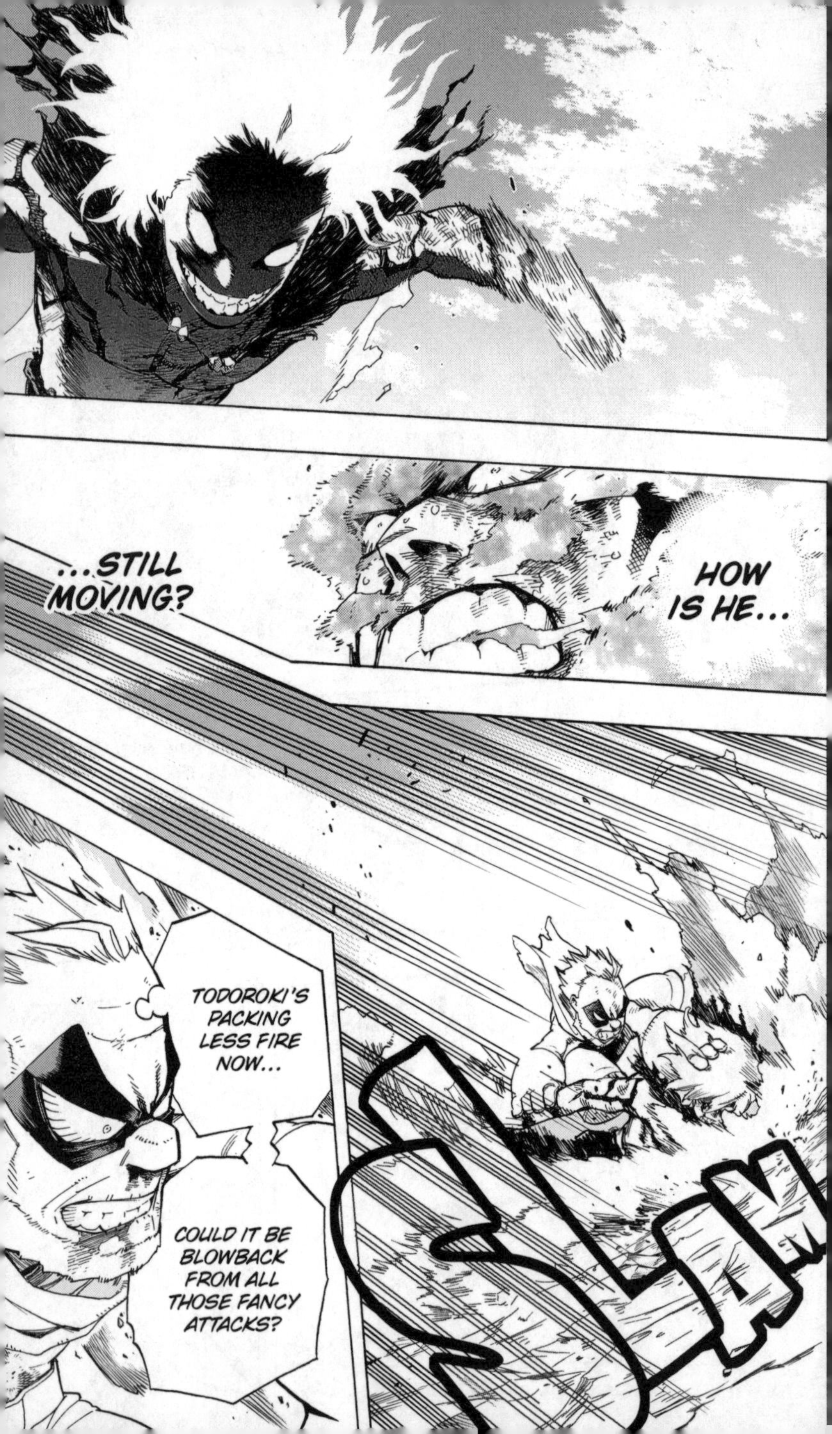
HOW IS HE...
...STILL MOVING?
SLAM
TODOROKI'S PACKING LESS FIRE NOW...
COULD IT BE BLOWBACK FROM ALL THOSE FANCY ATTACKS?

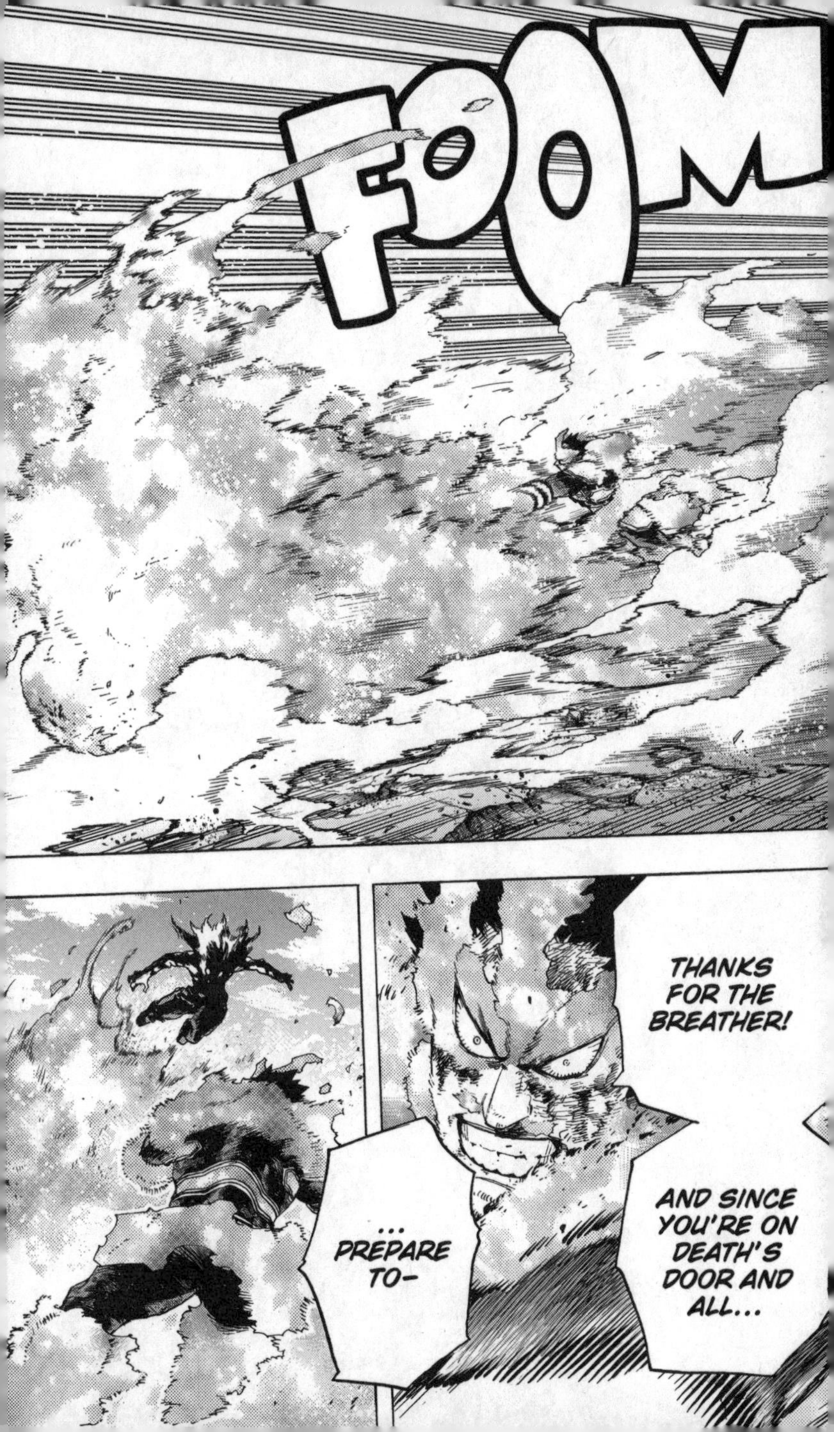
FOOM
THANKS FOR THE BREATHER!
AND SINCE YOU'RE ON DEATH'S DOOR AND ALL...
... PREPARE TO-

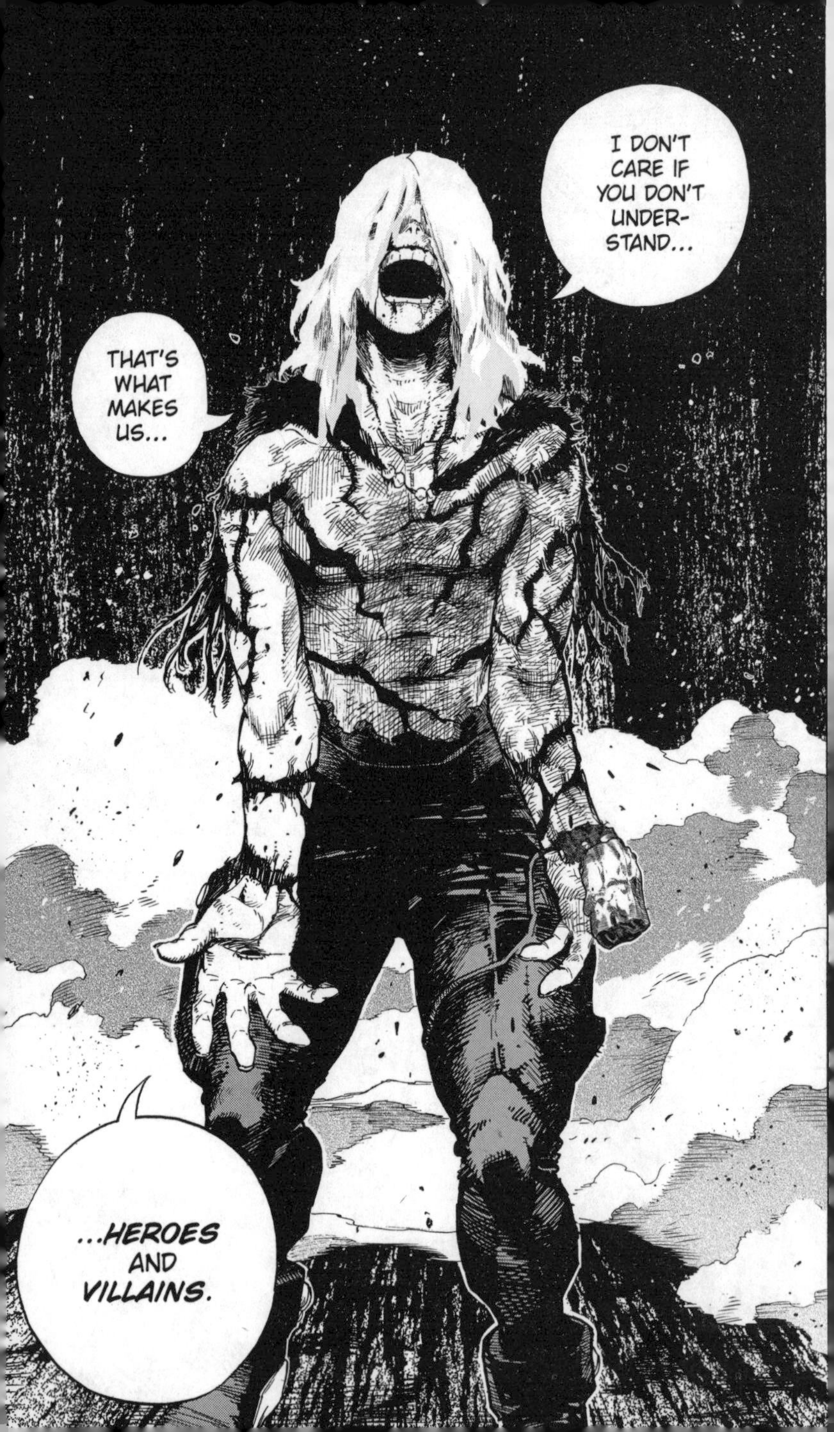
I DON'T CARE IF YOU DON'T UNDER-STAND...
THAT'S WHAT MAKES US...
...HEROES AND VILLAINS.

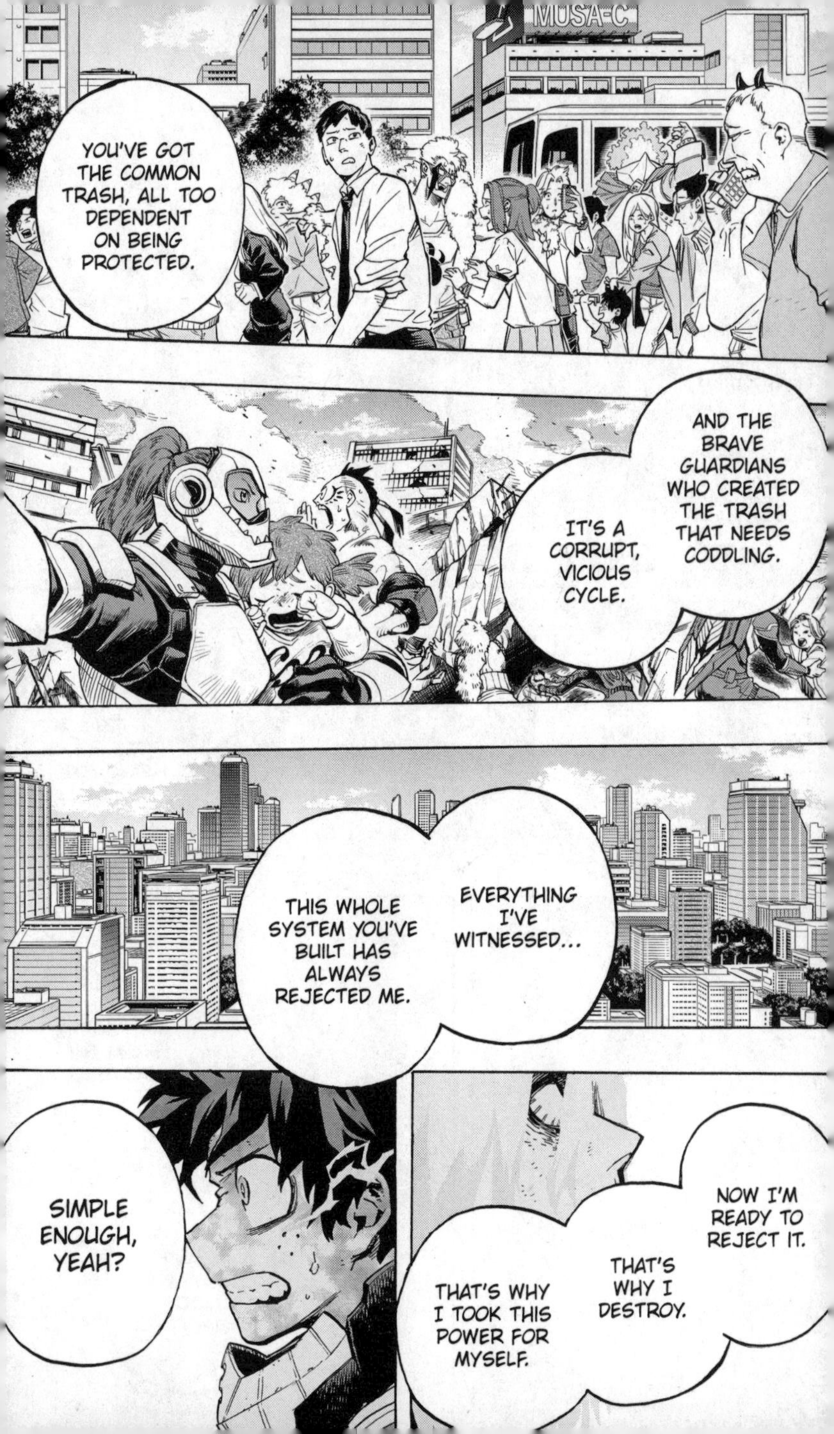
MUSA-C
YOU'VE GOT THE COMMON TRASH, ALL TOO DEPENDENT ON BEING PROTECTED.
AND THE BRAVE GUARDIANS WHO CREATED THE TRASH THAT NEEDS CODDLING.
IT'S A CORRUPT, VICIOUS CYCLE.
EVERYTHING I'VE WITNESSED...
THIS WHOLE SYSTEM YOU'VE BUILT HAS ALWAYS REJECTED ME.
NOW I'M READY TO REJECT IT.
THAT'S WHY I DESTROY.
THAT'S WHY I TOOK THIS POWER FOR MYSELF.
SIMPLE ENOUGH, YEAH?

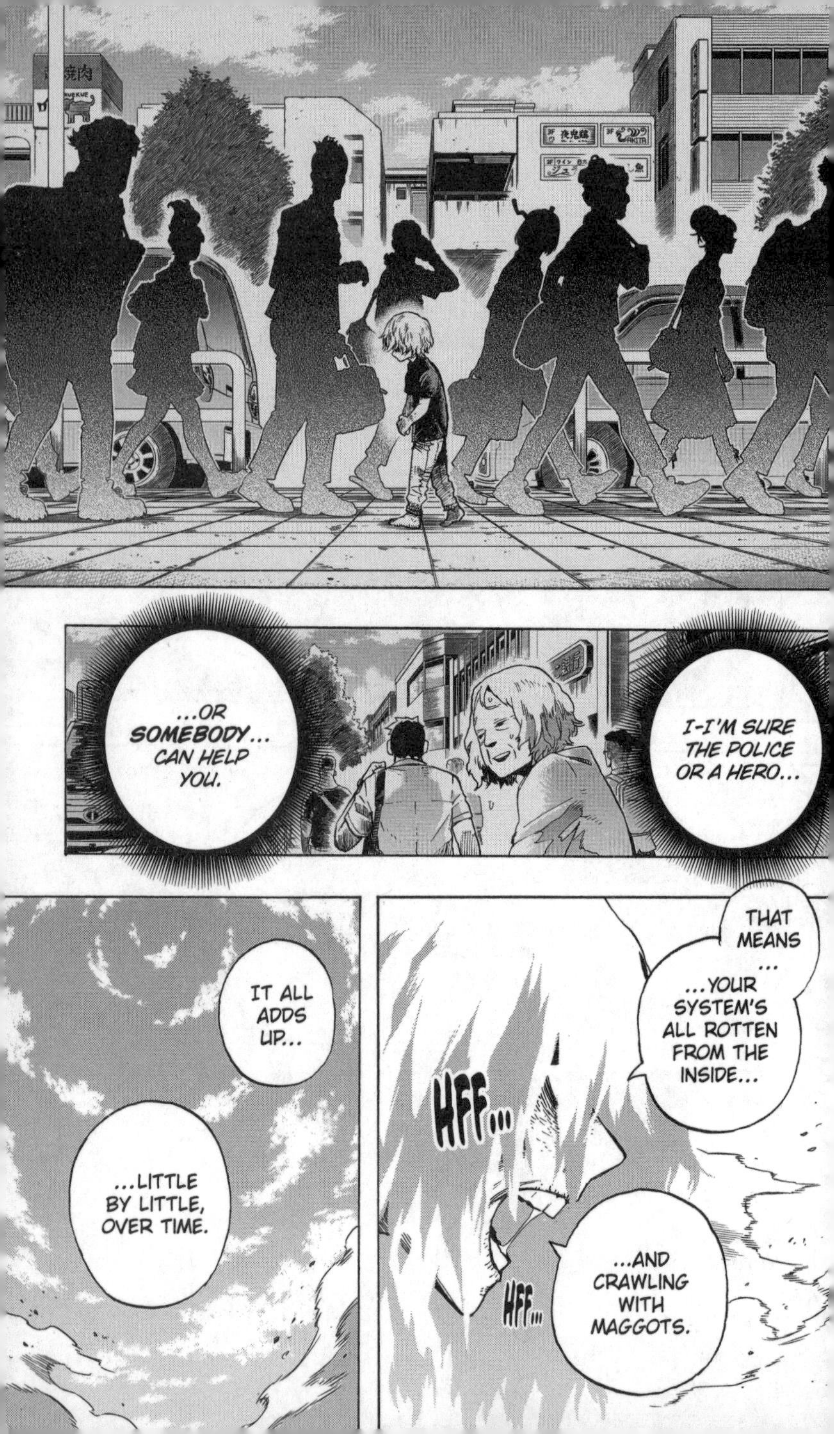
I-I'M SURE THE POLICE OR A HERO...
...OR SOMEBODY... CAN HELP YOU.
THAT MEANS ...
...YOUR SYSTEM'S ALL ROTTEN FROM THE INSIDE...
HFF...
HFF...
...AND CRAWLING WITH MAGGOTS.
IT ALL ADDS UP...
...LITTLE BY LITTLE, OVER TIME.

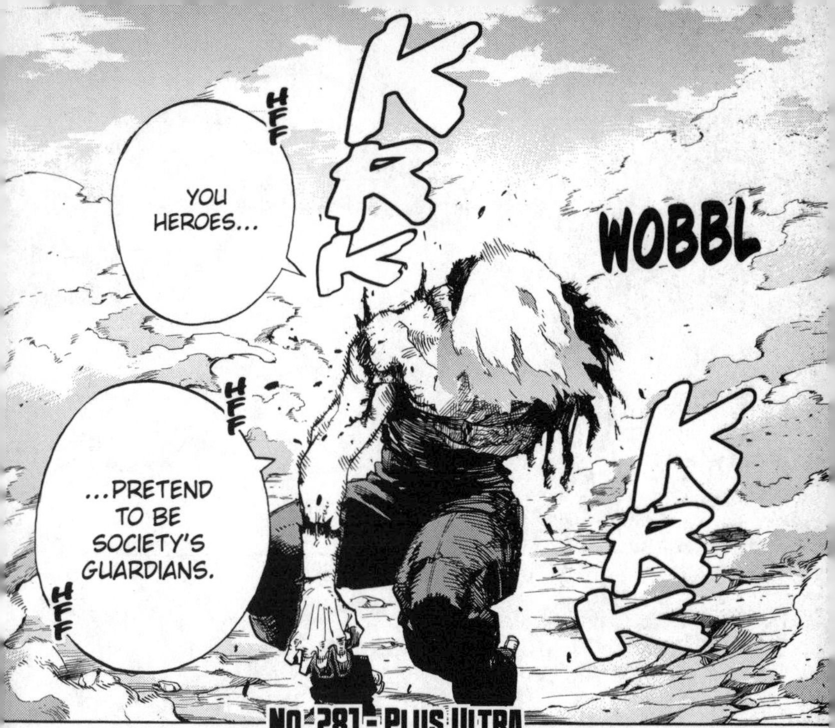
KRK
WOBBL
HFF
YOU HEROES...
HFF
KRK
...PRETEND TO BE SOCIETY'S GUARDIANS.
HFF

NO. 281 - PLUS ULTRA

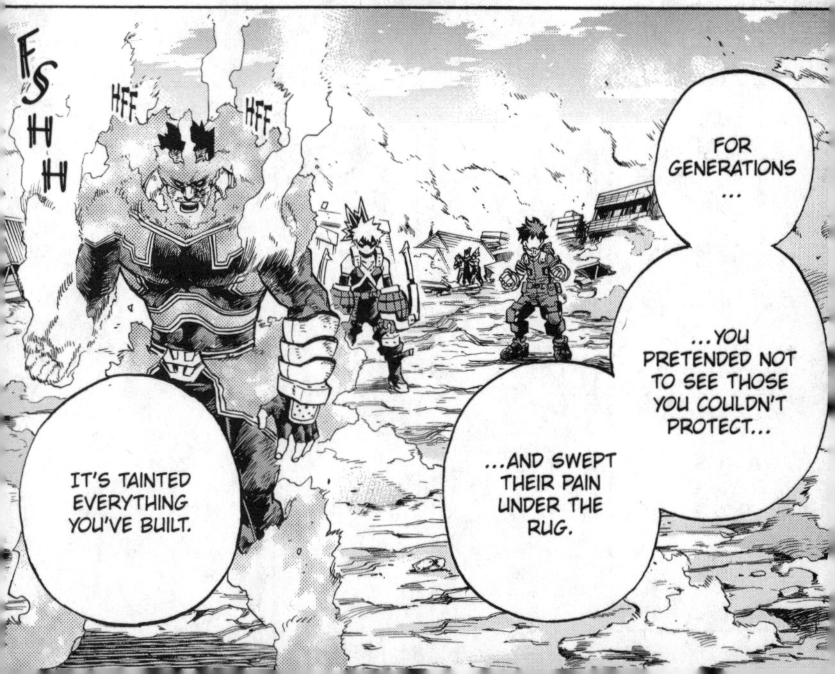
FOR GENERATIONS...
...YOU PRETENDED NOT TO SEE THOSE YOU COULDN'T PROTECT...
...AND SWEPT THEIR PAIN UNDER THE RUG.
HFF
HFF
FSHH
IT'S TAINTED EVERYTHING YOU'VE BUILT.

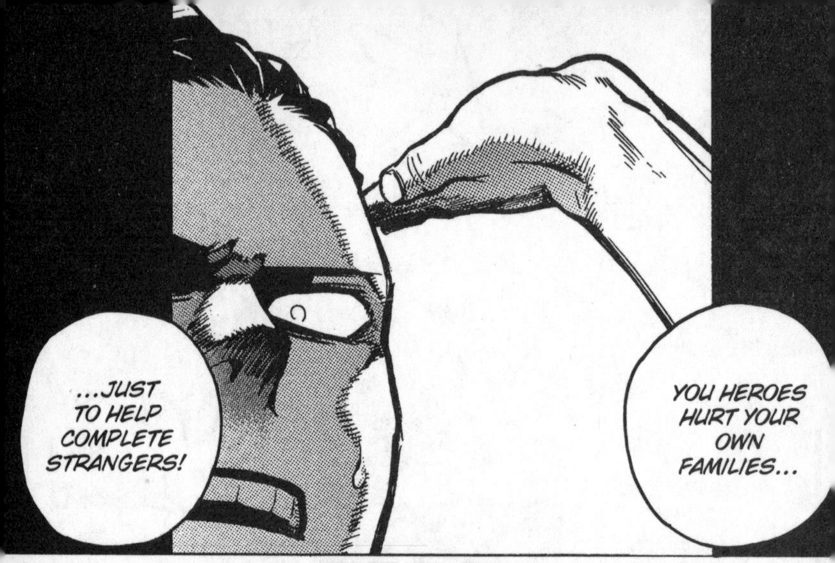
YOU HEROES HURT YOUR OWN FAMILIES...
...JUST TO HELP COMPLETE STRANGERS!

No. 281 - Plus Ultra

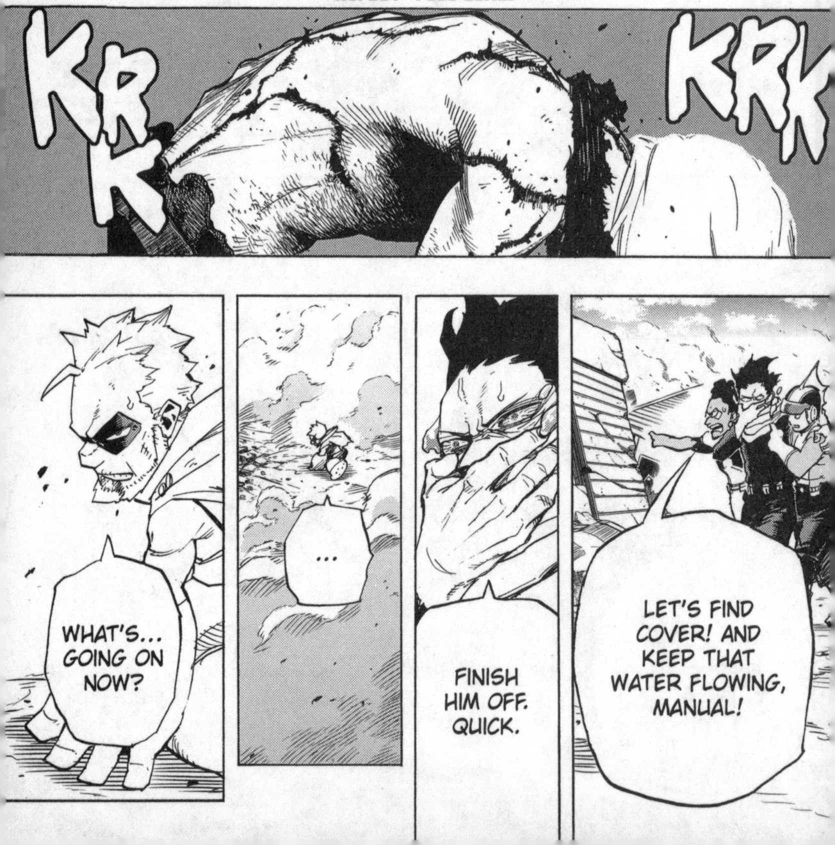
KRK
KRK
LET'S FIND COVER! AND KEEP THAT WATER FLOWING, MANUAL!
FINISH HIM OFF. QUICK.
...
WHAT'S... GOING ON NOW?

GIGANTOMACHIA

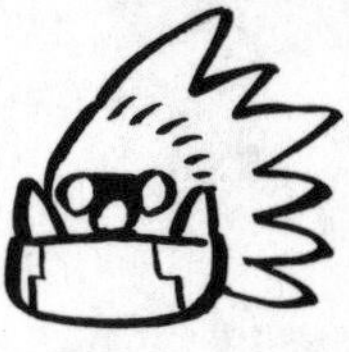

He was given six extra Quirks, which means he has seven in total (including his original one).

1. **Endurance:** His original Quirk. Makes him a stamina beast.
2. **Pain Blocker:** Can't feel pain.
3. **Gigantification:** Grows gigantic when agitated or excited.
4. **Dog:** Heightened senses of smell and hearing.
5. **Energy Saver:** Functions on very small amounts of nutrition and hydration.

   Doesn't need much sleep either.
6. **Fierce Gains:** His muscles are remarkably hard and tough.
7. **Mole:** A transformation that allows him to dig under the ground.

(Features include long claws, spines on his back that slide through earth more easily and a visor to shield his face.)

Machia wouldn't do so well with Quirks that require training or brainpower, so he was stuffed full of simplistic physical enhancements instead. Numbers 2 and 3 would only require a little training to control and adjust properly, but Machia always has them activated to some extent. It's a combination that automatically enhances the potential of 1.

All For One gave Machia number 7 specifically to allow him to lie dormant. Following his master's orders, the giant dug under the ground, deep in the mountains. When All For One was crippled by All Might and most of his flunkies were rounded up by the authorities, he employed the doctor and Machia to collect Quirks that he'd use to repair himself.

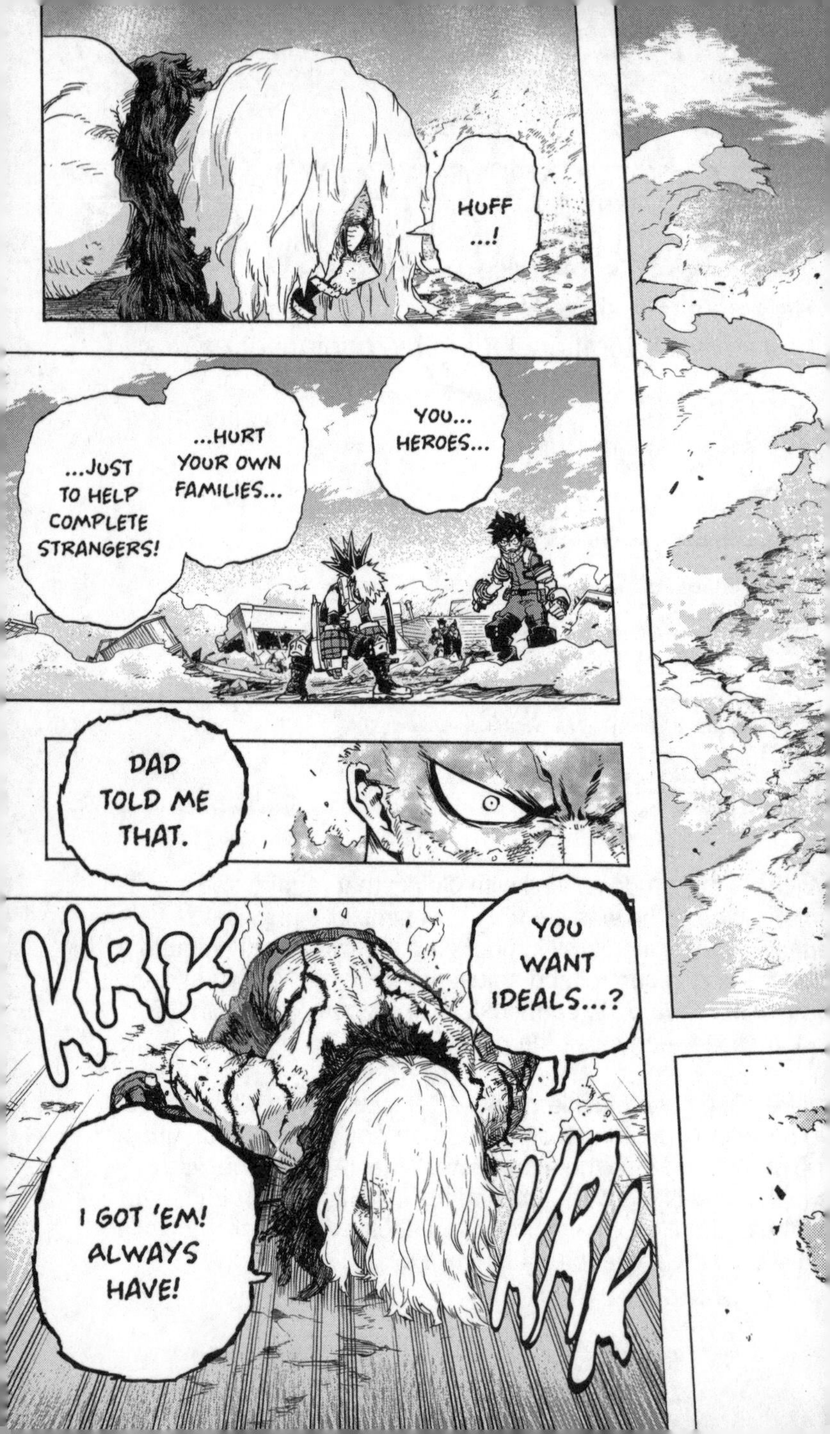
HUFF ...!
YOU... HEROES...
...HURT YOUR OWN FAMILIES...
...JUST TO HELP COMPLETE STRANGERS!
DAD TOLD ME THAT.
YOU WANT IDEALS...?
KRK
KRK
I GOT 'EM! ALWAYS HAVE!

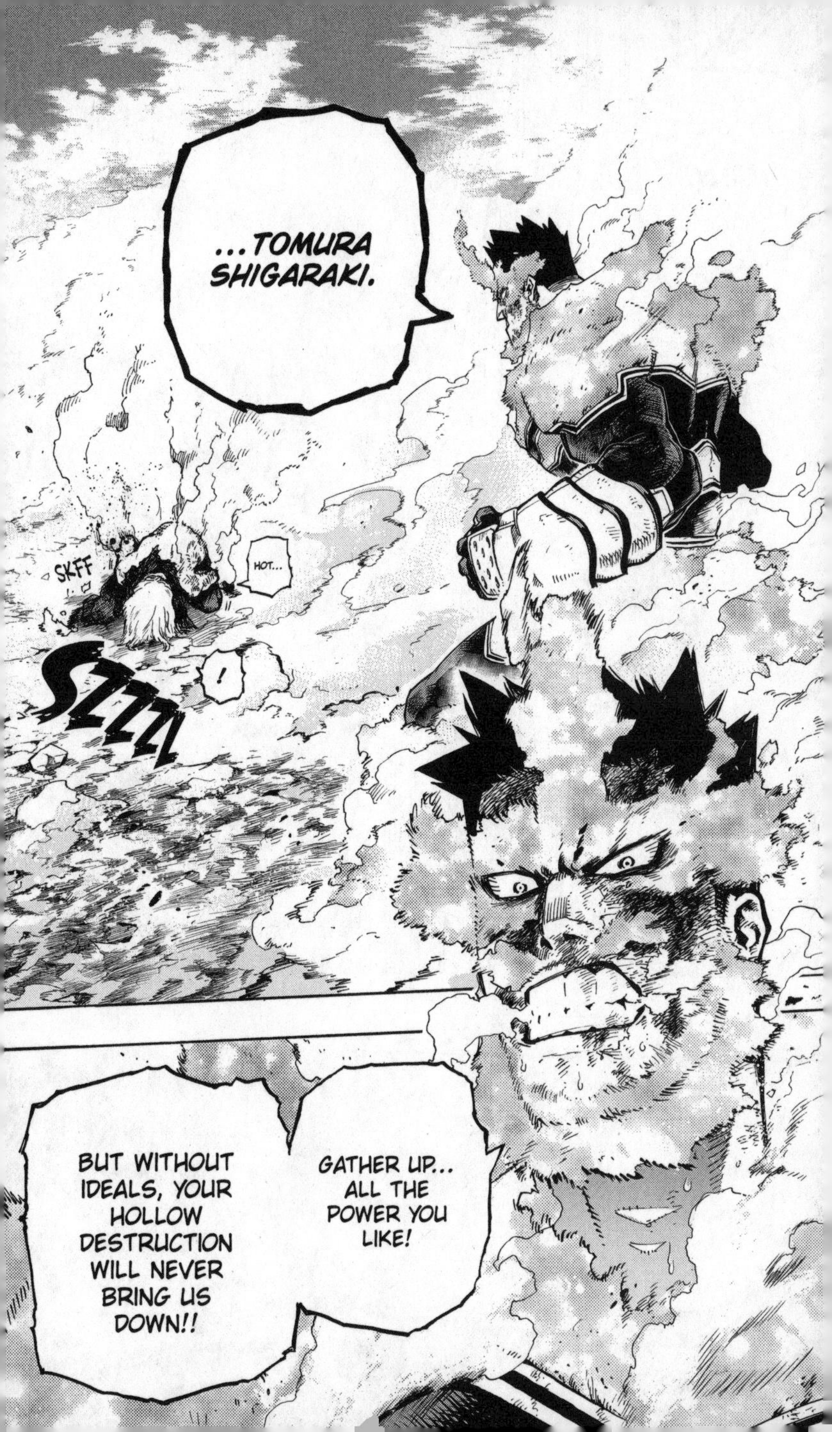
...TOMURA SHIGARAKI.
HOT...
SKFF
!
SZZZ
GATHER UP... ALL THE POWER YOU LIKE!
BUT WITHOUT IDEALS, YOUR HOLLOW DESTRUCTION WILL NEVER BRING US DOWN!!

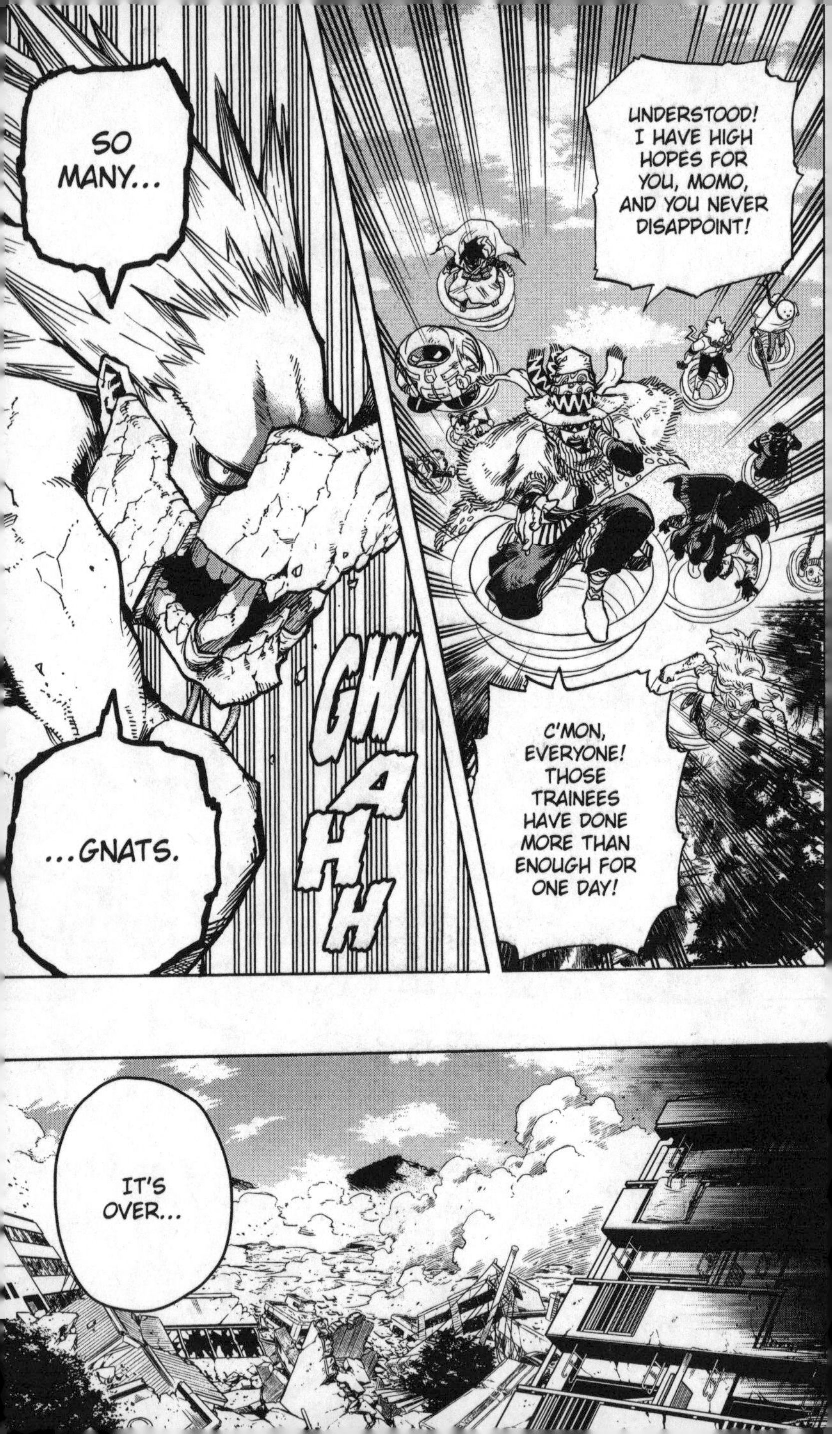
UNDERSTOOD! I HAVE HIGH HOPES FOR YOU, MOMO, AND YOU NEVER DISAPPOINT!
C'MON, EVERYONE! THOSE TRAINEES HAVE DONE MORE THAN ENOUGH FOR ONE DAY!
SO MANY...
GWAHH
...GNATS.
IT'S OVER...

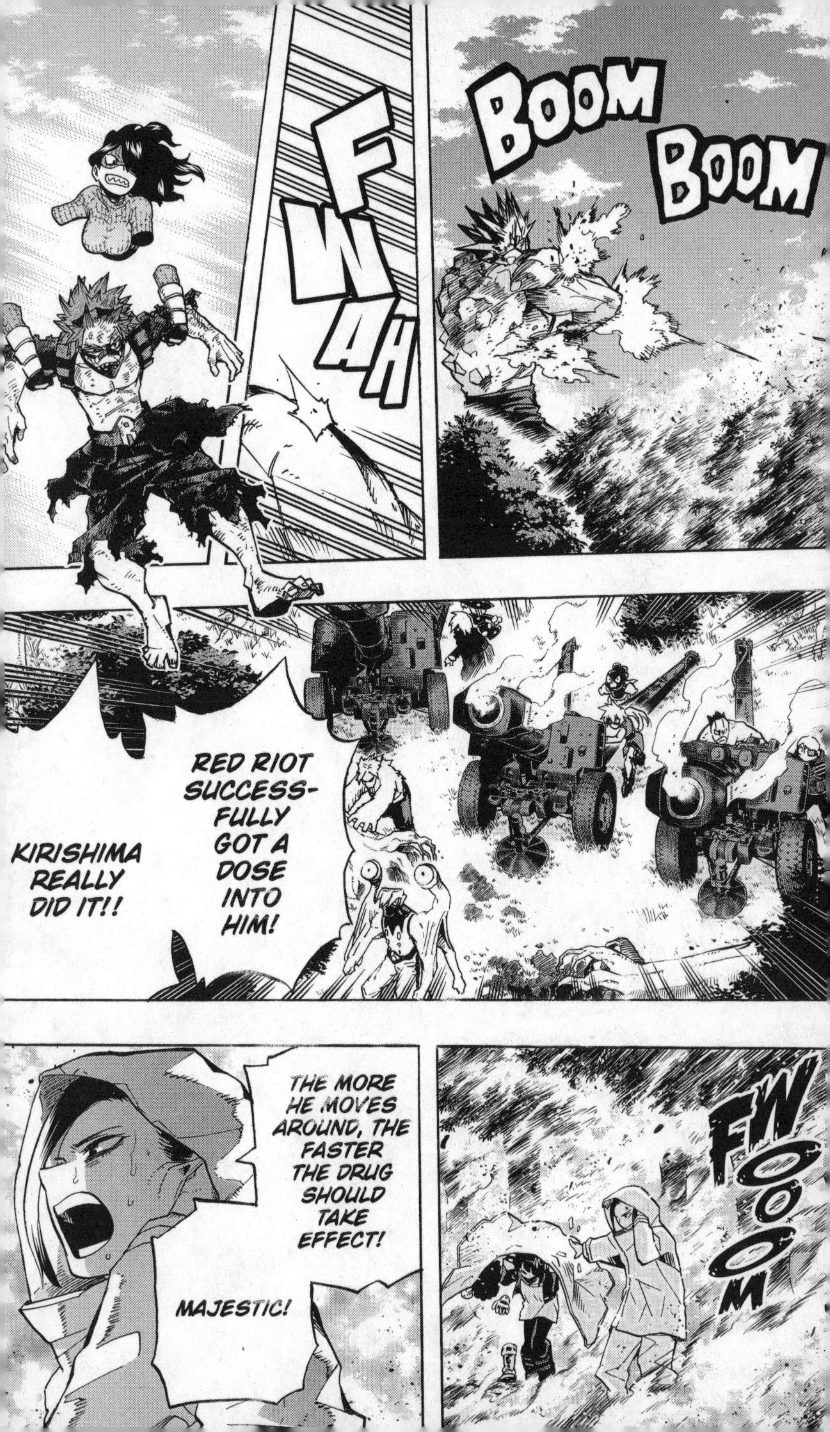
BOOM BOOM
FWAH
RED RIOT SUCCESS-FULLY GOT A DOSE INTO HIM!
KIRISHIMA REALLY DID IT!!
FWOOOOM
THE MORE HE MOVES AROUND, THE FASTER THE DRUG SHOULD TAKE EFFECT!
MAJESTIC!

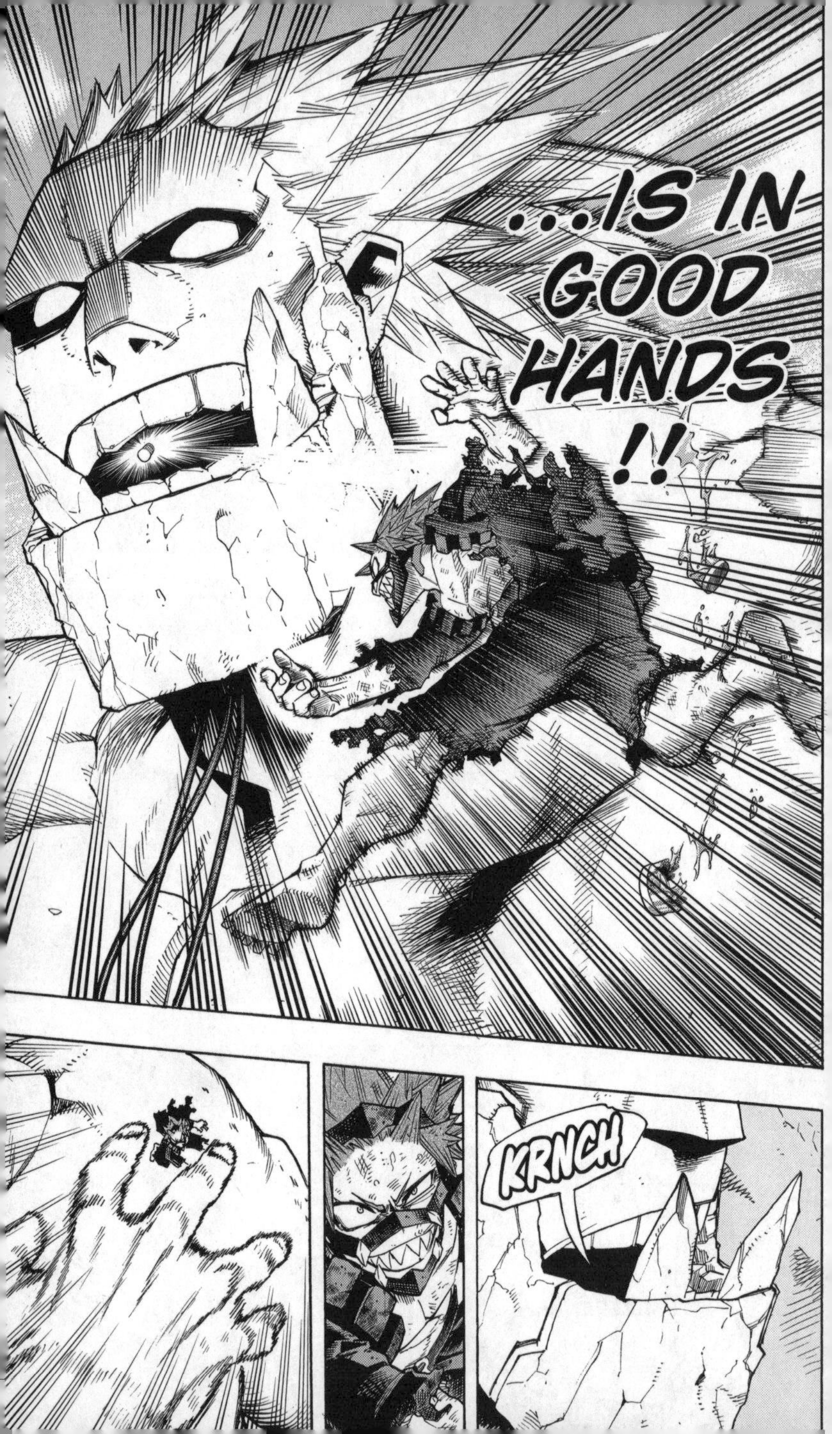
...IS IN GOOD HANDS!!
KRNCH

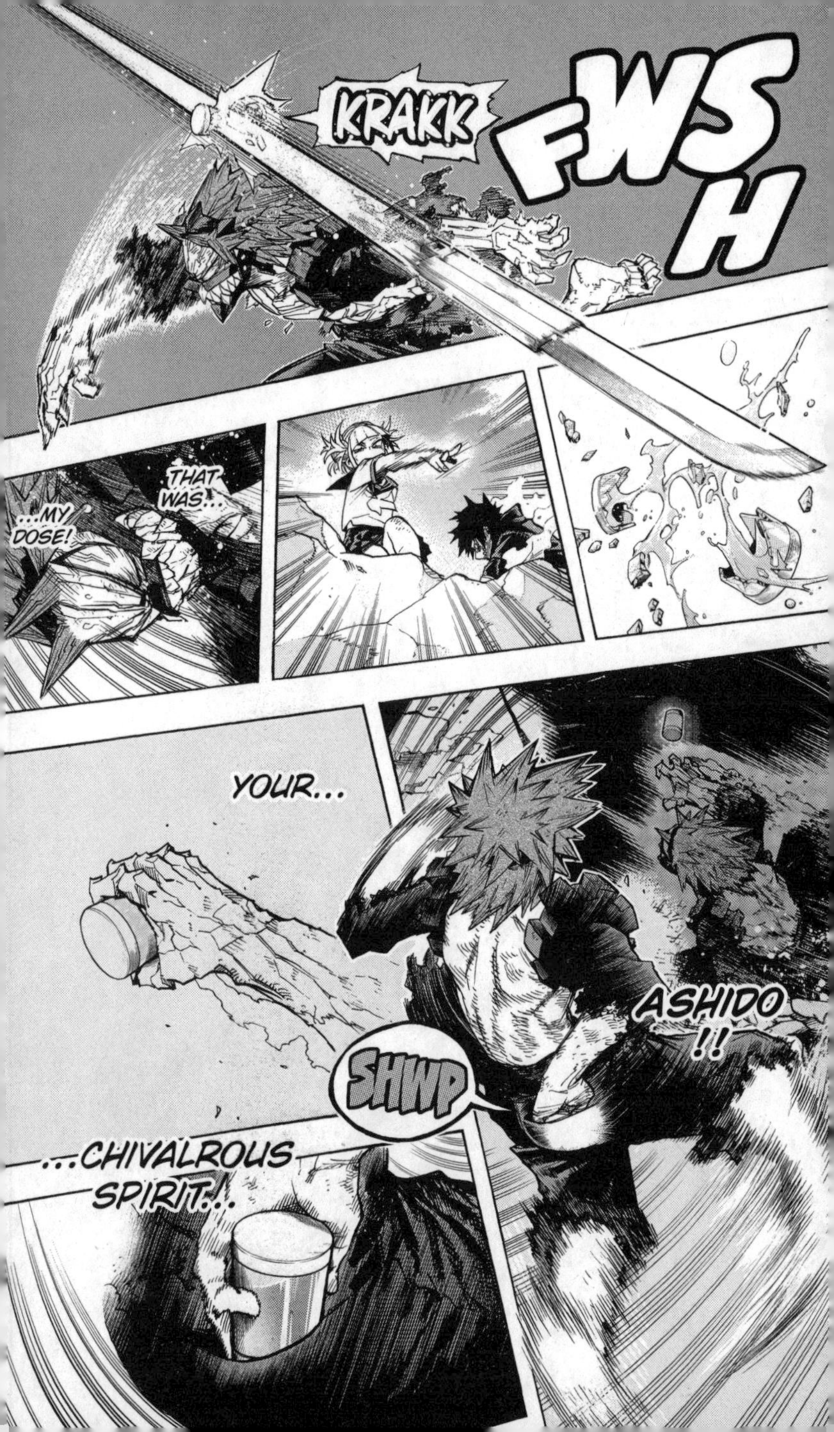
FWSH
KRAKK
THAT WAS...
...MY DOSE!
ASHIDO!!
SHWP
YOUR...
...CHIVALROUS SPIRIT...

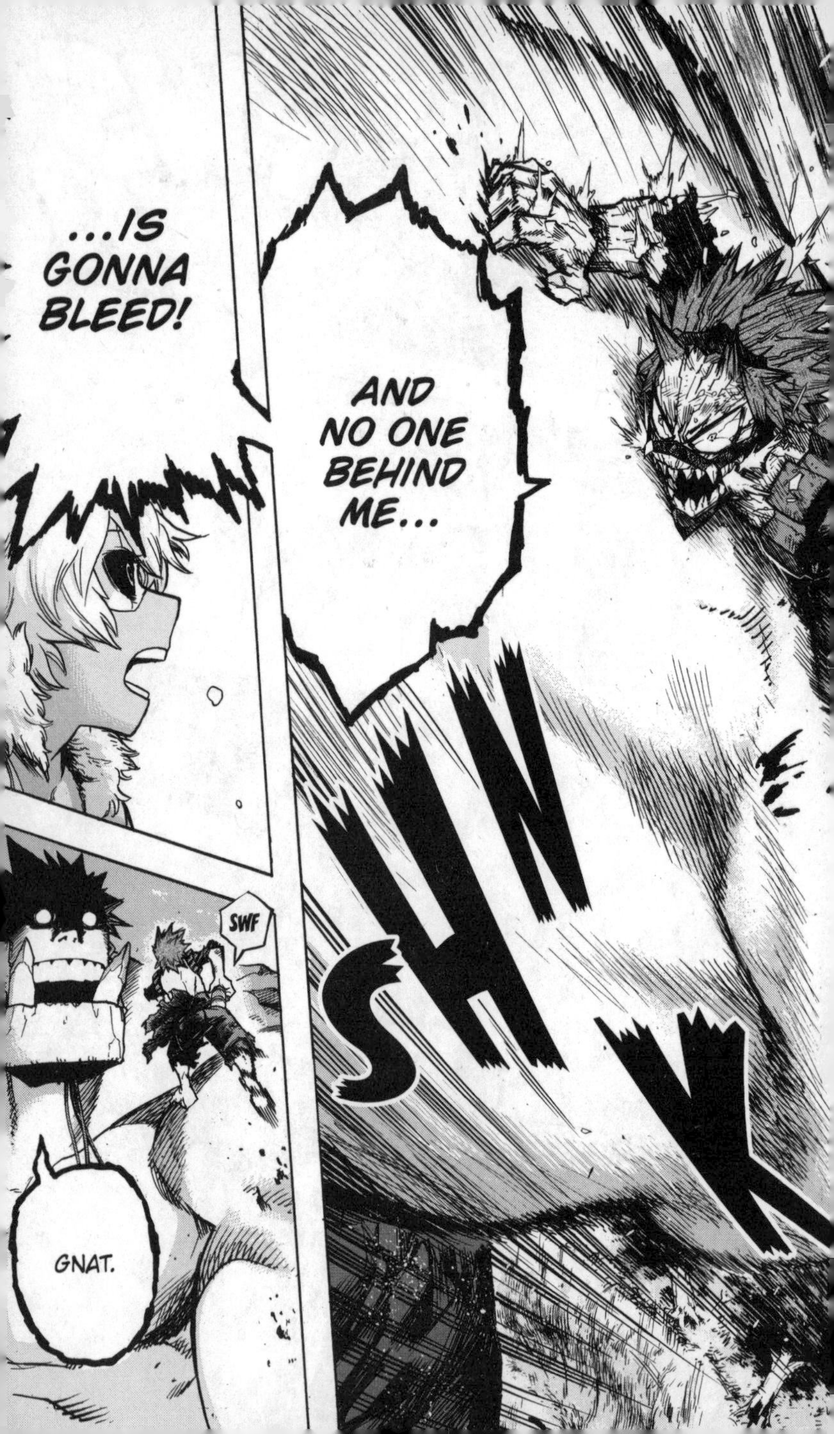
AND NO ONE BEHIND ME...
SHNK
...IS GONNA BLEED!
SWF
GNAT.

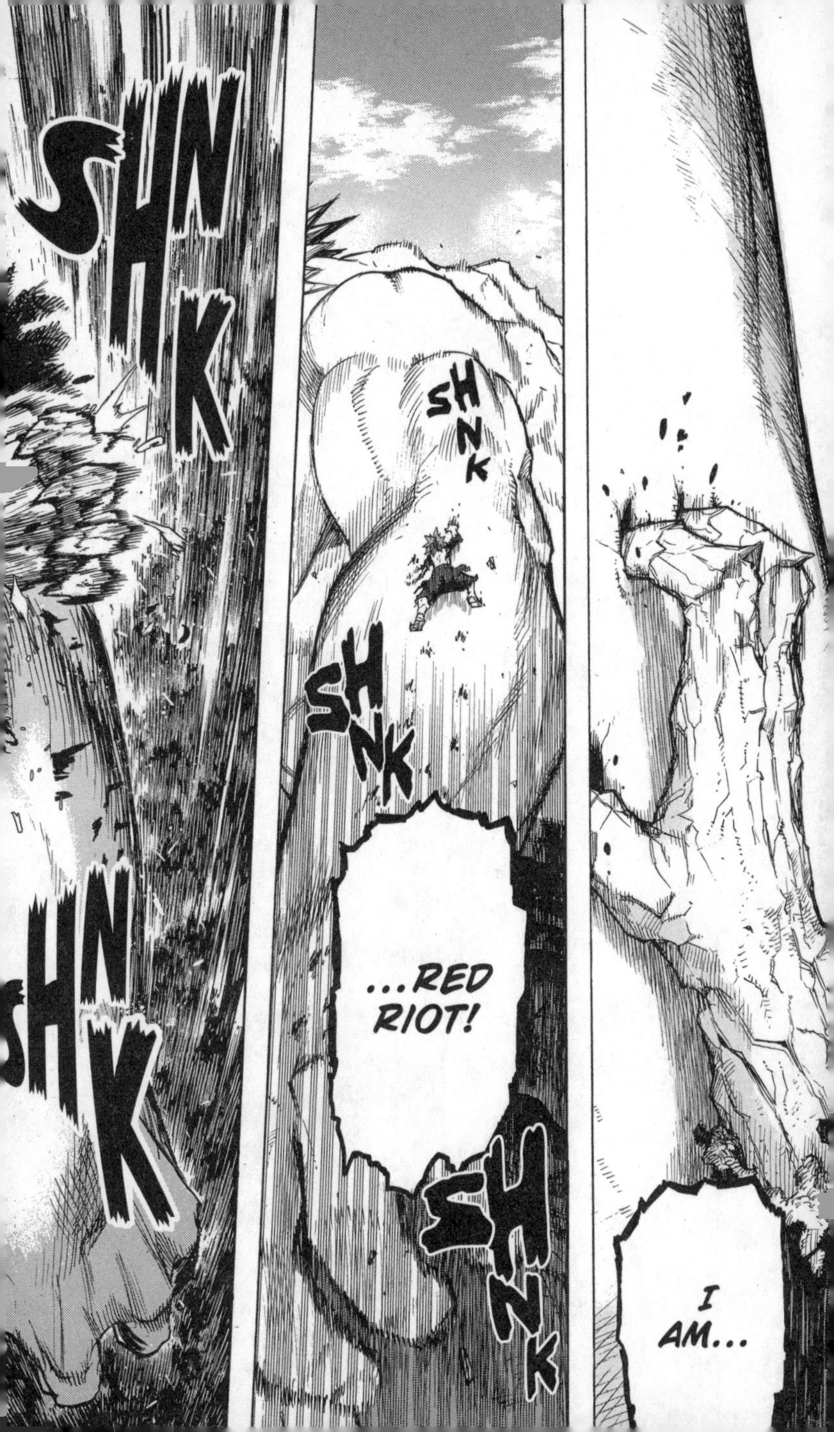
I AM...
SHNK
SHNK
...RED RIOT!
SHNK
SHNK
SHNK

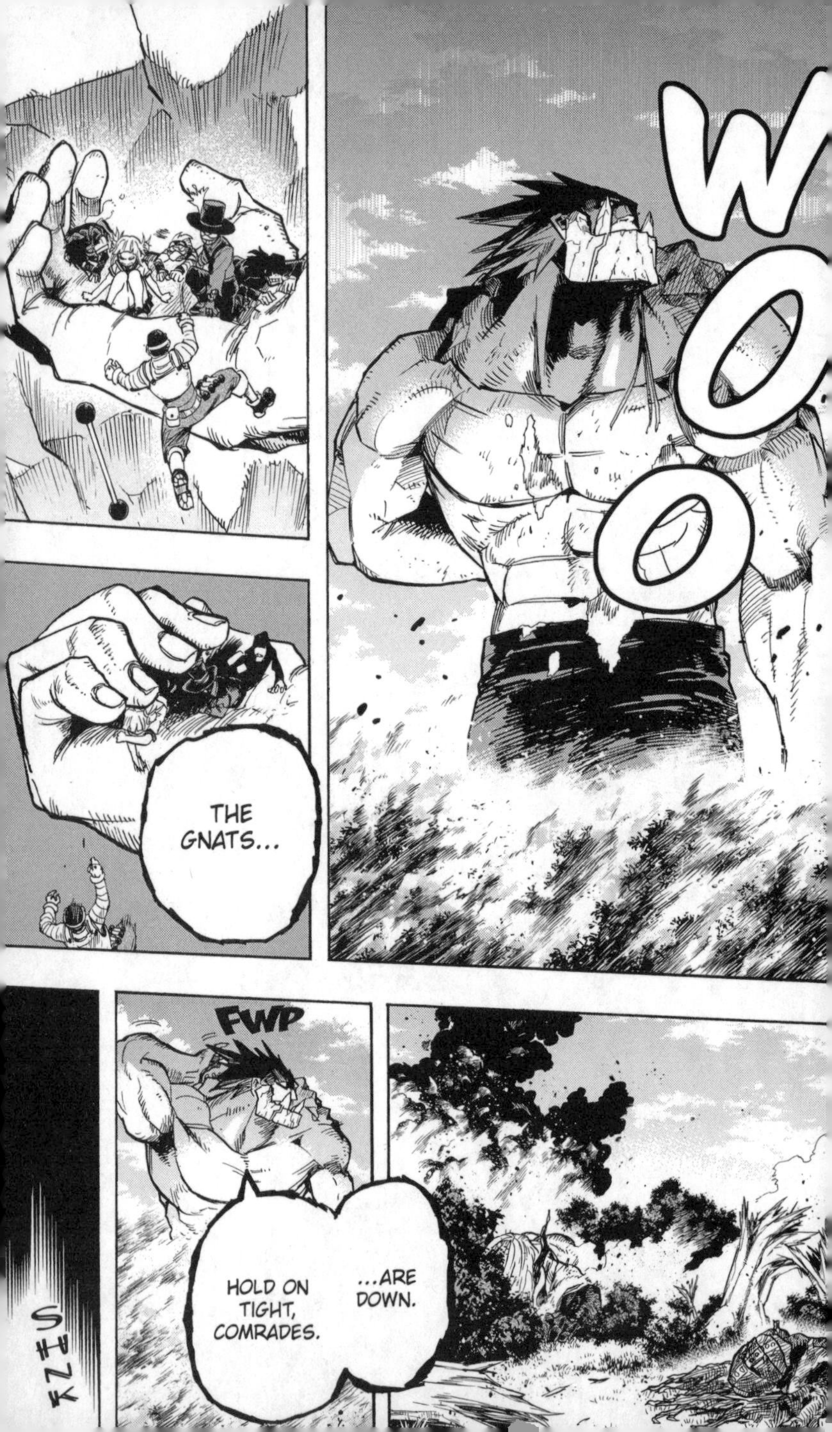
WOOO
THE GNATS...
...ARE DOWN.
FWP
HOLD ON TIGHT, COMRADES.
SHNK

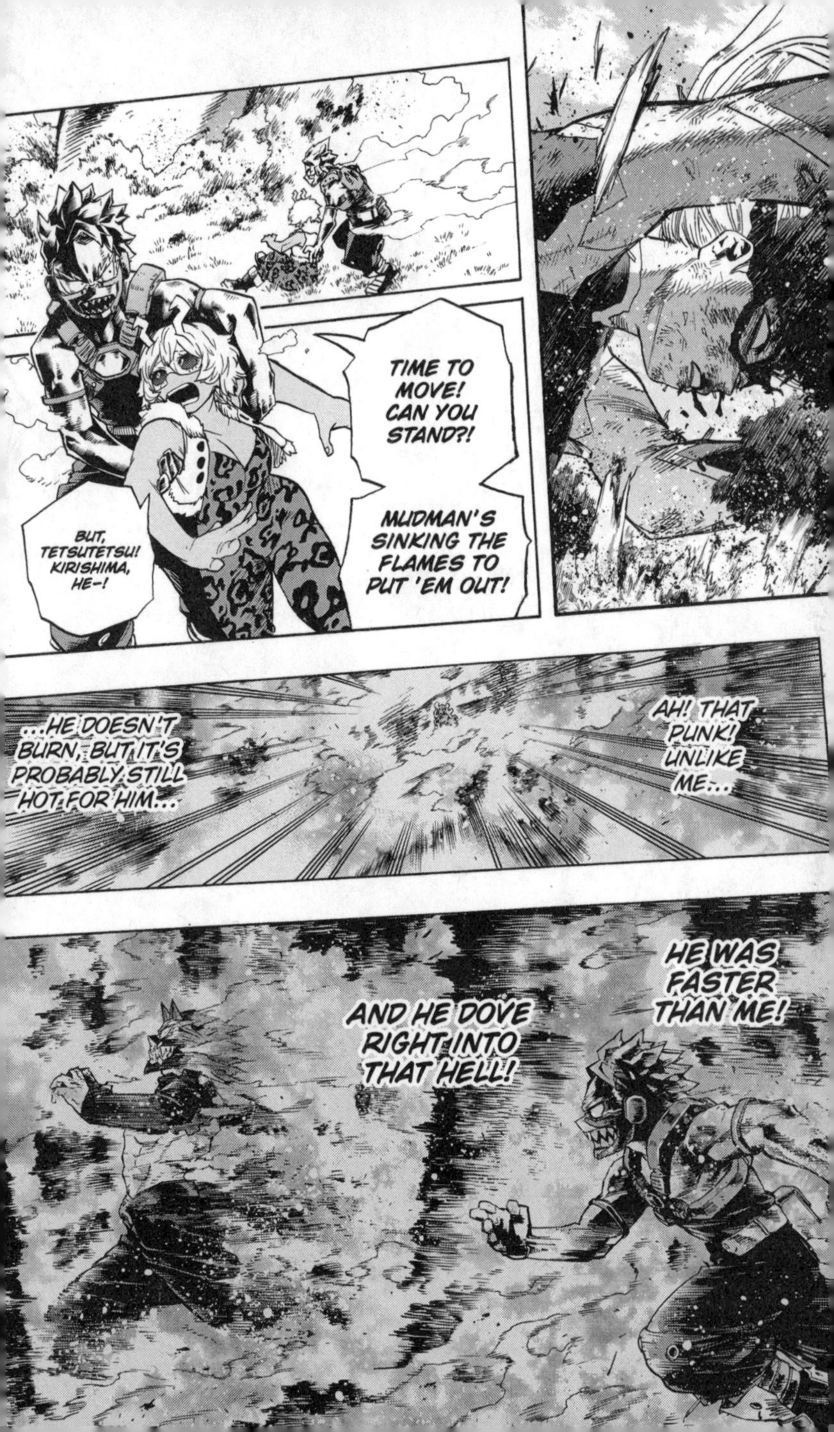
TIME TO MOVE! CAN YOU STAND?!
MUDMAN'S SINKING THE FLAMES TO PUT 'EM OUT!
BUT, TETSUTETSU! KIRISHIMA, HE-!
AH! THAT PUNK! UNLIKE ME...
...HE DOESN'T BURN, BUT IT'S PROBABLY STILL HOT FOR HIM...
HE WAS FASTER THAN ME!
AND HE DOVE RIGHT INTO THAT HELL!

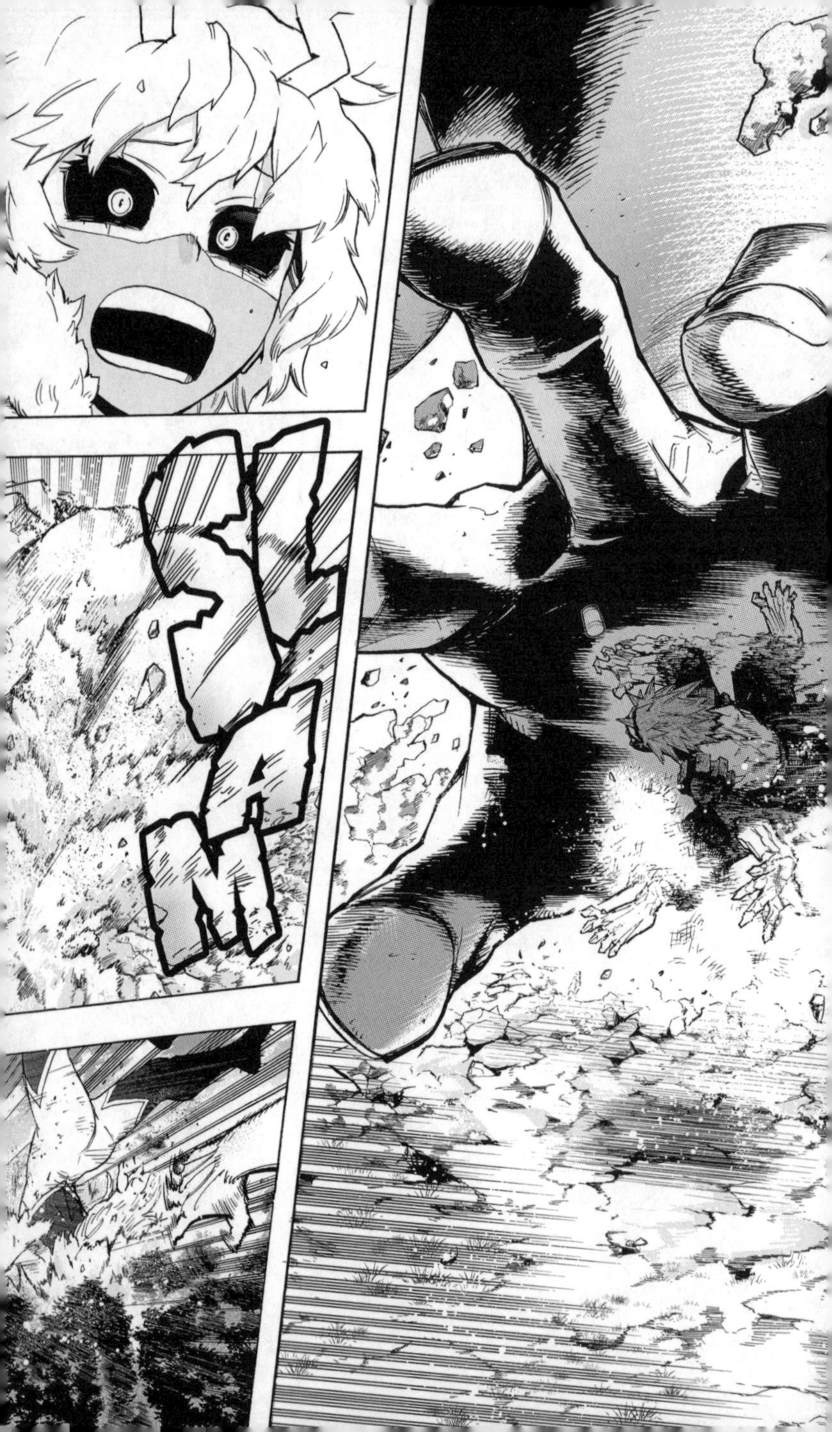
SLAM

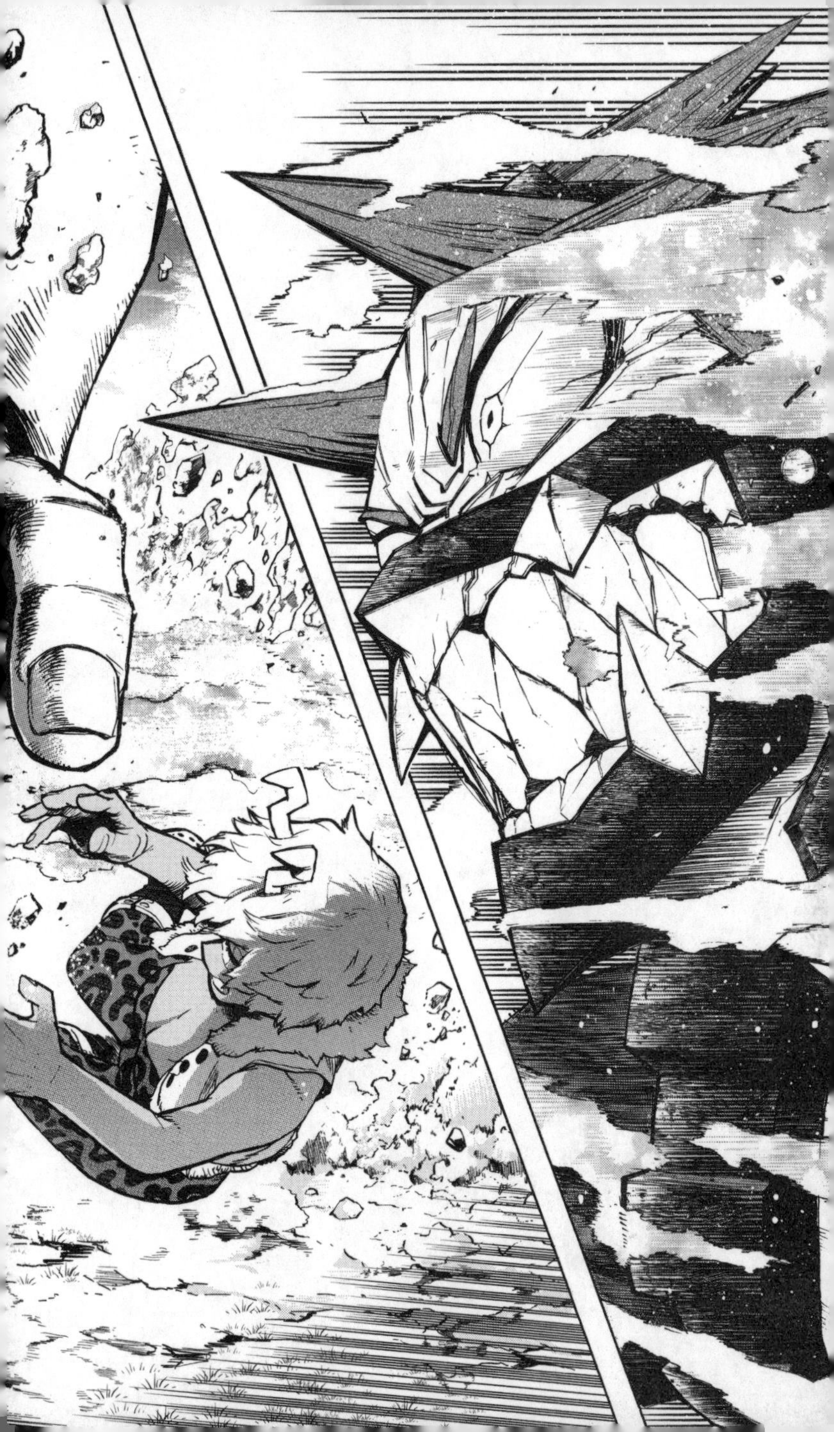

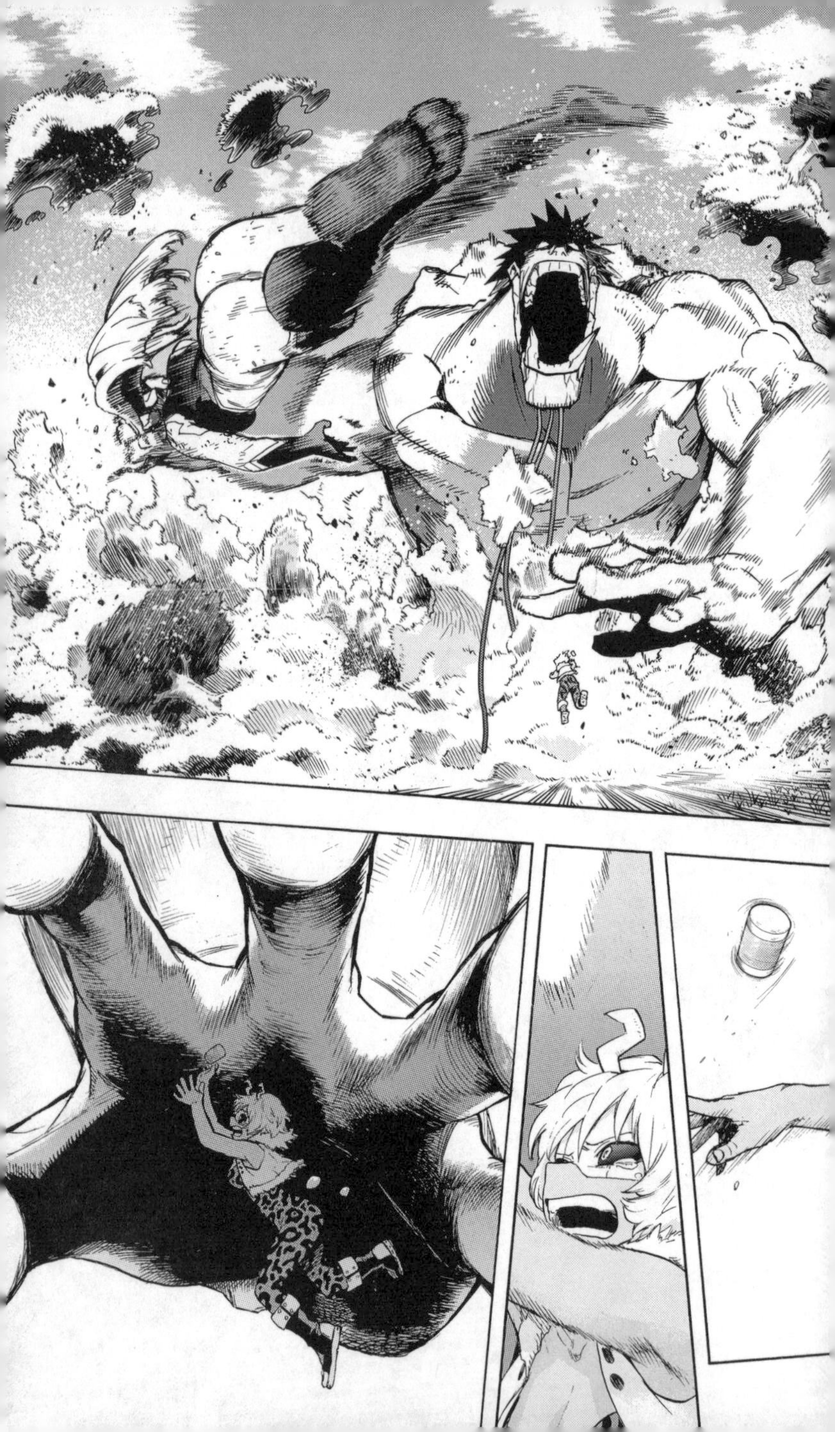

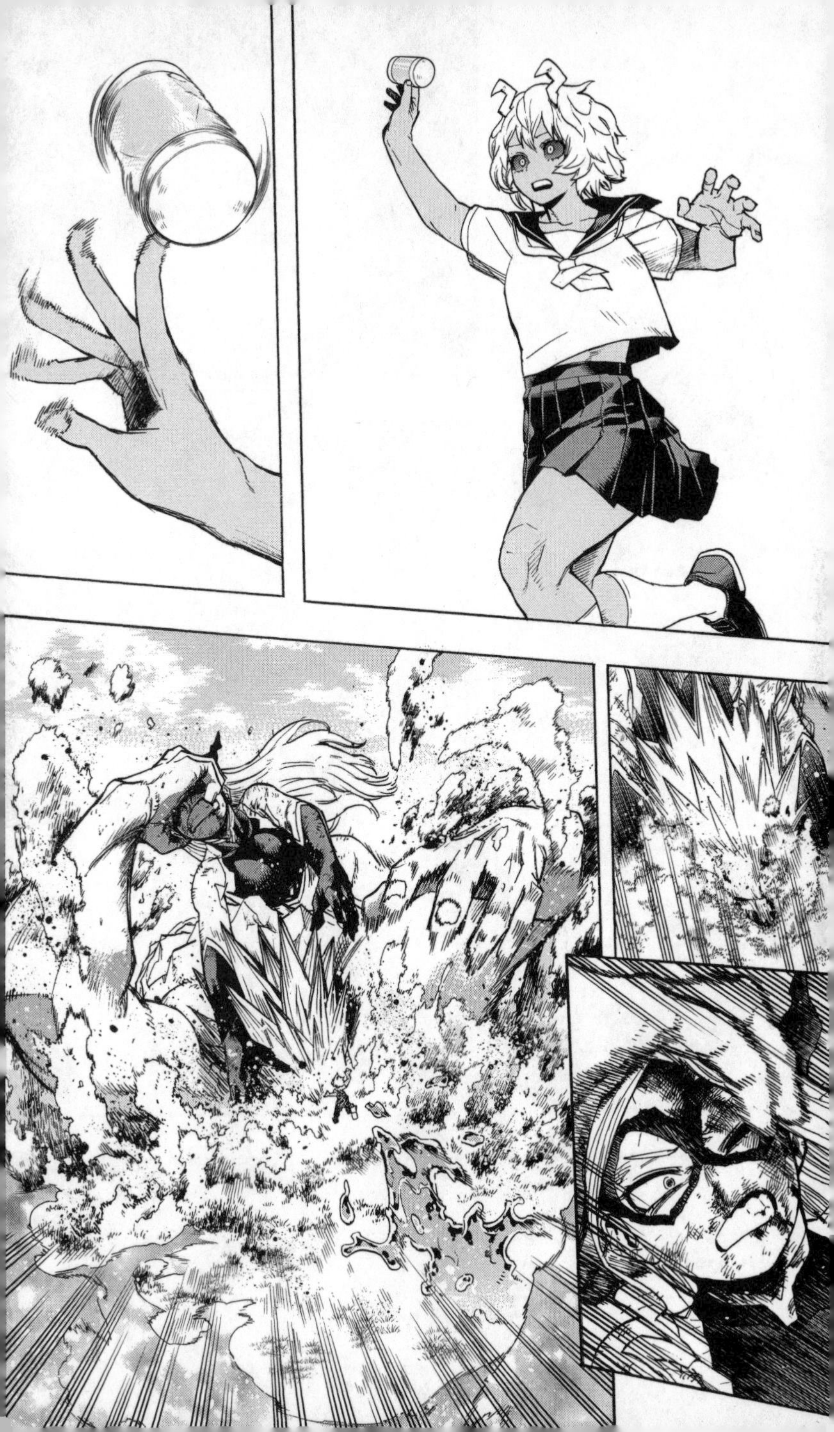

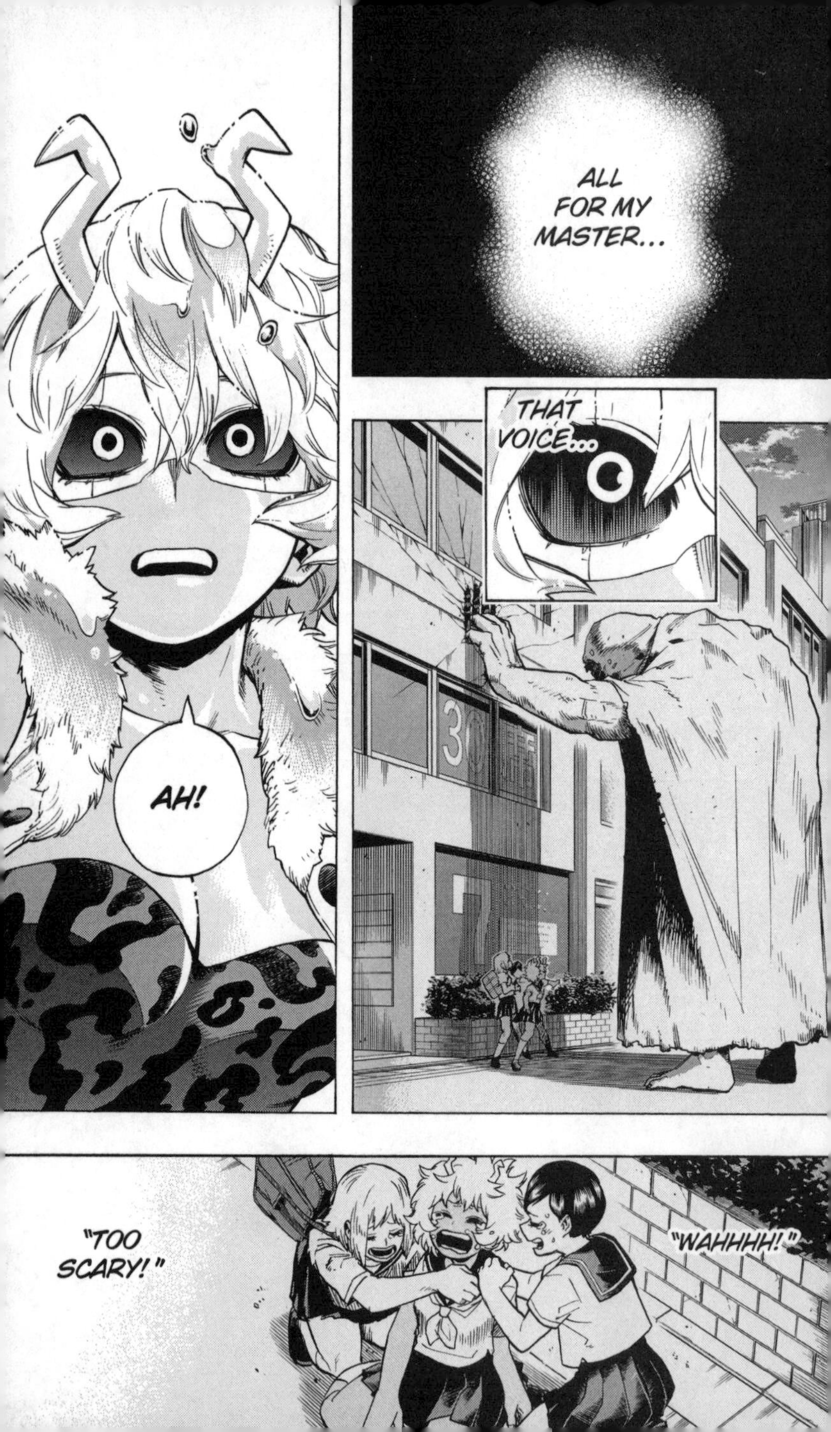
ALL FOR MY MASTER...
THAT VOICE...
AH!
"WAHHHH!"
"TOO SCARY!"

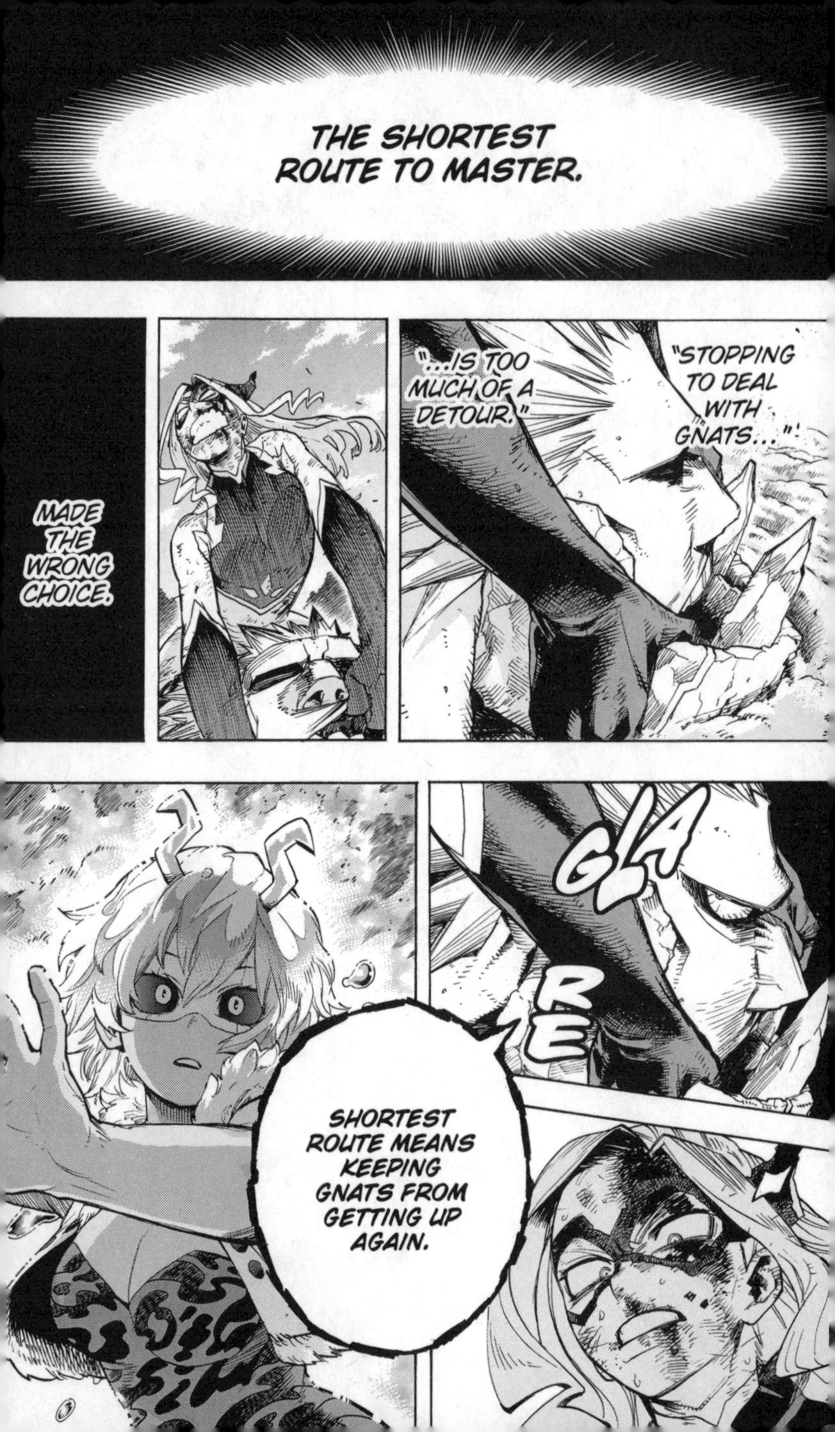
THE SHORTEST ROUTE TO MASTER.
"STOPPING TO DEAL WITH GNATS..."
"...IS TOO MUCH OF A DETOUR."
MADE THE WRONG CHOICE.
GLARE
SHORTEST ROUTE MEANS KEEPING GNATS FROM GETTING UP AGAIN.

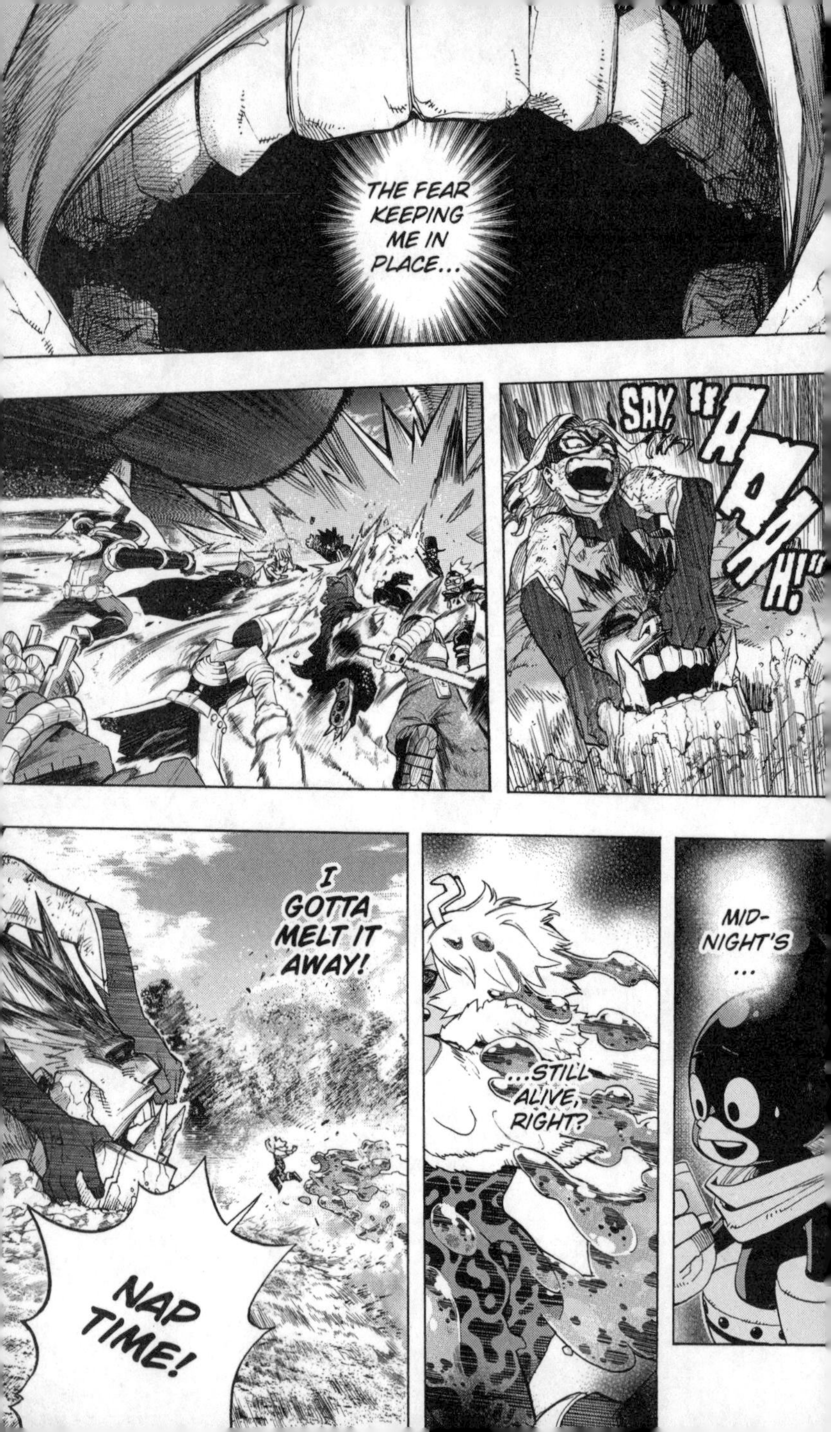
THE FEAR KEEPING ME IN PLACE...
SAY, "AAH!"
MID-NIGHT'S ...
...STILL ALIVE, RIGHT?
I GOTTA MELT IT AWAY!
NAP TIME!

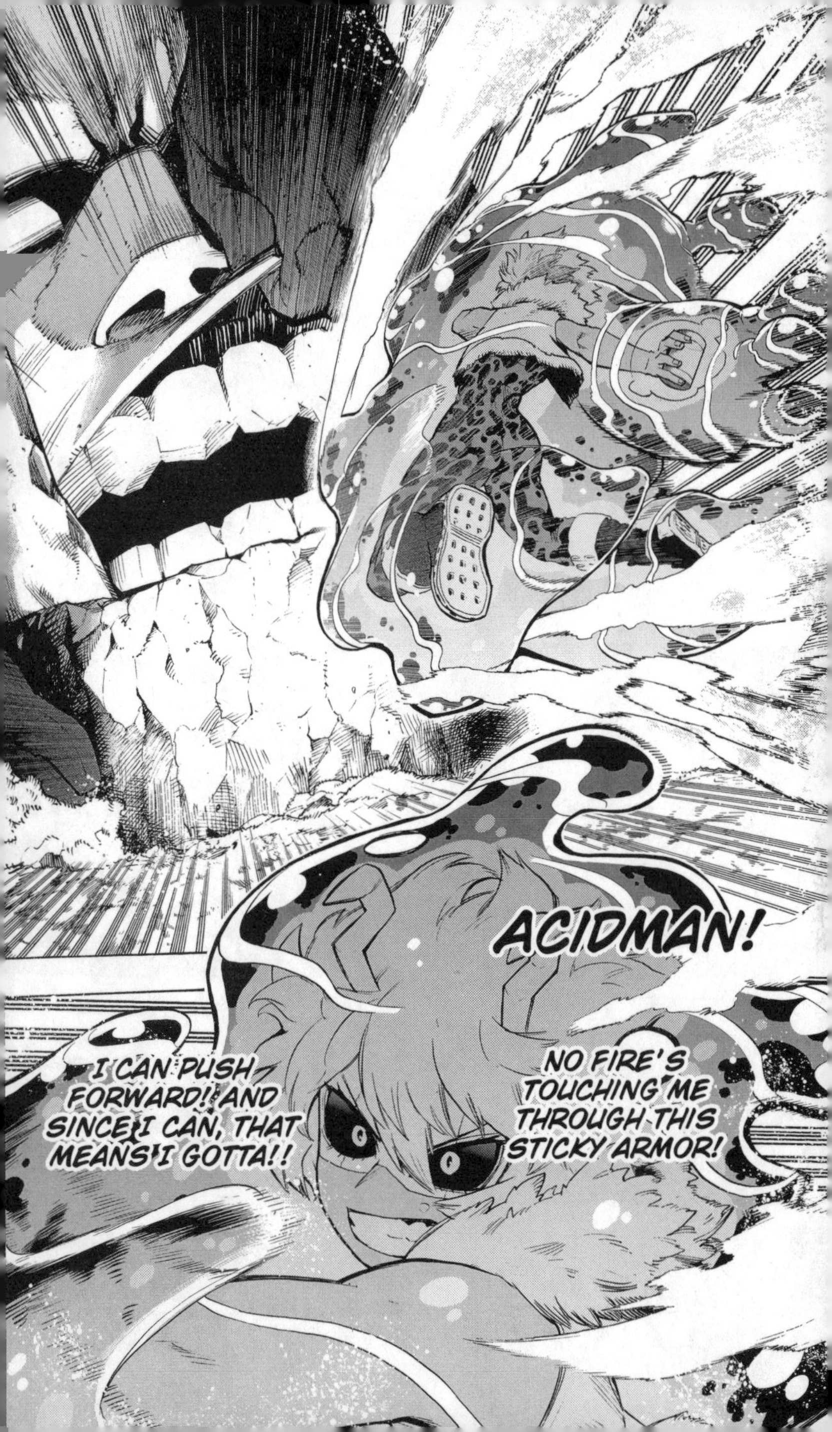
ACIDMAN!
NO FIRE'S TOUCHING ME THROUGH THIS STICKY ARMOR!
I CAN PUSH FORWARD!! AND SINCE I CAN, THAT MEANS I GOTTA!!

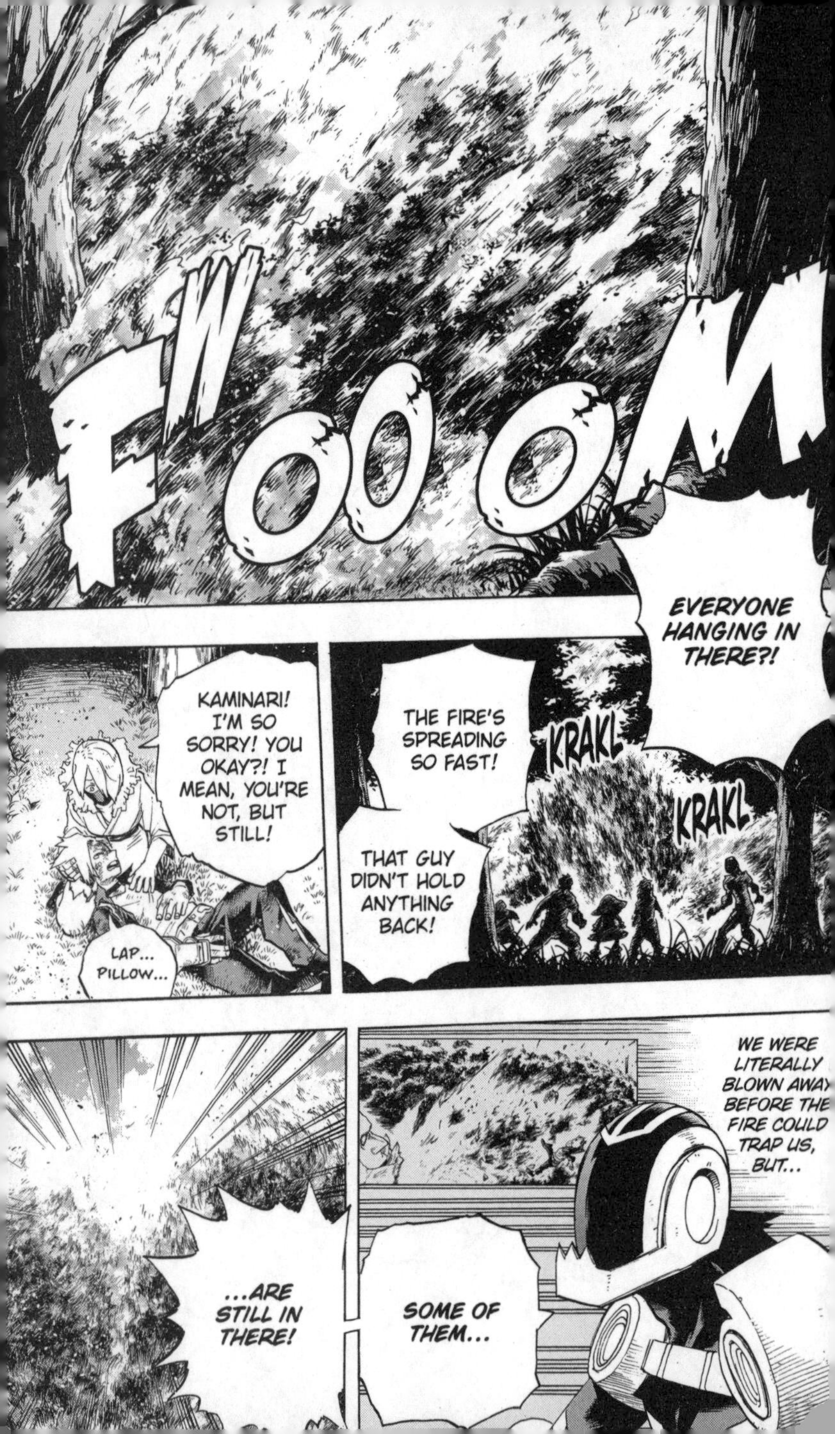
FWOOOM
EVERYONE HANGING IN THERE?!
KRAKL
KRAKL
THE FIRE'S SPREADING SO FAST!
THAT GUY DIDN'T HOLD ANYTHING BACK!
KAMINARI! I'M SO SORRY! YOU OKAY?! I MEAN, YOU'RE NOT, BUT STILL!
LAP... PILLOW...
WE WERE LITERALLY BLOWN AWAY BEFORE THE FIRE COULD TRAP US, BUT...
SOME OF THEM...
...ARE STILL IN THERE!

MY HERO
ACADEMIA

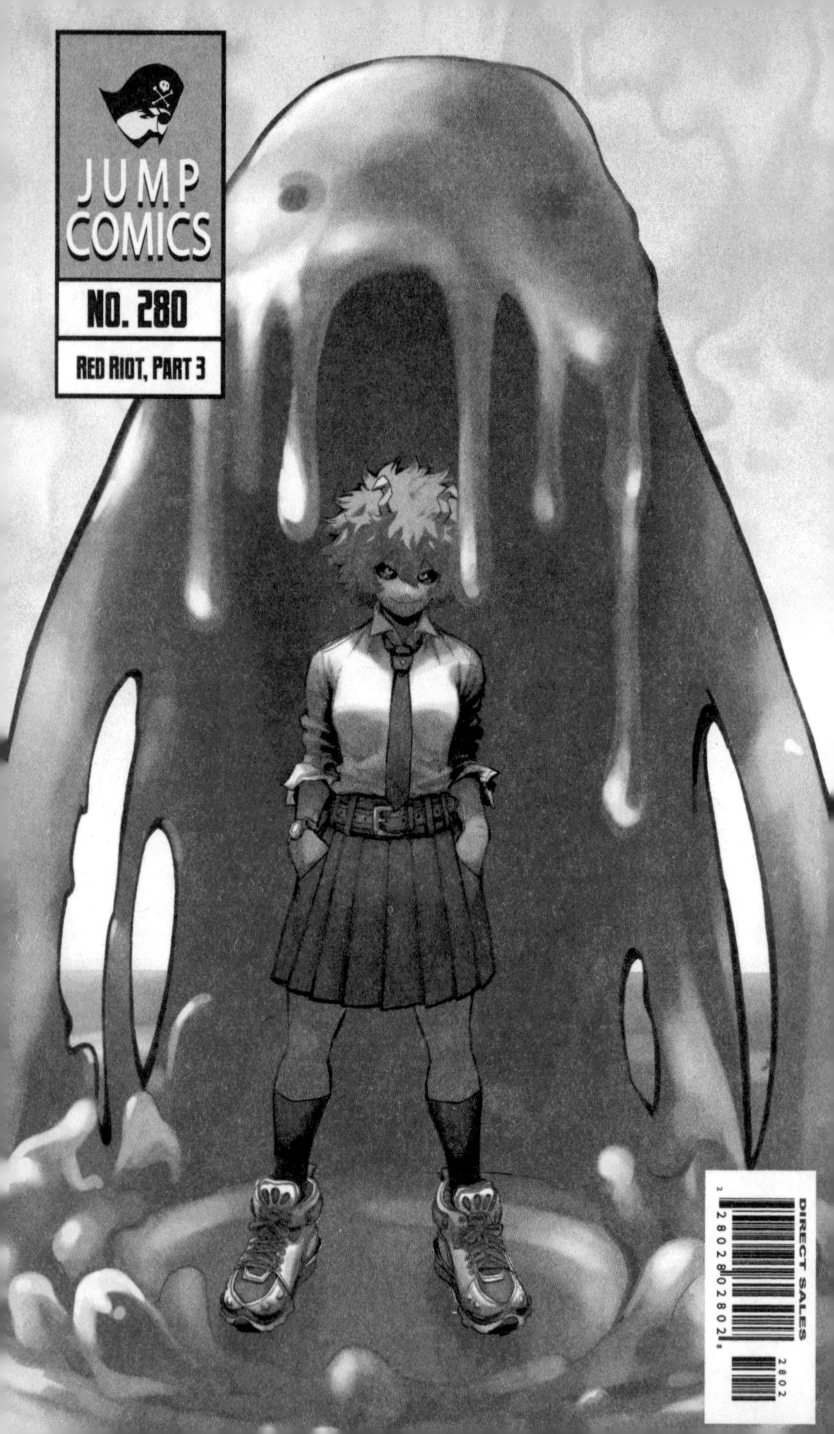
JUMP COMICS
NO. 280
RED RIOT, PART 3
DIRECT SALES

Honenuki was worried about Monoma, but he and the other members of class B who aren't on any of the main battlefields are just fine.

They were assigned to a hideout in a different area.

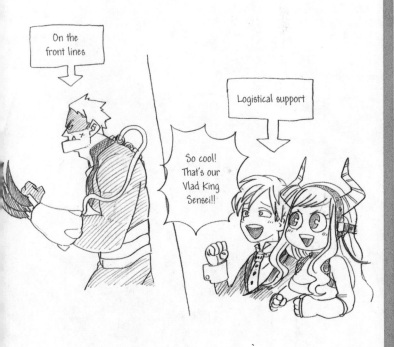

Logistical support
So cool! That's our Vlad King Sensei!!
On the front lines

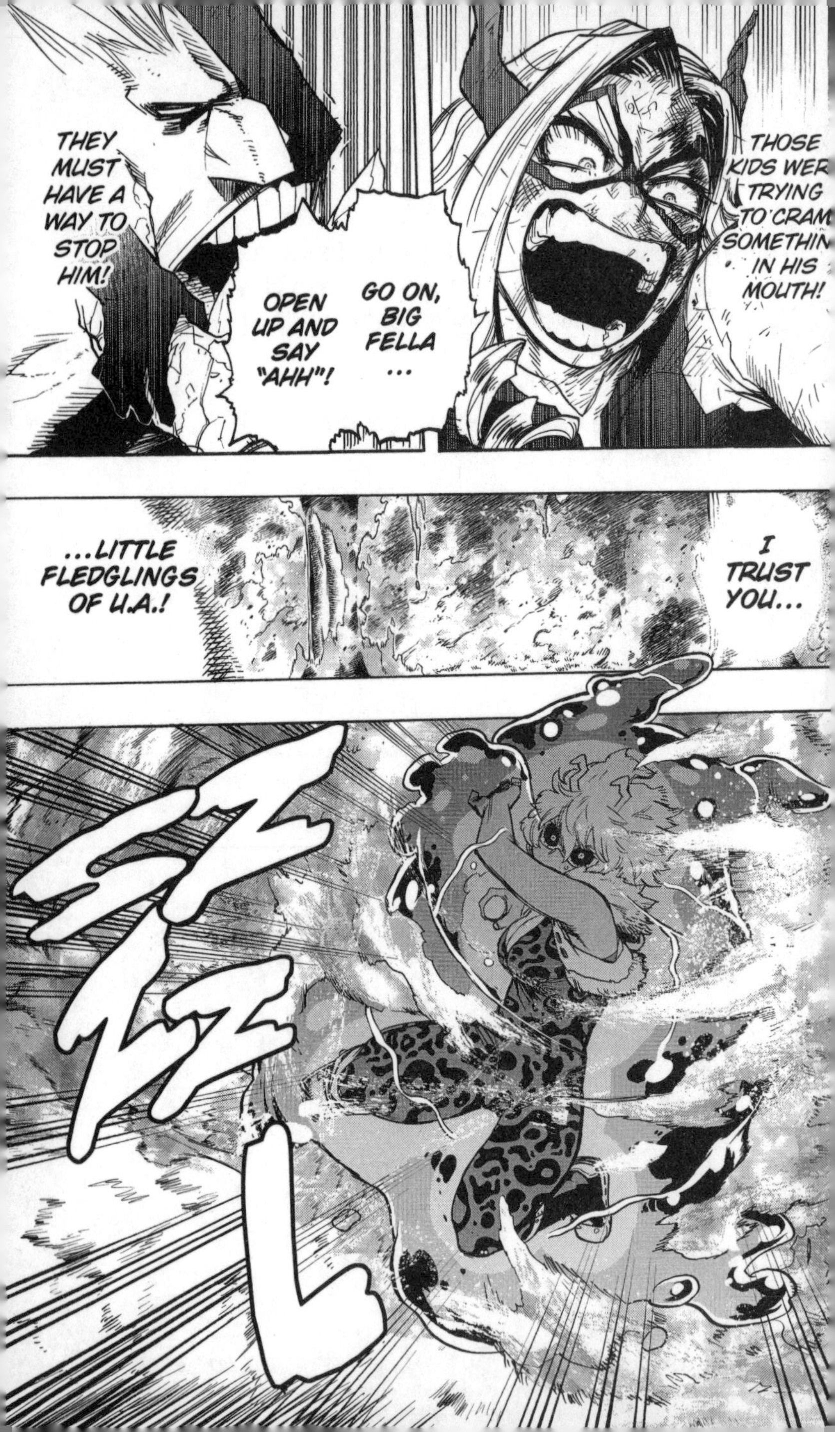
THOSE KIDS WER TRYING TO CRAM SOMETHIN IN HIS MOUTH!
GO ON, BIG FELLA ...
OPEN UP AND SAY "AHH"!
THEY MUST HAVE A WAY TO STOP HIM!
I TRUST YOU...
...LITTLE FLEDGLINGS OF U.A.!

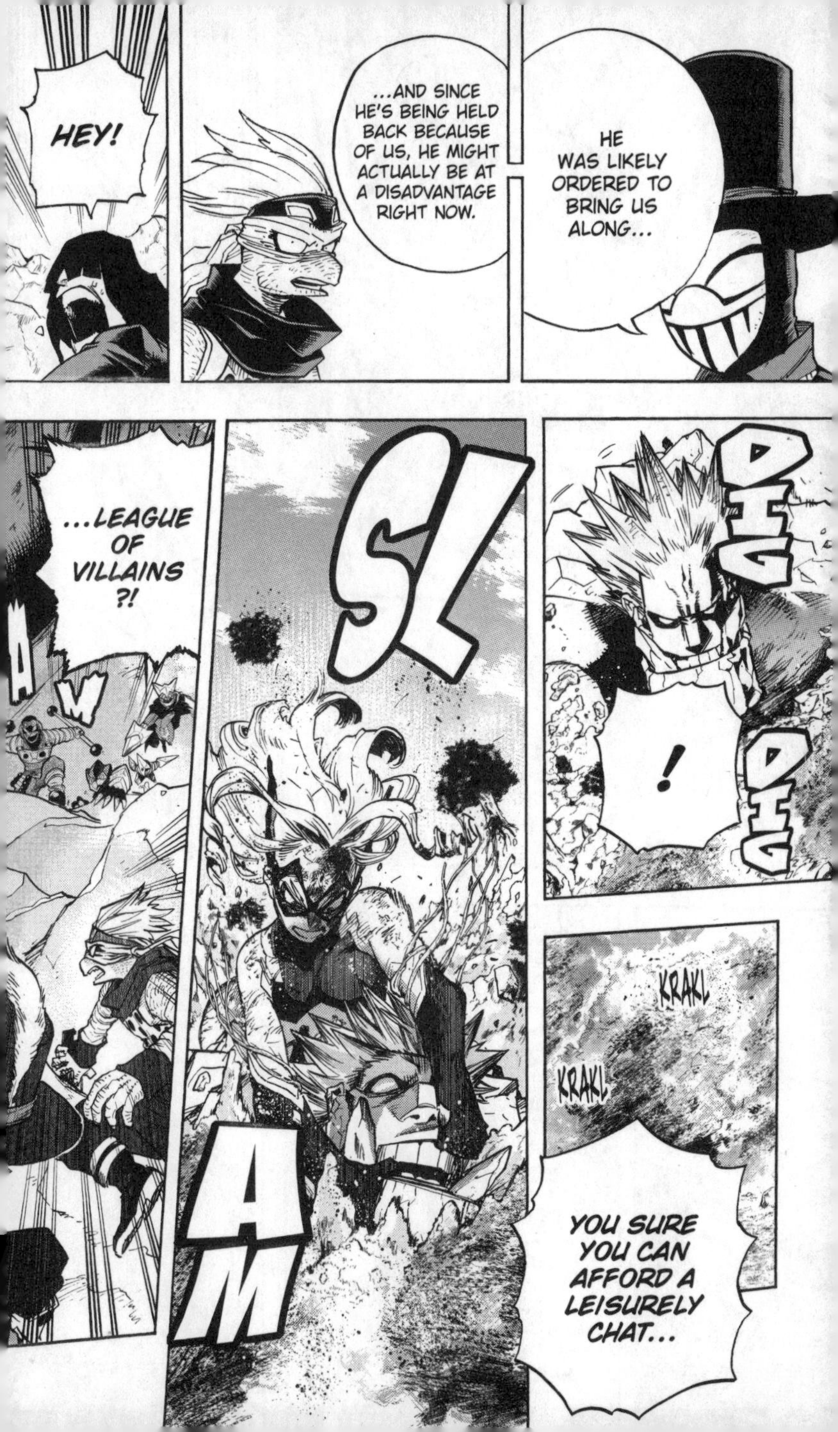
HE WAS LIKELY ORDERED TO BRING US ALONG...
...AND SINCE HE'S BEING HELD BACK BECAUSE OF US, HE MIGHT ACTUALLY BE AT A DISADVANTAGE RIGHT NOW.
HEY!
DIG DIG
!
KRAKL
KRAKL
YOU SURE YOU CAN AFFORD A LEISURELY CHAT...
SL
AM
...LEAGUE OF VILLAINS?!
AM

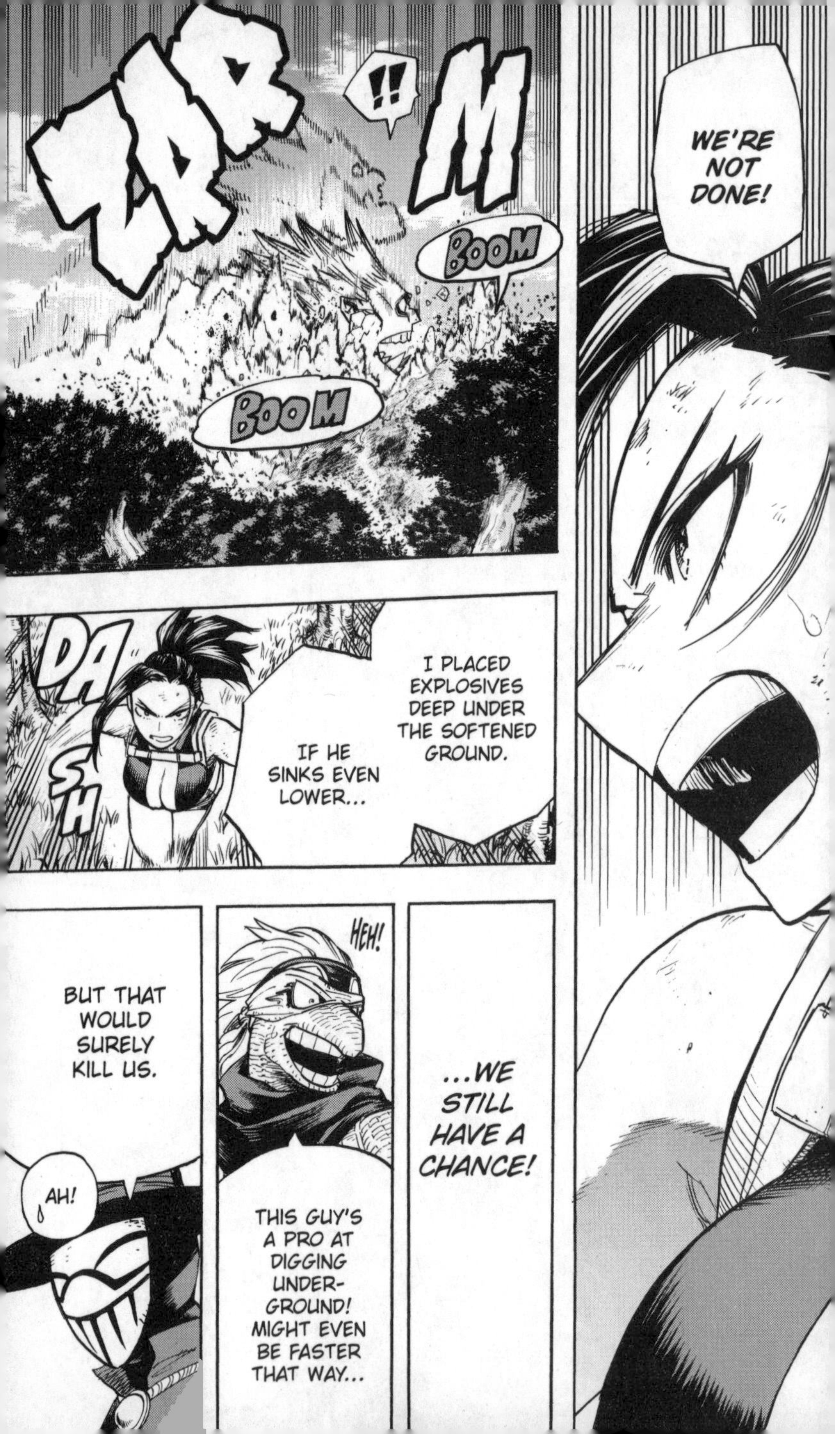

WE'RE NOT DONE!
ZA-!! BOOM
BOOM
BOOM
DASH
I PLACED EXPLOSIVES DEEP UNDER THE SOFTENED GROUND.
IF HE SINKS EVEN LOWER...
...WE STILL HAVE A CHANCE!
HEH!
THIS GUY'S A PRO AT DIGGING UNDER-GROUND! MIGHT EVEN BE FASTER THAT WAY...
BUT THAT WOULD SURELY KILL US.
AH!

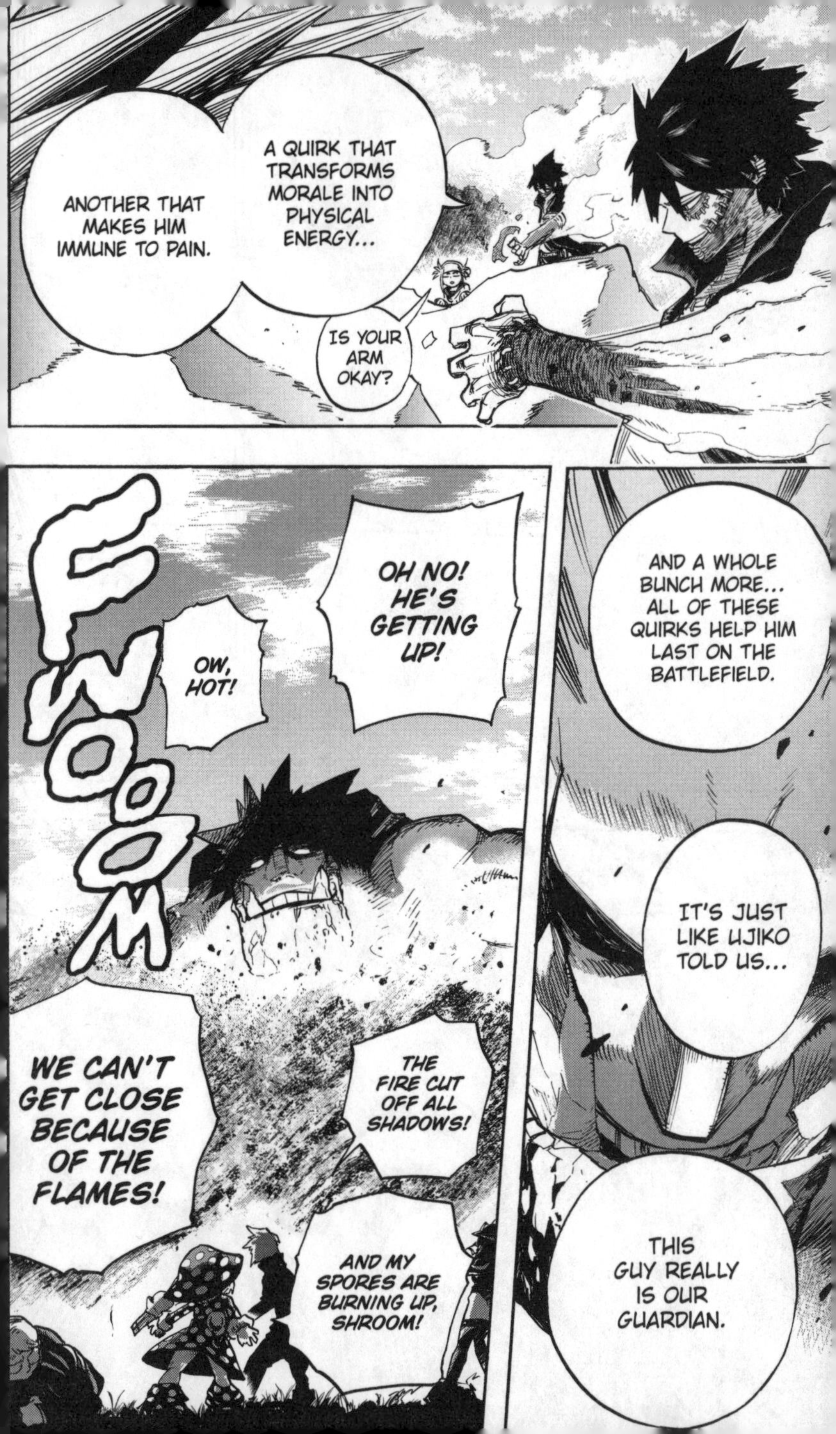
IS YOUR ARM OKAY?
A QUIRK THAT TRANSFORMS MORALE INTO PHYSICAL ENERGY...
ANOTHER THAT MAKES HIM IMMUNE TO PAIN.
AND A WHOLE BUNCH MORE... ALL OF THESE QUIRKS HELP HIM LAST ON THE BATTLEFIELD.
IT'S JUST LIKE UJIKO TOLD US...
THIS GUY REALLY IS OUR GUARDIAN.
OH NO! HE'S GETTING UP!
OW, HOT!
FWOOOM
THE FIRE CUT OFF ALL SHADOWS!
WE CAN'T GET CLOSE BECAUSE OF THE FLAMES!
AND MY SPORES ARE BURNING UP, SHROOM!

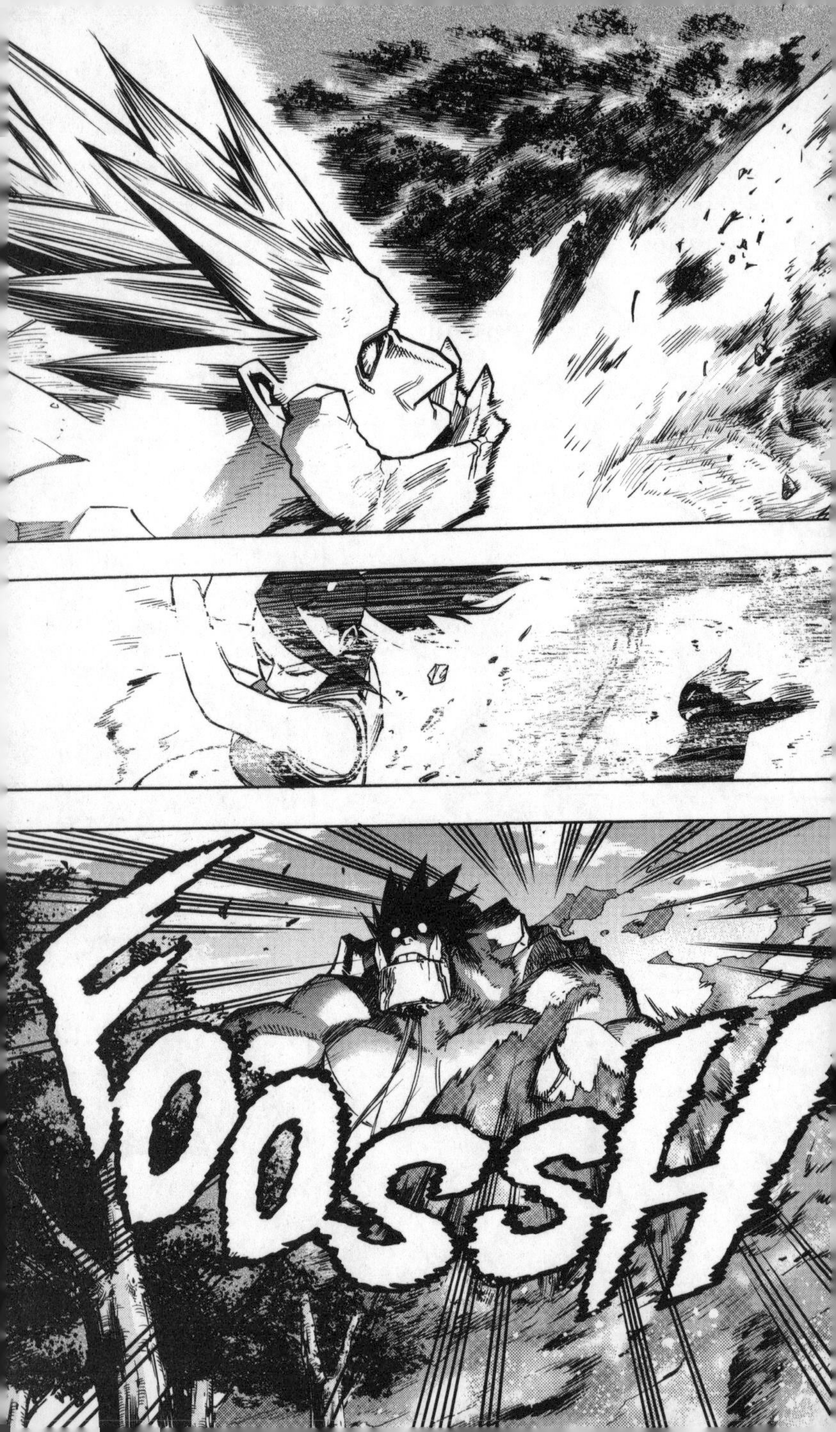
FOOSSH!

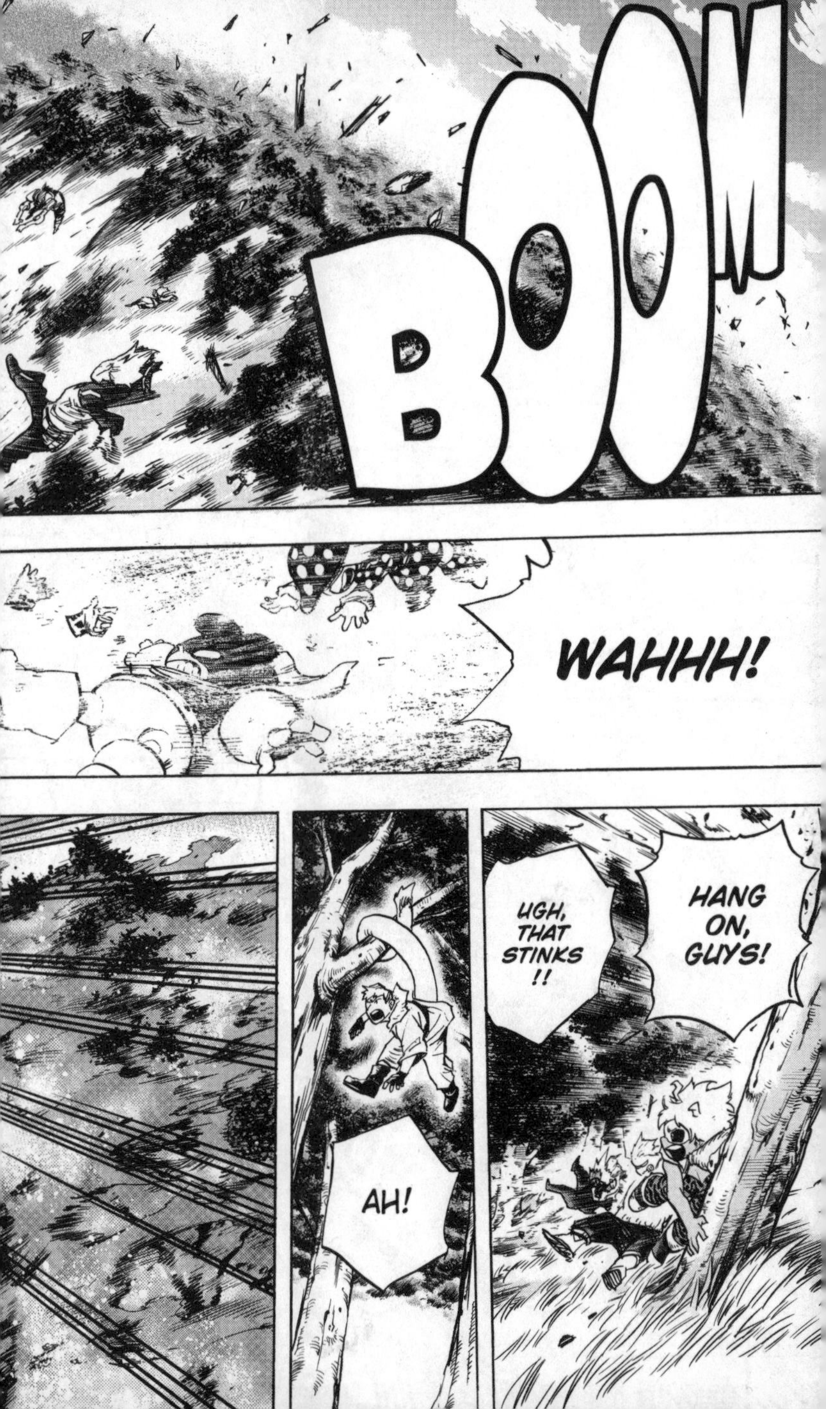
BOOM
WAHHH!
HANG ON, GUYS!
UGH, THAT STINKS !!
AH!

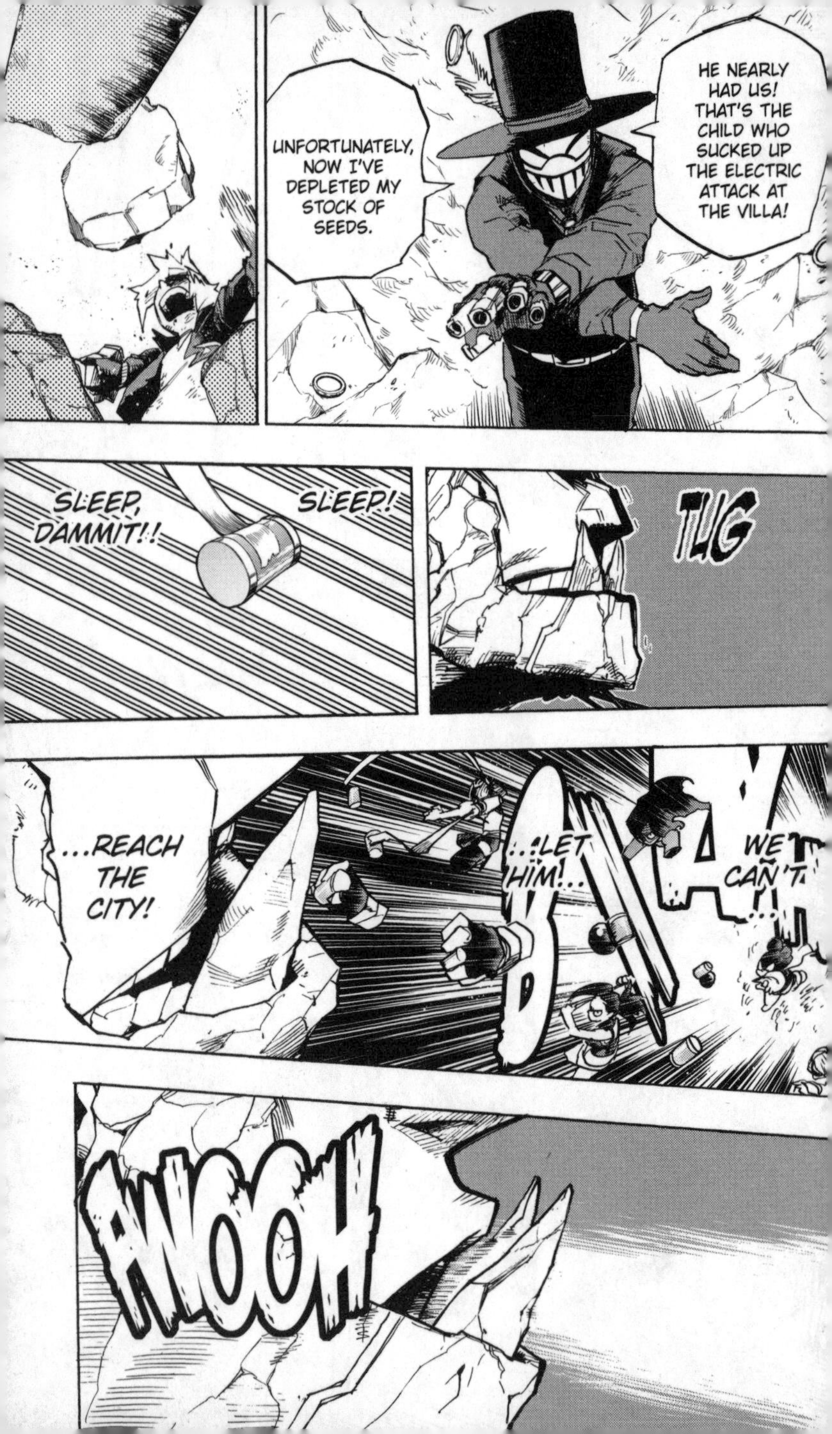
HE NEARLY HAD US! THAT'S THE CHILD WHO SUCKED UP THE ELECTRIC ATTACK AT THE VILLA!
UNFORTUNATELY, NOW I'VE DEPLETED MY STOCK OF SEEDS.
TUG
SLEEP!
SLEEP, DAMMIT!!
WE CAN'T...
...LET HIM!...
...REACH THE CITY!
FWOOH

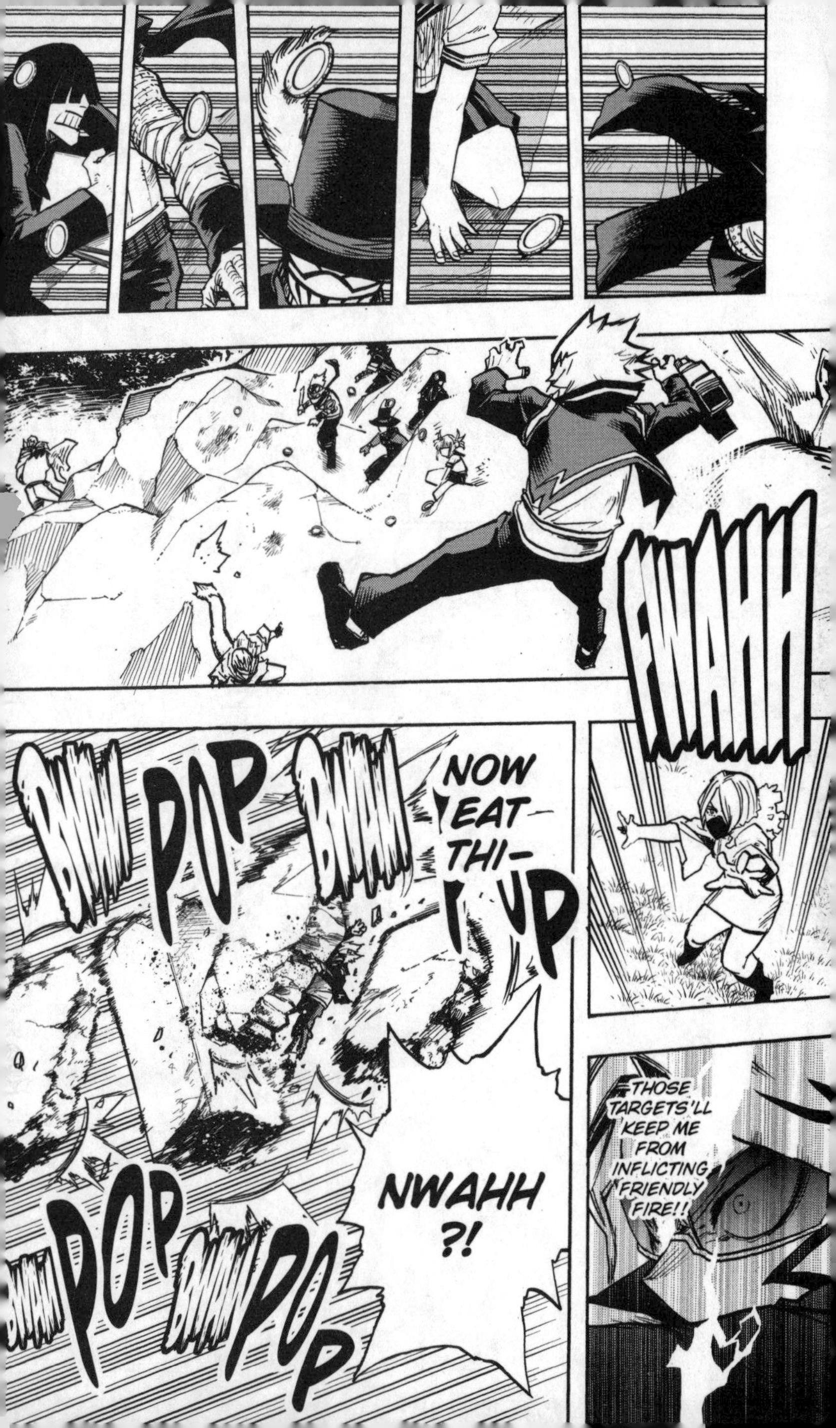
FWAHH
THOSE TARGETS'LL KEEP ME FROM INFLICTING FRIENDLY FIRE!!
NOW EAT THI-
BWAM
POP
BWAM
UP
NWAHH ?!
POP
BWAM
POP
BWAM
POP

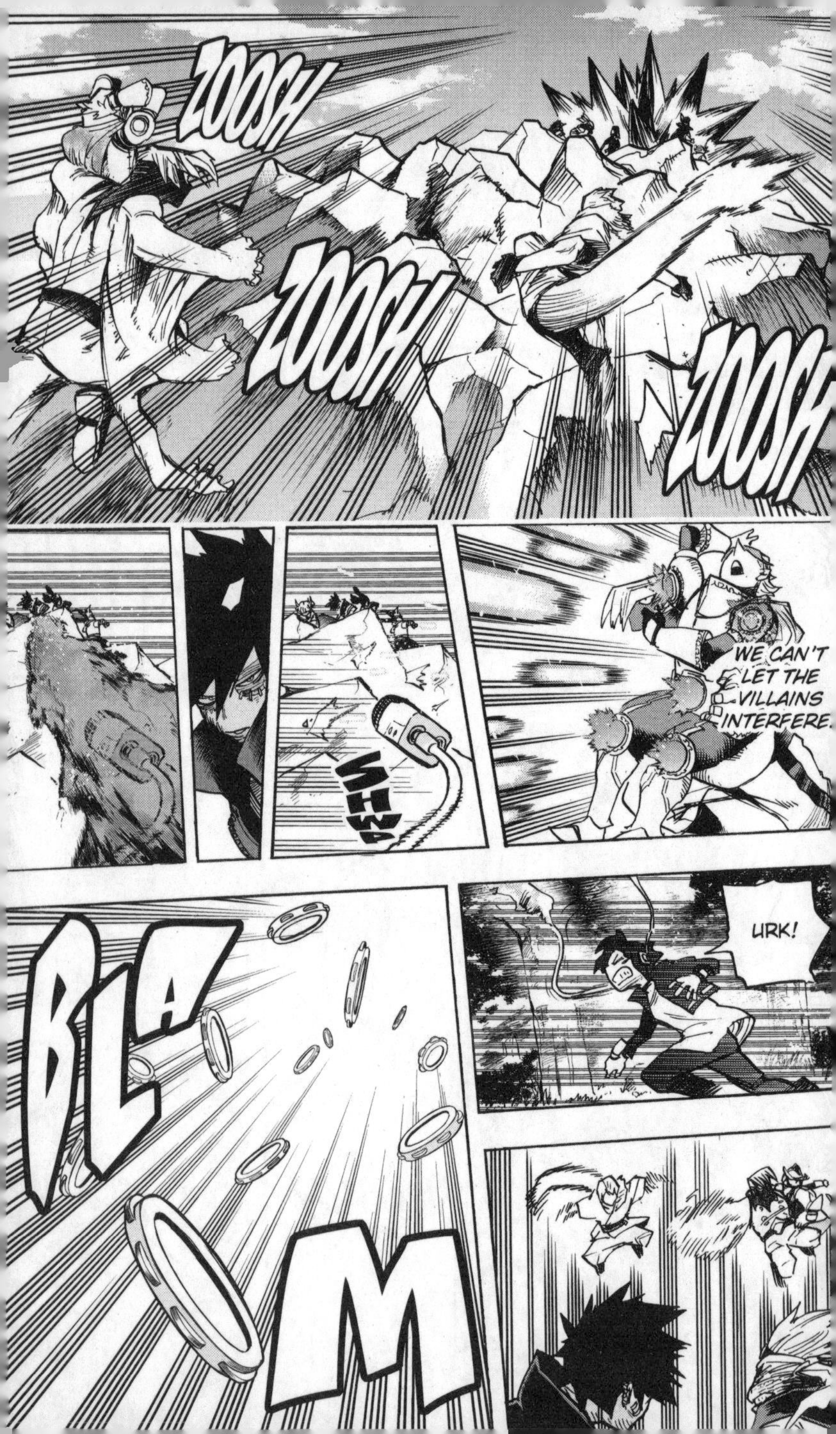
ZOOSH
ZOOSH
ZOOSH
WE CAN'T LET THE VILLAINS INTERFERE.
SHWP
URK!
BLAM

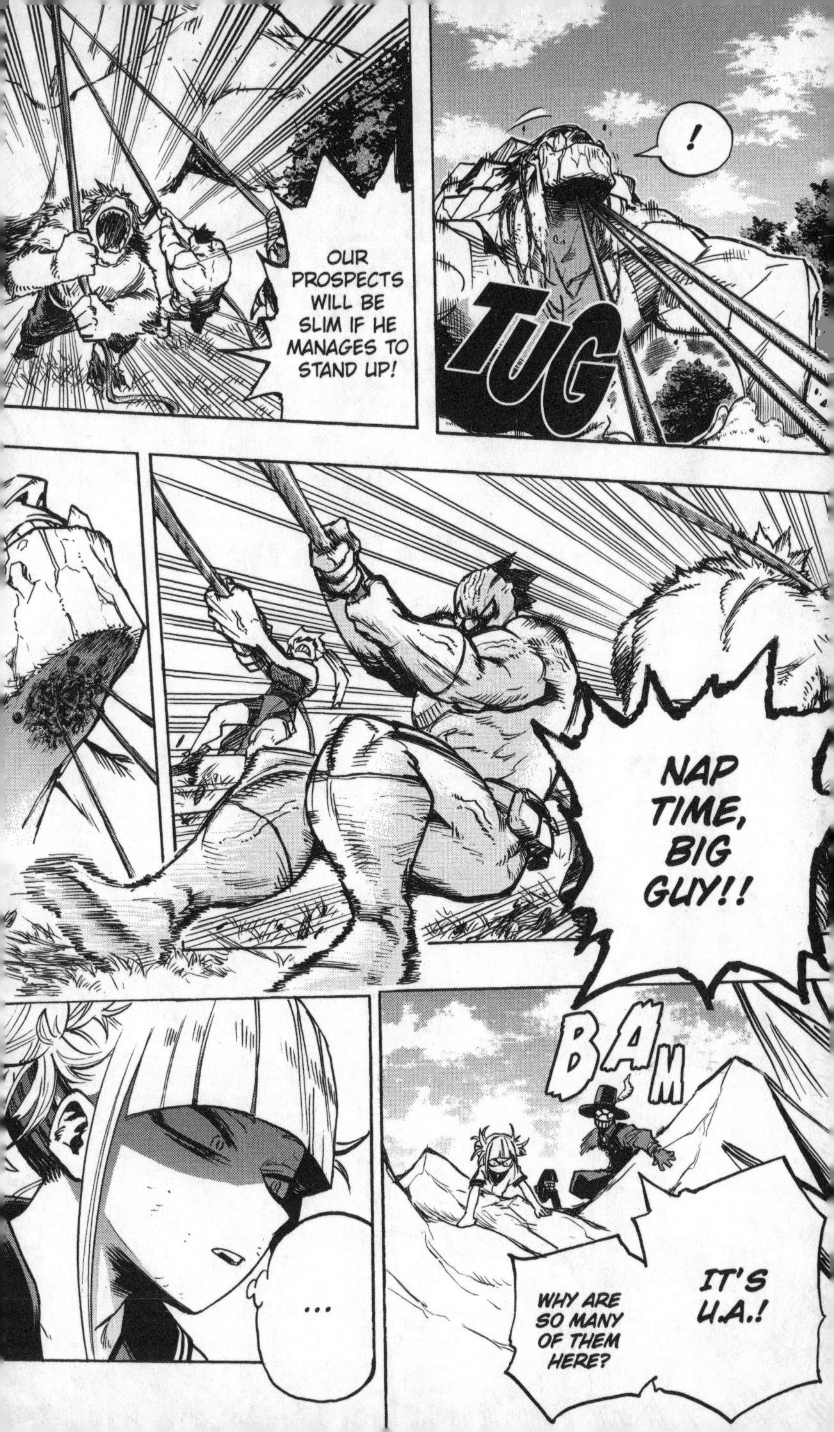
!
TUG
OUR PROSPECTS WILL BE SLIM IF HE MANAGES TO STAND UP!
NAP TIME, BIG GUY!!
BAM
IT'S U.A.!
WHY ARE SO MANY OF THEM HERE?
...

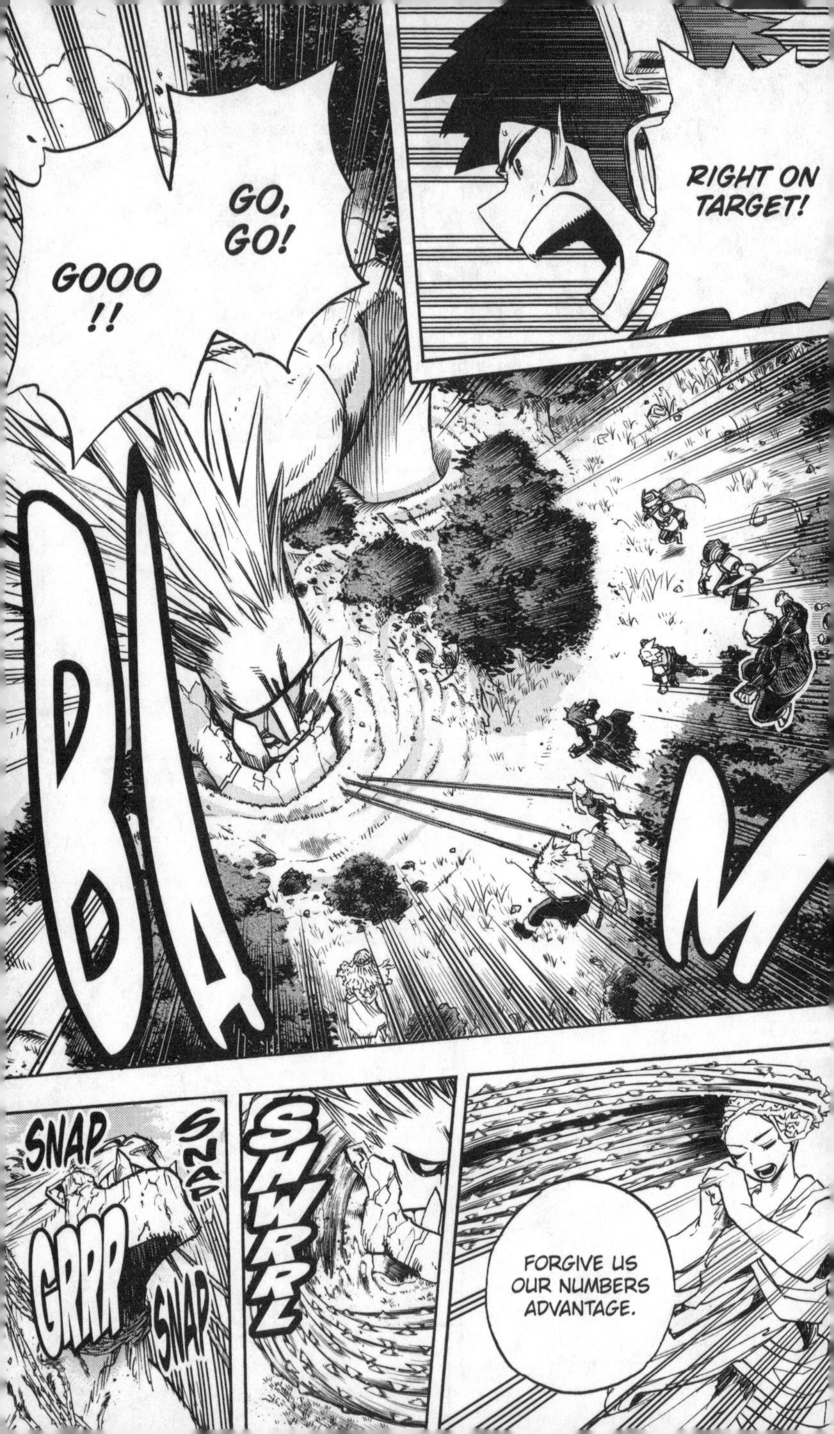

RIGHT ON TARGET!
GO, GO!
GOOO!!
BA
M
FORGIVE US OUR NUMBERS ADVANTAGE.
SHWRRL
SNAP
SNAP
GRRR
SNAP

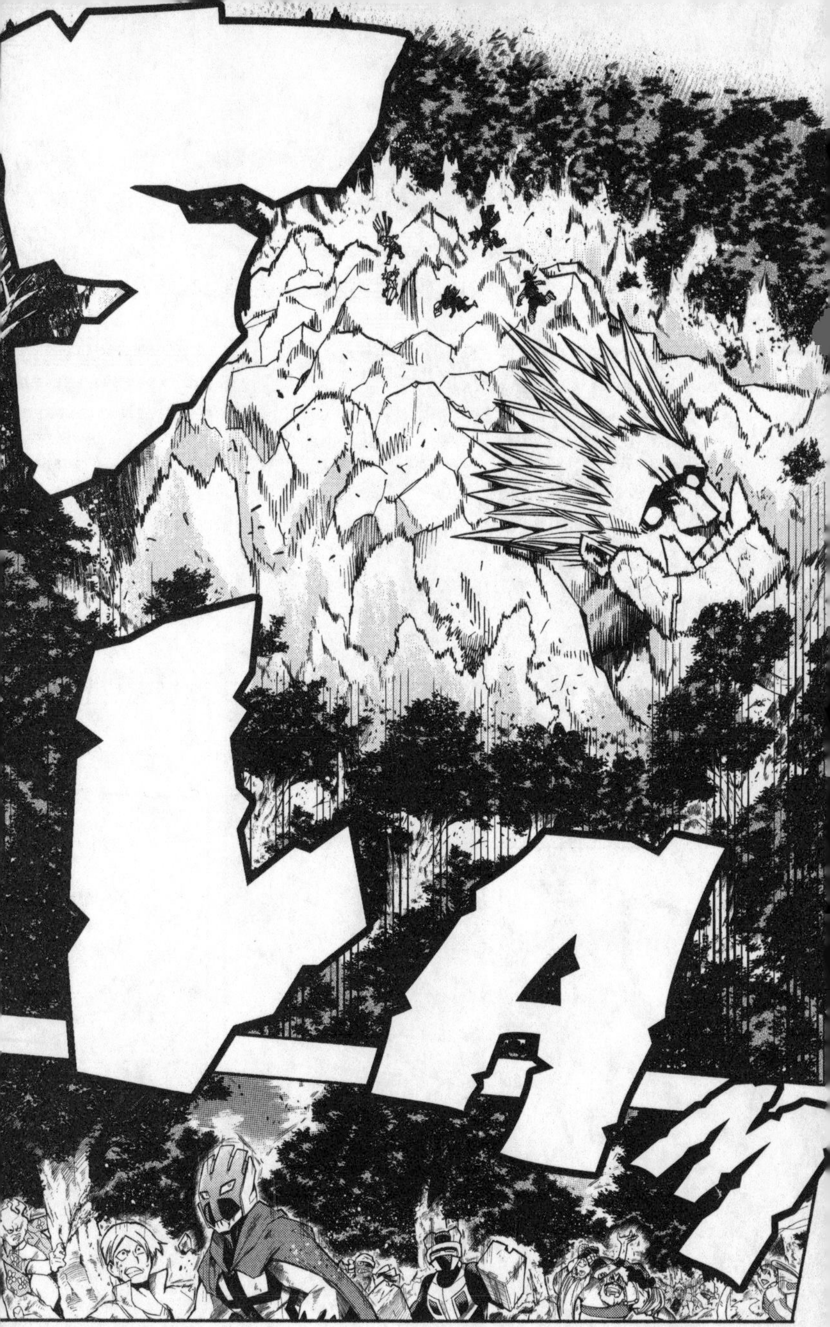

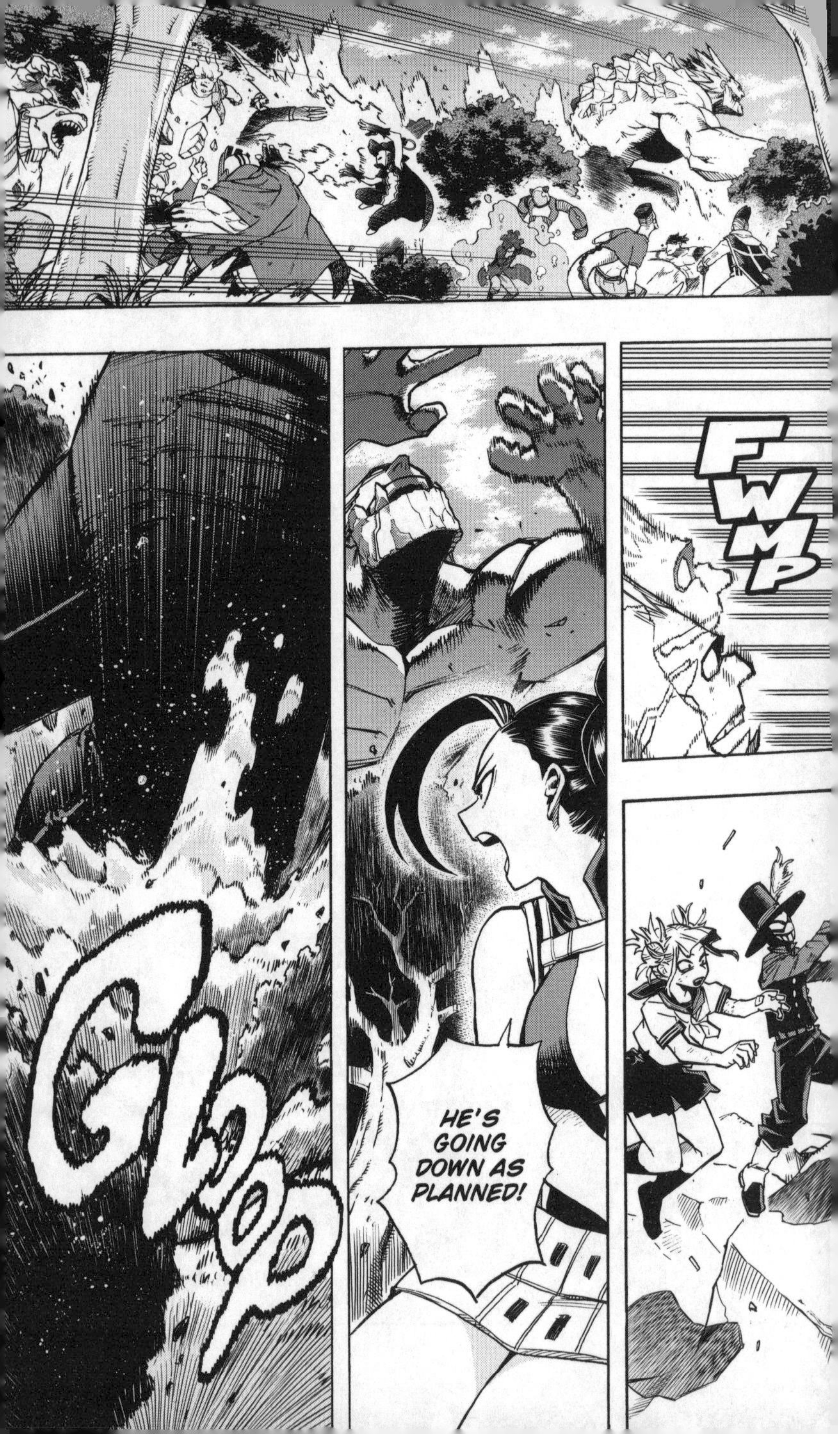
FWMP
HE'S GOING DOWN AS PLANNED!
GLOOP

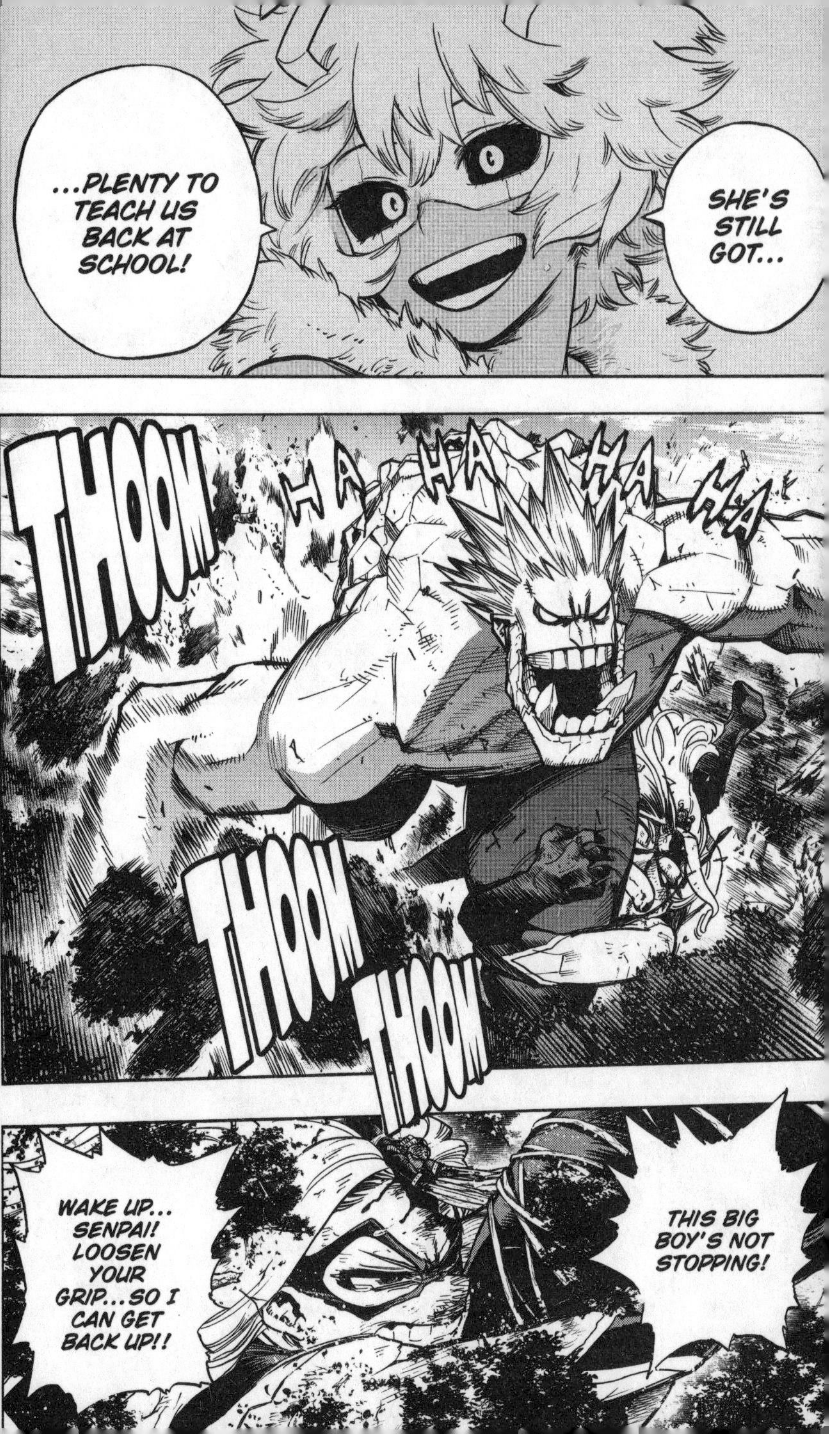
SHE'S STILL GOT...
...PLENTY TO TEACH US BACK AT SCHOOL!
HA HA HA HA
THOOM
THOOM
THOOM
THIS BIG BOY'S NOT STOPPING!
WAKE UP... SENPAI! LOOSEN YOUR GRIP... SO I CAN GET BACK UP!!

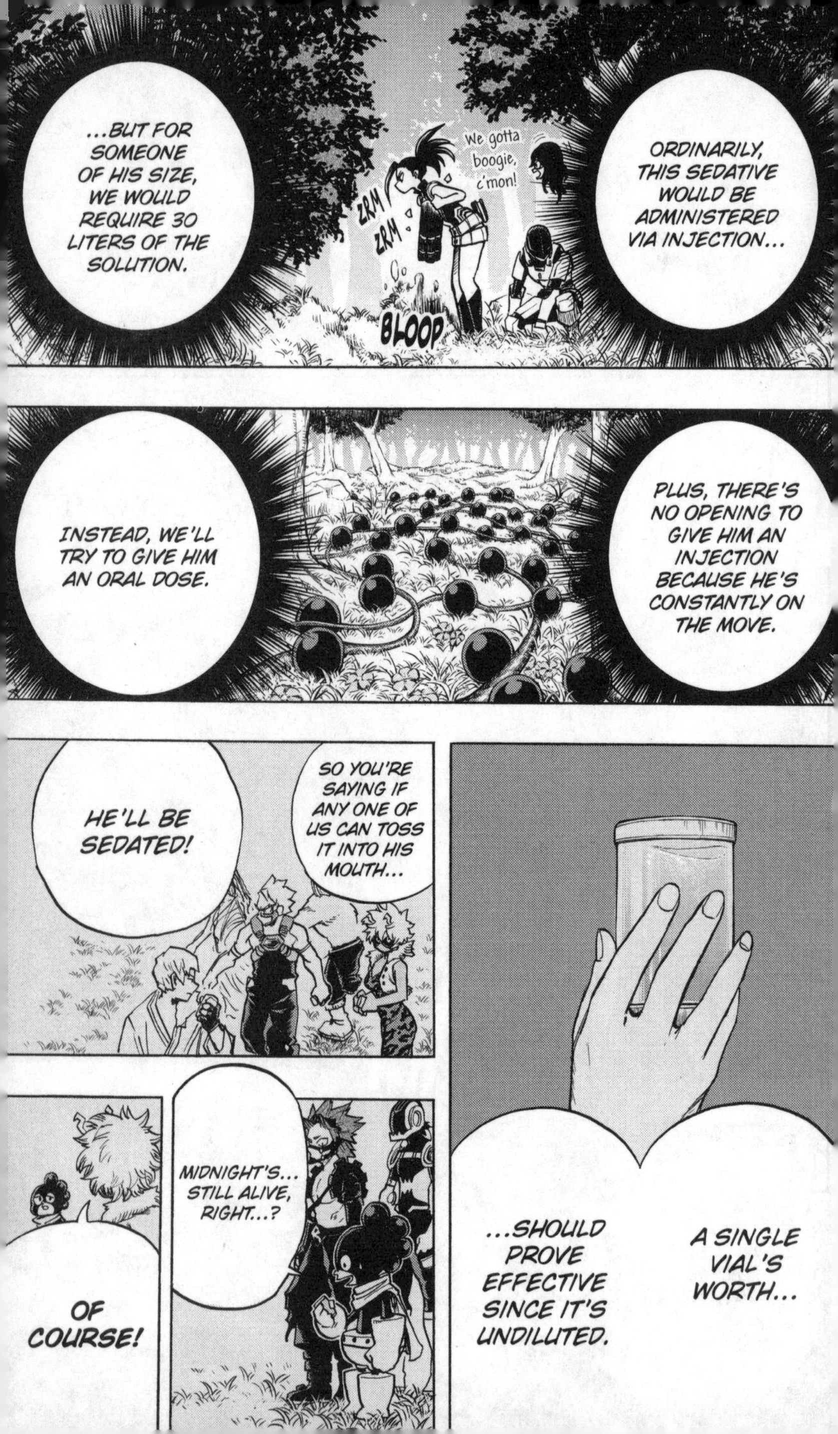
ORDINARILY, THIS SEDATIVE WOULD BE ADMINISTERED VIA INJECTION...
We gotta boogie, c'mon!
ZRM ZRM
BLOOP
...BUT FOR SOMEONE OF HIS SIZE, WE WOULD REQUIRE 30 LITERS OF THE SOLUTION.
PLUS, THERE'S NO OPENING TO GIVE HIM AN INJECTION BECAUSE HE'S CONSTANTLY ON THE MOVE.
INSTEAD, WE'LL TRY TO GIVE HIM AN ORAL DOSE.
A SINGLE VIAL'S WORTH...
...SHOULD PROVE EFFECTIVE SINCE IT'S UNDILUTED.
SO YOU'RE SAYING IF ANY ONE OF US CAN TOSS IT INTO HIS MOUTH...
HE'LL BE SEDATED!
MIDNIGHT'S... STILL ALIVE, RIGHT...?
OF COURSE!

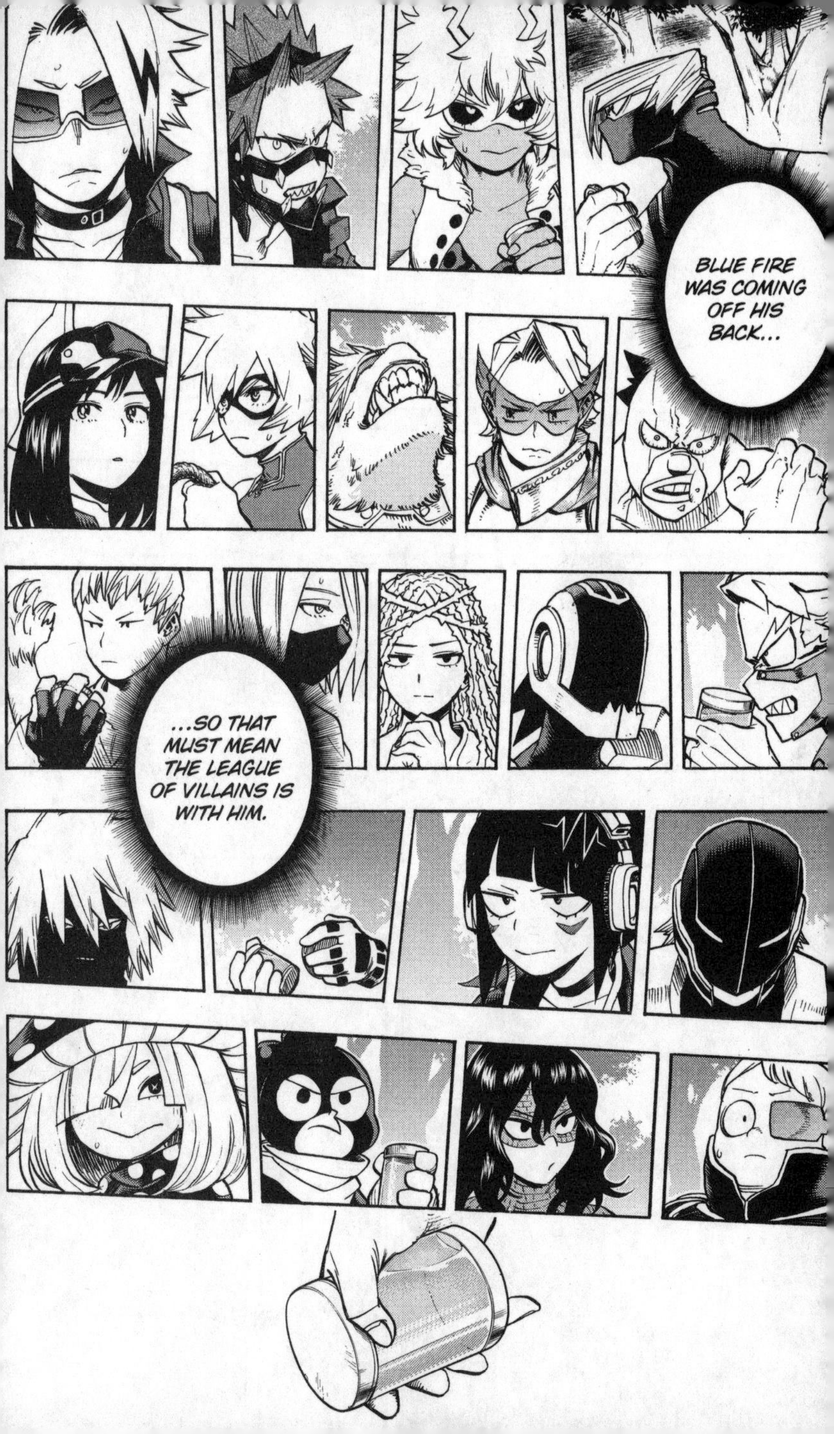
BLUE FIRE WAS COMING OFF HIS BACK...
...SO THAT MUST MEAN THE LEAGUE OF VILLAINS IS WITH HIM.

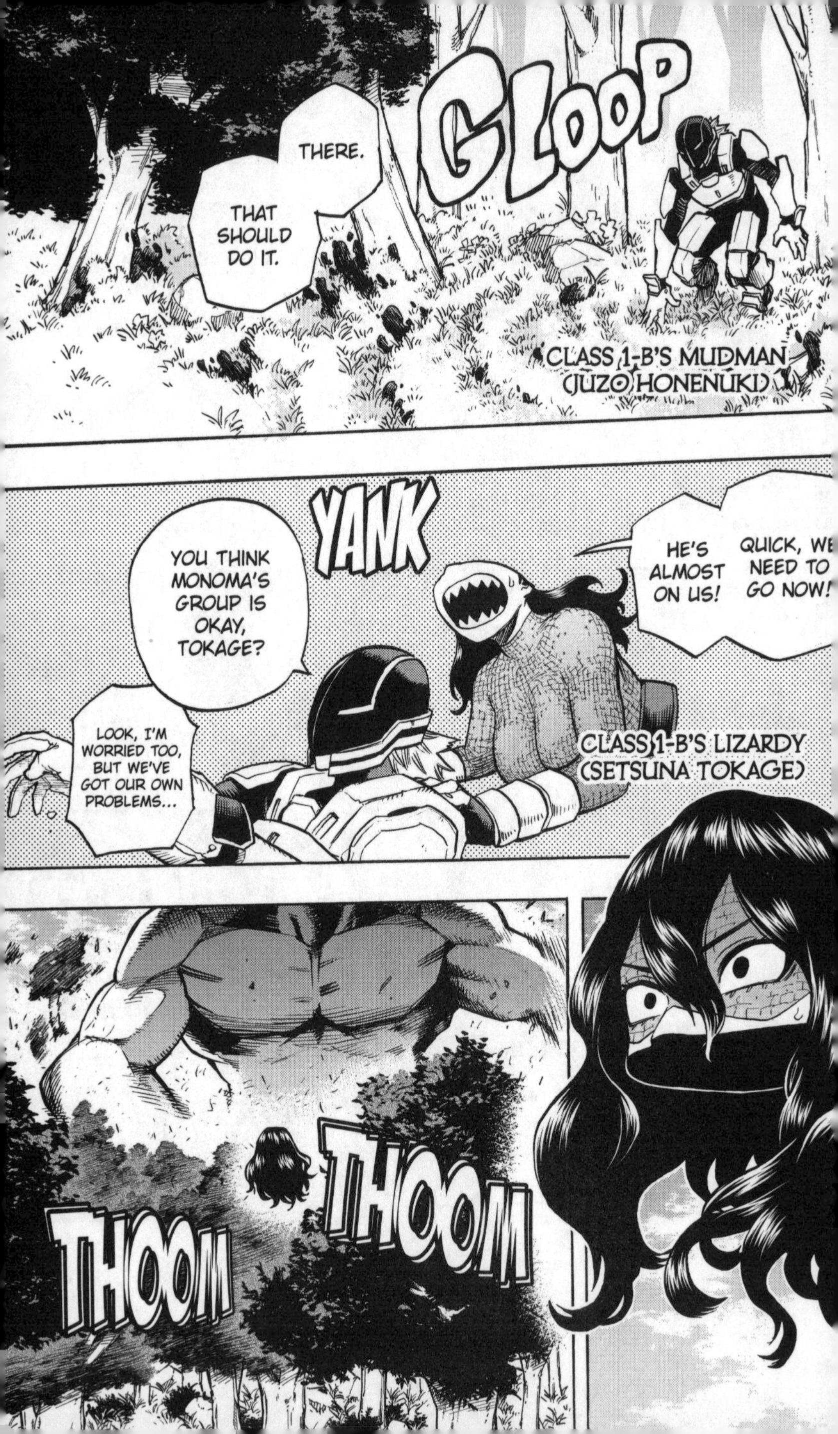
GLOOP
THERE.
THAT SHOULD DO IT.
CLASS 1-B'S MUDMAN (JUZO HONENUKI)
QUICK, WE NEED TO GO NOW!
HE'S ALMOST ON US!
YANK
YOU THINK MONOMA'S GROUP IS OKAY, TOKAGE?
CLASS 1-B'S LIZARDY (SETSUNA TOKAGE)
LOOK, I'M WORRIED TOO, BUT WE'VE GOT OUR OWN PROBLEMS...
THOOM
THOOM

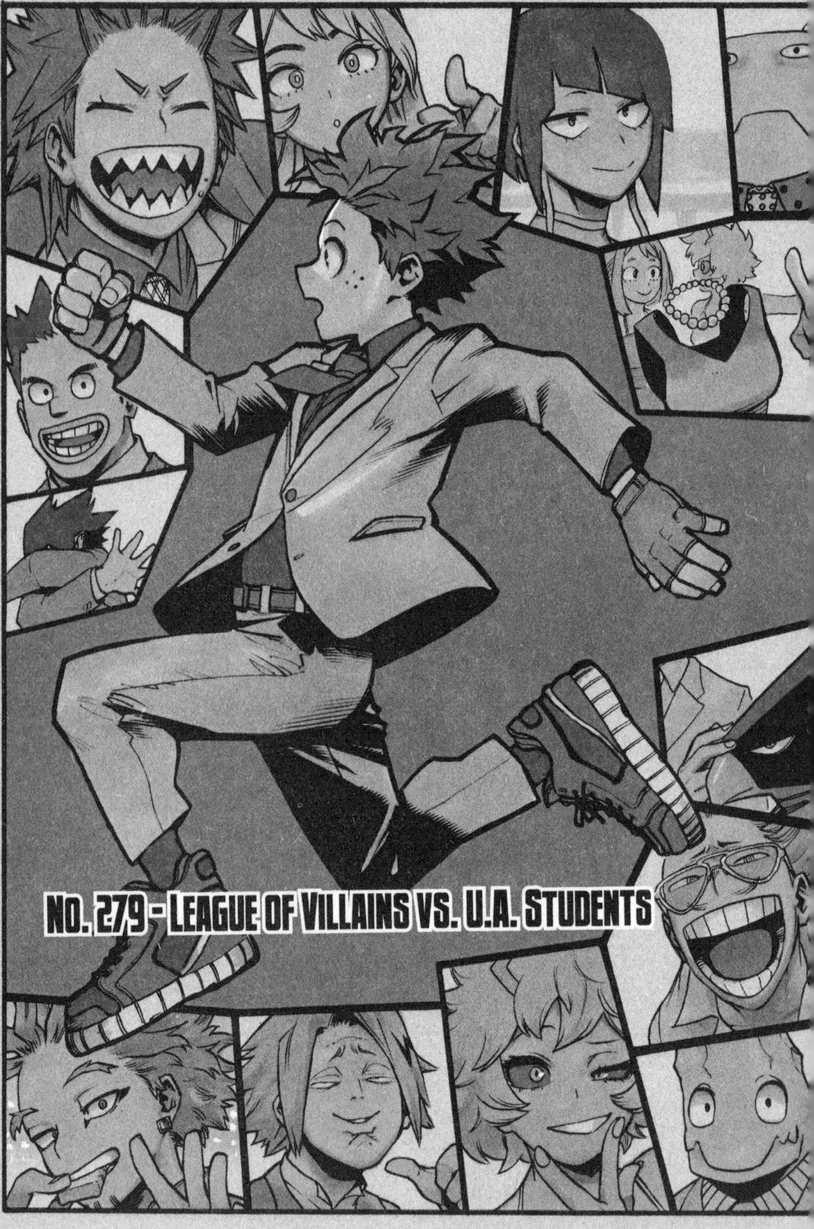
NO. 279 - LEAGUE OF VILLAINS VS. U.A. STUDENTS

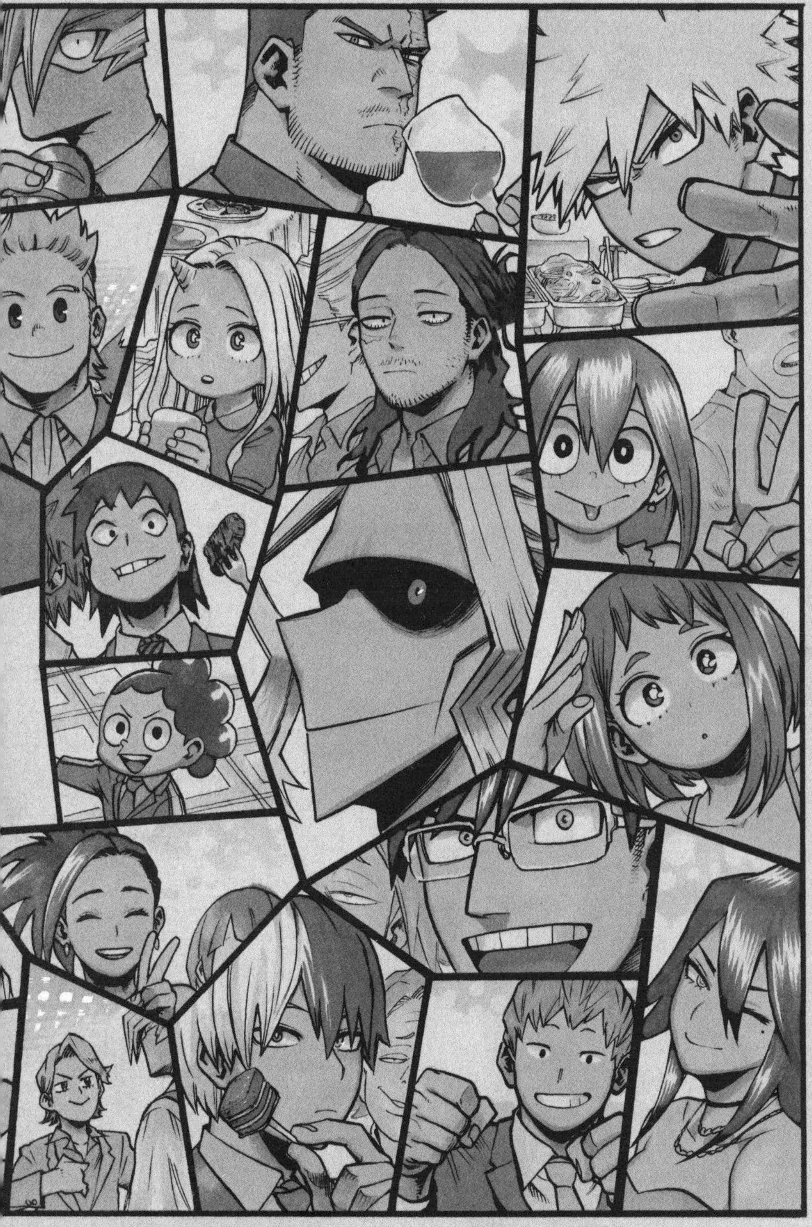

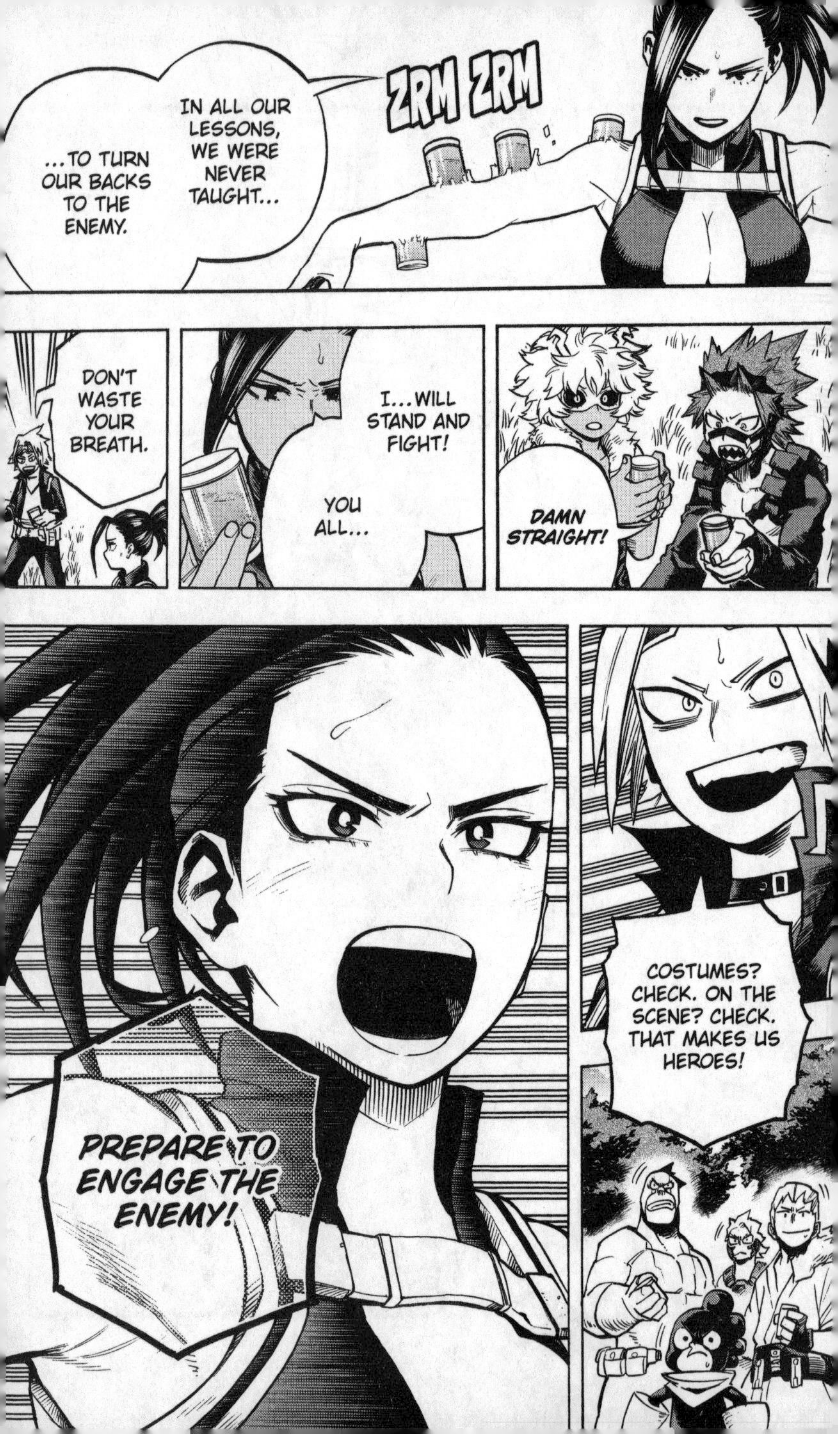
ZRM ZRM
IN ALL OUR LESSONS, WE WERE NEVER TAUGHT...
...TO TURN OUR BACKS TO THE ENEMY.
DAMN STRAIGHT!
I...WILL STAND AND FIGHT!
YOU ALL...
DON'T WASTE YOUR BREATH.
COSTUMES? CHECK. ON THE SCENE? CHECK. THAT MAKES US HEROES!
PREPARE TO ENGAGE THE ENEMY!

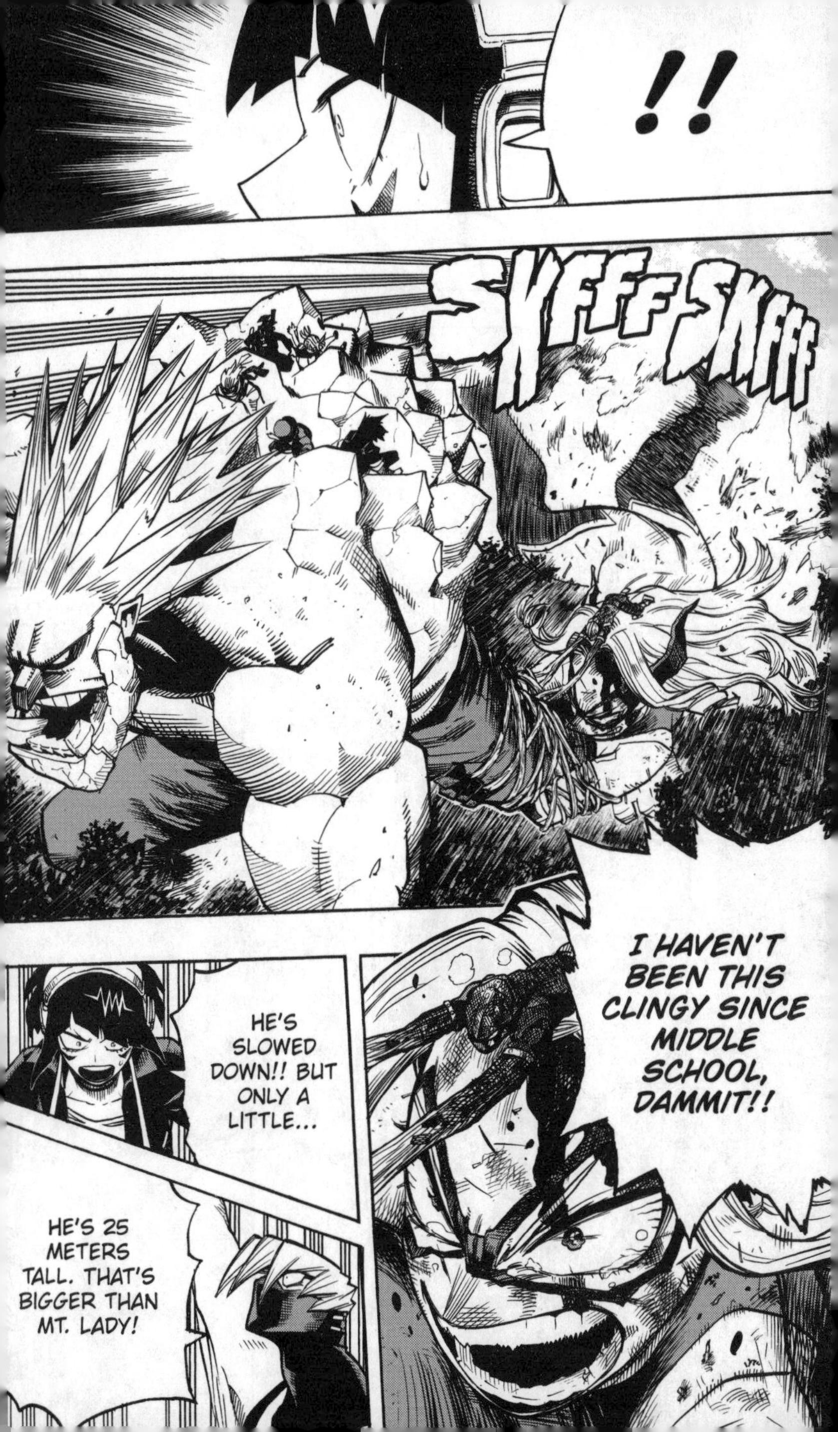
!!
SKFFF SKFFF
I HAVEN'T BEEN THIS CLINGY SINCE MIDDLE SCHOOL, DAMMIT!!
HE'S SLOWED DOWN!! BUT ONLY A LITTLE...
HE'S 25 METERS TALL. THAT'S BIGGER THAN MT. LADY!

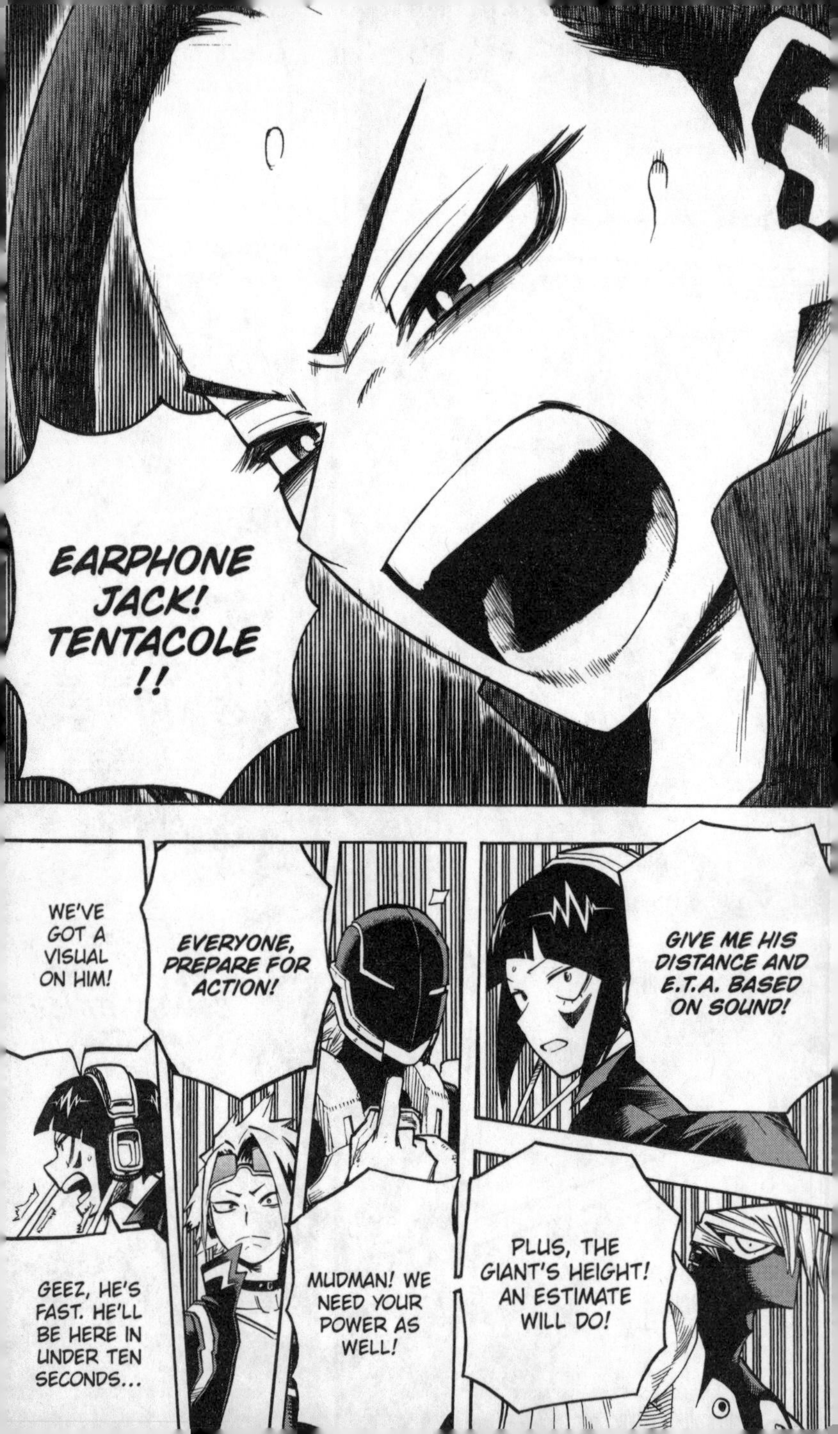
EARPHONE JACK! TENTACOLE !!
GIVE ME HIS DISTANCE AND E.T.A. BASED ON SOUND!
PLUS, THE GIANT'S HEIGHT! AN ESTIMATE WILL DO!
MUDMAN! WE NEED YOUR POWER AS WELL!
EVERYONE, PREPARE FOR ACTION!
WE'VE GOT A VISUAL ON HIM!
GEEZ, HE'S FAST. HE'LL BE HERE IN UNDER TEN SECONDS...

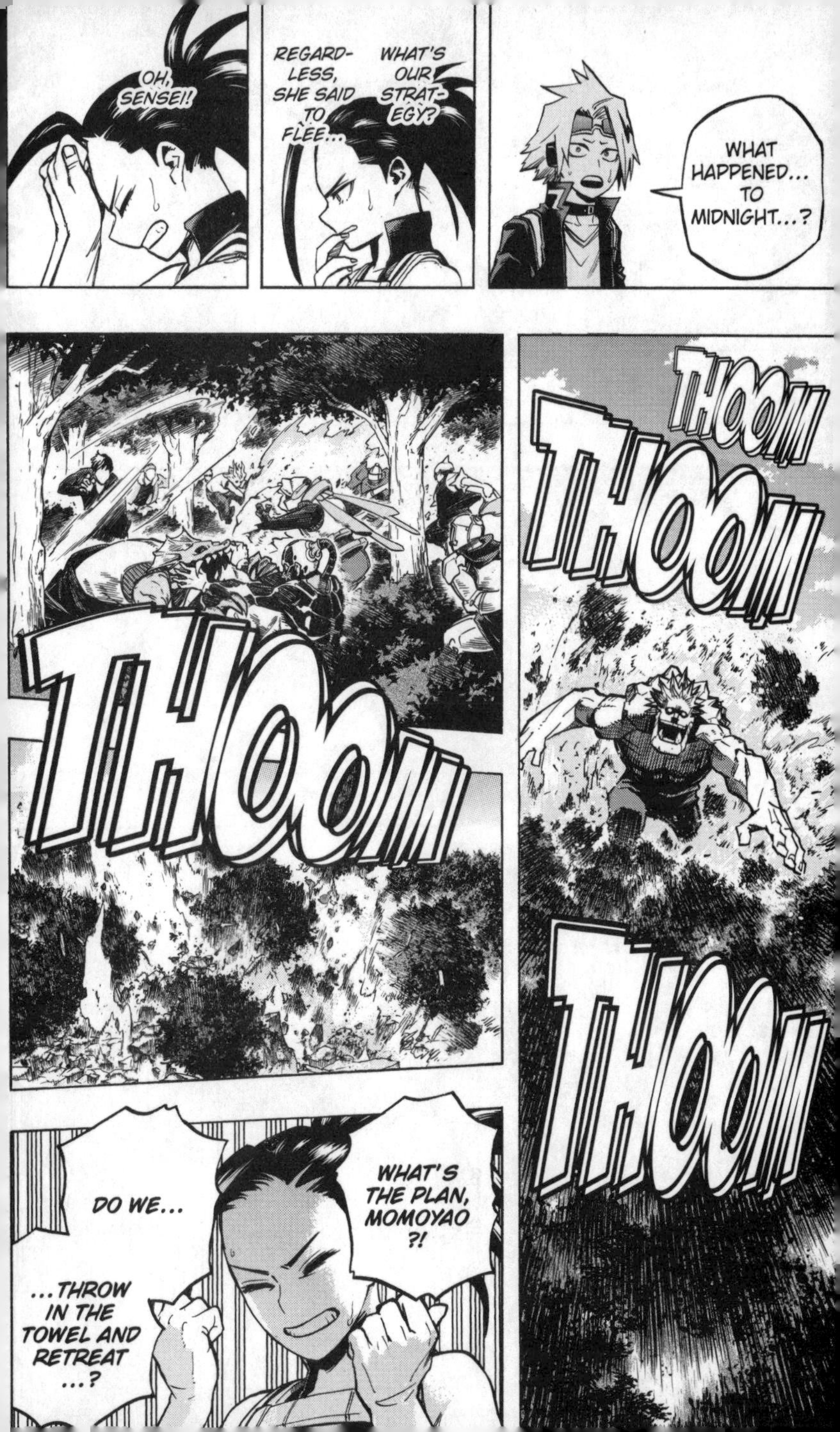
WHAT HAPPENED... TO MIDNIGHT...?
WHAT'S OUR STRATEGY?
REGARDLESS, SHE SAID TO FLEE...
OH, SENSEI!
THOOM
THOOM
THOOM
THOOM
WHAT'S THE PLAN, MOMOYAO?!
DO WE...
...THROW IN THE TOWEL AND RETREAT...?

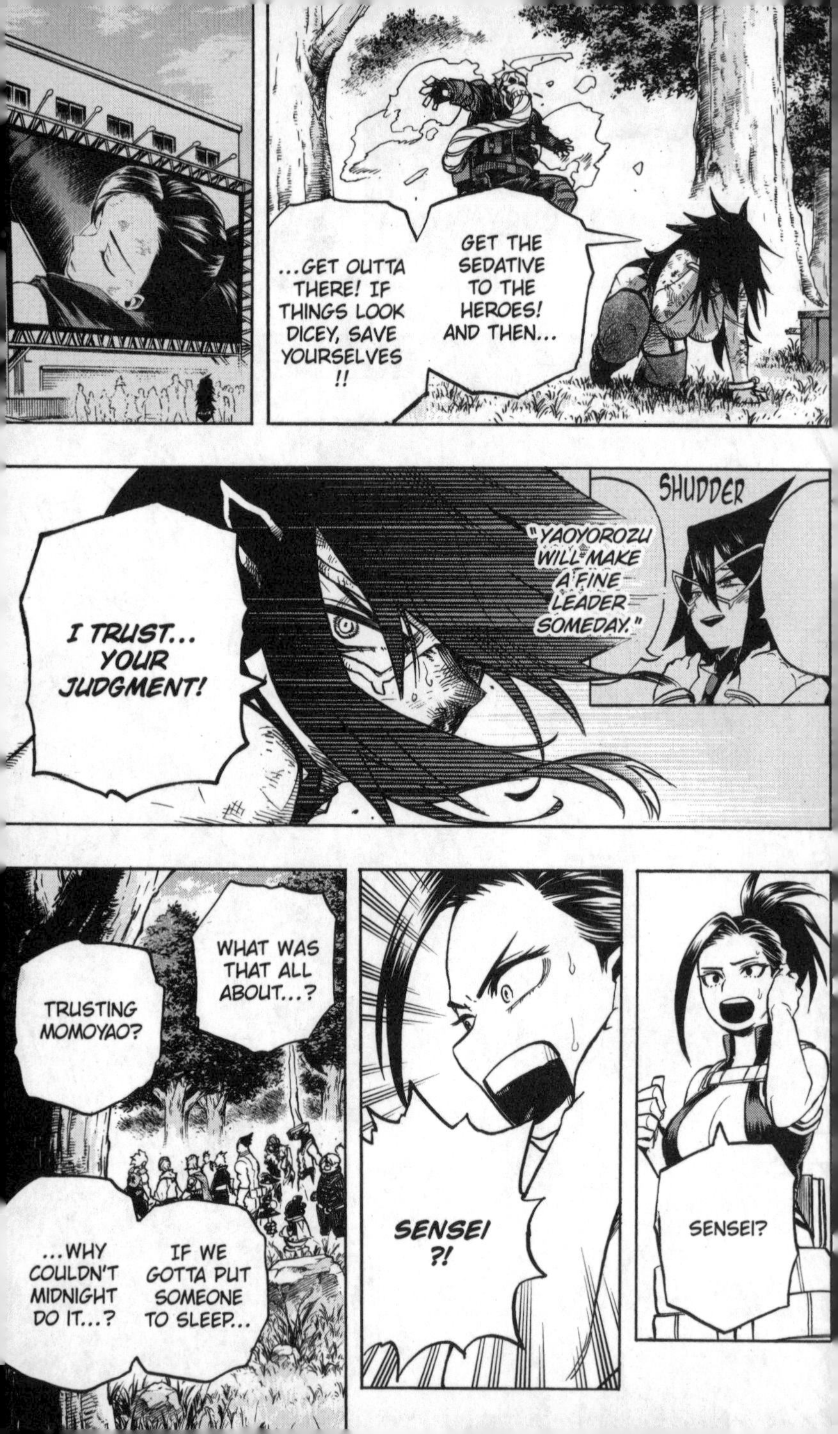
GET THE SEDATIVE TO THE HEROES! AND THEN...
...GET OUTTA THERE! IF THINGS LOOK DICEY, SAVE YOURSELVES !!
SHUDDER
"YAOYOROZU WILL MAKE A FINE LEADER SOMEDAY."
I TRUST... YOUR JUDGMENT!
SENSEI?
SENSEI ?!
WHAT WAS THAT ALL ABOUT...?
TRUSTING MOMOYAO?
IF WE GOTTA PUT SOMEONE TO SLEEP...
...WHY COULDN'T MIDNIGHT DO IT...?

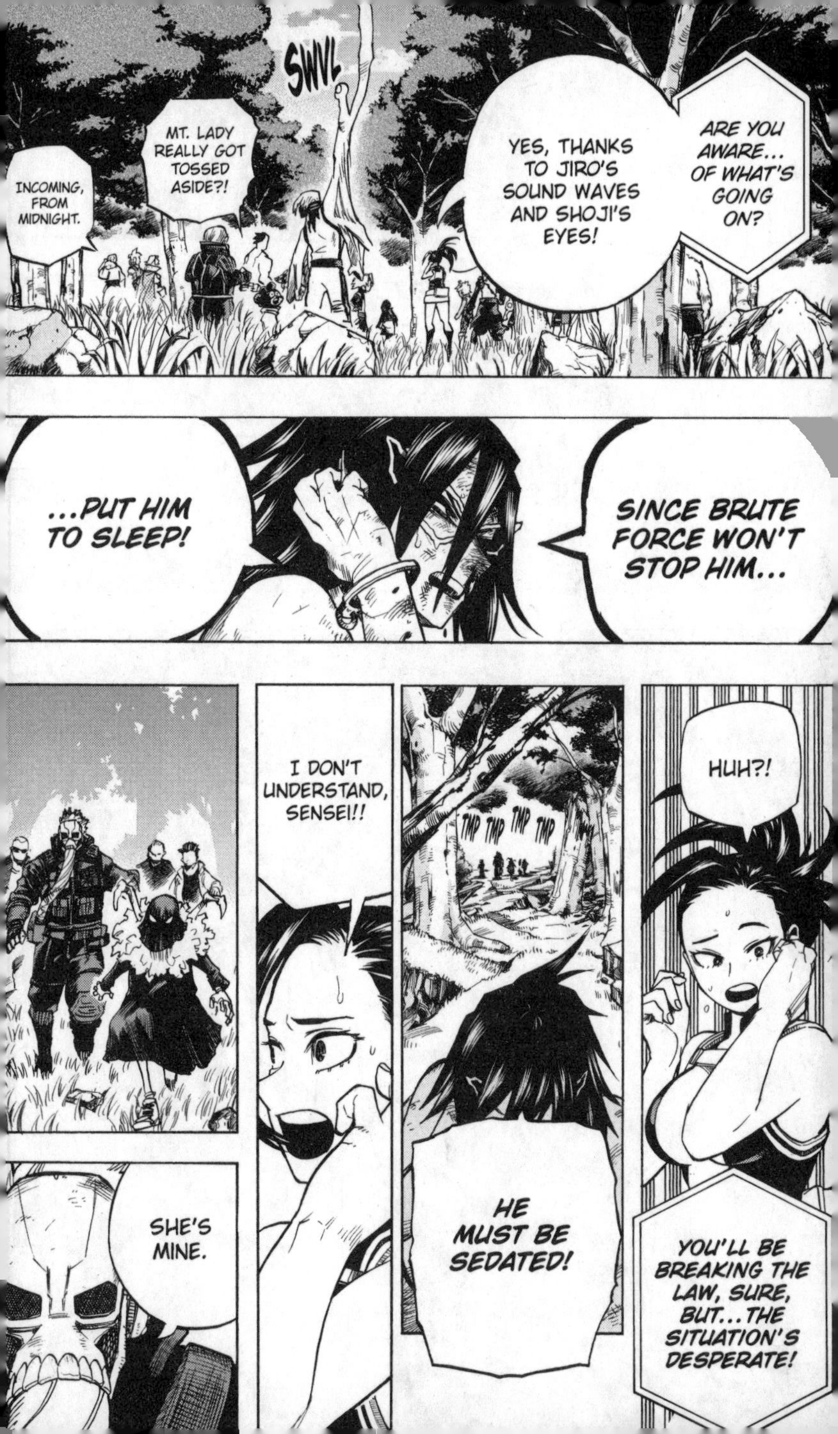
ARE YOU AWARE... OF WHAT'S GOING ON?
YES, THANKS TO JIRO'S SOUND WAVES AND SHOJI'S EYES!
SWVL
MT. LADY REALLY GOT TOSSED ASIDE?!
INCOMING, FROM MIDNIGHT.
SINCE BRUTE FORCE WON'T STOP HIM...
...PUT HIM TO SLEEP!
HUH?!
YOU'LL BE BREAKING THE LAW, SURE, BUT... THE SITUATION'S DESPERATE!
TMP TMP TMP TMP
HE MUST BE SEDATED!
I DON'T UNDERSTAND, SENSEI!!
SHE'S MINE.

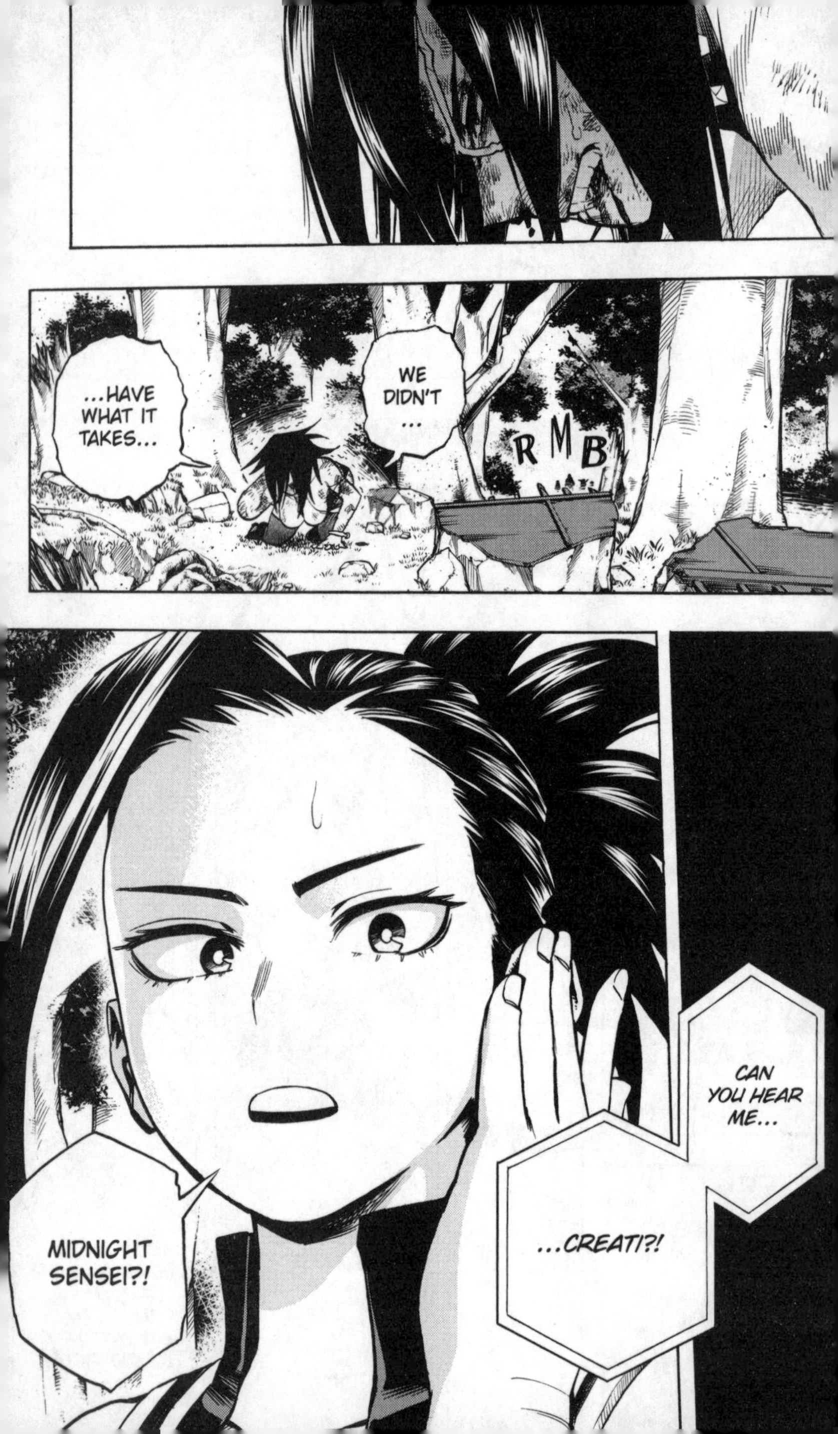
RMB
WE DIDN'T ...
...HAVE WHAT IT TAKES...
CAN YOU HEAR ME...
...CREATI?!
MIDNIGHT SENSEI?!

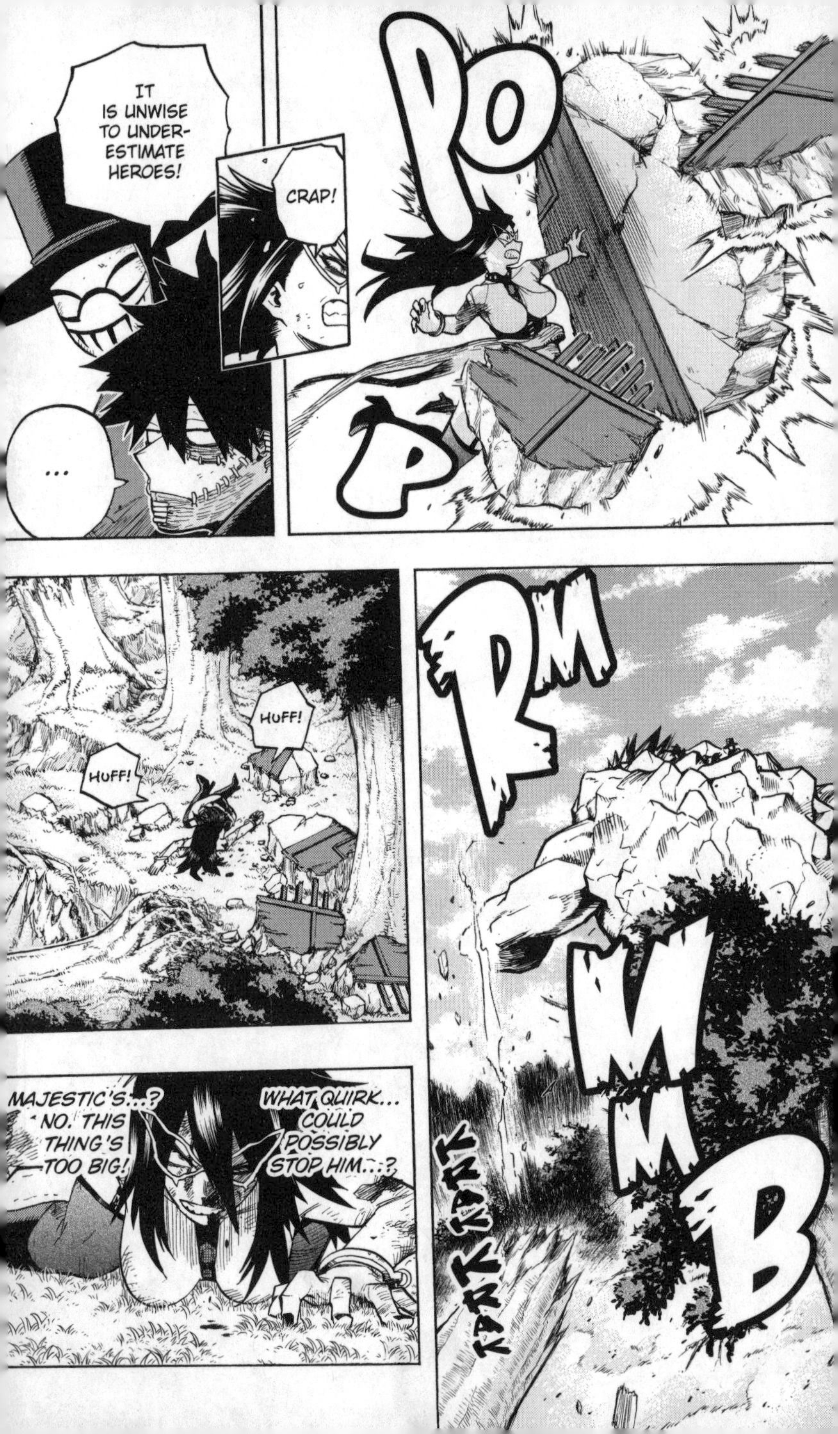

PO
P
CRAP!
IT IS UNWISE TO UNDER-ESTIMATE HEROES!
...
RM
M
M
B
KRAK KRAK
HUFF!
HUFF!
WHAT QUIRK... COULD POSSIBLY STOP HIM...?
MAJESTIC'S...? NO. THIS THING'S TOO BIG!

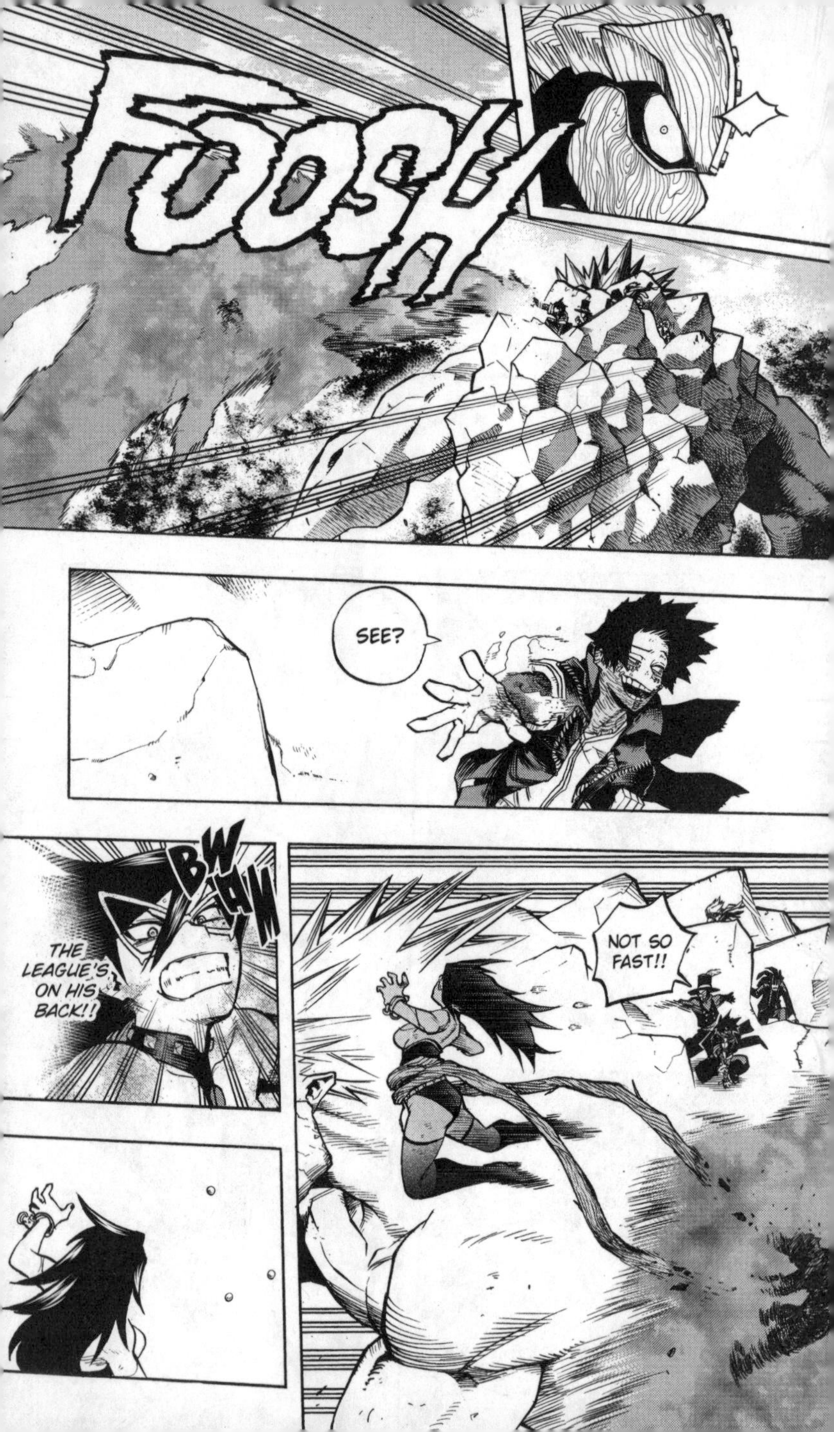
FOOSH
SEE?
NOT SO FAST!!
BWHAM
THE LEAGUE'S ON HIS BACK!!

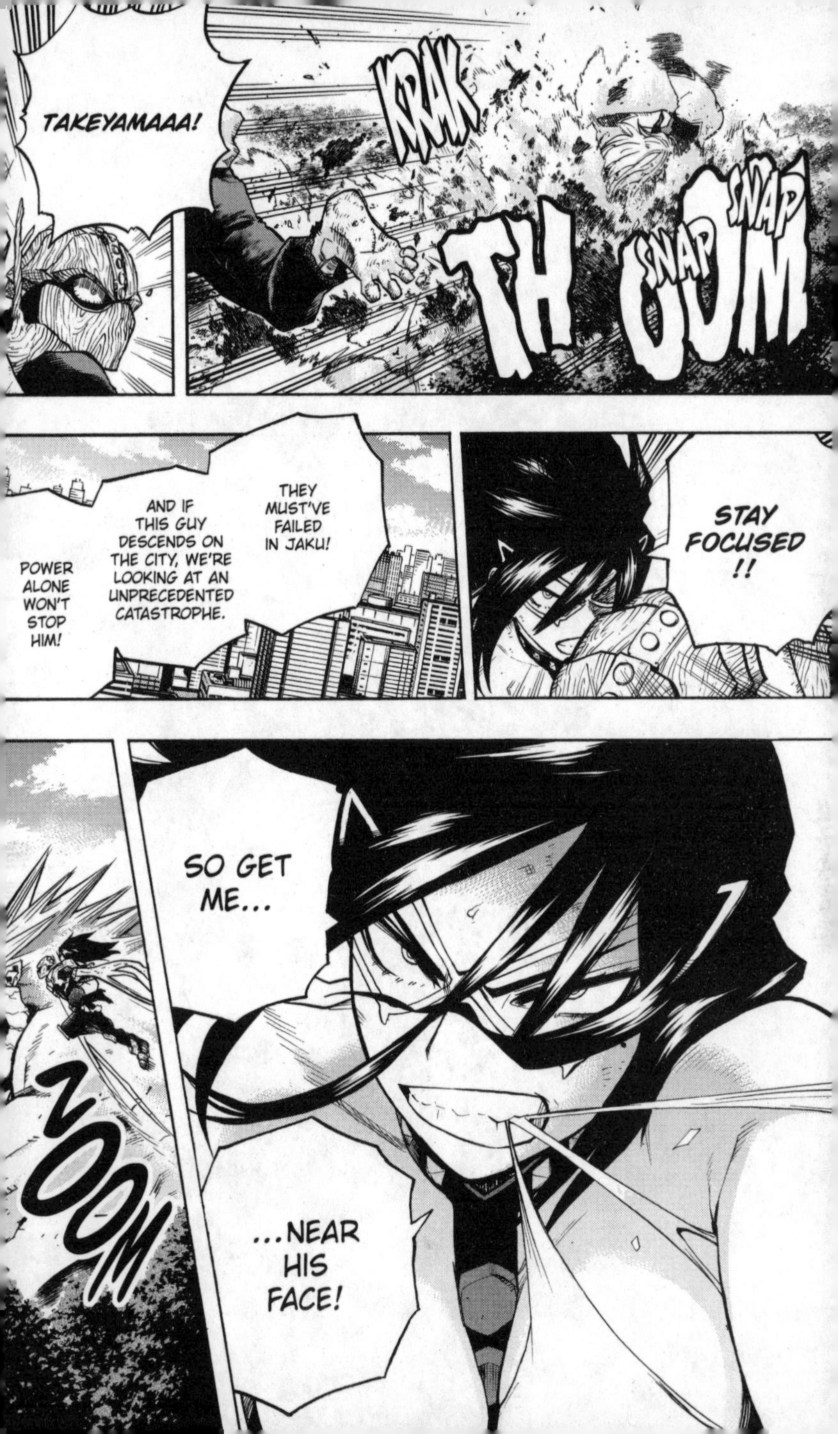
KRAK
SNAP
SNAP
THOOM
TAKEYAMAAA!
STAY FOCUSED!!
THEY MUST'VE FAILED IN JAKU!
AND IF THIS GUY DESCENDS ON THE CITY, WE'RE LOOKING AT AN UNPRECEDENTED CATASTROPHE.
POWER ALONE WON'T STOP HIM!
SO GET ME...
...NEAR HIS FACE!
ZOOOM

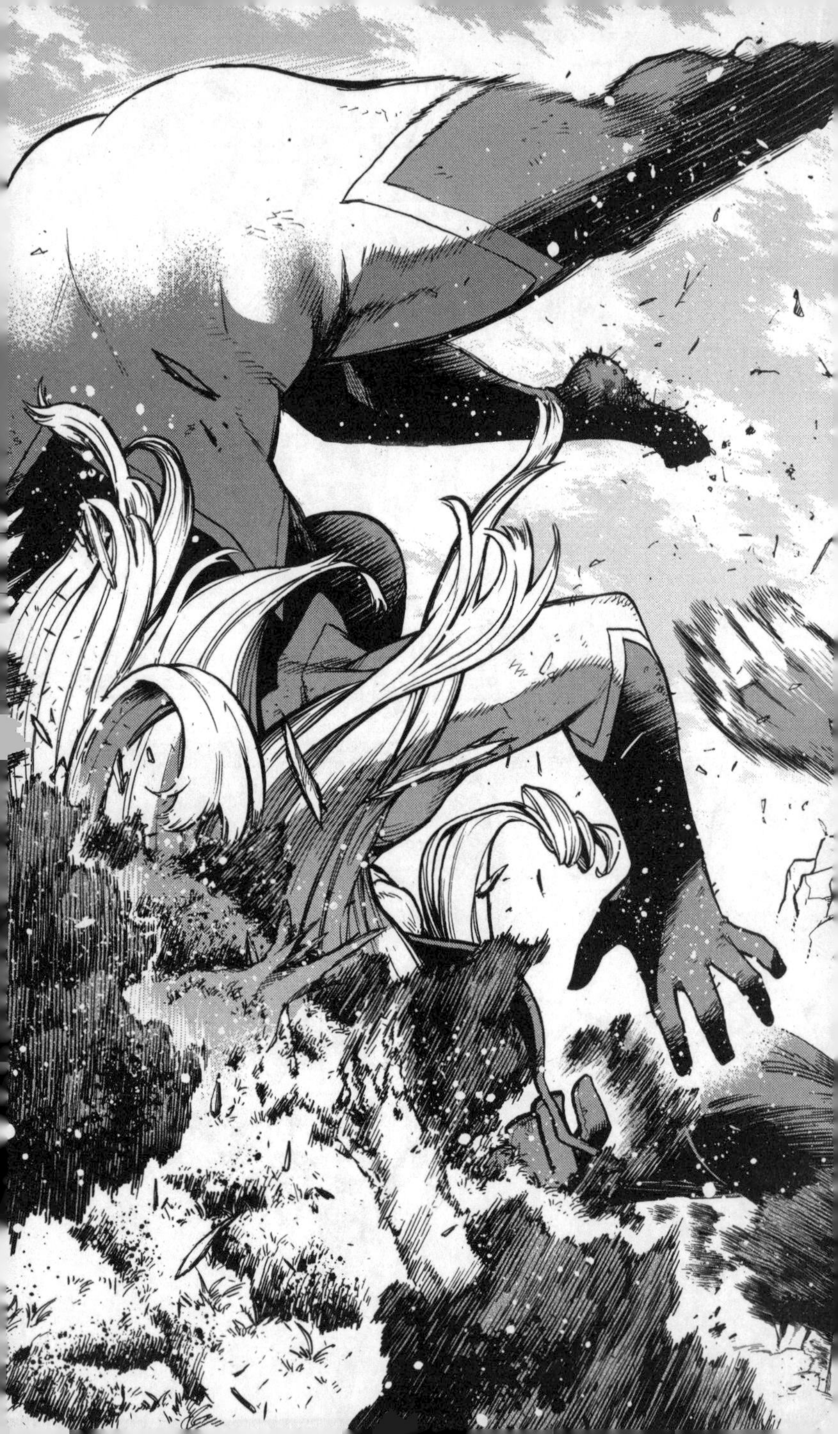

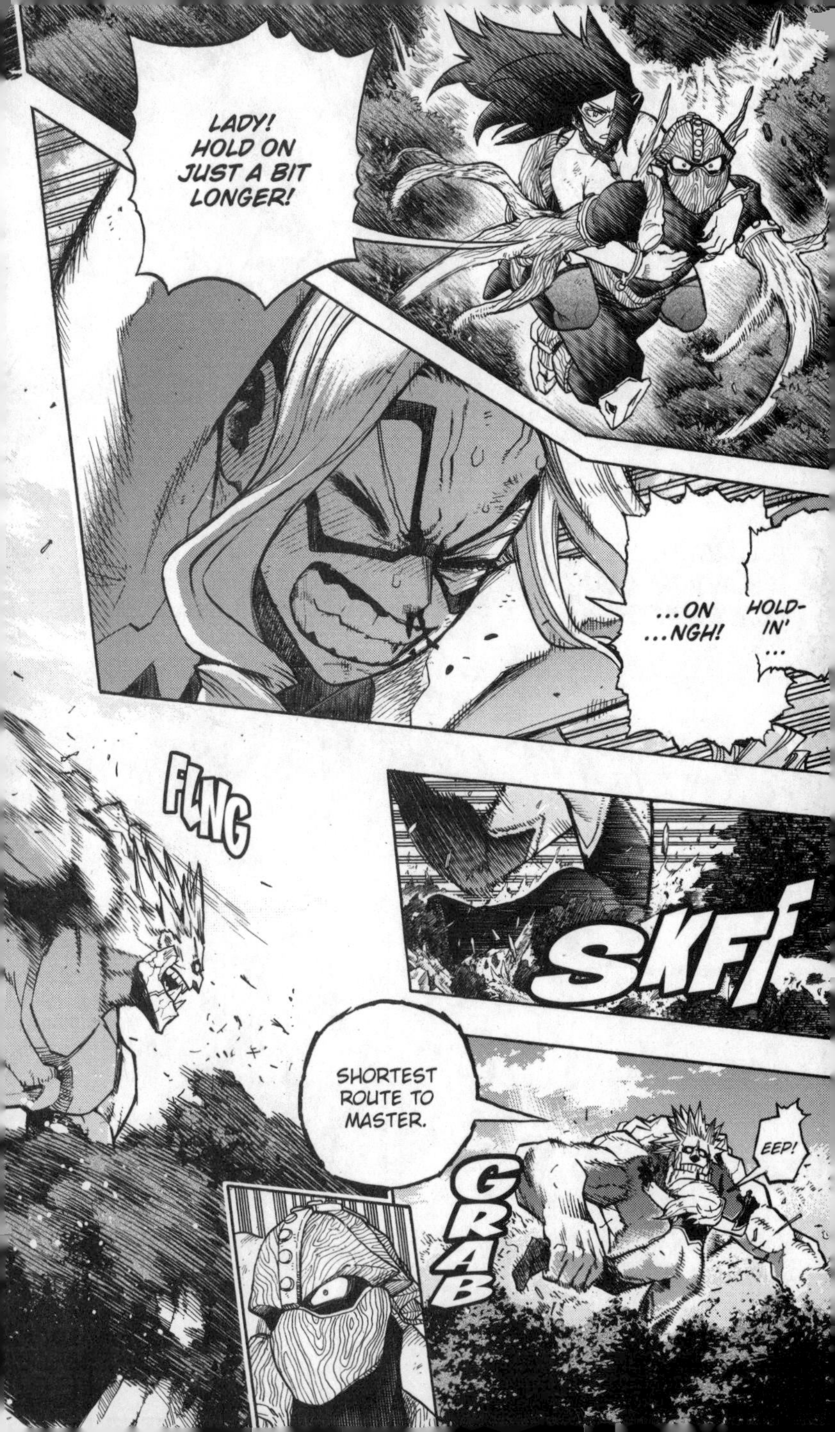
LADY! HOLD ON JUST A BIT LONGER!
HOLDIN' ...
...ON ...NGH!
SKFF
FLING
EEP!
GRAB
SHORTEST ROUTE TO MASTER.

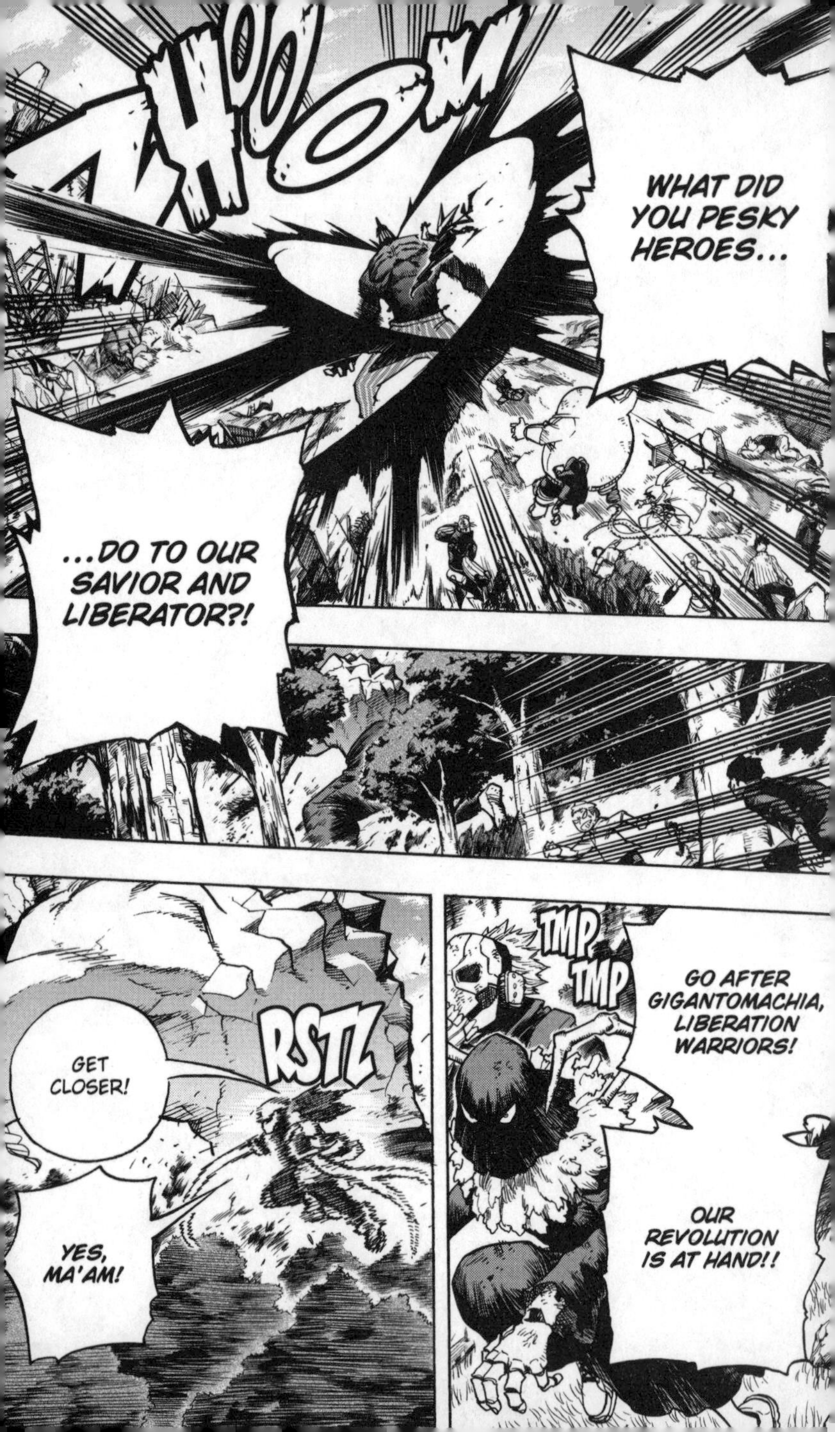
ZHOOOOM
WHAT DID YOU PESKY HEROES...
...DO TO OUR SAVIOR AND LIBERATOR?!
TMP TMP
GO AFTER GIGANTOMACHIA, LIBERATION WARRIORS!
OUR REVOLUTION IS AT HAND!!
RSTL
GET CLOSER!
YES, MA'AM!

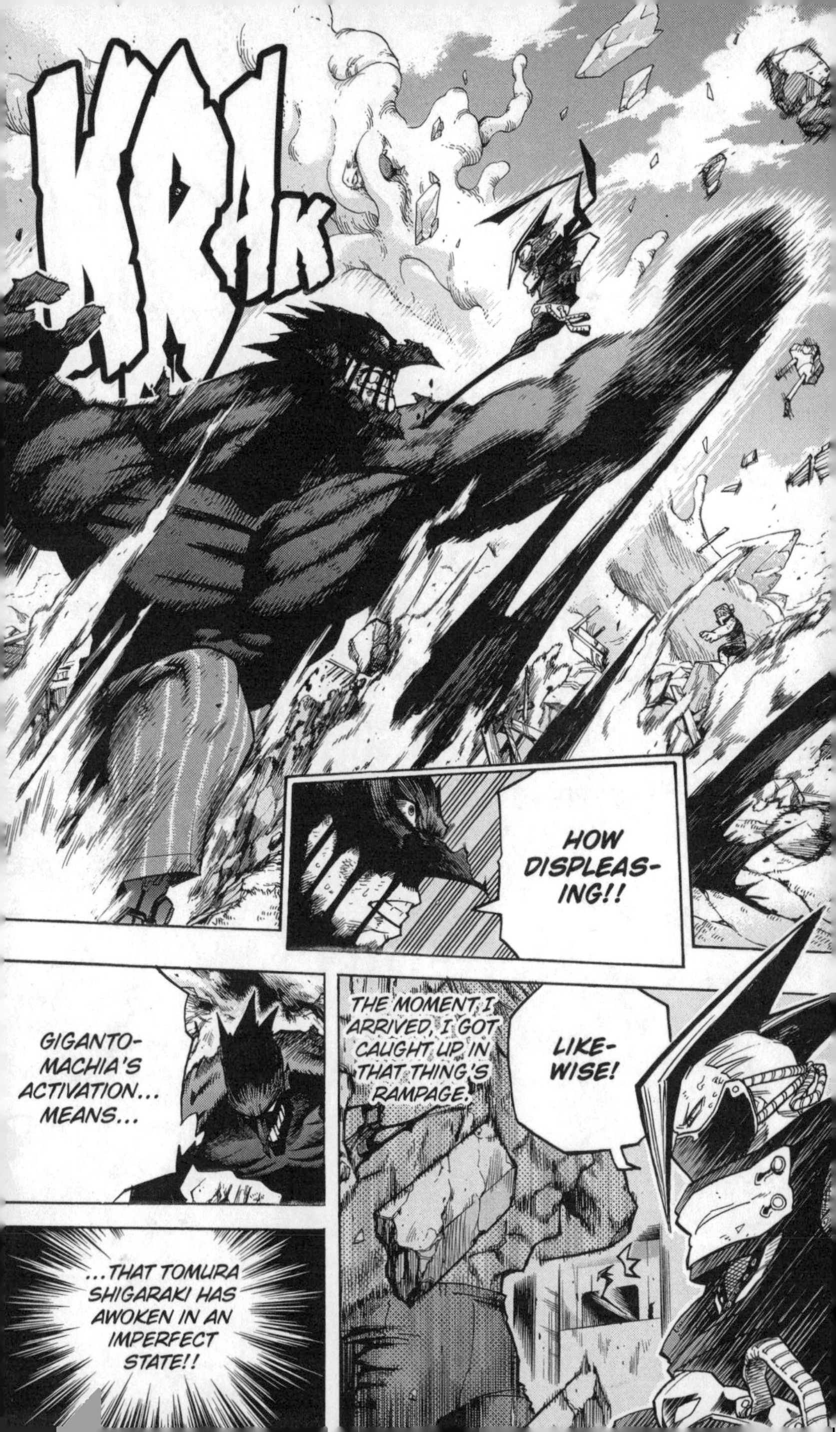
KRAK
HOW DISPLEASING!!
LIKE-WISE!
THE MOMENT I ARRIVED, I GOT CAUGHT UP IN THAT THING'S RAMPAGE.
GIGANTO-MACHIA'S ACTIVATION... MEANS...
...THAT TOMURA SHIGARAKI HAS AWOKEN IN AN IMPERFECT STATE!!

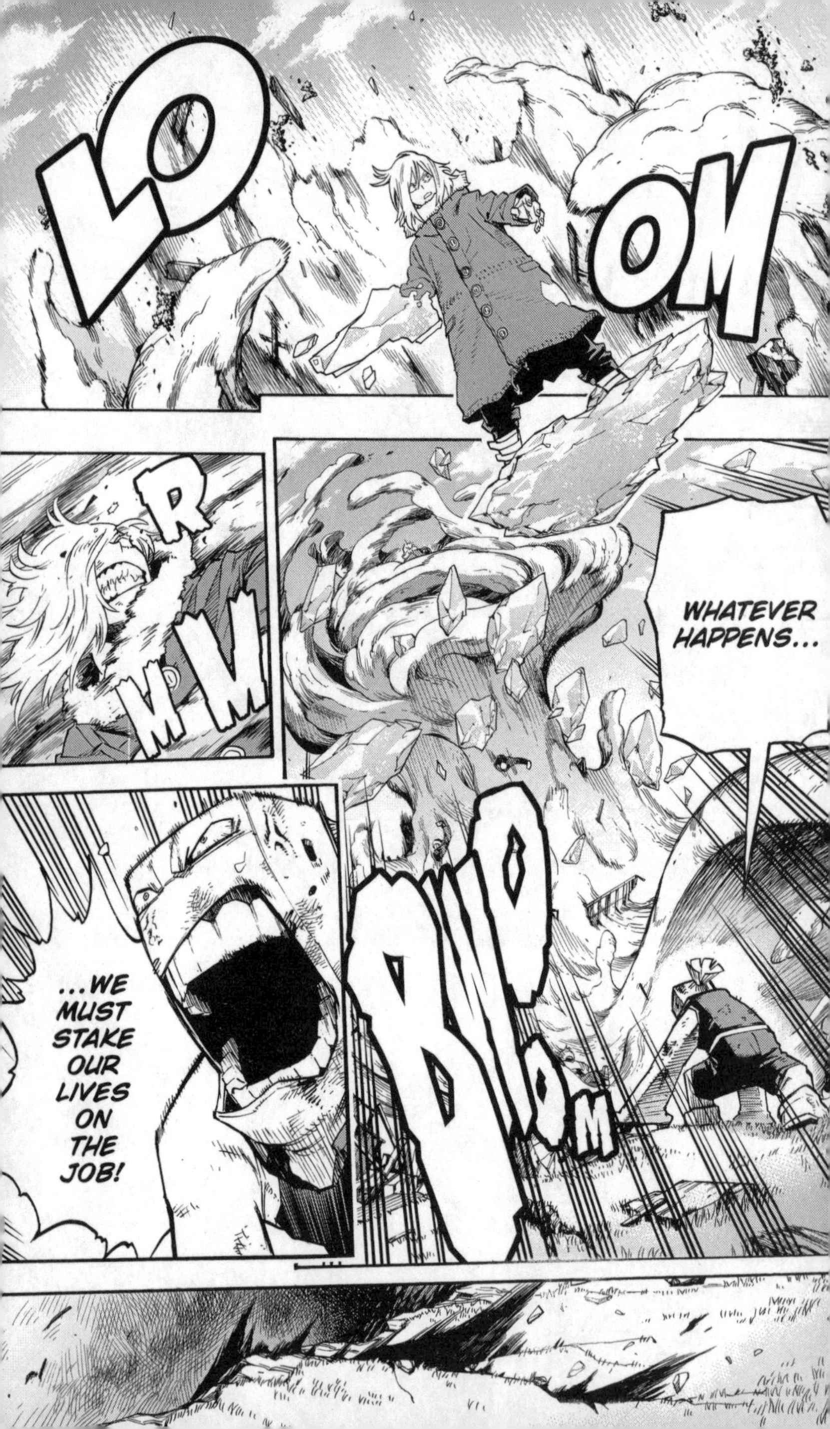
WHATEVER HAPPENS...
...WE MUST STAKE OUR LIVES ON THE JOB!

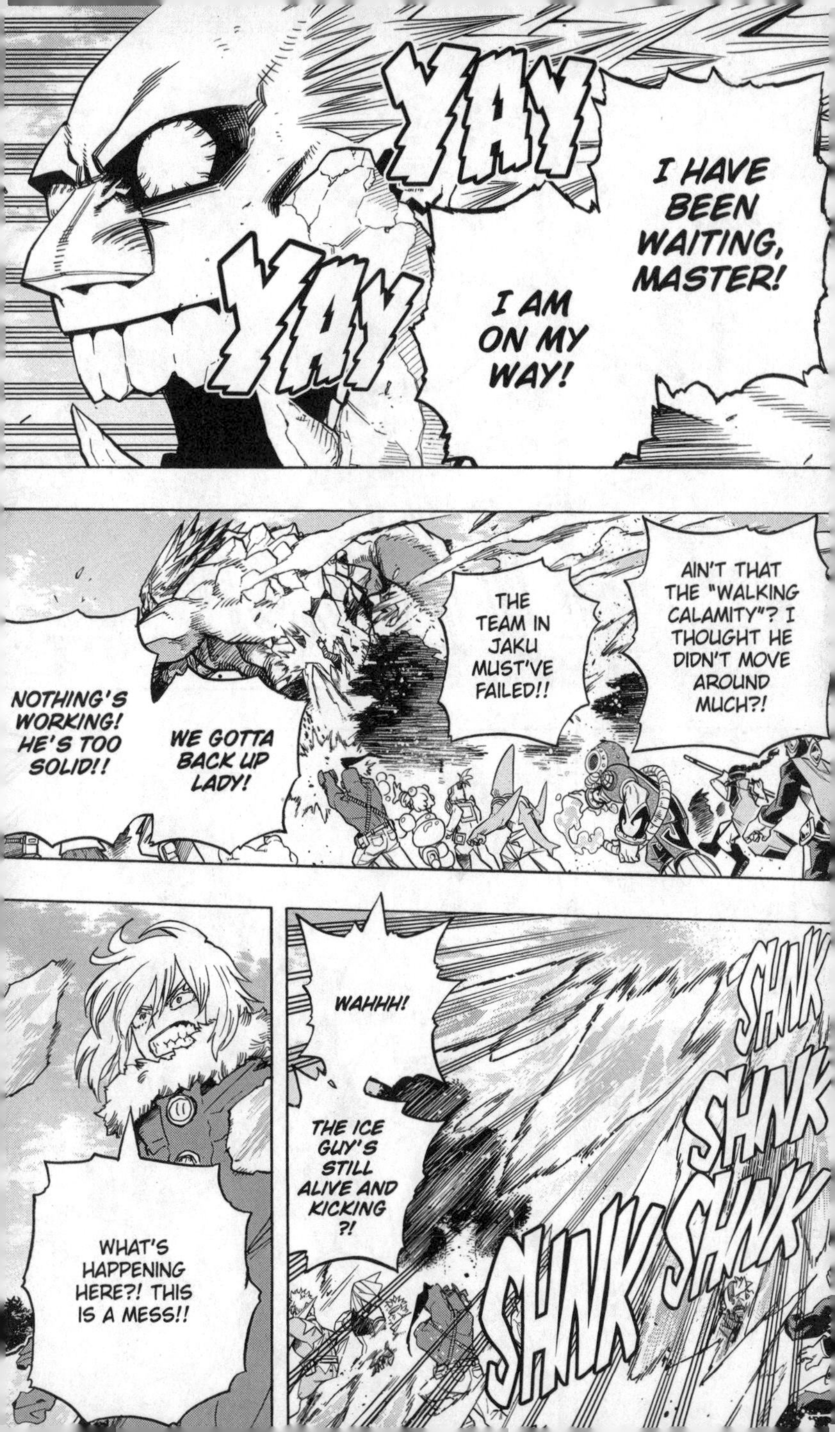
YAY
YAY
I HAVE BEEN WAITING, MASTER!
I AM ON MY WAY!
AIN'T THAT THE "WALKING CALAMITY"? I THOUGHT HE DIDN'T MOVE AROUND MUCH?!
THE TEAM IN JAKU MUST'VE FAILED!!
WE GOTTA BACK UP LADY!
NOTHING'S WORKING! HE'S TOO SOLID!!
SHNK
SHNK
SHNK
SHNK
WAHHH!
THE ICE GUY'S STILL ALIVE AND KICKING ?!
WHAT'S HAPPENING HERE?! THIS IS A MESS!!

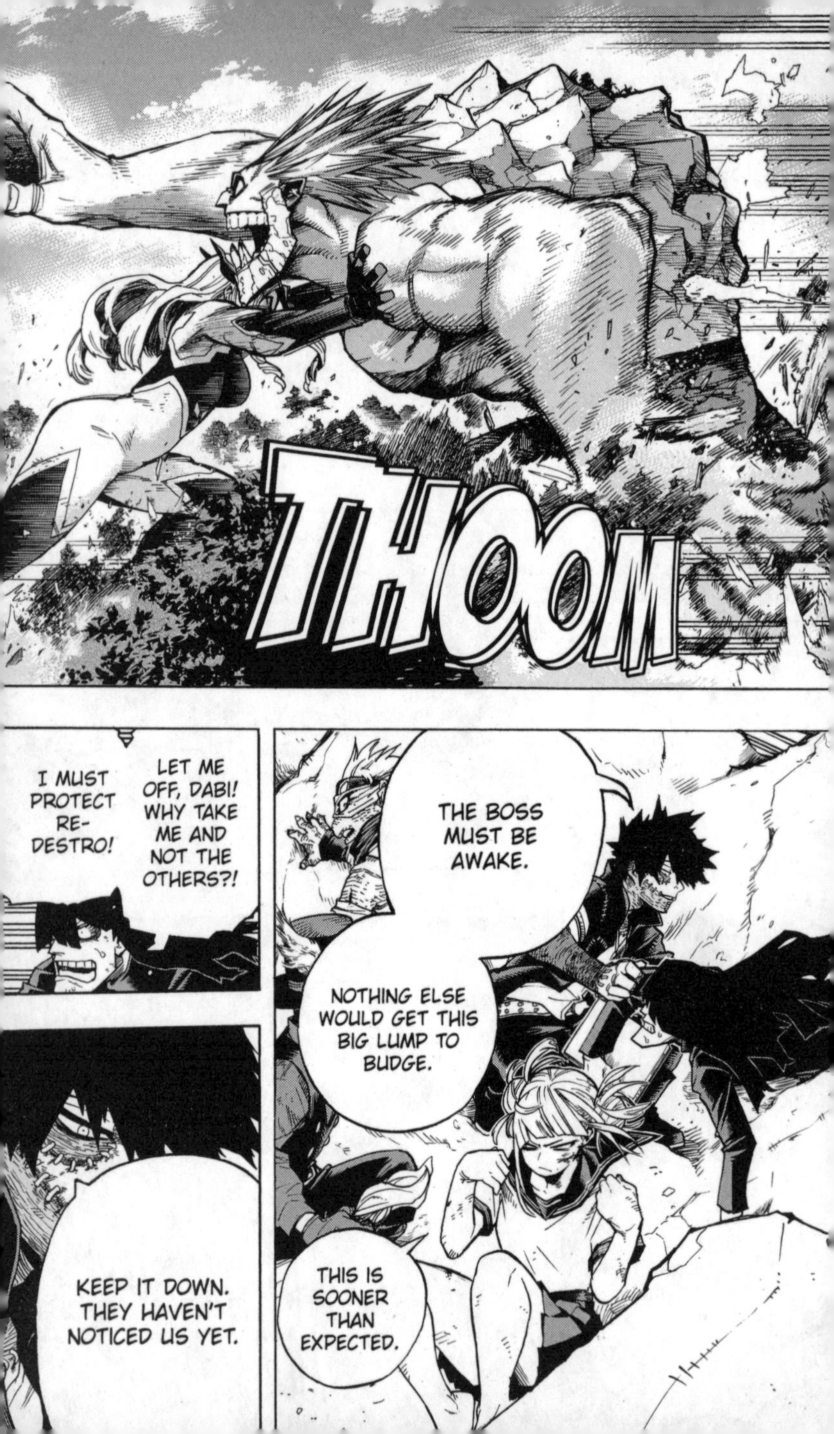
THOOM
THE BOSS MUST BE AWAKE.
NOTHING ELSE WOULD GET THIS BIG LUMP TO BUDGE.
THIS IS SOONER THAN EXPECTED.
LET ME OFF, DABI! WHY TAKE ME AND NOT THE OTHERS?!
I MUST PROTECT RE-DESTRO!
KEEP IT DOWN. THEY HAVEN'T NOTICED US YET.

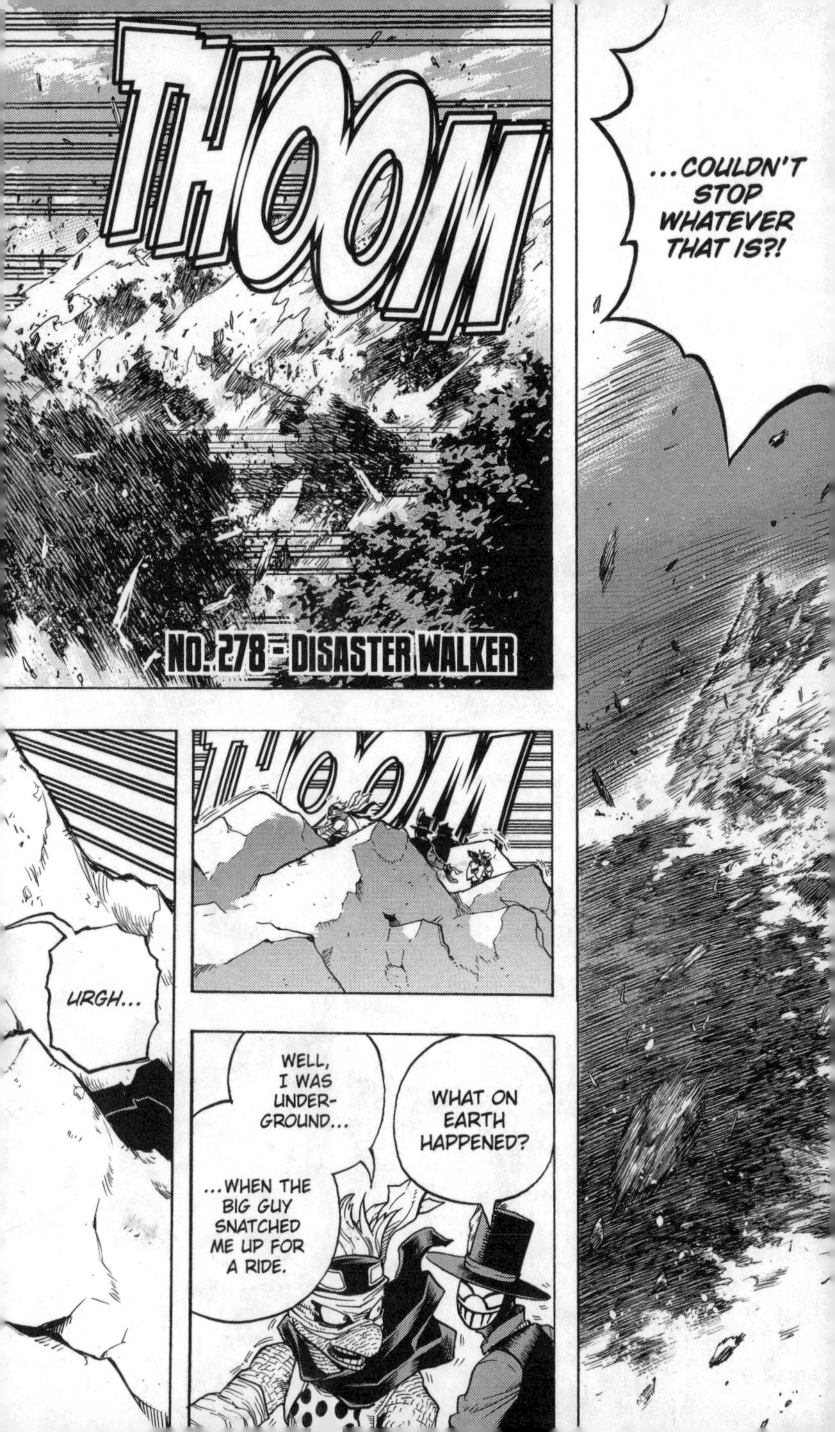
...COULDN'T STOP WHATEVER THAT IS?!
THOOM
NO. 278 - DISASTER WALKER
THOOM
WHAT ON EARTH HAPPENED?
WELL, I WAS UNDER-GROUND...
...WHEN THE BIG GUY SNATCHED ME UP FOR A RIDE.
URGH...

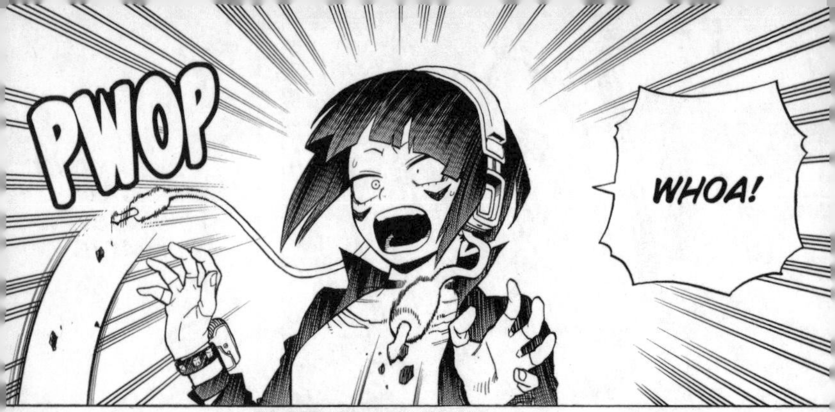
WHOA!
PWOP

NO. 278 - DISASTER WALKER

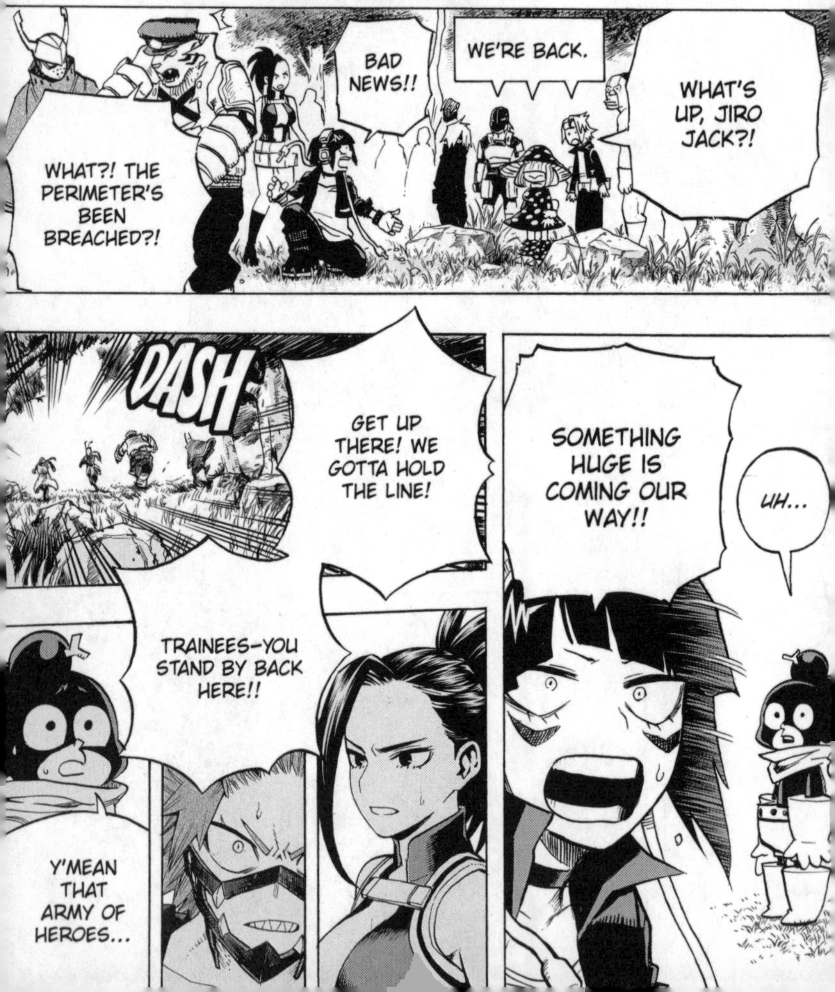
WHAT'S UP, JIRO JACK?!
WE'RE BACK.
BAD NEWS!!
WHAT?! THE PERIMETER'S BEEN BREACHED?!
SOMETHING HUGE IS COMING OUR WAY!!
UH...
GET UP THERE! WE GOTTA HOLD THE LINE!
DASH
TRAINEES—YOU STAND BY BACK HERE!!
Y'MEAN THAT ARMY OF HEROES...

For chapter 273, in the previous volume… (When Machia's giant arm rose up behind Toga. That part. If you don't remember, check out volume 28!!)

This is a scene I wanted to include, and it made me weep to have to cut it. These sorts of deleted scenes are born when I just draw the whole chapter however I want first, and then have to adjust things to account for page count. Consider this a bonus supplement.

16
Argh! Just a moment! What are you thinking?!
DADOOM
Machia's left hand
KRAK
Dabi
KRAK
AHHHH!
Machia's front
RMMMBL
Hrm? Where's Dabi?
Here, I packed extra clothing for you.
17
Shigaraki must've woken up!
And you sniffed him out? So now you're scooping us up...
Dabi, running downstairs...
Just a sec, Machia.
RMMMBL
There's someone else I'll be needing!!
Lower Level
Dabi
GRAB
Huh?!
From the day we met, I knew you'd be perfect for this.
Eek!
What's this about?!

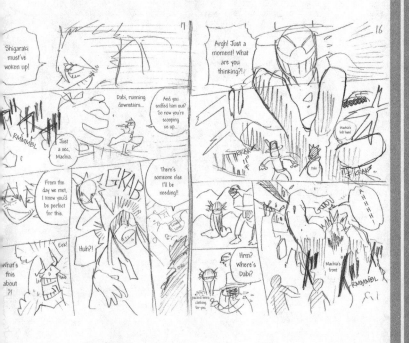

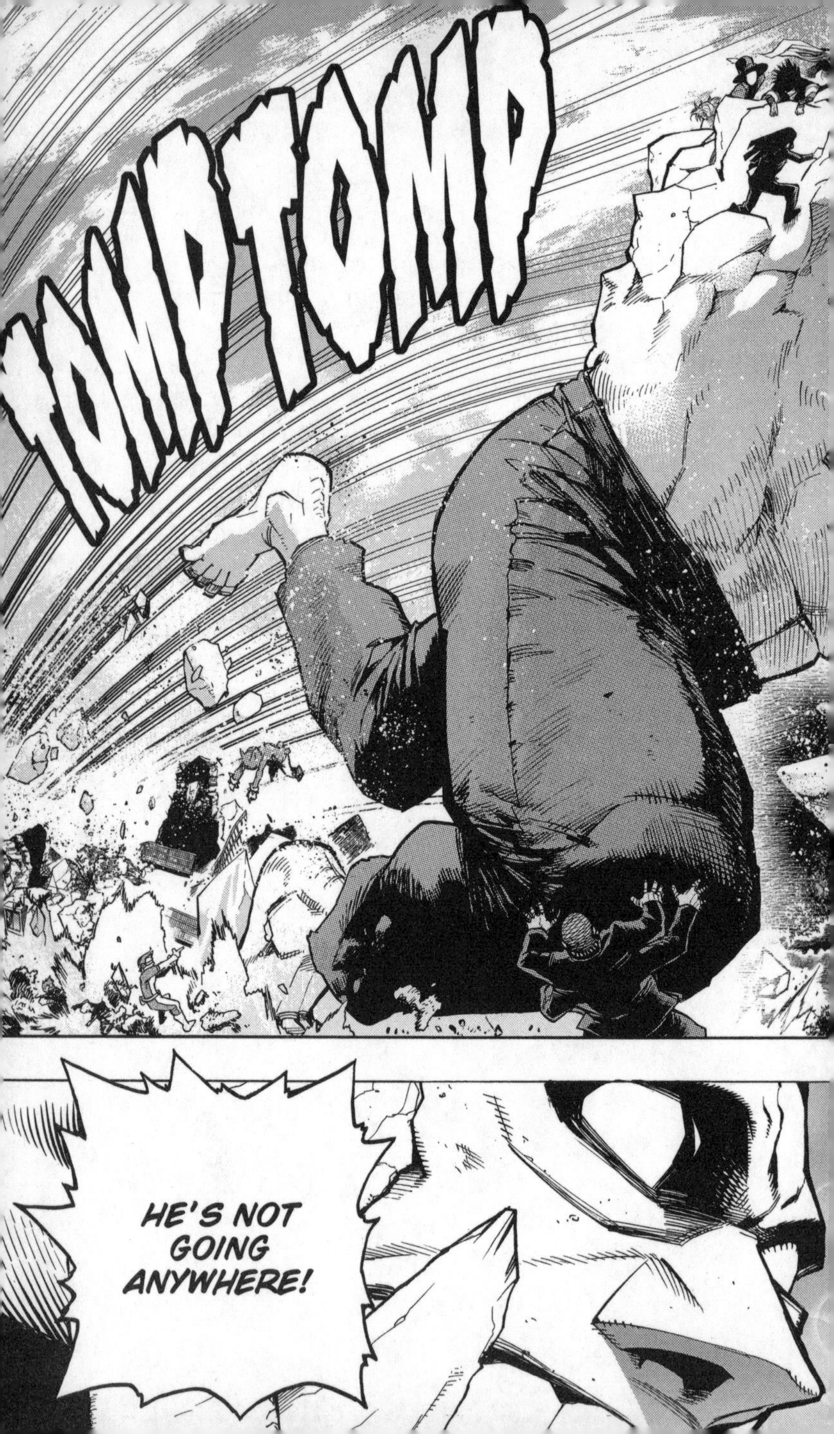
TOMP TOMP
HE'S NOT GOING ANYWHERE!

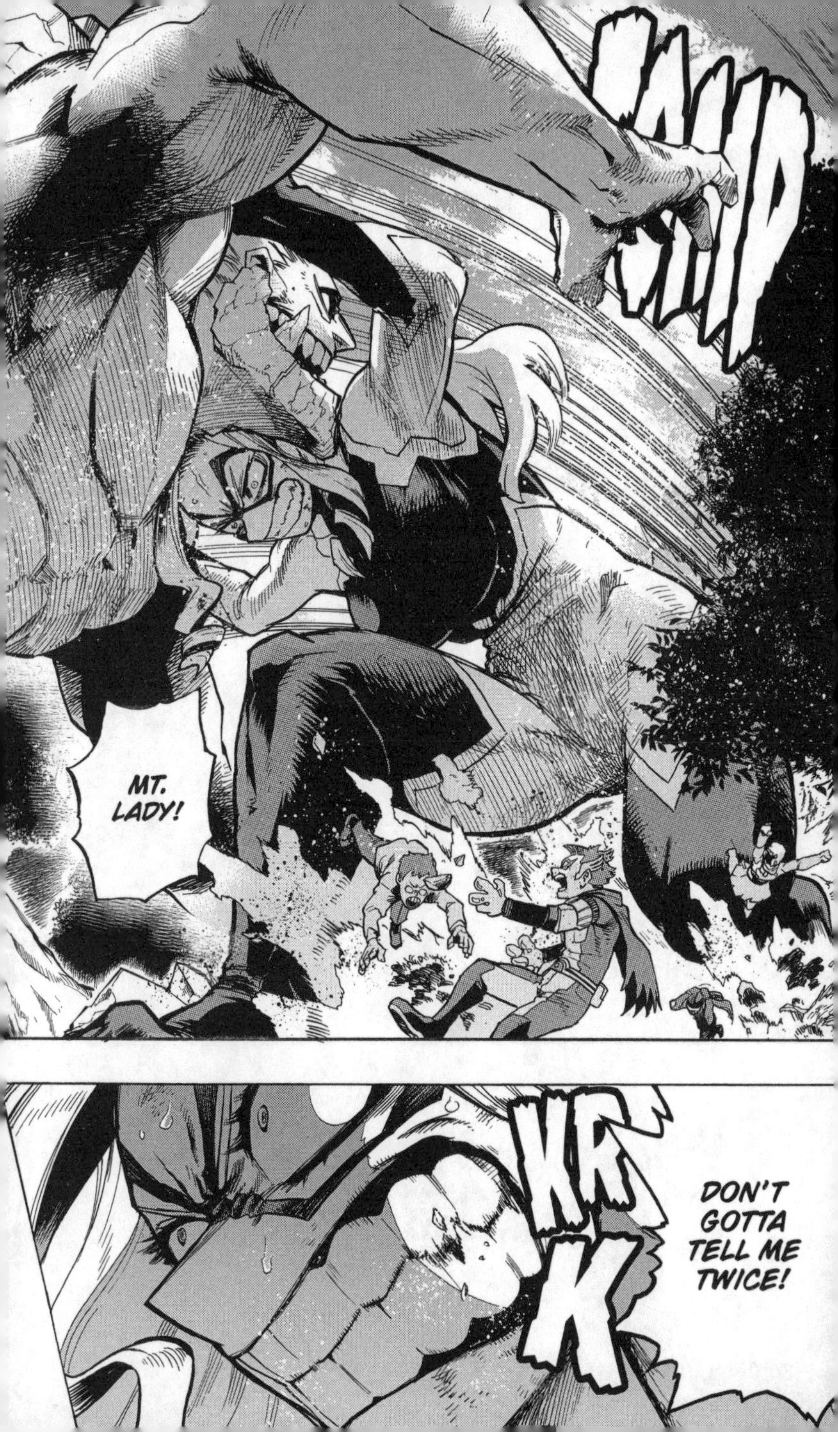
MT. LADY!
KRK
DON'T GOTTA TELL ME TWICE!

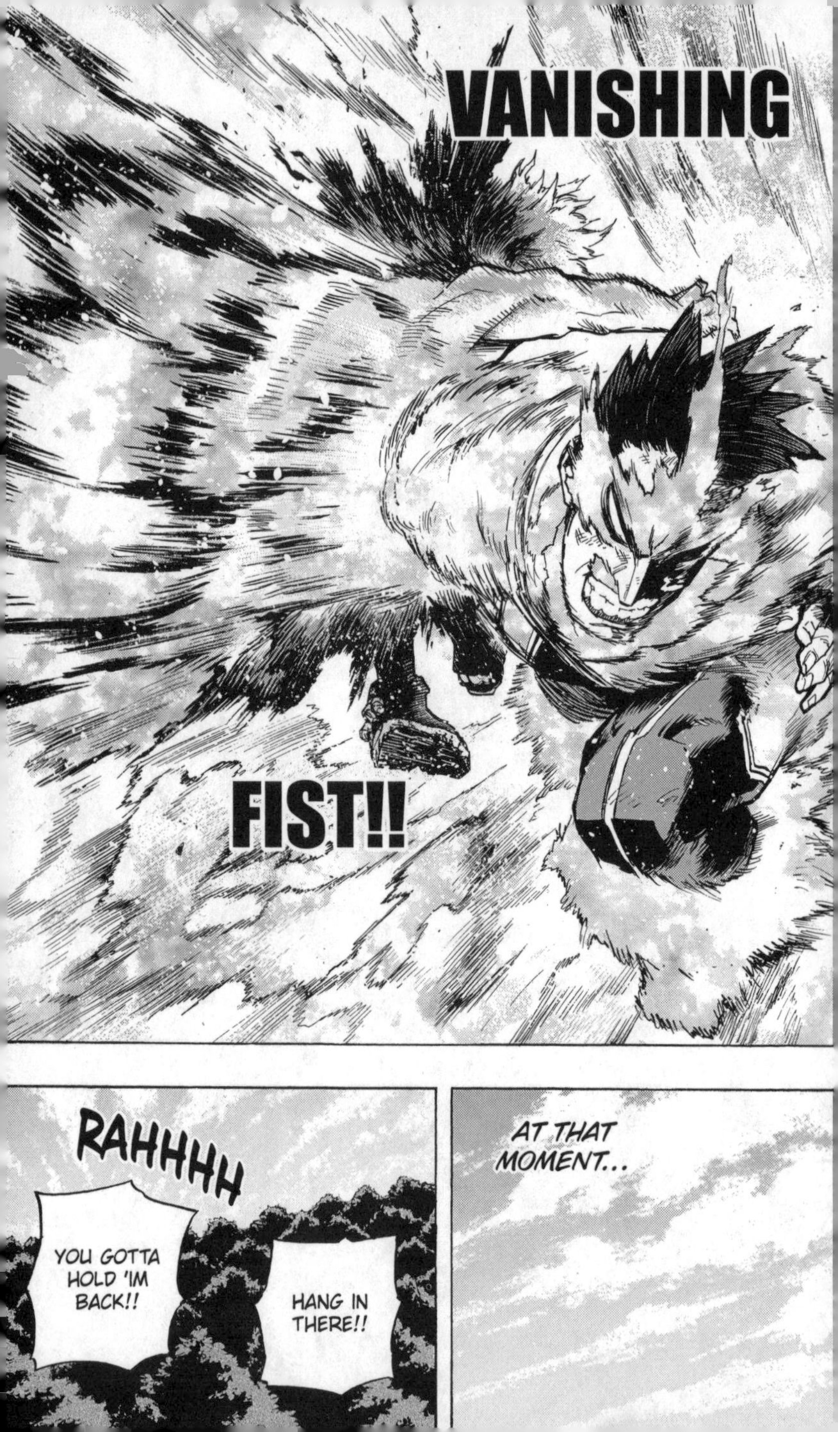
VANISHING
FIST!!
AT THAT MOMENT...
RAHHHH
HANG IN THERE!!
YOU GOTTA HOLD 'IM BACK!!

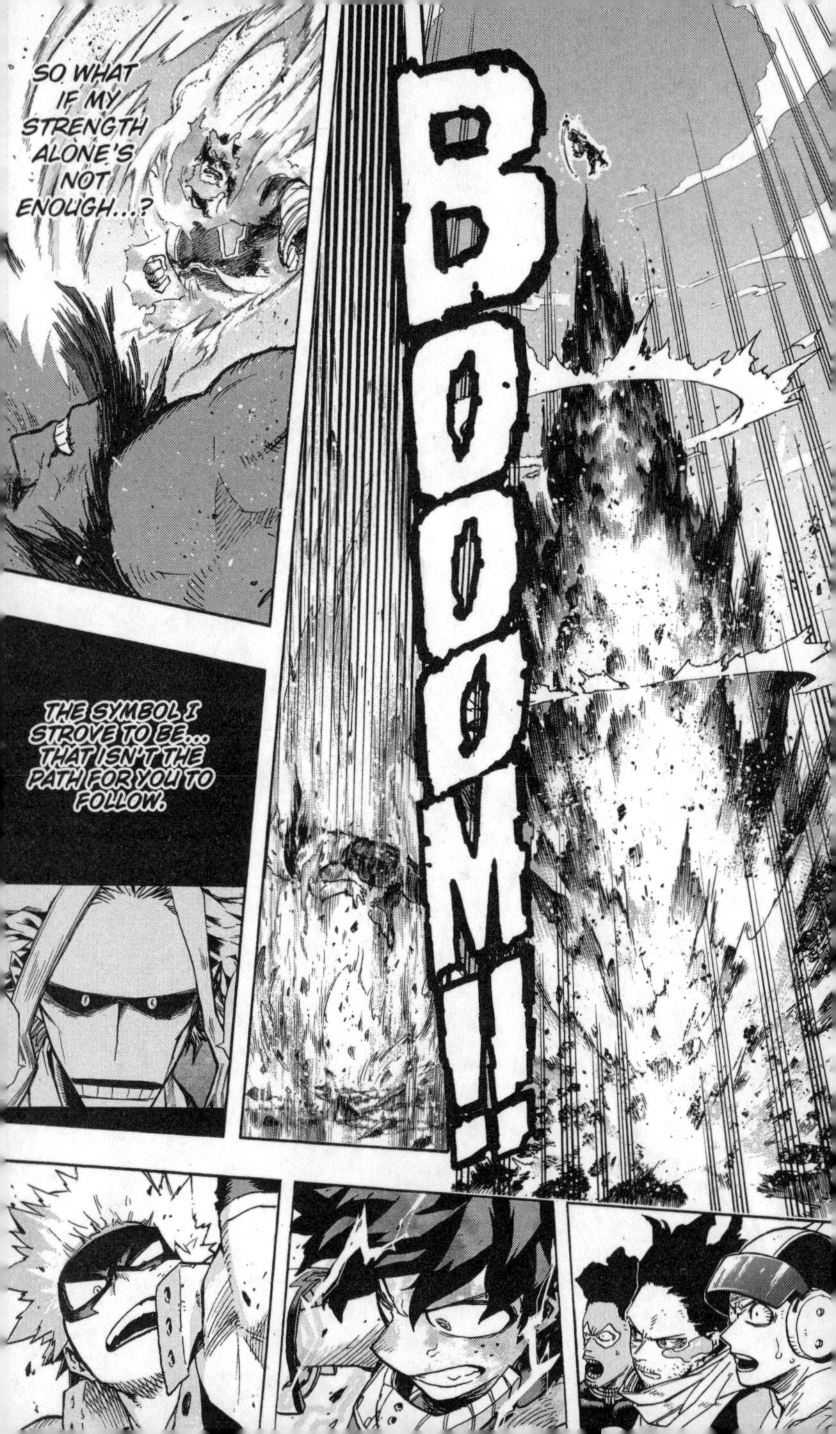
BOOOOM!!
SO WHAT IF MY STRENGTH ALONE'S NOT ENOUGH...?
THE SYMBOL I STROVE TO BE... THAT ISN'T THE PATH FOR YOU TO FOLLOW.

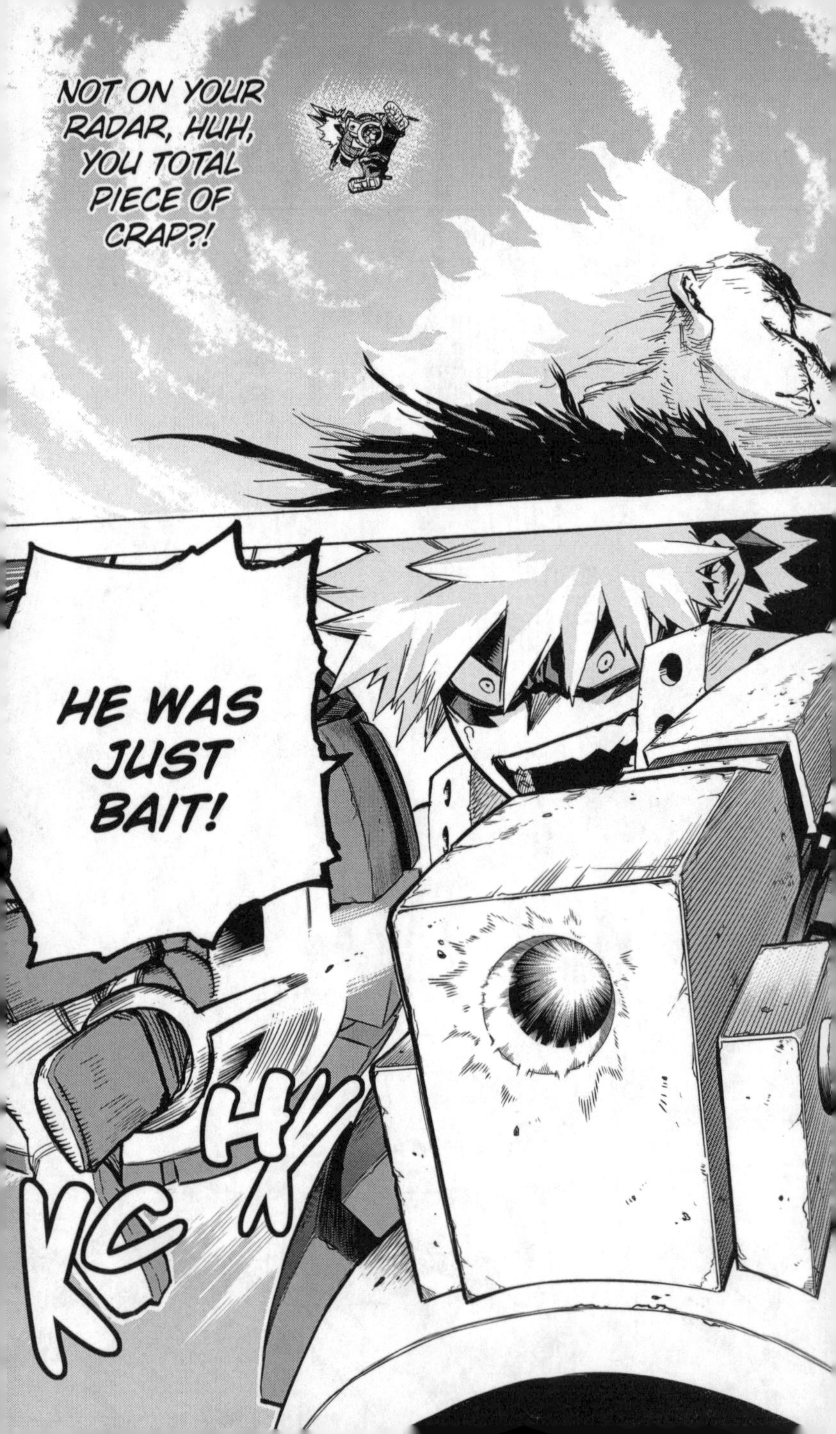
NOT ON YOUR RADAR, HUH, YOU TOTAL PIECE OF CRAP?!
HE WAS JUST BAIT!
KCHHH

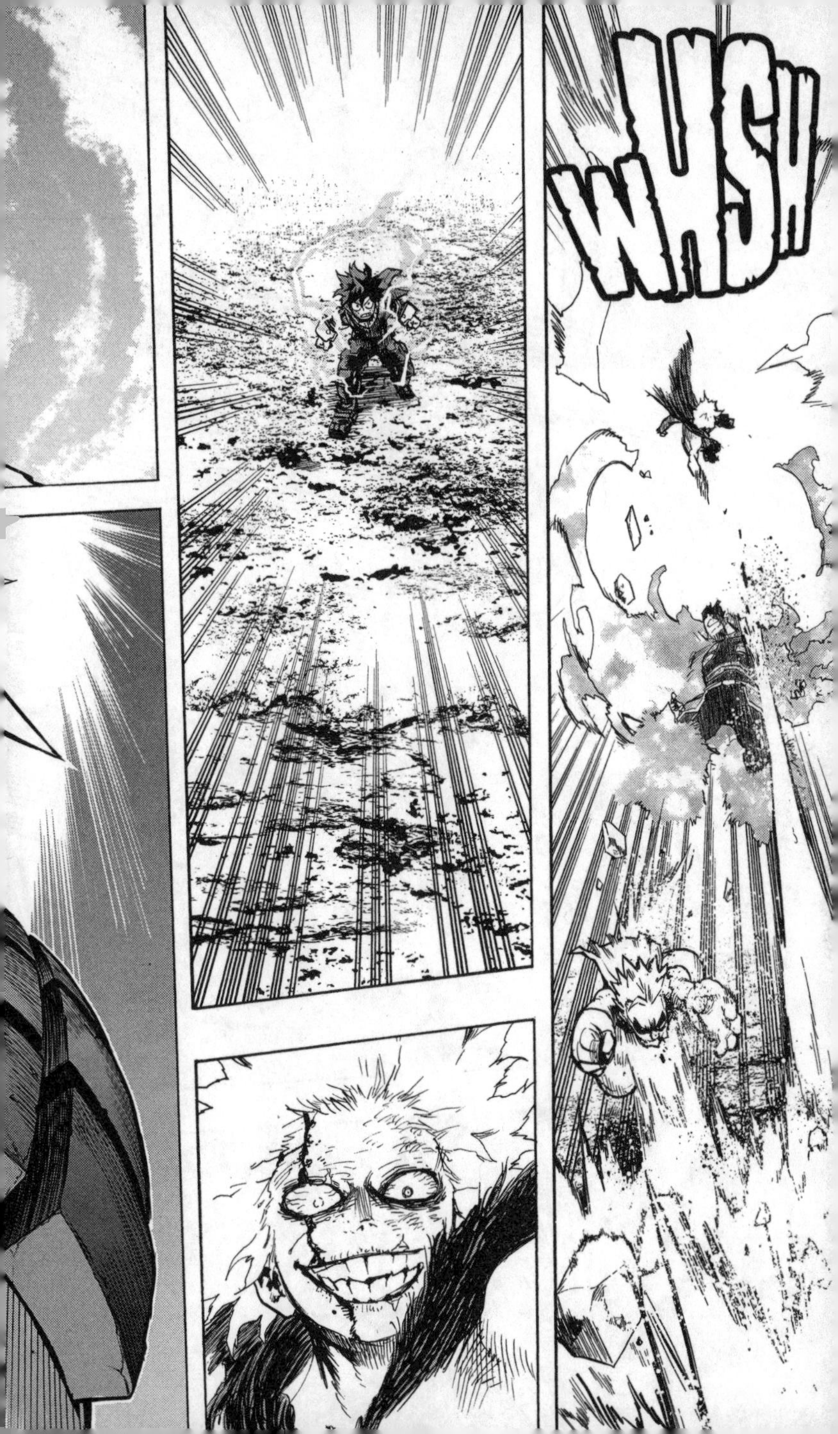
WHSH

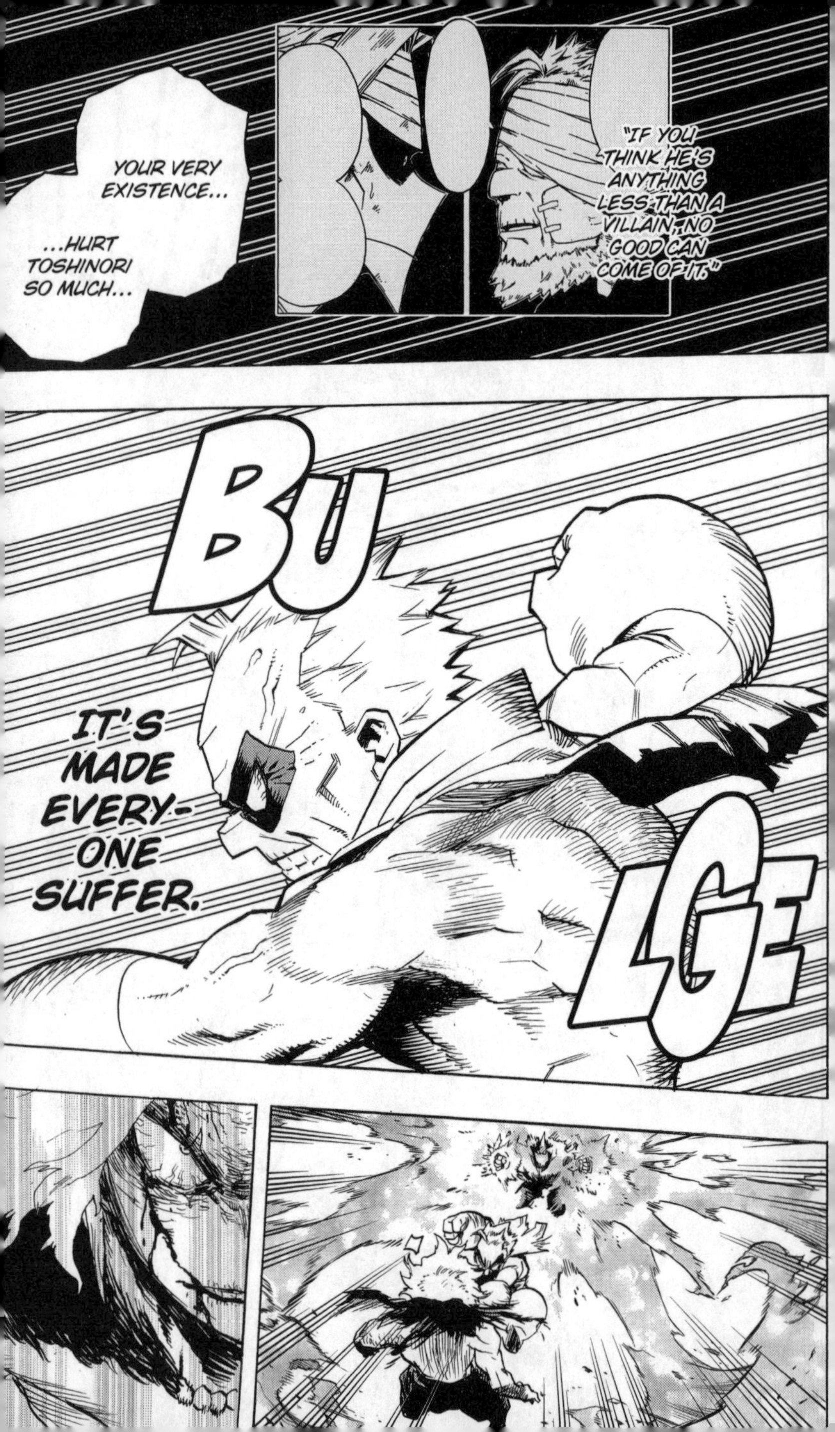
"IF YOU THINK HE'S ANYTHING LESS THAN A VILLAIN, NO GOOD CAN COME OF IT."
YOUR VERY EXISTENCE...
...HURT TOSHINORI SO MUCH...
BULGE
IT'S MADE EVERY-ONE SUFFER.

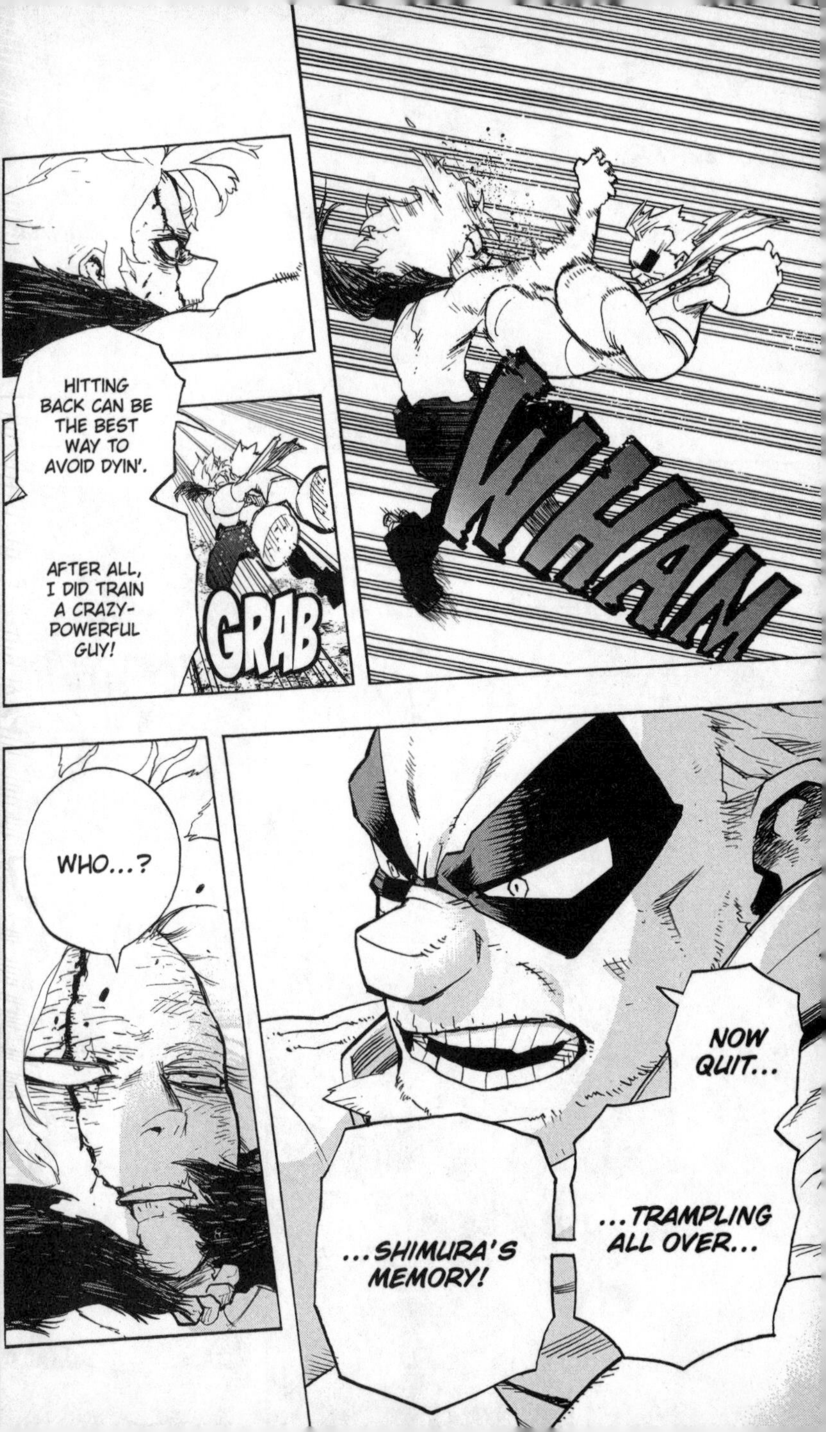
WHAM
HITTING BACK CAN BE THE BEST WAY TO AVOID DYIN'.
AFTER ALL, I DID TRAIN A CRAZY-POWERFUL GUY!
GRAB
NOW QUIT...
...TRAMPLING ALL OVER...
...SHIMURA'S MEMORY!
WHO...?

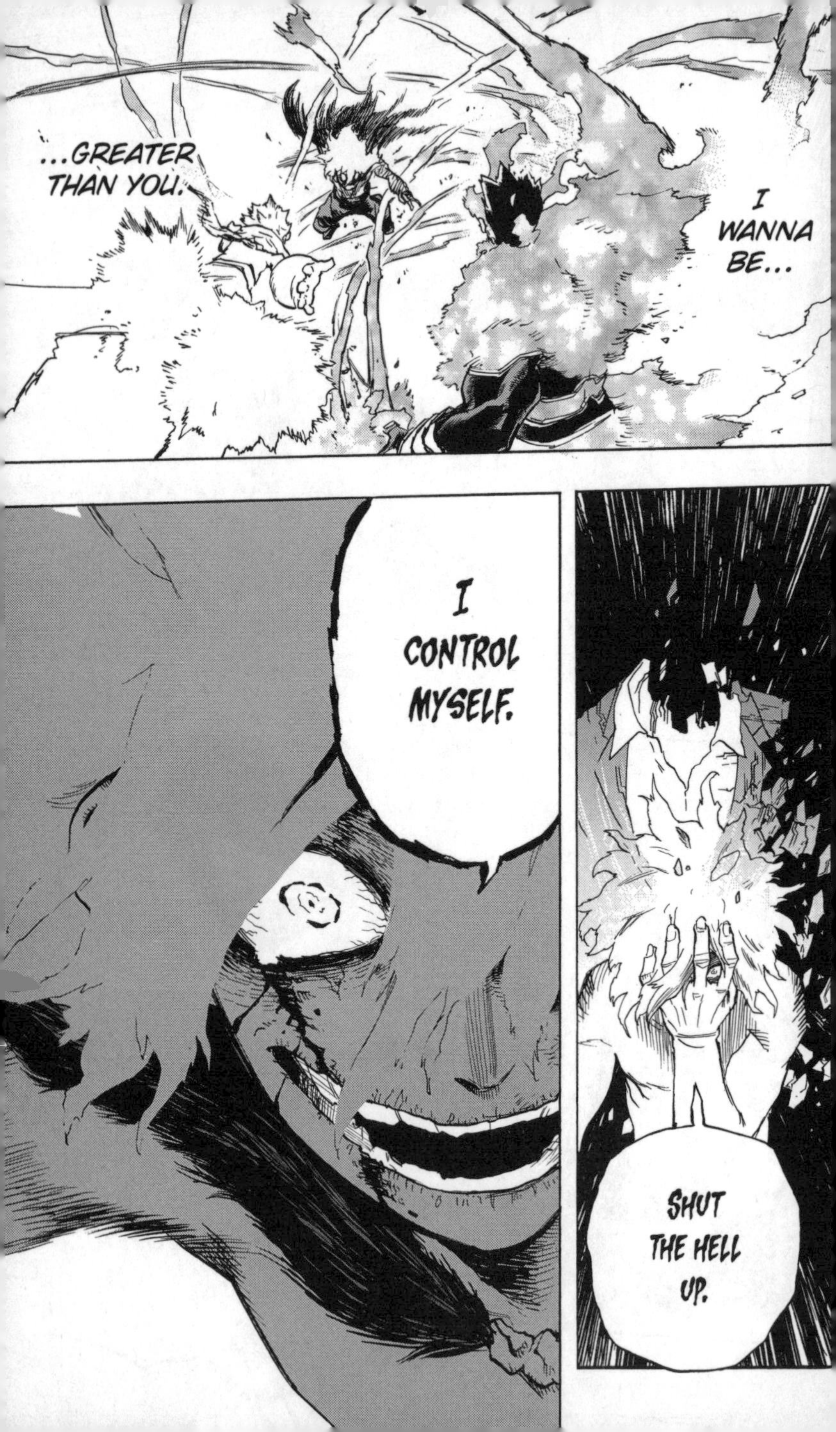
I WANNA BE...
...GREATER THAN YOU.
SHUT THE HELL UP.
I CONTROL MYSELF.

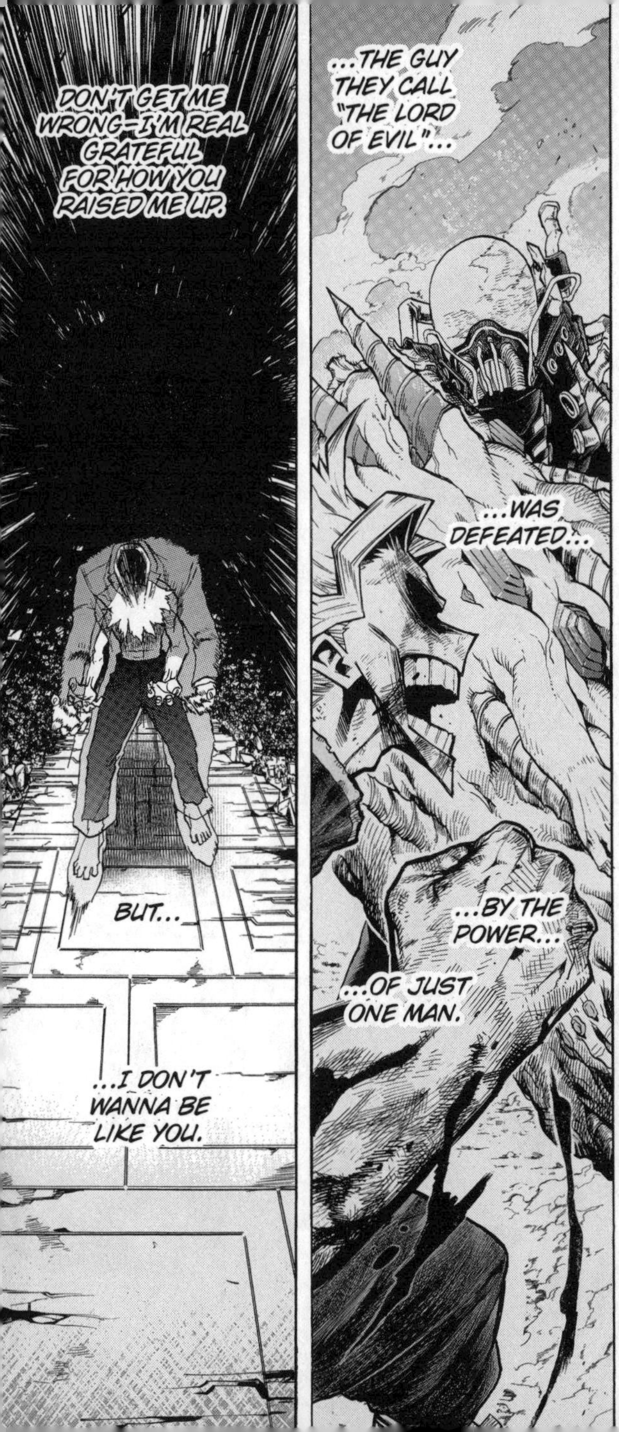
...THE GUY THEY CALL "THE LORD OF EVIL"...
...WAS DEFEATED...
...BY THE POWER...
...OF JUST ONE MAN.
DON'T GET ME WRONG—I'M REAL GRATEFUL FOR HOW YOU RAISED ME UP.
BUT...
...I DON'T WANNA BE LIKE YOU.

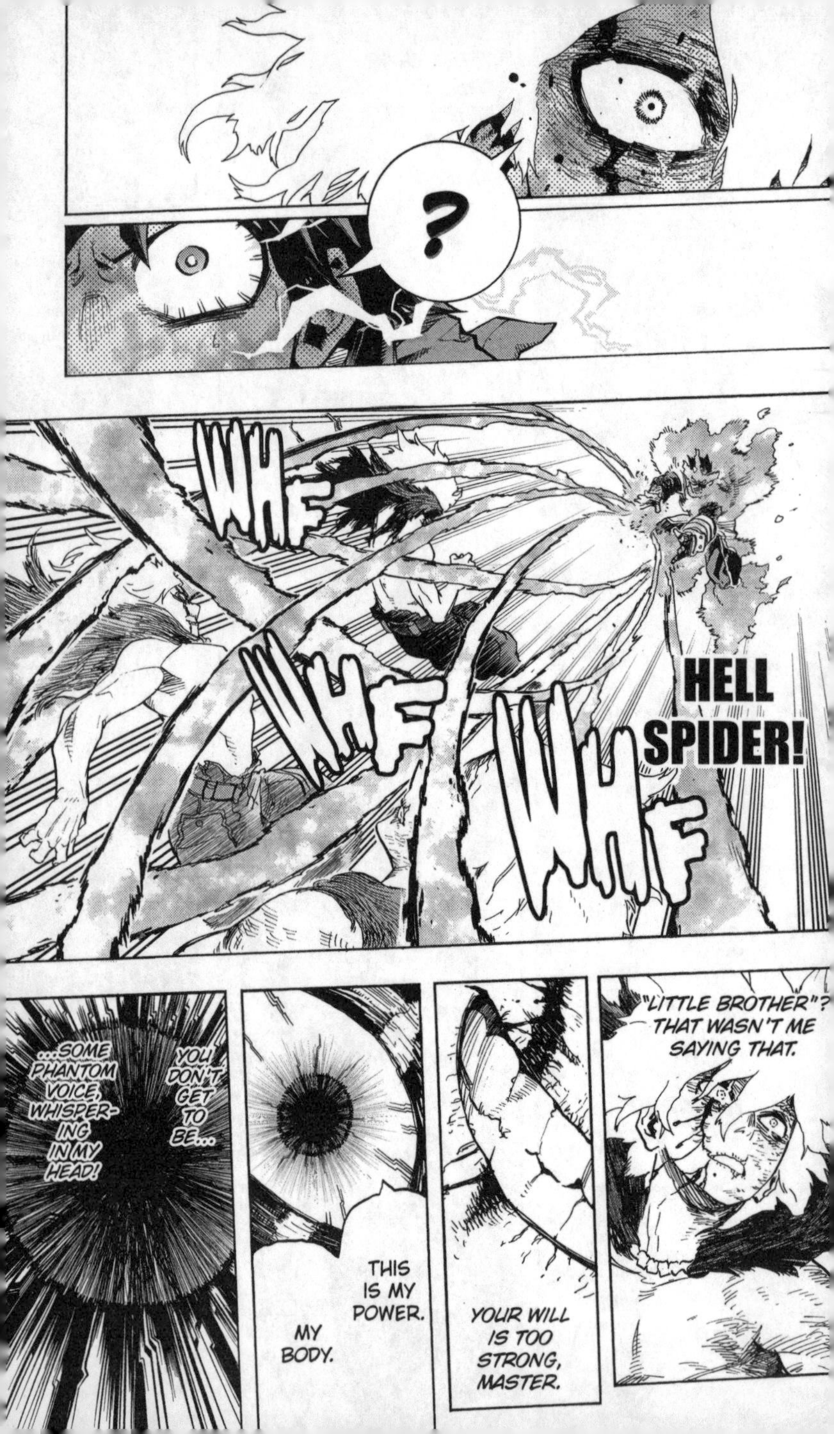
?
WHF
HELL SPIDER!
WHF
WHF
"LITTLE BROTHER"? THAT WASN'T ME SAYING THAT.
YOUR WILL IS TOO STRONG, MASTER.
THIS IS MY POWER.
MY BODY.
YOU DON'T GET TO BE...
...SOME PHANTOM VOICE, WHISPER-ING IN MY HEAD!

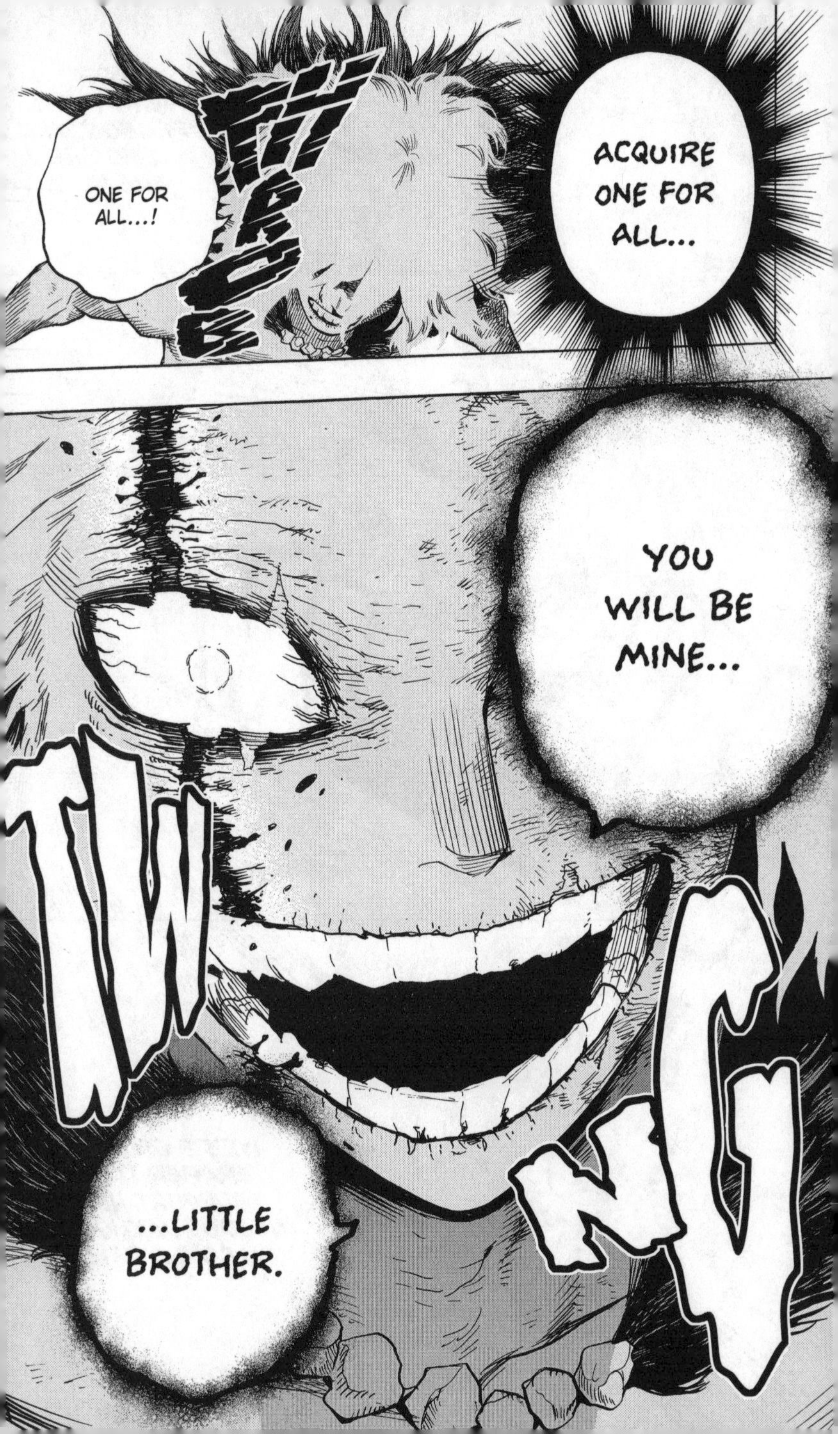
ACQUIRE ONE FOR ALL...
ONE FOR ALL...!
YOU WILL BE MINE...
...LITTLE BROTHER.

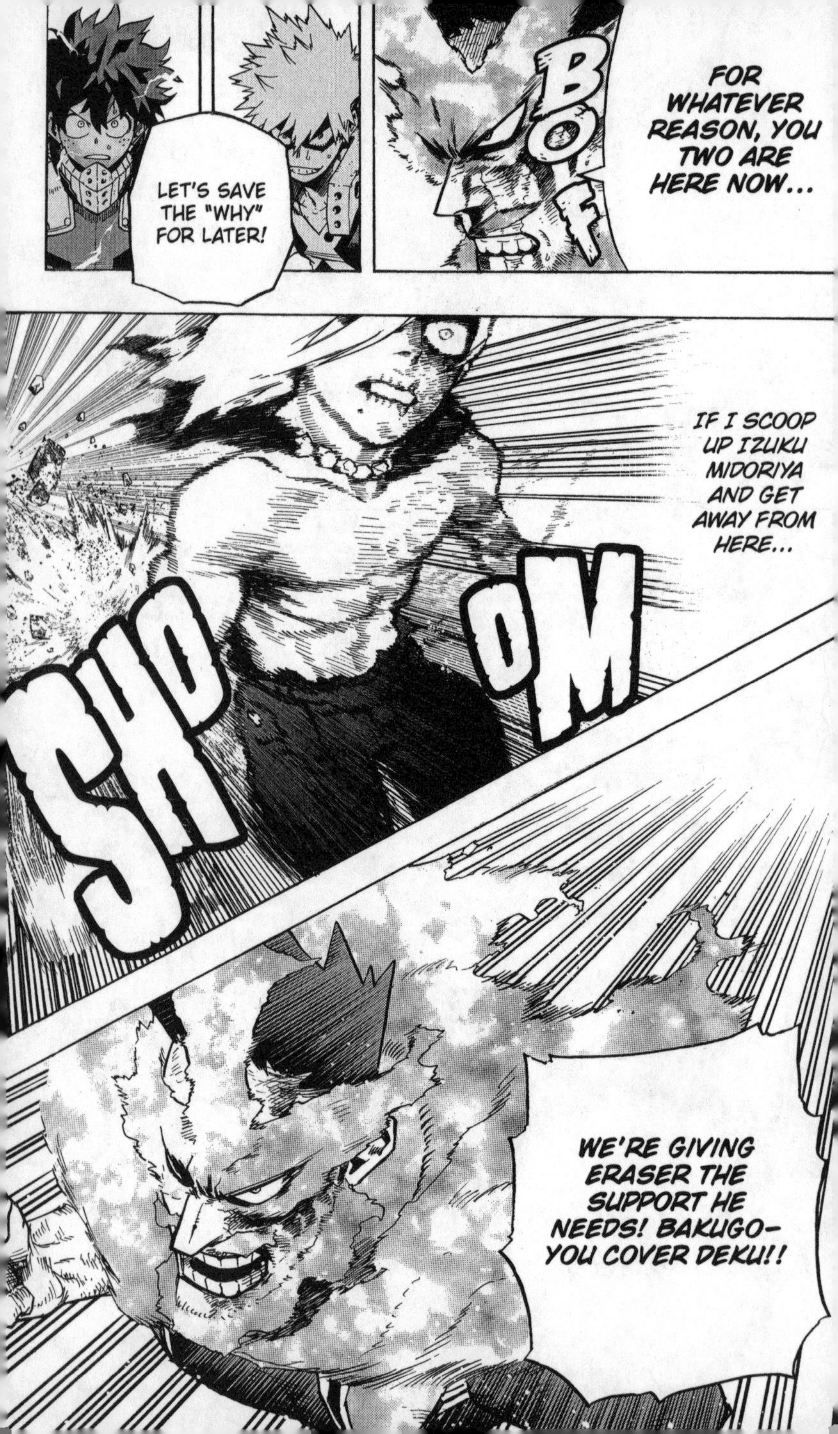
FOR WHATEVER REASON, YOU TWO ARE HERE NOW...
BOF
LET'S SAVE THE "WHY" FOR LATER!
IF I SCOOP UP IZUKU MIDORIYA AND GET AWAY FROM HERE...
SHOOM
WE'RE GIVING ERASER THE SUPPORT HE NEEDS! BAKUGO-YOU COVER DEKU!!

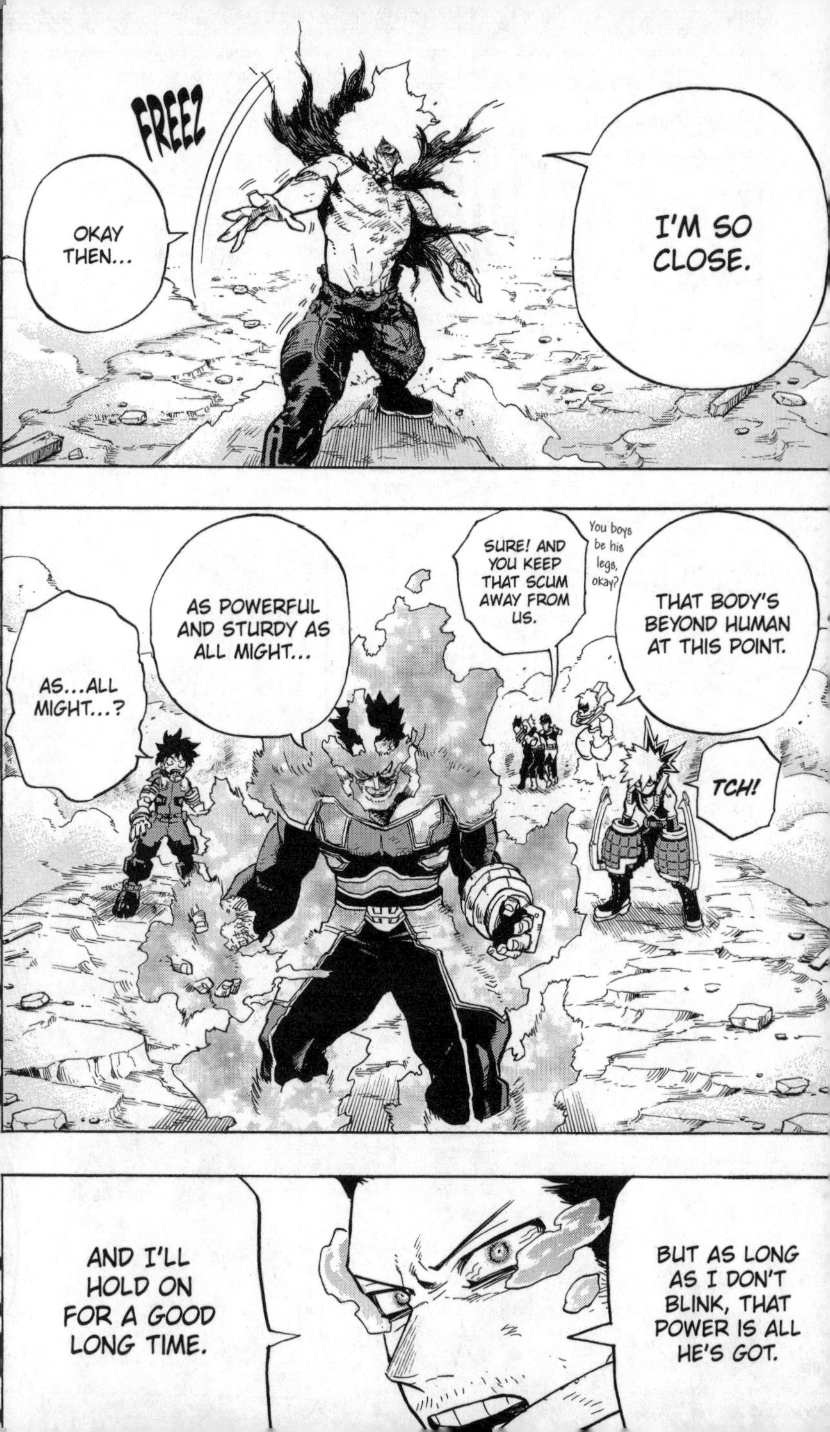
I'M SO CLOSE.
FREEZ
OKAY THEN...
THAT BODY'S BEYOND HUMAN AT THIS POINT.
You boys be his legs, okay?
SURE! AND YOU KEEP THAT SCUM AWAY FROM US.
TCH!
AS POWERFUL AND STURDY AS ALL MIGHT...
AS...ALL MIGHT...?
BUT AS LONG AS I DON'T BLINK, THAT POWER IS ALL HE'S GOT.
AND I'LL HOLD ON FOR A GOOD LONG TIME.

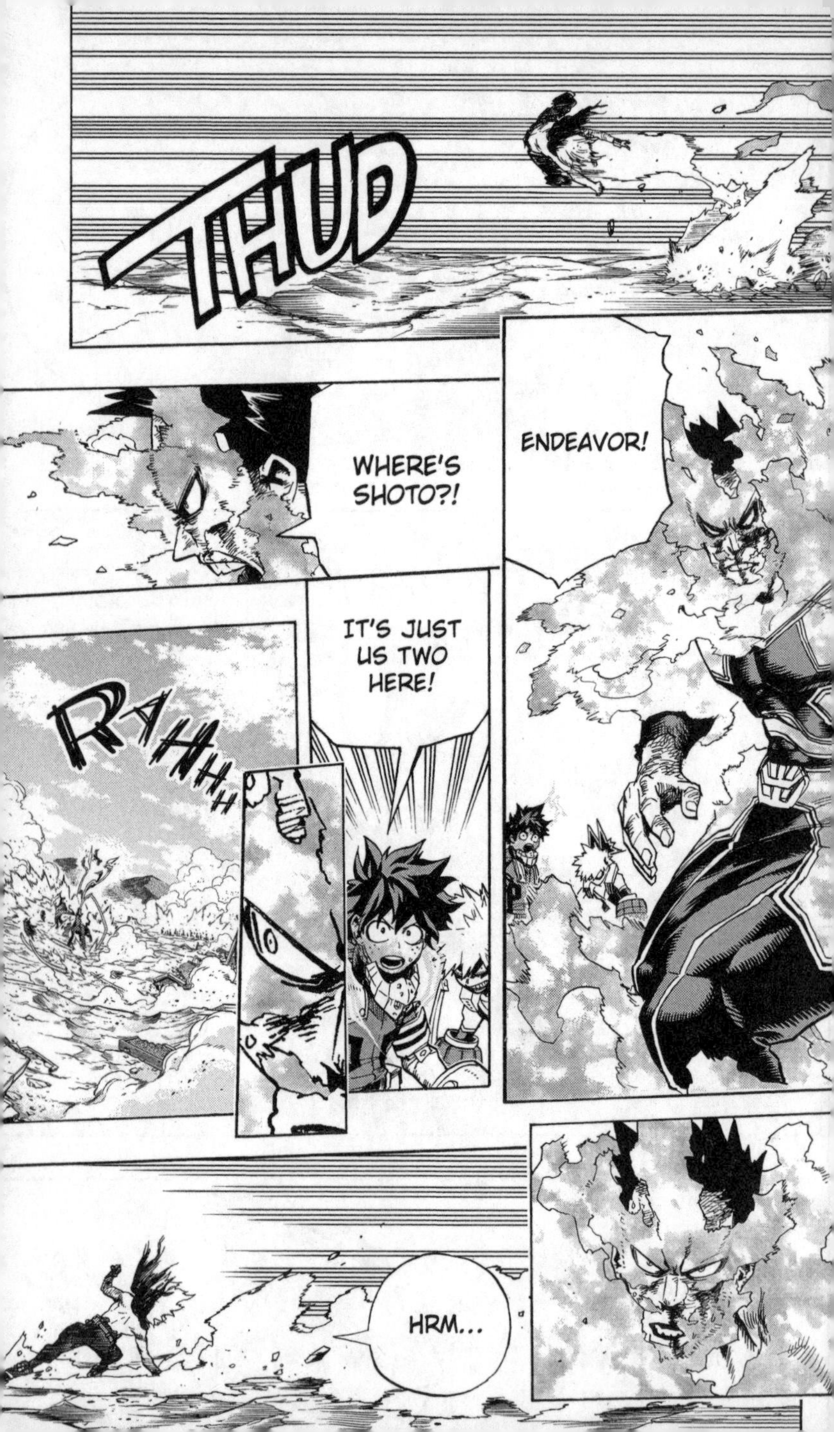
THUD
ENDEAVOR!
WHERE'S SHOTO?!
IT'S JUST US TWO HERE!
RAHHHH
HRM...

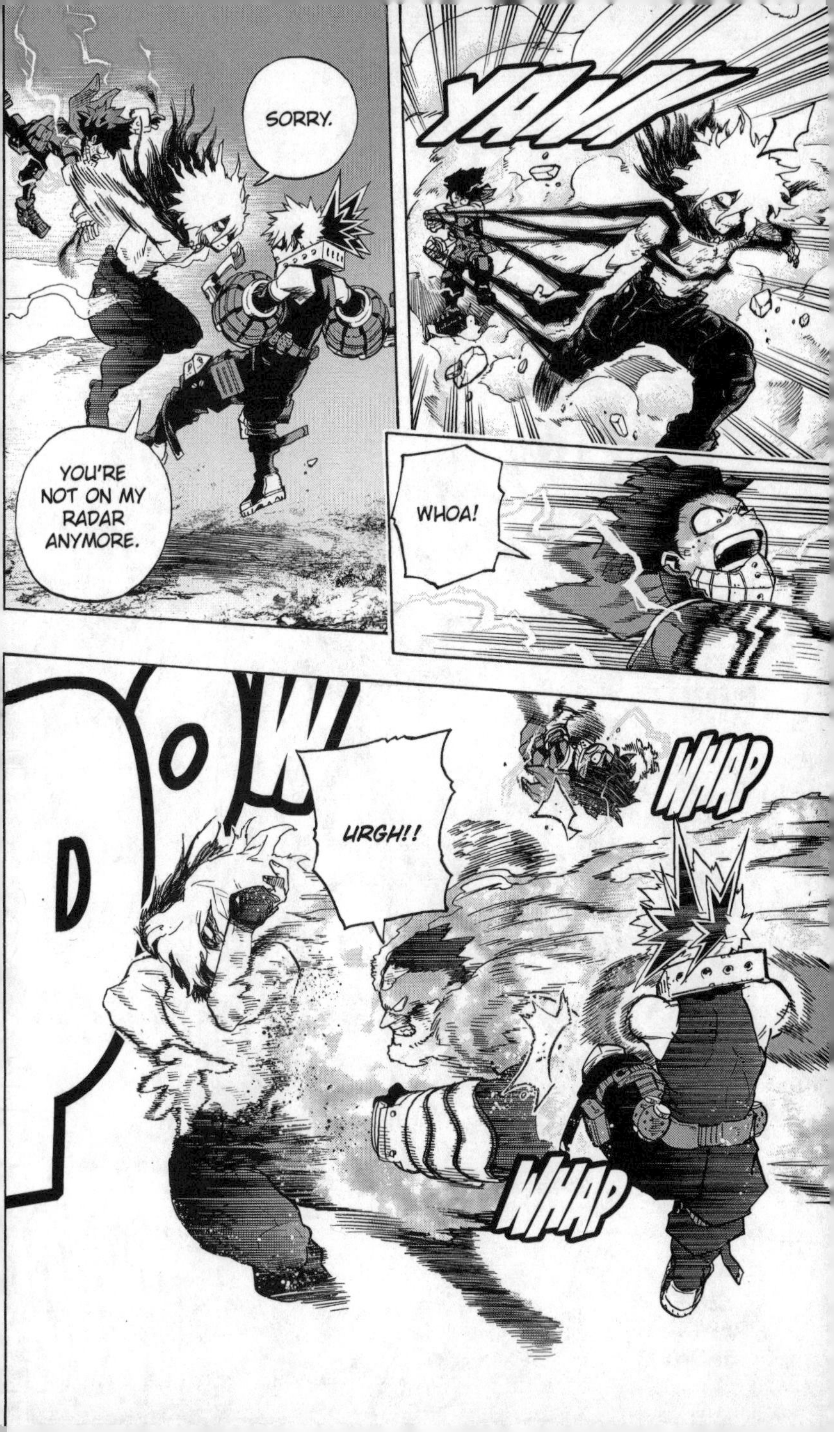
YANK
WHOA!
SORRY.
YOU'RE NOT ON MY RADAR ANYMORE.
WHAP
URGH!!
POW
WHAP

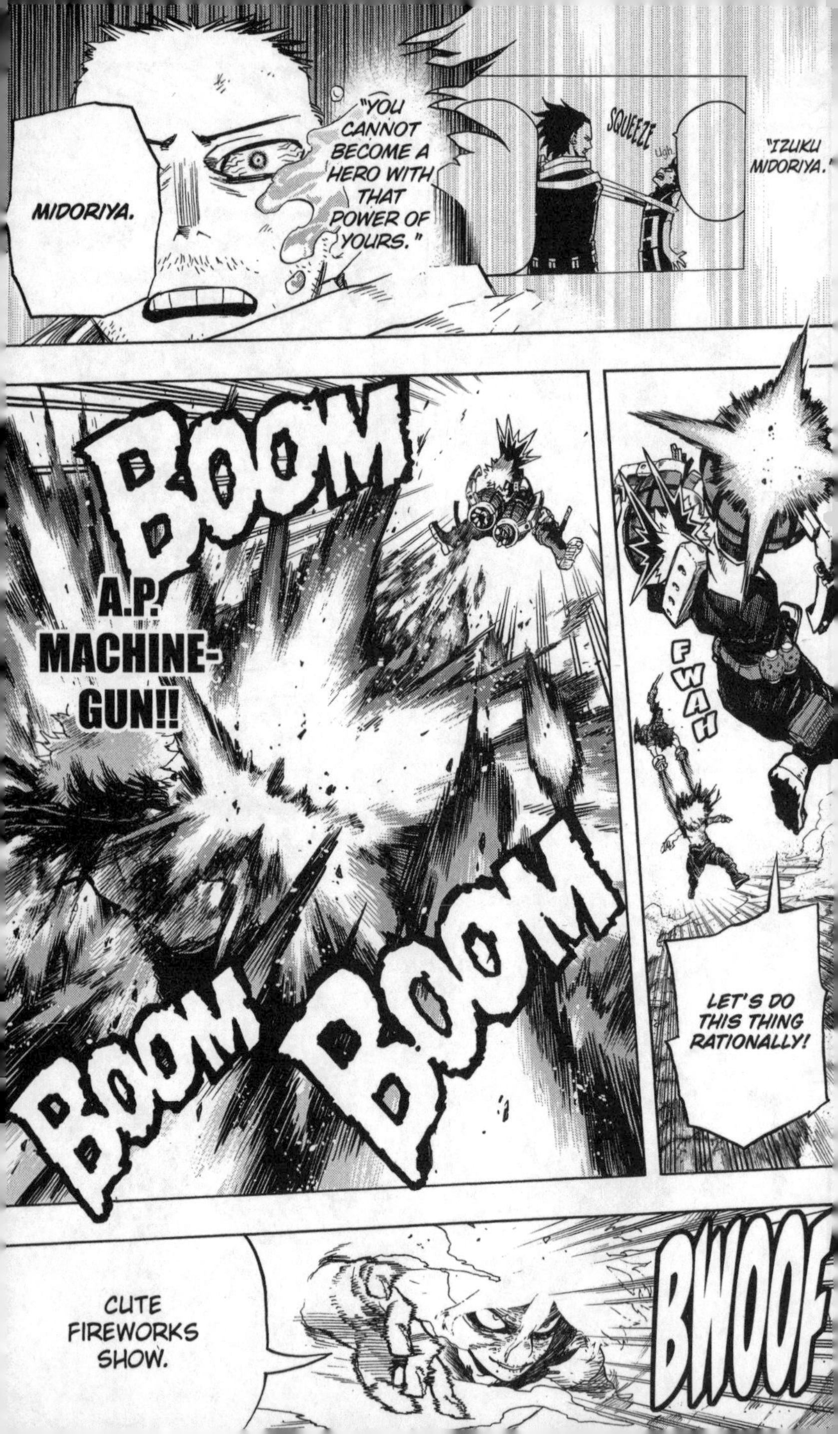
"IZUKU MIDORIYA."
SQUEEZE
Ugh
"YOU CANNOT BECOME A HERO WITH THAT POWER OF YOURS."
MIDORIYA.
FWAH
LET'S DO THIS THING RATIONALLY!
BOOM
A.P. MACHINE-GUN!!
BOOM
BOOM
BWOOF
CUTE FIREWORKS SHOW.

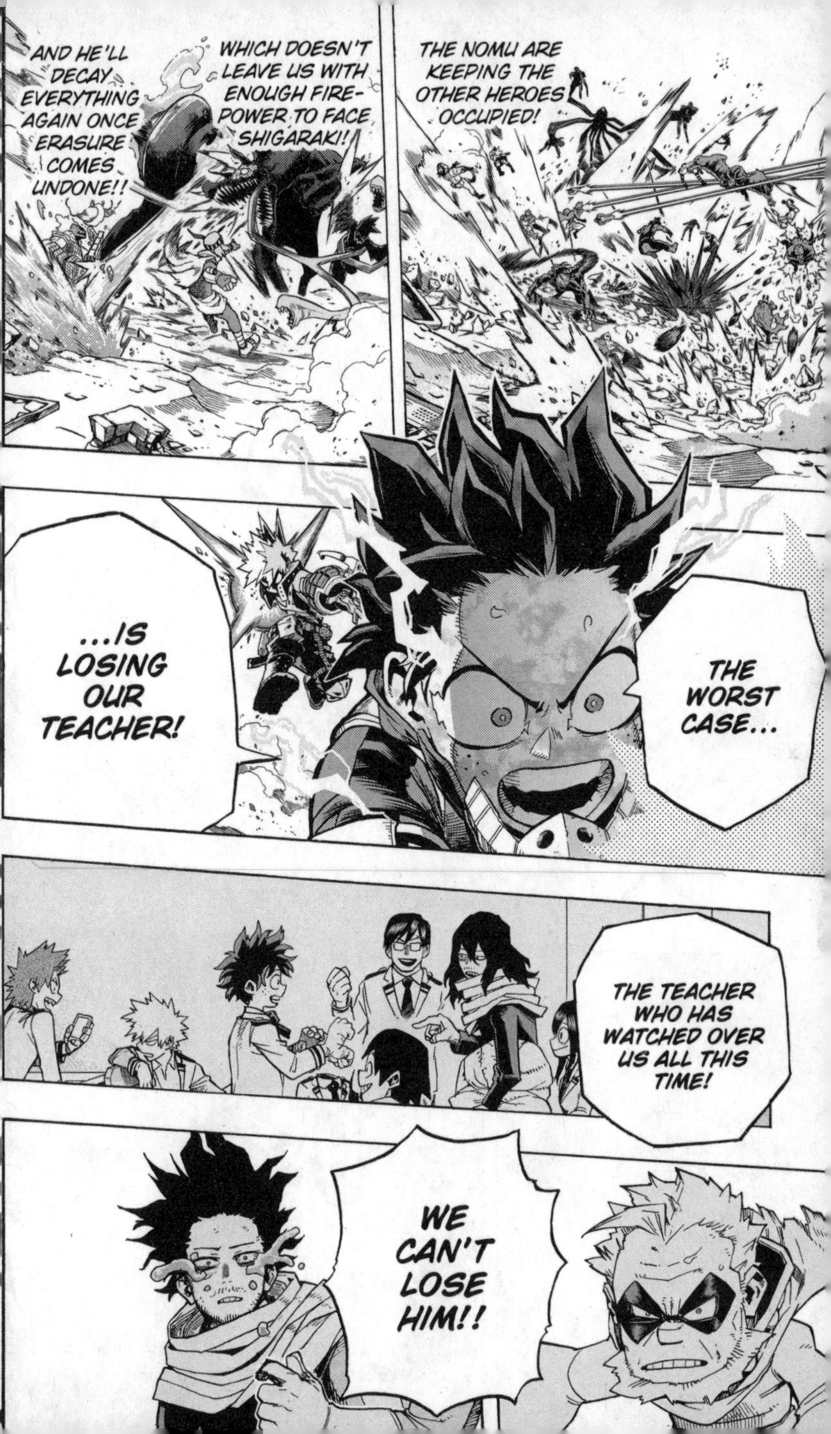
THE NOMU ARE KEEPING THE OTHER HEROES OCCUPIED!
WHICH DOESN'T LEAVE US WITH ENOUGH FIRE-POWER TO FACE SHIGARAKI!!
AND HE'LL DECAY EVERYTHING AGAIN ONCE ERASURE COMES UNDONE!!
THE WORST CASE...
...IS LOSING OUR TEACHER!
THE TEACHER WHO HAS WATCHED OVER US ALL THIS TIME!
WE CAN'T LOSE HIM!!

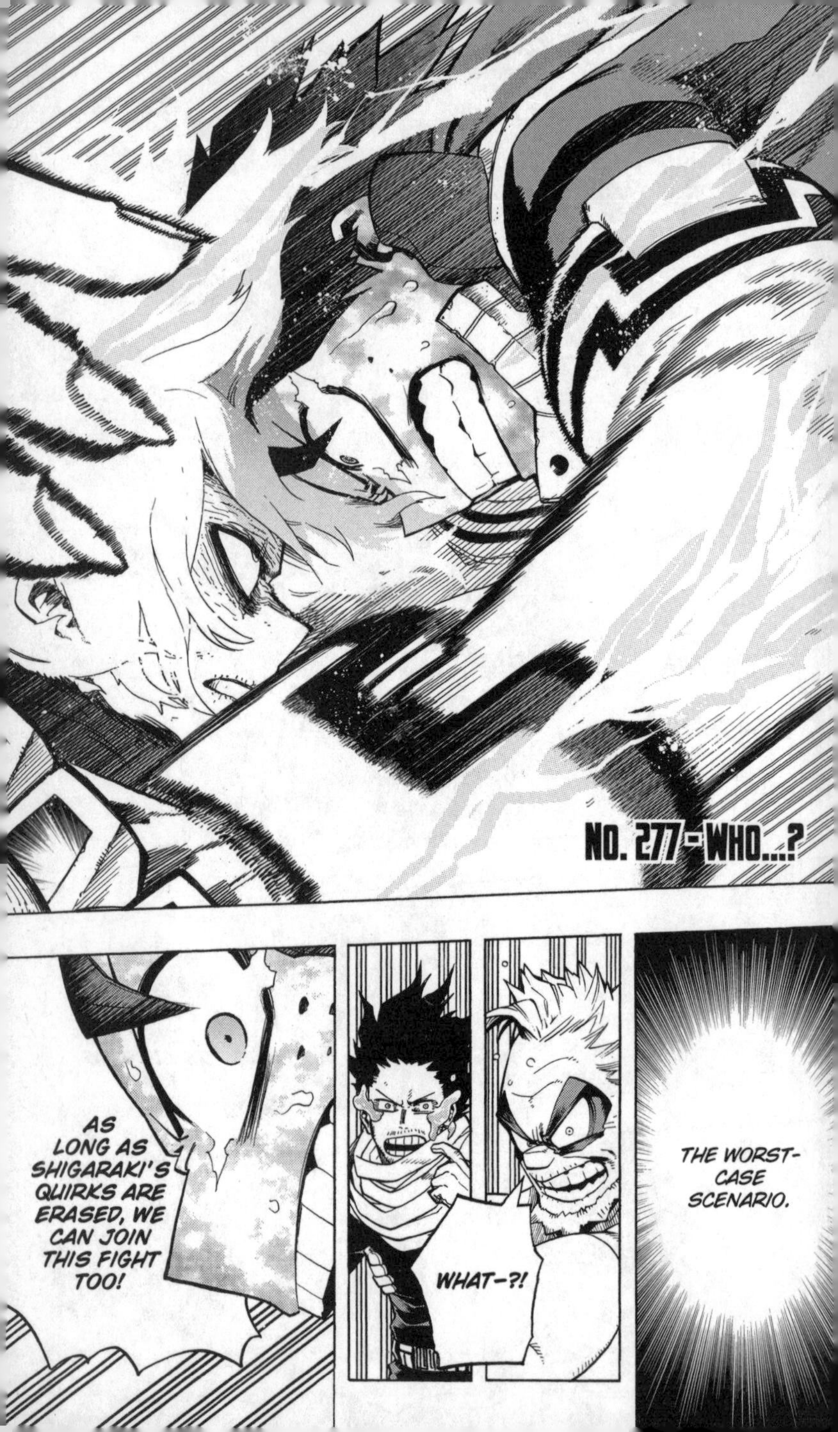

NO. 277 - WHO...?
THE WORST-CASE SCENARIO.
WHAT-?!
AS LONG AS SHIGARAKI'S QUIRKS ARE ERASED, WE CAN JOIN THIS FIGHT TOO!

MY HERO ACADEMIA

Vol. 29

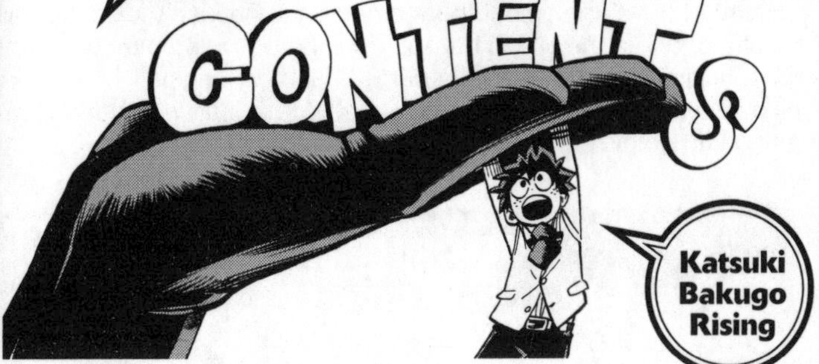
CONTENTS
Katsuki Bakugo Rising

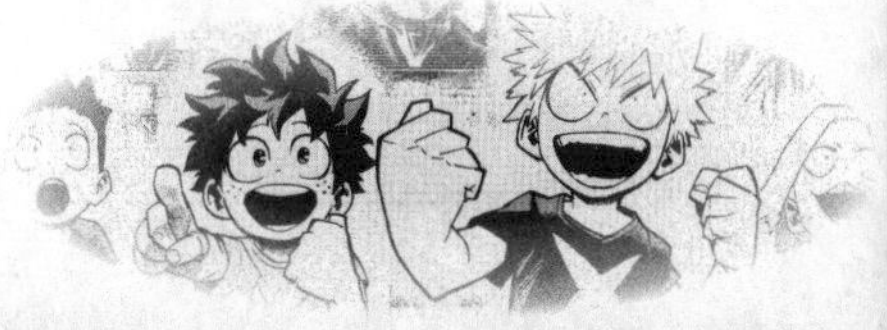

One day, people began manifesting special abilities that came to be known as "Quirks," and before long, the world was full of superpowered humans. But with the advent of these exceptional individuals came an increase in crime, and governments alone were unable to deal with the situation. At the same time, others emerged to oppose the spread of evil! As if straight from the comic books, these heroes keep the peace and are even officially authorized to fight crime. Our story begins when a certain Quirkless boy and lifelong hero fan meets the world's number one hero, starting him on his path to becoming the greatest hero ever!

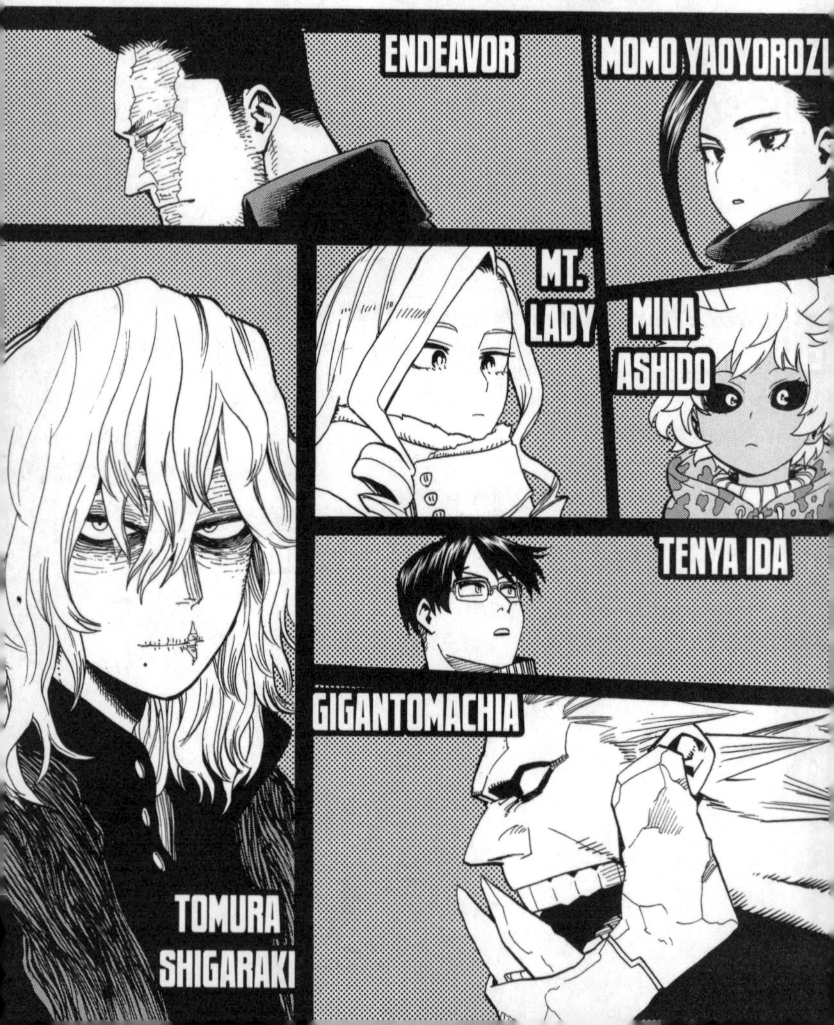
MOMO YAOYOROZU
ENDEAVOR
MINA ASHIDO
MT. LADY
TENYA IDA
GIGANTOMACHIA
TOMURA SHIGARAKI

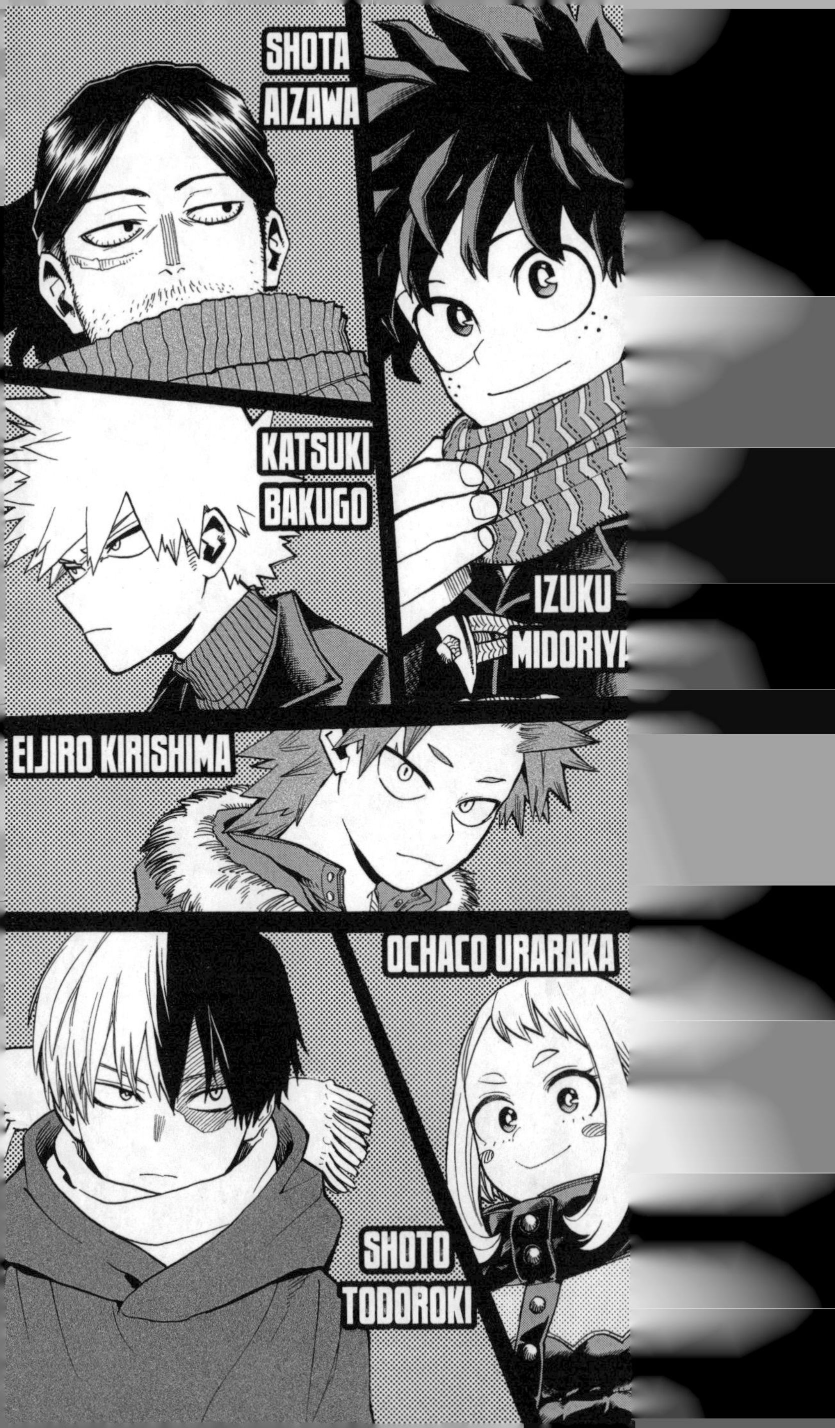
IZUKU MIDORIYA
SHOTA AIZAWA
KATSUKI BAKUGO
EIJIRO KIRISHIMA
OCHACO URARAKA
SHOTO TODOROKI

MY HERO ACADEMIA vol.29

Katsuki Bakugo Rising

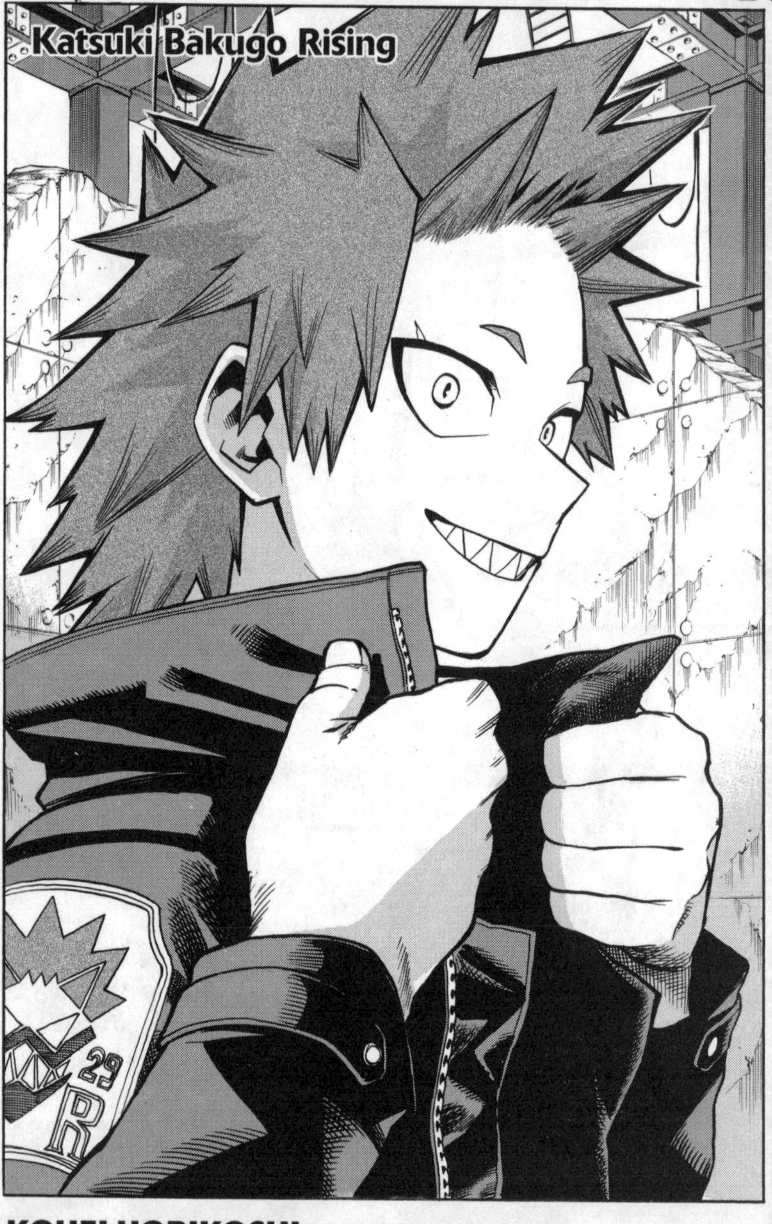
29
R

KOHEI HORIKOSHI

SHONEN JUMP Manga Edition

STORY & ART **KOHEI HORIKOSHI**

TRANSLATION & ENGLISH ADAPTATION **Caleb Cook**
TOUCH-UP ART & LETTERING **John Hunt**
DESIGNER **Julian [JR] Robinson**
SHONEN JUMP SERIES EDITOR **John Bae**
GRAPHIC NOVEL EDITOR **Mike Montesa**

BOKU NO HERO ACADEMIA © 2014 by Kohei Horikoshi
All rights reserved.
First published in Japan in 2014 by SHUEISHA Inc., Tokyo.
English translation rights arranged by SHUEISHA Inc.

The stories, characters and incidents mentioned in this publication are entirely fictional.

Printed in the U.S.A.

Published by VIZ Media, LLC
P.O. Box 77010
San Francisco, CA 94107

10 9 8 7 6 5 4 3 2 1
First printing, September 2021

PARENTAL ADVISORY
MY HERO ACADEMIA is rated T for Teen
and is recommended for ages 13 and up.
This volume contains fantasy violence.

It's volume 29! Thanks for purchasing!
Sometimes I chow down on fresh salad at 3 a.m.,
and honestly, I'm not sure if it's good or bad for
my health!!

KOHEI HORIKOSHI